The Copyright Protection of Computer Software in the United Kingdom

DR STANLEY LAI

LLB (Hons) (Leicester), LLM (Cantab), PhD (Cantab)
Barrister-at-Law (Lincoln's Inn), Advocate and Solicitor (Singapore)

·H A R T·
PUBLISHING

OXFORD – PORTLAND OREGON
2000

Hart Publishing
Oxford and Portland, Oregon

Published in North America (US and Canada) by
Hart Publishing c/o
International Specialized Book Services
5804 NE Hassalo Street
Portland, Oregon
97213-3644
USA

Distributed in the Netherlands, Belgium and Luxembourg by
Intersentia, Churchillaan 108
B2900 Schoten
Antwerpen
Belgium

Hart Publishing Ltd is a specialist legal publisher based in Oxford, England.
To order further copies of this book or to request a list of other
publications please write to:

Hart Publishing Ltd, Salter's Boatyard,
Folly Bridge, Abingdon Road, Oxford OX1 4LB
Telephone: +44 (0)1865 245533 or Fax: +44 (0)1865 794882
e-mail: mail@hartpub.co.uk

British Library Cataloguing in Publication Data
Data Available
ISBN 1 84113–087–7 (cloth)

Typeset by Hope Services (Abingdon) Ltd.
Printed in Great Britain on acid-free paper
by Biddles Ltd, Guildford and King's Lynn.

Contents

Acknowledgements

I wish to thank Professor William Cornish for being untiring in his support, encouragement and insightful guidance throughout his supervision of my research in Cambridge. I am also most grateful to the Lee Foundation, Singapore, for its generous financial grant in support of this project.

Dedicated to my parents,

SL
August 1999
Singapore

Table of Cases

Table of Legislation

Table of EU Directives

1

Introduction

I. AIMS AND OBJECTIVES

This work investigates the scope of copyright protection for computer software **1.1** in the United Kingdom. It aims to make a reasoned and well-argued case for the incorporation of US infringement methodology into UK software copyright analysis. Where appropriate, a comparative study is made between both systems, in relation to particular areas in the field, such as reverse engineering and user interface protection. At these points, the book will suggest that perceived differences in the copyright law of both systems are capable of reconciliation.

The study also seeks to clarify the scope of software copyright protection in **1.2** the United Kingdom. It pays particular attention to infringement methodology, the legal issues surrounding reverse engineering practice and the range and parameters of the defences which avail the copyright defendant. Finally some of the future challenges which confront this subject are addressed.

II. ISSUES FOR INVESTIGATION

It is not the purpose of this book to provide a detailed historical account of soft- **1.3** ware copyright protection.[1] Several generations of copyright decisions have passed through the USA and the United Kingdom. In the first generation of decisions, courts had to deal with the literal copying of computer programs. The issue was not whether the act of copying or appropriation constituted an infringement, but which forms of "computer programs" were protected by copyright; source code, object code, or both.

Towards the mid-1980s, broad protection for computer programs was recog- **1.4** nised by US courts,[2] following the 1980 Amendments to the US Copyright Act

---

[1] For a concise history of US software protection generally, see Samuelson "A Case Study on Computer Programs" in Wallerstein, Mogee and Schoen (eds) *Global Dimensions of Intellectual Property Rights in Science and Technology* (Nat Academy Press, 1993) at pp 284–294.

[2] See *Apple Computer v Formula* 562 F.Supp 575 at 778–780 (1983) (where it was held that computer programs are protected in any form, fixed in any medium, regardless of their purpose and function. Object code was said to be protected despite only indirectly communicating to the user through the hardware, since US law did not require that a computer program communicate its expression directly to the user); *Williams Electronics v Arctic International* 685 F.2d 870 at 975 (3d Cir 1982) (where it was said that the "copyrightability of computer programs [was] firmly established after the 1980 amendments to the Copyright Act" and that the expression of a program in source and object codes is protected as a "copy" under s.101 USCA) and *Apple Computer v Franklin* 545 F.Supp 812 (1982).

(USCA) and the work of CONTU.[3] In the United Kingdom the question of copyright protection of object code was resolved in *Sega Enterprises v Richards,*[4] where the plaintiff applied for an interlocutory injunction and the Court proceeded on the basis that copyright vested in the software of the "Frogger" game, even though the program was in machine-readable assembly code.[5] Protection given to a computer program as a literary work was subsequently confirmed by section 1 of the Copyright (Computer Software) Amendment Act 1985,[6] and made even clearer by section 3(1) of the Copyright, Designs and Patents Act 1988 (CDPA).[7] In neither country was it disputed that copyright protection extends as much to object code as to source code, and even, micro-code.[8] Moreover the international resolution of these issues has also emerged through Treaty intervention.[9]

1.5   More controversially, the second generation of software decisions has addressed the copyright protection of "non-literal" elements. Non-literal elements refer to features that are behaviourally and functionally similar between programs even if their underlying coding is different. The question has turned to the protection which should be accorded to the "structure, sequence and organisation"[10] of software elements, "interfaces"[11] and "interface specifications".[12]

---

[3] Acronym for the National Commission on New Technological Uses of Copyright Works, set up by Congress in 1974 to consider major public policy questions of concern in the copyright field. Among the problems considered by the Commission was the extent to which computer programs should be protected by copyright. The Final Report was issued in 1978, and recommended, inter alia, that computer programs be treated as a proper subject for copyright protection (CONTU at pp 14–15).

[4] [1983] FSR 73. Courts generally proceeded on the basis that a computer program was eligible for copyright protection as a literary work but experienced difficulties in determining software copyright infringement: eg Megarry VC in *Thrustcode Ltd v WW Computing Ltd* [1983] FSR 502 at 505.

[5] Courts in other jurisdictions have not always accepted that all forms of computer programs are protected by copyright; see *Computer Edge Pty Limited v Apple Computer* (1986) 65 ALR 33, where it was held that copyright did not vest in the object code form of original source code programs—the position has been subsequently amended by statute.

[6] However in actions proceeding under the Copyright Act 1956, it was still sometimes argued that at least before the 1985 amendment, the Act did not protect computer software: *Milltronics v Hycontrol Ltd* [1990] FSR 273.

[7] The wording under the CDPA makes it completely clear that computer programs are literary works and not simply to be protected as though they were literary works.

[8] *NEC v Intel* 643 F.Supp 590 (ND Cal 1986).

[9] Art 10(1) TRIPS Agreement; Art 4 WIPO Copyright Treaty 1996.

[10] Generic language that was used in the now disapproved case of *Whelan v Jaslow*, but never specifically contradicted as a phrase.

[11] At the highest level of generality, an operating system is the "interface" between an application program and computer hardware. It refers to the functional characteristic of an element's interaction with other elements of the computer system, eg permissible output or control (*infra*, n 55). See also Report of the US Congress, OTA, "Finding a balance: Computer Software, Intellectual Property and the Challenge of Technological Change" OTA-TCT 527, May 1992 at p 126 ("OTA Report"), in which a program's interface is defined as "the conventions for communications between the program and other programs".

[12] The rules which govern a program's interaction with other elements of the computer.

To this end Chapter 2 discusses how the protection of non-literal elements **1.6** reached its apogee with the decision of *Whelan v Jaslow*. Subsequent US decisions have opted for a more dissective approach, as exemplified by the Second Circuit's opinion in *Computer Associates v Altai* and its deployment of the abstraction-filtration-comparison test.[13] In this context, under UK copyright law, the applicable methodology is in dispute, as evidenced from two UK High Court decisions, *John Richardson v Flanders*, and *Ibcos v Barclays Mercantile Finance*.[14]

Quite apart from the protection of interfaces, which are program "internal" **1.7** elements, another development in the jurisprudence has been the protection that should be accorded to the user interfaces,[15] or the "look and feel" of a computer program.[16] The user interface of a computer program relates to the screen displays, keystroke sequences and configurations; specifically how a user interacts at a temporal level with a computer program. The third generation of software cases has ushered the decline of "look and feel" protection and concurrent emergence of a dissective analysis towards graphical user interfaces,[17] and in the case of *Lotus v Borland*, the exclusion of a particular user interface element from protection altogether.[18] Apart from analysing the provisions of the CDPA which are relevant to the protection of screen displays as separate subject-matter, this work argues that *Lotus v Borland* raises a "threshold" question of protection which UK courts can ill afford to ignore, especially with copyright's exclusion of ideas, procedures, methods of operation or mathematical concepts attaining the status of an international norm.[19]

In the early 1990s much of the debate revolved around software reverse engi- **1.8** neering. Attention focused, on the one hand, on the stressful evolution of the Council Directive for the Protection of Computer Programs ("Software Directive") and its uneasy implementation in the United Kingdom; and on the other, the operation of the Fair Use doctrine in the USA (excusing acts of disassembly when undertaken to secure interoperability between programs)[20] and other Commonwealth developments. In this endeavour, the scope of copyright defences also becomes relevant. In particular, the continued operation of the UK fair dealing defence[21] to forms of reverse engineering falling outside the

---

[13] *Infra*, para 2.42 *et seq.*

[14] *Infra*, para 2.49 and references therein.

[15] The terms "user interface" and "look and feel" are interchangeable, and are a matter of definition. See Brian Johnson "An analysis of the copyrightability of the "look and feel" of a computer program: *Lotus v Paperback Software*" 52 Ohio St LJ 947 at 955 *et seq* (1991). In this work user interfaces and the "look and feel" of a program are treated as identical notions, and quite apart from the non-literal elements of software.

[16] Addressed in Chapter 4.

[17] *Apple v Microsoft*, *infra*, paras 4.19–4.23.

[18] First Circuit's treatment of Lotus' menu command hierarchy in *Lotus v Borland*, *infra*, paras 4.24–4.32.

[19] *Infra*, para 4.39. See s 102(b) USCA; Art 2 WIPO Copyright Treaty 1996; Art 9(2) TRIPS; recitals 13–15, Art 1(2) Software Directive.

[20] See Chapter 6.

[21] Research or private study, see Chapter 7.

decompilation provisions of the CDPA,[22] and the probing of such questions as whether fair use considerations assist in determining whether a dealing is "fair" under the CDPA.[23] Recent case law has also further restricted the scope of the *British Leyland* "spare parts" defence, and some discussion is also devoted to this,[24] and its impact on software copyright litigation.

1.9   Today the subject is facing challenges brought by the dissemination of digital technology. HTML programming, executable coding (eg Java and its use of applets) and object-orientated programming[25] raise questions as to which provisions of the CDPA remain relevant. Given the considerable case law and legislation in relation to the above topics, the work focuses specifically on the copyright protection of websites and links, both of which have acquired considerable prominence following *Shetland Times v Wills*,[26] explores other potentially applicable provisions in the CDPA covering web-programming activity, and scrutinises the latest initiatives which dominate the digital agenda.[27]

1.10   The last two chapters discuss database protection[28] and the copyright-contract interface.[29] Chapter 9 turns to the recent EC Directive[30] which introduces a new copyright/*sui generis* regime for the protection of both the schematic arrangements of database collections, as well as content. Attention is directed at the anomalies of implementation,[31] particularly in relation to computer-generated works,[32] and how the new database right is capable of protecting non-copyright database components within the computer programs.[33]

1.11   Chapter 10 addresses, in the first instance, the validity of shrink-wrap licences, subject to the provisions within the CDPA that prohibit the negation by exclusory contract of certain rights as provided by the Software Directive.[34] Secondly, it identifies the implied licence as becoming a fashionable defence in software disputes, observing the dangers of using such a device to supplant the exclusive rights of the copyright owner.[35]

[22] Art 5(3) Software Directive; s 50B CDPA.
[23] *Infra*, paras 7.23–7.24.
[24] *Infra*, para 7.35 *et seq*.
[25] See eg Verity and Schwartz "Software made simple: will object-oriented programming transform the computer industry?" *Business Week*, 30 September 1991 at 92, 94.
[26] [1997] FSR 604.
[27] *Infra*, para 8.30 *et seq*.
[28] See Chapter 9.
[29] See Chapter 10.
[30] Council Directive on the Legal Protection of Databases, 96/9/EC of 11 March 1996, OJ L77/20 ("Database Directive").
[31] Copyright and Rights in Database Regulations 1997 (SI 1997 No 3032).
[32] *Infra*, paras 9.8–9.9.
[33] *Infra*, paras 9.16–9.21.
[34] *Infra*, paras 10.10–10.12; 10.15–10.31.
[35] *Infra*, para 10.42 *et seq*.

III. APPROACH

The last two decades have been dominated by a debate as to whether copyright **1.12** is the suitable vehicle for software protection. Critics have varied from those who argue that no form of computer software is fit for copyright protection;[36] those who argue that the level of protection for software should be reduced;[37] to those who favour patent protection,[38] an alternate system of "utility patent protection"[39] or the creation of *sui generis* legislation.[40]

It is not the purpose of this work to rehearse the above arguments[41]—the **1.13** work prefers to adhere to legislative realities,[42] and discusses a re-orientation of

[36] See eg Stallman and Garfinkel "Viewpoint: Against User Interface Copyright" Comm ACM November 1990 at 18. See Dworkin, "The Nature of Computer Programs" in Lahore, et al *Information Technology: The Challenge of Copyright* (Sweet & Maxwell, 1984) (widening the debate by stating "the application of copyright law to industrial articles is conceptually inappropriate").

[37] See eg Karjala "Copyright, Computer Software and the New Protectionism" Jurimetrics J 33 at 50 (Fall 1987); Menell "An Analysis of the Scope of Copyright Protection for Application Programs" (1989) 41 Stan L Rev 1045 at 1085.

[38] See eg Chisum "The Patentability of Algorithms" (1986) 47 U.Pitt L Rev 959 (in defence of the patentability of programs); cf Samuelson "Benson revisited: The Case against Patent Protection for Algorithms and Other Computer Program-related Inventions" (1990) 39 Emory LJ 1025. At present it appears that programs contained within carefully drafted claims will satisfy the requirements for patentable subject-matter in the USA: *In Re Alappat* 35 F.3d 1526, 1542–43 (Fed Cir 1994); *Arrhythmia Research Tech v Corazonix Corp* 958 F.2d 1053, 1057–58 (Fed Cir 1992); Examination Guidelines for Computer-Related Inventions 61 Fed Reg 7478, 7481–86 (1996).

[39] Stern "Is the Centre Beginning to hold in US Software Copyright Law?" [1993] 2 EIPR 39.

[40] See eg Paul Goldstein "Infringement of Copyright in Computer Programs" (1986) 47 U.Pitt L Rev 1119, 1125–26; Reichman "Computer Programs as Applied Scientific Knowhow: Implications of copyright Protection for Commercialised University Research" (1989) 42 Vand L Rev 639 at 662–667. Professor Samuelson has in particular championed this cause in her writings, eg "CONTU Revisited: The case against Copyright Protection for computer programs in machine-readable form" (1984) Duke LJ 663, 664, 703–704; "Modifying Copyrighted Software: Adjusting Copyright Doctrine to Accommodate a Technology" Jurimetrics J 179 at 188–192 (Winter 1988). The most influential work to date on this subject has been Samuelson, *et al*, "A Manifesto concerning the Legal Protection of Computer Programs" (1994) 94(8) Columbia L Rev 2308.

[41] See Professor Miller's treatment of the critics, which he divides into four categories; "functionality" (since computer programs are "utilitarian" works, according them full copyright protection may result in a patent-like protection of valuable processes), "access" (since the inner workings of a computer program are incomprehensible to an ordinary user, copying should be permitted to gain access to the program's ideas), "standardisation" (argument that the most efficient use of technology involves relaxing copyright law so as to permit the standardisation of computer programs; see further Stern "The Paperback Case: Part 3, Misconceptions about Functionality" IEEE Micro, February 1991 at 49; Samuelson "Reverse engineering someone else's software: is it legal?" IEEE Micro, January 1990 at 90) and "competence" (raised by .technologists who challenge the ability of judges to comprehend the intricacies of computer programs; Stern "The Paperback Case, Part 4" IEEE Micro, April 1991 at 30, 32–33). See further Miller "Copyright Protection for Computer Programs, Databases and Computer-generated works: is anything new since CONTU?" (1993) 106 Harvard L Rev 977 at 986–991.

[42] *Supra*, n 9. See Dworkin "Copyright, Patents and/or sui generis: what regime best suits computer programs?" in Hugh Hansen (ed) *International Intellectual Property Law & Policy* Vol.1 (Jurvis Publishing, Sweet & Maxwell, 1996) at ch 21. Professor Dworkin observes that "we have succumbed to the full copyright approach" (at p 168), but supports giving full consideration to proposals for alternative paradigms and mechanisms for software protection.

the scope of protection within copyright through the evolving jurisprudence on the subject. It is the author's view that the basic copyright structure is sound, given that the UK copyright system has managed over time to accommodate new technologies; computer programs[43] and digital dissemination being the latest manifestation of this recurring phenomenon. One is reminded of the words of Oliver Wendell Holmes:

> "The development of our law has gone on for nearly a thousand years, like the development of a plant, each generation taking the inevitable step, mind, like matter, simply obeying a law of spontaneous growth".[44]

1.14   There is a strong case for a change of infringement methodology in the United Kingdom, in favour of a narrower scope of copyright protection for software in future. The subject is further elaborated by a consideration of the copyright issues which arise in the context of reverse engineering and the scope of copyright defences.

IV. PROPOSED INFRINGEMENT METHODOLOGY

1.15   My thesis primarily argues that a limiting approach of dissection, when judiciously applied to features of both the internal (interfaces) and external (user interfaces) elements of programs, will assist a UK judge in determining substantial similarity between the non-literal elements of rival programs.[45] The *Altai* test calls for filtration of abstracted elements, through the application of limiting doctrines such as merger and *scènes à faire*. Chapter 3 discusses the inception of these doctrines, and establishes that they are sufficiently well grounded under UK law for application, notwithstanding their apparent US persuasion.

1.16   A successive filtering process, when applied to individual program elements (internal and external), will assist a UK judge in the definition of the proper scope of protection for computer software. In the UK law there is an urgent need to displace the present test of "overborrowing" of the plaintiff's skill labour,[46] which this study argues, is not only fraught with uncertainty and imprecision, but lends itself to overprotection.[47]

1.17   There is a conspicuous absence of thorough discussion in UK texts on the potential application of US infringement techniques, and it is in this area that the work aims to make a substantial contribution, in the critical evaluation, inter alia, of *Computer Associates v Altai*, and its progeny in US courts. The

---

[43] Professor Miller makes a similar pronouncement for literary copyright protection of software in the USA; *supra*, n 41 at 982.

[44] Oliver W Holmes, "The Path of the Law" (1897) 10 Harv L Rev 457 at 468.

[45] The assistance which an *Altai* analysis can bring to determining such similarity is "not without resonance": Cornish *Intellectual Property*, 3rd edn (1996) at 13–29.

[46] Per Jacob J in *Ibcos*, discussed *infra* at paras 2.31–2.33.

[47] Paras 2.54; 3.24–3.25.

book attempts to identify, from recent jurisprudence, the generic features of software that qualify for protection under the prescribed methodology.

V. JUSTIFICATIONS

The various propositions advanced by this book support a narrow scope of copyright protection for computer software. Several reasons account for this. First, although computer programs are treated in copyright as literary works, they do not fit easily into such a categorisation. The inherent functionality of computer software advances a utilitarian *raison d'etre*, that to accord it broad copyright protection may permit patent-like monopolisation of valuable processes without satisfying the more demanding prerequisites of patent law. Functionality as a concept is not per se a bar to British copyright (even if problems existed in the past),[48] but in pursuing the distinction between "functional" and "expressive" works,[49] computer software may dominate the former, but appropriate credit must also be also be given for its "expressive" aspects.[50] **1.18**

Secondly, it is not denied that software programming is a creative process,[51] but UK copyright has thus far, with the limited exception of *John Richardson v Flanders*, not developed a coherent approach to separate protectable and unprotectable elements[52] of computer software.[53] The burden of developing standards for the application of copyright concepts to software is best left to the judiciary, in the face of evolving technology,[54] and this study attempts to contribute to this realisation. **1.19**

---

[48] Notably in the sphere of design protection, where the combined effect of the Copyright Act 1956 and Design Copyright Act 1968 was generous artistic copyright protection for functional designs that otherwise could not qualify for registered design protection. See further, Laddie, Prescott and Vitoria, *Modern Law of Copyright and Designs*, Vol 1, paras 29.39–29.40; 46.4. The introduction of the unregistered design right (s 213 CDPA) removed functional designs from the ambit of copyright, thus offering implicit justification for the methodology proposed by this work.

[49] In the USA this inquiry has been reduced to a cruder categorial distinction between "books" and "machines", which do not provide clear resolution. See Weinreb "Copyright for Functional Expression" (1998) 111 Harvard L Rev 1149 at 1180–1210.

[50] The USA has faced similar challenges. In the seminal case of *Baker v Selden* 101 US 99 (1880), the Supreme Court, although drawing a distinction between works "having their final end in application and use" and those "[whose] essence consists only in their statement" (at 104), found expression in both categories to be eligible for protection (ibid).

[51] Explored by Miller, *supra*, n 41, at 983–984; cf Karjala, who takes the view that the policy basis for protecting software under copyright is not creativity, but inexpensive and easy piracy: (1997) 66 U Cinn L Rev 53 at 55, 67, 69.

[52] That is, programming elements which can be discounted by limiting doctrines and standard programming practice. See Chapter 3.

[53] This is particularly apparent from *Ibcos v Barclays*, discussed *infra* at paras 2.31–2.33, 2.65.

[54] In the USA, this was recognised by CONTU, who decided against compiling a detailed list of protectable and non-protectable program elements (CONTU, Final Report at 22–23).

1.20   Thirdly, the methodology advanced by this work addresses the interoperability[55] concerns of software programming[56] (objectives which are addressed by the Software Directive),[57] which would otherwise be ignored if traditional infringement tests were followed in the United Kingdom.

1.21   Finally, a narrow scope of protection for software also serves the public interest[58] through the stimulation of competition,[59] judicial recognition of the sanctity of the public domain,[60] the merits of standardisation[61] and consequent avoidance of monopoly stagnation.

VI.   THE RELEVANCE OF COMPETITION LAW

1.21   Apart from the issues discussed, the book recognises the profound impact of EC competition law[62] on the scope of software copyright in the United Kingdom, particularly after *Magill*.[63] This is true particularly of the extent to which Article 86 EC Treaty may prevent the assertion of copyright where it will restrict access to and use of software interfaces[64] by a third party, as seen from the *IBM Settlement*,[65] which provided the bedrock for the launch of the Software Directive.[66] For example, in pursuit of the "imperative of interoperability", as a

---

[55] An ideal that is rigorously pursued in the USA; see Band, Katoh, *Interfaces on Trial* (Westview Press, 1995) ch 1.

[56] Particularly in the "interfaces" which support interconnectivity and compatibility between programs, and between software and hardware. See *Interfaces on Trial*, ibid at ch 3.

[57] Articles 5, 6, 9 and accompanying recitals.

[58] See Linder "A Recommended Copyright Test for Computer Program User Interfaces" (1993) 66 Temple L Rev 969 at 970–971; 973–74.

[59] Controversially, the author's interest is a "secondary consideration", and "[t]he ultimate aim, is . . . to stimulate artistic creativity for the general public good". See *Computer Associates v Altai* 982 F.2d at 696 (2nd Cir, 1992); cf *Whelan v Jaslow*, where it was said that a broad scope of protection "would provide the proper incentive for programmers by protecting their most valuable efforts": 797 F.2d 1222 at 1237 (3rd Cir 1986). The latter rationale is questionable since it suggests protecting the "sweat of the brow", a defunct basis for copyright protection in the USA after *Feist*. *Infra*, para 2.7.

[60] The importance of which is overlooked with the expansion of intellectual property rights. See Boyle, *Shamans, Software and Spleens* (HUP, 1996) at pp141–143.

[61] *Infra*, paras 3.52–3.53.

[62] Articles 85, 86 EC Treaty. On Art 85 and Software Licensing, see generally Vinje "Compliance with Article 85 in Software Licensing" [1992] 4 ECLR 165 at 166–167; Dolmans "Software Licensing in Europe—Do we need a group exemption?" in Hansen (ed) *International Intellectual Property Law and Policy* (Sweet & Maxwell, 1996).

[63] [1995] FSR 530; [1995] 4 CMLR 718.

[64] Areas where Art 86 potentially "interacts" with the Software Directive are (i) access to interfaces which enable a third party to create an interoperable software product; (ii) access to information for the maintenance of software; (iii) reproduction of an existing user interface and (iv) the dissemination of information in networks. See further Robbie Downing, "Magill and the Software Directive: are they interoperable?" [1995] 4 Web JCLI.

[65] [1984] 3 CMLR 147; see further *Bulletin of the European Communities* (10–1984) at 96.

[66] In 1980 the Commission investigated IBM's alleged dominant position with respect to its System/370 Computer. IBM's activities was held by the Commission to constitute an abuse of Art 86 in three respects (i) combining main memory storage and an operating system with System/370, thus depriving competitors of the opportunity of marketing these components to System/370

consequence of *Magill*, Article 86 may provide a basis for intervention where the de facto control over user interfaces may allow a dominant vendor to extend the economic benefits from its primary copyright to a downstream market.[67]

Notwithstanding the importance of Articles 85 and 86, particularly where **1.22** broad copyright protection is asserted,[68] this work will not contain further discussion on this topic, for reason of its focus on selected aspects of copyright law and licensing.

VII. METHOD AND PLAN

The book divides into four parts, (1) The Subsistence of Copyright and **1.23** Infringement Methodology;[69] (2) The Scope of Copyright Protection of User Interfaces;[70] (3) Reverse Engineering and Defences[71] and (4) Challenges for the Future.[72]

On the subject of exclusive rights,[73] I have chosen to concentrate on the adap- **1.24** tation[74] and reproduction rights[75] (being the most relevant rights to the topics discussed), devoting less discussion to other rights,[76] and moral rights.[77] Authorship, Ownership and Term have been excluded from the scope of this book.

---

purchases; (ii) refusing to supply manufacturers of plug-compatible equipment with the interface information they required in order to begin manufacture of such equipment; (iii) refusing to supply software installation services to users of non-IBM computers. IBM denied that these activities constituted abuse, but gave undertakings to the Commission in return for a suspension of any further investigation (first, interface information would be made available by the earlier of four months from the announcement of the new product or the date it became generally available and secondly, the System/370 would be supplied with only the minimum memory necessary to undertake diagnostic tests). This settlement implicitly contributed to the need for a European harmonising effort surrounding software copyright protection, while buttressing the Commission's monopoly-policing role. See further Vinje, "History of the EC Software Directive" in Lehmann, Tapper (eds) *A Handbook of European Software Law* (Oxford, 1992), at pp 44–45.

[67] See further Vinje "Magill: its Impact on the Information Technology Industry" [1992] 11 EIPR 397 at 400–401; Vinje, "The Final Word on Magill" [1995] 6 EIPR 297 at 302–303.

[68] Hence providing another justification for narrowing substantive copyright protection, the effect of which would be to minimise the invasive intervention of Art 86, post-*Magill*.

[69] Chapters 2 and 3.

[70] Chapters 4 and 5.

[71] Chapters 6 and 7.

[72] Chapters 8–10.

[73] For a discussion of Secondary Infringement, see paras 2.16–2.18.

[74] *Infra*, paras 6.4–6.7.

[75] *Infra*, para 2.29 *et seq.*

[76] See *infra*, para 2.15.

[77] *Infra*, paras 2.19–2.21.

Part 1

Subsistence of Copyright and Infringement Methodology

2

Subsistence of Copyright and Infringement Analysis under US and UK laws

I. INTRODUCTION

This chapter sets out the fundamentals of software copyright protection in the **2.1** United Kingdom with reference to the relevant exclusive rights of the copyright owner. Infringement methodology in the USA and United Kingdom are introduced after a discussion of the underpinning notions of "originality" and the "idea-expression dichotomy". The chapter discusses recent US developments in non-literal protection, and the trends that are emerging between different US courts. The proposition is ultimately advanced, that US infringement methodology, as exemplified by the test introduced in *Computer Associates v Altai*, should be applicable in the United Kingdom, for it prescriptively assists a British judge in determining scope of protection in respect of what is largely functional subject-matter.

II. SUBSISTENCE OF COPYRIGHT

(a) Computer Programs as Protectable Works

The first generation of software cases considered basic issues of copyright pro- **2.2** tection of object as opposed to source code programs with varied results between different jurisdictions.[1] Subsequent statutory,[2] EC Directive[3] and

---

[1] eg in *Computer Edge Pty Limited v Apple Computer Inc*(1986) 65 ALR 33 the High Court of Australia decided that copyright did not vest in the object code form of original source code programs, a decision subsequently reversed by statute. In the USA, doubts were expressed at first instance in *Apple Computer v Franklin* as to the protectability of object code, but this was subsequently rejected by the Third Circuit: 454 F.Supp 812 (ED Pa 1982), rev'd 714 F.2d 1240 (3rd Cir 1983). US Courts have had no difficulty protecting ROM-stored Microcode: *NEC v Intel* 645 F.Supp 590 (ND Cal 1986); see further Colin Tapper, *Computer Law*, 4th edn. (1989) at 38–39 and references therein.

[2] See s3(1) CDPA which includes computer programs as protectable literary works, and s 1(1) Copyright (Computer Software) Amendment Act 1985, which amended the 1956 Act.

[3] Article 1(1) and recital 7, Software Directive.

Treaty[4] intervention have rendered computer programs primarily protected as literary works.

2.3   The CDPA carries no definition for computer software,[5] thus leaving UK courts the flexibility to adapt to new technologies[6] but the Software Directive has expanded the scope of "computer programs" to include preparatory design material. By apparently responding to a perceived problem of protecting material that may be the result of much labour and skill,[7] the Software Directive skirts perilously close to protecting ideas, "extending protection beyond how the preparatory design material expresses the logical steps to be taken to the what of the logic itself, arguably following processes and functions within the copyright paradigm as traditionally conceived".[8]

2.4   However the CDPA now classifies "preparatory design material" as a separate class of literary work.[9] Prior to the post-Directive amendments,[10] specifications, flow charts and diagrams, layouts and other materials relating to the design and production of a computer program would have been protected as literary or artistic works as appropriate.[11]

2.5   This different classification might mean that the provisions[12] applicable to computer programs would not apply to such preliminary material. For example one will not be able to make a back-up copy of a computer manual, unless some other permitted act was available under the CDPA. On the other hand the paternity right would avail preparatory design work,[13] but not computer programs.[14] Further, flow charts and diagrams, which previously would have been protected as artistic works, will now be protected as "literary works", with their attendant requirements, such as recording, in "writing or otherwise".[15]

---

[4] Article 10(1) TRIPS agreement states that "Computer programs, whether in source or object code, shall be protected as literary works under the Berne Convention (1971)". See also Art 4 WIPO Copyright Treaty (1996) and Lai "The Impact of the Recent WIPO Copyright Treaty and other Initiatives on Software Copyright in the United Kingdom" [1998] 1 IPQ 35 at 39–40.

[5] cf s 10 Australian Copyright Act. Attempts have been made to torture the meaning; see for example *Powerflex v Data Access* (1997) 37 IPR 436, where the Full Federal Court had to consider whether user interface commands (being mere ciphers) could be "computer programs". In the Irish case of *News Datacom Ltd v Satellite Decoding Systems* [1995] FSR 201 (Irish High Court), it was accepted that a "smartcard" decoder for use with scrambled satellite television broadcasts was a computer program.

[6] eg HTML programs, see Chapter 8.

[7] Laddie, Prescott and Vitoria, *Modern Law of Copyright and Designs*, Vol 1 at paras 20.9 to 20.21. The authors observe that when program developers have got this far they have done a great deal if not most of their work and the task of expressing the preparatory work in machine-readable code is often delegated to more junior personnel.

[8] Comment by Louise Longdin "Copyright Protection for Computerized Compilations: A Cautionary Tale from New Zealand" (1998) 5(3) Int J of Law and Information Technology 249 at 272.

[9] See s 3(1)(c) CDPA.

[10] Copyright (Computer Programs) Regulations 1992.

[11] For a discussion on the protection of ancillary material, see Bainbridge *Intellectual Property* (1992) at pp 172–177.

[12] See ss 50A–50C CDPA.

[13] Ibid s 77.

[14] Ibid s 79.

[15] Ibid s 3(2).

(b) Originality

(i) Originality in the USA and the United Kingdom

Whilst a work consists of its particular form, the uncontroversial observation **2.6** can be made that not every aspect of this form owes its origin to the author.[16] The US Supreme Court laid down the marker for "originality" and its relationship with the idea-expression dichotomy[17] in the well-known "compilations" decision of *Feist Publications v Rural Telephone Service Co*,[18] where it reconsidered the originality to mean:

> "that the work was independently created by the author (as opposed to copied from other works), and that it possess at least *some minimal degree of creativity*"[19] (emphasis added).

These four words arguably introduce a new standard of originality into US law,[20] requiring that at the very least, the author must have exercised some choice in determining an aspect of the form of a work before that part of the form can be said to have originated from him or her.

The stringency of this criteria is suspect. From the view point of copyright- **2.7** ability, in *Feist* the US Supreme Court pronounced that a vast majority of compilations will pass the test, and there only remained a narrow category of works in which "the creative spark is uttlerly lacking or so trivial as to be virtually non-existent".[21] Indeed this has been confirmed in successive decisions at both appellate[22] and district court levels.[23] In relation to factual compilations, the US

---

[16] *Miller v Universal City Studios* 650 F.2d 1365 at 1368 (5th Circuit 1981). The Fifth Circuit stated that the dichotomy between facts and their expression derives from the concept of originality.

[17] Discussed *infra*, paras 2.22–2.28.

[18] 113 L Ed 358 (1991).

[19] Ibid at 369.

[20] The court did accept that the 1976 Act was intended to incorporate without change the old standard of originality established under the 1909 Act; ibid at 375. For a different interpretation, see Ang, "The Idea -Expression Dichotomy and Merger Doctrine in the Copyright Laws of the US and the UK" [1993] 2 Int J of Law and Information Technology 111 at 127.

[21] *Supra*, n 18 at 377.

[22] *BellSouth Advertising and Publishing Corp v Donnelly Information Publishing Inc*. 933 F.2d 952 (11th Cir 1991) (*infra* at n 24); *Key Publications v Chinatown Today Publishing Enterprises* 945 F.2d 509 at 513–514 (2nd Cir 1993) (yellow pages of a Chinese–American directory were held copyrightable); *Kregos v Associated Press* 937 F.2d 700 at 703 (2nd Cir 1991) (the plaintiff's "pitching form" was protectable). cf cases in which copyright was denied for want of creativity; *Victor Lalli Enterprises v Bog Red Apple* 936 F.2d 671 at 673 (2d Cir 1991) (compilation of "lucky numbers" used in gambling); followed in *Thomas Distribs v Green Line Distribs* 41 USPQ 2d 1382 (6th Cir 1986) (a catalogue of replacement belts "organized in a manner unknown to the industry prior to its publication" was insufficiently creative to qualify for copyright protection).

[23] See eg *Mathew Bender v West Pub Co*. 1997 US Dist Lexis 6915 (SDNY, 19 May 1997) (ruling that West's pagination of reported cases was not copyrightable, its editorial revision of cases not entailing copyrightable authorship); *Oasis Pu Co. v West Pub Co* 924 F.Supp 918 (D.Minn 1996) (copyright in the compilation of cases reported in West's Southern Reporter; and finding that the defendant's use of the star pagination to West's page numbers constituted infringement); *National Council on Compensation v Insurance Data Resources* 40 USPQ.2d 1362 (SD Fla 1996) (finding that a manual comprising job codes and formats used by insurance raters was unprotectable).

position appears to be that the selection, co-ordination or arrangement of a particular work of authorship must not be something so mechanical or routine, entirely typical or obvious as to require no creativity whatsoever.[24]

2.8   "Originality" also galvanises the distinction between expression and ideas. In the USA, where the dichotomy is the subject of more sophisticated judicial discussion,[25] largely because of explicit statutory recognition,[26] limiting concepts to copyright protection are justified on grounds of originality or rather the lack thereof. For example, the *scènes à faire* has also been said to be based on the premise that where a particular expression is common to the treatment of a particular idea, process or discovery, it is lacking in the originality that is the *sine qua non* of copyright protection.[27]

2.9   In the United Kingdom it is clear that the originality requirement does not demand novelty or merit, merely that the work should originate from the author, and should not have been copied from another source.[28] Taking this "minimalist interpretation"[29] further, under UK law it does not matter that the various elements comprising a collective whole have all been copied from other sources, provided that the particular combination has not itself been copied, and has involved the application of the compiler's own skill, labour and judgment.[30]

2.10   In relation to computer programs, as a result of the undemanding requirements for copyright originality both in Anglo and American traditions, exhaustive consideration of the level of creativity or intellectual or aesthetic content is absent from many software decisions.[31] In the United Kingdom, the observation

[24] Particularly vulnerable are comprehensive factual databases covering an entire universe of information, where the element of selection is lacking and the arrangement obvious; *Warren Pub v Microdos Data Corp* 115 F.3d 1509 (11th Cir 1997); *American Rental Association v Delta Dental Plains Assoc* 39 USPQ.2d 1714 (ND Ill. 1996). A contrast may be provided by creative selection and formatting, which is deserving of copyright protection. In *Bell South Advertising and Publishing v Donnelly Information Publishing Inc.* (*supra* n 22) the 11th Circuit held that the publisher of a "Yellow Pages" telephone directory had exercised selection in selecting geographical criteria, a directory close date and other business classifications. The publisher also cros-referenced listings with different categories. Such activities were held to be sufficiently creative for the publisher's format of its directory to be copyrightable.

[25] eg *Computer Associates v Altai*, discussed at *infra* para 2.42 *et seq.*

[26] See s 102(b) USCA, discussed at paras 2.25–2.28.

[27] See *Gates Rubber v Brando American Inc.* 9 F.3d 823 (10th Cir 1993). Also Sookman, "International differences in Copyright Protection for Software" [1995] 5 CTLR 142 at 143 *et seq.* See para 3.36.

[28] See the much repeated words of Peterson J in *London University Press v University Tutorial Press* [1916] 2 Ch 601 at 608. Although minimal, it is still possible for some works originated by an author to fall beneath the threshold, especially in the area of compilations. See for example, the diary in *Cramp v Smythson* [1944] AC 329 (*de minimis* case; the gathering of existing pocket diary tables was not sufficient).

[29] So described by Professor Colin Tapper, writing on "The Software Directive: A UK Perspective" in Lehman, Tapper (eds) *A Handbook on European Software Law* (Oxford, 1992) at p 147.

[30] Usually the standard for secondary work based on existing sources; see eg *Macmillan v Cooper* (1923) 40 TLR 186.

[31] See observations of Dreier "Copyright Protection for Computer Programs in Foreign Countries: Legal Issues and Trends in Judicial Decisions and Legislation" (1989) 20 IIC 803 at 809. There is an obvious lack of discussion in *Richardon v Flanders* [1993] FSR 497 at 515–516.

has been made that because of the limited approach towards originality, the efforts to distinguish between ideas and expression find occasional place in the determination of copyright subsistence.[32] Against this limited approach has been a rigorous European campaign to remove the British originality criterion in favour of the "author's intellectual creation".[33]

(ii) The "author's intellectual creation"

Continental traditions follow a personality-oriented concept of originality. Not **2.11** only must origination be present, but the author's own personality must find its expression in the work.[34] In the context of software, on one extreme, the German Supreme Court when applying a test of originality, did not only require individuality as compared with pre-existing programs, but also that the ability shown in the engineering process considerably surpassed average programming ability.[35]

National differences between various Member States have led the European **2.12** Commission to adopt a common definition of originality in the Software Directive, that is founded on the "author's intellectual creation"[36] adding that "[n]o other criteria shall be applied to determine its eligibility for protection".[37] When implementing the Software Directive, the United Kingdom's implementing regulations did not include it, the draftsman's presumption being that UK originality was consistent and needed no clarification. This is highly suspect.[38]

---

[32] Cornish, *Intellectual Property*, 3rd edn (1996) at para 10–10.

[33] See Cohen Jehoram "The EC Directives, Economics and Author's Rights" (1994) 25 IIC 821 at 828–829, where this definition of copyright originality has been championed as the main justification for the Software Directive; and is also a "horizontal" provision, which prejudices future directives and the whole of an emerging European Copyright Law.

[34] See Drexl "What is protected in a computer program?" IIC Studies, Vol 15 at pp 76–79. Compare Art 6bis of the Japanese Copyright Act 1986, which confers protection on "database works, which by reason of the selection or systematic construction of information contained therein, constitute intellectual creations".

[35] See *Inkassoprogram* (1986) 17 IIC 681; *Betriebssystem* (1990) 22 IIC 723. A German Court has issued a decision overruling the *Inkasso*; *Buchhaltungsprogramm* CR 1993 at 752 *et seq* (comment by Michael Lehmann).

[36] This criterion currently exists for computer programs, databases and photographs (see Art 6 and Recital 17 of the Term Directive (93/98/EEC of 29 October 1993, OJ L 290/9 (24 November 1993), which speaks of "the author's own intellectal creation reflecting his personality").

[37] Article 1(3) Software Directive. Recital 8 states that "in respect of the criteria to be applied in determining whether or not a computer program is an original work, no tests as to the qualitative or aesthetic merits of the program should be applied". This is understood to be direct reaction from the Commission to the high level of originality required by the German Federal Supreme Court, which in making comparisons with average programming ability invariably imposes a standard of quality. See Drexl, *supra*, n 34 at 96. It is worth noting that the original proposal for a Directive expressly equated originality in respect of computer programs with originality in respect of other literary works, but Art 1(3) in its final form was adopted, deliberately aimed at minimising national variation. For a history of Art 1(3), see Dreier (1991) 4 Comp L&Pr 178.

[38] Seeing that many modern computer programs are effectively compilations of standard modules. See Commission Proposal for the Directive 89/C/91/05, para 2.7.

2.13   More recently the operative phrase has been written into the CDPA by the Copyright and Related Rights (Databases) Regulations 1997,[39] albeit applicable only to "database copyright" as defined by these regulations. It remains to be seen whether UK judges are likely to be persuaded that this standard should also be applied to computer software as a rule of interpretation,[40] and read such a change as justifying a wholesale reformulation of the originality requirement in UK law.[41] Such a move may be regarded as bold but at the same time would chime with concerns over the over-extension of the copyright monopoly.[42] However the express amendment of the CDPA as regards databases simpliciter is more likely to be interpreted as signifying the maintenance of the existing originality standard for other works.[43] Even though UK law recognises a "double test" for assessing originality, ie that the work is not copied, and that it involves an investment of skill and labour, it has been said that the phrase "skill and labour" does not necessarily quadrate with the "sweat of the brow" doctrine (rejected by the US Supreme Court). Arguably "skill" carries an extensive import, covering creative endeavour. Hence a UK judge should have no difficulty in applying the test of skill as requiring intellectual creation.[44]

2.14   If, on the other hand, the threshold of originality for the United Kingdom is raised by the above words, there is an arguable case for undertaking filtration for non-originality[45] when determining substantial similarity between two programs. Holyoak and Torremans[46] have argued for the imposition of this standard of originality in software cases in support of Jacob J's approach in *Ibcos v Barclays Mercantile Highland Finance*, where his Lordship rejected the application of US infringement methodology in preference for a general test of "over-borrowing" of the plaintiff's skill, labour and judgment.[47]

---

[39] See reg 6. Indeed the implementation of the phrase may generally be viewed as an exercise of European appeasement by the British; see Chalton, Rees (eds) *Database Law* (Jordans, 1998) at pp 85–86.

[40] See Chapter 9; Lai [1998] 1 IPQ 32 at 33–34.

[41] See eg the suggestion for some level of minimal creativity by Ricketson "The Concept of Originality in Anglo–Australian Copyright Law" (1991) 9(2) *Copyright Reporter* 1 at 16.

[42] See Laddie [1996] 5 EIPR 253 at 260.

[43] A view confirmed by Ian McCartney, Minister of State, DTI, at the Fourth Standing Committee on Delegated Legislation, 3 December 1997.

[44] Sterling, "Creator's Right and the Bridge between Author's Right and Copyright" (1998) 29 IIC 302 at 305. The phrase can equally be read to refer to a "not copied" test; see Cornish, *supra*, n 32 at para 13–25.

[45] The principle of filtration for non-originality has been long accepted in English law, particularly in respect of compilations (*Ladbroke v Hill* [1964] 1 WLR 273) and secondary works (*Warwick Film Production v Eisinger* [1969] 1 Ch 508).

[46] Holyoak and Torremans *Intellectual Property law* (1995), p 420. The authors argue that a proper application of the originality criterion specified in the Software Directive would result in a core of protectable expression, the equivalent result achieved by applying the *Altai* test (discussed *infra* at para 2.42 *et seq*).

[47] [1994] FSR 275 at 302. See further Stone, "Software Law—Lessons for America: Filtration for Functionality from Software Copyright" (1997) CLSR 15–21.

(c) Other Prohibited Acts under Section 16 CDPA

This work focuses on the reproduction[48] and adaptation[49] (in the context of **2.15** reverse engineering) rights. It is the author's view that they most directly affect and define the scope of copyright protection for software. Other prohibited acts which are applicable to computer software include issuing copies of the work to the public;[50] performing, showing or playing the work in public;[51] broadcasting and inclusion in a cable programme service;[52] and most recently, rental and lending.[53]

(d) Secondary Infringement of Copyright

(i) Classes of secondary infringement

Unlike primary infringement, secondary infringement of copyright in software **2.16** and other works is predicated upon the guilty knowledge[54] of the defendant. Three broad classes of secondary infringement exist; first the dealings[55] with "infringing copies",[56] secondly, the provision of the means for the manufacture of infringing copies,[57] and thirdly the sanctions for provision of the means for infringing performances of a copyright to take place.[58]

Bandey has observed that a more modern species of secondary infringement **2.17** is that concerned with the use of devices designed to circumvent copy protection.[59] It is the author's view that the anti-circumvention legislation and recent

---

[48] See ss 16(1)(a), 17 CDPA.

[49] Ibid ss 16(1)(e), 21(3)(ab), 21(4). See further *infra*, para 6.4.

[50] Ibid ss 16(1)(b), 18(3) (incorporating EU-wide exhaustion).

[51] Ibid ss 16(1)(c), 19.

[52] Ibid ss 16(1)(d), 20.

[53] As amended by the Copyright and Related Rights Regulations 1996 (SI 1996 No 2967) implementing the Rental and Lending Rights Directive. See ss 16(1)(ba) and 18A CDPA. For further analysis of these provisions, and Art 7 of the WIPO Copyright Treaty (1996), see Lai [1998] 1 IPQ 35 at 40–42.

[54] Easier to establish under the CDPA 1988, by the addition of the words "reason to believe" in ss 22 and 23. Further guidance is offered by Morritt J in *Gear Incorporated v Hi-Tec Sports Plc* [1992] FSR 121 at 129: "it seems to me that 'reason to believe' must involve the concept of knowledge of facts from which a reasonable man would arrive at the relevant belief. Facts from which a reasonable man might suspect the relevant conclusion cannot be enough . . . the phrase does connote the allowance of a period of time to enable the reasonable man to evaluate those facts so as to convert the facts into reasonable belief."
This dicta was approved in *Hutchinson Personal Communications v Hook Advertising* [1995] FSR 365 at 378.

[55] See s 23 CDPA. Dealings in infringing copies also include importation; see ibid s 22.

[56] Defined in ibid ss 23 and 27.

[57] Ibid s 24(1).

[58] Ibid s 26(2).

[59] See Bandey *International Copyright in Computer Program Technology* (CLT, 1996) at pp 192–195.

proposals so affect primary rights that they warrant treatment in a separate chapter of this work.[60]

(ii) Transmission of computer software

2.18 An important, but oft-forgotten provision, especially in the context of digital dissemination, is section 24(2) CDPA, which states that copyright in a work is also infringed by a person, who, without the licence of the copyright owner, transmits the work by means of a telecommunications system.[61] This provision is highly relevant for transmission of computer software or collections of sub-programs across computer networks (whether in the form of the internet or intranets), or computer bulletin boards or via electronic mail-providing services.

(e) Moral Rights

2.19 Under the CDPA neither the rights of paternity[62] nor integrity[63] apply to computer software.[64] These moral rights do however apply to flowcharts, specifications, and other preparatory design material, which qualify as literary works under section 3 CDPA.[65] It is doubtful whether these moral rights apply to user interfaces such as the menu command hierarchy of Lotus 1–2–3, or the Microsoft windows environment, since these items may be regarded as part of a computer program.[66]

2.20 An anomaly lies in the retention of the right against false attribution,[67] which applies to all forms of work. If it is important to the author of a computer program not to have his work falsely attributed, it is difficult to see why it is not important for him to be attributed as the author in the first place.

2.21 With the fast-encroaching culture of deploying "rights management information"[68] in digital disseminations, authorial information will increasingly be embedded in computer software for the purposes of both online and off-line dissemination. It may be opportune to reassess the continued relevance of moral rights exclusions in relation to computer programs.

---

[60] *Infra*, para 8.23 *et seq.*

[61] Defined in s 178 CDPA as a system for conveying visual images, sounds or other information by electronic means.

[62] The right to be identified as author: ibid s 77.

[63] The right to object to derogatory treatment: ibid s 80.

[64] Ibid ss 79(2); 81(2).

[65] Note the disparity in implementing the Software Directive, which states that "preparatory design material" is protected as part of the computer program (Art 1(1) Software Directive).

[66] This is the view of Bainbridge, *Software Copyright Law*, 3rd edn (1997) at 22–23.

[67] By virtue of there being the absence of any exclusionary provision on this point in the CDPA; see ibid s 84.

[68] See Art 12 WIPO Copyright Treaty (1996), in which the definition of "Rights Management Information" is expanded to include information about the terms and conditions set by the owner for use of the work, as well as "numbers or codes that represent such information".

III. THE IDEA/EXPRESSION DICHOTOMY

(a) The Realm of "Ideas"

The unprotectable nature of an "idea" is trite to copyright law,[69] and yet its dis- **2.22**
tinction from expression is most difficult to ascertain,[70] particularly in software
cases. Amongst the many commentaries which have remarked on the ambiguous nature of the term "ideas" is Allen Rosen's "Reconsidering the Idea/
Expression Dichotomy".[71] He suggests that "idea" comprises four distinctions;
the style-content distinction, the fixed idea-unfixed idea distinction, the mental
idea-linguistic expression distinction and the general-specific idea distinction.[72]
Rosen identifies the last of these distinctions as the most important and concludes that the ambiguity is inherent and arbitrary but adds that this is actually
advantageous as "a means of balancing the public interest in a free flow of ideas
against the need to provide rewards and incentives for creative work".[73]

A commonly employed meaning of "idea", which is gathering increasing **2.23**
prominence in the software copyright field, places it as part of a continuum in
which any "expression" can be restated in more abstract terms until a point of
abstraction is reached, where all further abstractions are deemed unprotectable
ideas.[74] The consequence of this approach is that the idea/expression dichotomy
is thus transformed into an infinitely malleable device, enabling a court to strike
a balance between rewarding and encouraging creative contribution and the
interest of the public in using aspects of such contributions,[75] in relation to different works.[76]

---

[69] *LB (Plastics) v Swish Products* [1979] RPC 551at 629.

[70] Remembering the famous words of Learned Hand J in *Nichols v Universal Pictures* 45 F.2d 119
at 121 (2nd Cir 1930). "Nobody has ever been able to fix that boundary, and nobody ever can".
Elsewhere the dichotomy has been descrbied as "a distinction with an ill-defined boundary". See
Cornish, *Intellectual Property: Patents, Copyright, Trade Marks and Allied Rights*, 2nd edn (1989)
at p 289; unhelpfully described by Laddie, Prescott and Vittoria as a "cautious understatement"
(*Modern Law of Copyright and Designs*, 2nd edn, Vol 1 at p 62). The latter work takes the view that
the dichotomy is in fact a fallacy, since "expression" does not mean the actual form of expression
employed: "There is merely a series of gradations ranging from the very abstract to the utterly concrete all of which will fit equally well on any given work" (p 62).

[71] 26 UBC L.Rev 263 (1992) at 266–277.

[72] Ibid at 279.

[73] Ibid at 276.

[74] See *Nichols, supra* n 70; *Lotus v Paperback*, discussed *infra*, para 2.41; *Computer Associates v
Altai infra*, para 2.42.

[75] Rosen, *supra*, n 71 at 276; Teter, "Merger and Machines: An analysis of the Pro-Compatibility
Trend in Computer Software Copyright Cases" (1993) 45 Stanford L Rev 1061 at 1074–1075.

[76] *Atari v North American Philips Consumer Electronics* 672 F.2d 607 at 617 (7th Cir) cert denied
459 US 880 (1982); Band and Katoh *Interfaces on Trial* (1995) at pp 62–63.

(b) Dichotomy under Threat

2.24 Most significantly UK law does not have the equivalent of section 102(b) USCA.[77] Much is made of this difference by Jacob J in *Ibcos Computers Ltd v Barclays Mercantile Finance*[78] in considering US authorities and methodology to be unhelpful to the endeavours of UK software copyright law. His Lordship prefers a distinction between a "general" as opposed to "specific" idea, where only the latter qualifies for copyright protection.[79] This work argues that the consequence of not entrenching a firm judicial basis for application of the dichotomy in the United Kingdom, particularly in relation to software, is undesirable over-protection, as seen in *Ibcos*. Although the dichotomy has come under scathing criticism,[80] the principle is not without foundation under English law.[81]

(c) Basis for Applying the Dichotomy in the United Kingdom

2.25 As a general observation, a partial extraction of section 102(b) USCA now features in the language of many treaties, the latest being Article 2 of the recently concluded WIPO Copyright Treaty (1996). Article 2 Copyright Treaty reiterates the elements of a copyright protectable work—that copyright protection does

---

[77] USCA s102(b) provides "In no case does copyright protection for an original work of authorship extend to any idea, procedure, process, system, method of operation, concept, principle, or discovery, regardless of the form in which it is described, explained, illustrated or embodied in such work". This is a codification and expansion of the principle in *Baker v Selden* 101 US 99 (1879), that systems and their constituent parts, even if embodied in a specific pattern or arrangement of words, are not protectable by copyright.

[78] [1994] FSR 275. See discussion *infra* at para 2.31–2.33.

[79] Ibid at 291–292; an approach endorsed by Laddie, *et al Modern Law of Copyright and Designs*, Vol 1 at para 20.78.

[80] See Laddie, *et al, supra*, n 79 at paras 2.73–2.78. In their usual felicity and customary clarity the authors primarily argue that unless by "expression" one means the actual form of expression employed, then philosophically speaking there is no such dichotomy; only a series of conceivable gradations ranging from the very abstract to the utterly concrete, all of which will fit equally well on any given work. See further Dworkin [1979] EIPR 117.

[81] See s 51 CDPA (which removes the protection of ordinary copyright in an artistic work, being a design of an article which is not itself an artistic work, in relation to articles made to that design); and s 213 CDPA (excluding from unregistered design protection features and articles which are essentially functional; discussed *infra*, para 3.31, in relation to merger). UK judges have recognised and affirmed the existence of the dichotomy; see *LB (Plastics) v Swish* [1979] RPC 611 at 629 (per Lord Hailsham); *Donoghue v Allied Newspapers Ltd* [1938] Ch 106 at 109–110 (per Farwell J); and *Total Information Processing Systems v Daman* [1992] FSR 171 at 181 (Judge Paul Baker); *Geo Ward (Moxley) v Sankey* [1988] FSR 66 (Whitford J); *John Richardson v Flanders* [1993] FSR 497 (Ferris J). cf *Plix v Winstone* [1986] FSR 63 at 92–94, in which a New Zealand court, while accepting the proposition that copyright does not extend to ideas, sought to reconcile it with the formula that "copyright subsists only in the form of expression" by saying in effect that the protected ideas are considered to be part of the expression (upheld on appeal [1986] FSR 608). But this statement was made in the different context of copyright protection for functional designs under liberal rules protecting such material.

not extend to "any idea, procedures, methods of operation or mathematical concepts as such". The wording of Article 2 is in part material to Article 9(2) TRIPS. Both these provisions carry important ramifications for software copyright in the United Kingdom, in that they place a real and substantial limitation[82] on the scope of copyright protection of computer software: every idea, procedure, method of operation or mathematical concept is freely available for use by others. By its exclusory approach, Article 2 arguably goes even further than Article 1(2) Software Directive and its accompanying recitals. In this regard it is noteworthy that the *Ibcos* judgment was handed down in 1994, but it dealt with infringements dating from 1986 (before the Software Directive). The judgment itself makes no reference to the Directive or its implementing Regulations. Whatever its status as a declaration of a purely English approach operating prior to the Software Directive, the decision arguably cannot represent current UK law.[83]

Enactments like Article 2 WIPO Copyright Treaty pave the way for doctrines **2.26** like merger and *scènes à faire*[84] to achieve a prominence in UK law which has thus far been denied them.

As the following sections will show, these limiting doctrines[85] serve to aid the **2.27** adjudication of software copyright, particularly in defining what constitutes a "substantial taking".[86] The dichotomy affirms the fundamental tension when a court is called upon to protect expression that is inseparable from a useful article, or is inherently part of a "procedure", a "method of operation"[87] or "mathematical concept". Although computer programs may in some instances be imbued with the creativity of the programmer, they are also highly functional in that they are the actual steps followed by a computer to produce a required result. For many types of software, output information may only be presented in one of a few ways.[88]

---

[82] Gervais, *The TRIPs Agreement* (1998) at pp 77–79, 81. Although another interpretation is that the statement in Art 2 refers *only* to copyright protection within the scope of the Copyright Treaty. This is arguably too restrictive a reading of Art 2.

[83] See Stone "Software Law—Lessons from America: Filtration of Functionality from Software Copyright" (1997) 13(1) CLSR 15 at 20.

[84] These doctrines are discussed in detail in the next chapter.

[85] Forming part of a "filtration" process, as illustrated in by the Second Circuit in *Computer Associates v Altai* 982 F.2d 693 (2nd Cir, 1992). For a comprehensive summary and references to some of the literature on this subject, see Rowland, MacDonald *Information Technology Law* (Cavendish, 1997) at pp 31–53. See discussion in Chapter 3.

[86] The abstraction-filtration-comparison test was endorsed and applied by Ferris J in *John Richardson v Flanders* [1993] FSR 497 at 550, 553. His Lordship, while admitting a difficulty in applying the test (ibid at 527, 549), did not see any conflict between US authorities such as *Computer Associates v Altai* (ibid) (in extracting a "core of protectable expression") and UK jurisprudence (ibid at 526–527). This approach, which is argued to be fundamentally sound, is to be contrasted with that of Jacob J in *Ibcos* [1994] FSR 275 at 301–302.

[87] As it has been held by the First Circuit in respect of Lotus' menu command hierarchy: *Lotus v Borland* 49 F.3d 807 (1st Cir 1995). In this endeavour, Art 2 Copyright Treaty may also serve to define whether user interfaces or aspects thereof are copyrightable subject matter. See Lai [1998] 1 IPQ at 38–39, and further discussion in Chapter 4.

[88] In *Richardson v Flanders* [1993] FSR 497, Ferris J found this to be true of the "date option" in the plaintiff's program (at 550). His Lordship observed that the similarity of label entries sequenced

2.28   At least in relation to computer software, such utilitarian considerations will surely fetter the determination of substantial copying,[89] quite apart from the originality (or otherwise) of the material copied.

IV. INFRINGEMENT METHODOLOGY: A PRESCRIPTIVE ANALYSIS OF
SUBSTANTIAL SIMILARITY

(a) Copyright Infringement of Computer Software: Literal Copying

2.29   As with any other literary work, copyright in computer software is infringed, by making, without authorisation, a copy of the program or a substantial part thereof.[90] It is trite that substantiality is ultimately an adjudication of quality—whether in "essence" the plaintiff's program has been copied, no matter how small.[91]

(i) *Literal copying of software*

2.30   Literal copying is the direct reproduction of another's work, with very little subtlety.[92] In this instance a UK court addresses three axiomatic issues. First, it tests for subsistence of copyright in the plaintiff's program.[93] Secondly, it determines whether the defendant copied in fact.[94] Thirdly, it asks whether the reproduc-

in both programs were the result of a "common sense choice . . . between very restricted alternatives"(at 553). Further, the display of minimum stock figures on screen was regarded to be the only practical means by which the idea could be expressed (at 555–557).

[89]   See eg Sterling "Testing for Subsistence and Infringement of Copyright in Computer Programs: some US and UK cases" [1995] 11 CLSR 119 at 124; Richard Arnold [1993] EIPR 250 at 253.

[90]   See s 16 CDPA.

[91]   For example in *MS Associates v Power* [1988] FSR 242, the defendant's program contained 43 similarities out of a total of 9,000 lines. This was however sufficient to justify an arguable case that a substantial part of the original program had been taken.

[92]   In the software context this is usually revealed by line-by-line comparisons of respective source codes. See *Ibcos, infra*, n 96; *Accounting Systems 2000 v CCH Australia* [1993] FSR at 480 (Australian High Court); *Microsoft Corporation v Electro-wide Ltd* [1997] FSR 580 at 590–594 (summary judgment obtained by Microsoft in respect of straightforward censed preloading of its operating system software). See also *Cantor Fitzgerald International & Anr v Tradition (UK) Limited & Others* (Judgment of Pumfrey J dated 15 April 1999). In resolving a copyright claim over the computer programs of a City bond-broking system, the court had to consider a line-by-line analysis of 77,000 lines of code, at the end of which a mere 2,952 lines of code were shown (and admitted) to have been copied.

[93]   A test of "originality" after identification of the work.

[94]   The court will draw an inference of copying based on the similarity of two works. The onus then shifts to the defendant to rebut the inference. Several explanations may be offered, eg both parties derived the material from a common source (third party or public domain); the similarity arises from a functional necessity, or that the plaintiff copied from the defendant's work. See further *Ibcos, infra*, n 96 at 298–297. Moreover, it is the presence of trivial inconsequential matter that traps the unwary copyist: "It is the resemblances in inessentials, the small, redundant, even mistaken elements of the copyright work which carry the greatest weight. This is because they are least likely to have been the result of independent design". (So rightly observed by Hoffmann J in *Billhöfer Maschinenfabrik GmbH v Dixon Ltd* [1990] FSR 105 at 123.)

tion, if not whole, is substantial. An affirmative response to each of these questions gives rise to infringement, subject to a defence or permitted act.[95]

(ii) Ibcos v Barclays Mercantile Finance

Ibcos v Barclays Mercantile Finance[96] was the first case in the United Kingdom **2.31**
to consider seriously the literal copying of computer software. The case is
prominent in this book, largely because of the surprising rejection by Jacob J of
US authorities as being irrelevant and incapable of assisting a UK judge in deciding the scope of copyright of a computer program, for the purposes of determining substantial similarity.[97] The contrary position is advanced by this
work.[98]

The plaintiff owned a suite of computer programs known as the "Agriculture **2.32**
Dealing System". A competing suite, called UNICORN was subsequently
designed by a former partner, written in different variants of the same programming language. Jacob J concluded that there had been disk to disk copying.[99] Regarding copyright subsistence, his Lordship took the view that not only
were the individual programs protected by copyright, but the suite in question
was protected as a compilation.[100]

Turning to the issue of substantiality, Jacob J concluded that 28 out of 55 of **2.33**
the defendant's programs infringed the plaintiff's copyrights, as to program
structure and design features and sub-programs, both individually and as a compilation.[101] A crude test for substantial copying was stated as follows:

> "*It is a question of degree where a good guide is the notion of overborrowing of skill,
> labour and judgment which went into the copyright work*".[102] (emphasis added)

With respect it is submitted that this test of "overborrowing of skill, labour
and judgment", while possibly carrying some descriptive merit, fails as a prescriptive solution, because it lacks precision, and if left unchecked, results in
over-protection of computer programs in the United Kingdom.[103]

[95] Addressed in Chapter 7.
[96] [1994] FSR 275.
[97] Ibid at 301–304. Bainbridge has issued an appropriate warning about Jacob J's comments about the use of US precedents and non-literal copying, since *Ibcos* is strictly a literal copying case; see Bainbridge *Intellectual Property*, 3rd edn (1996) at p 181.
[98] Including the deployment of relevant limiting doctrines, such as merger in the United Kingdom; also spurned by Jacob J. See also Stone (1997) 13(1) CLSR 15 at 16.
[99] *Supra*, n 96 at 296–301.
[100] *Infra*, para 9.15. The plaintiff's computer software comprised 335 programs, 171 record layout files and 46 screen layouts.
[101] *Supra*, n 96 at 304–314.
[102] *Supra*, n 96 at 302.
[103] This may be illustrated by his Lordship's approach towards the copying of data divisions of programs as possibly "substantial" (disagreeing with Judge Baker's views in *Total Information Processing v Daman*)—a direct consequence of applying the sole criteria of skill, labour and judgment (ibid at 303) and taking no notice of any other factors and technical constraints. More recently in *Cantor Fitzgerald v Tradition* (*supra*, n 92), Pumfrey J also took the view that "overborrowing" was not of assistance in forming a view as to substantiality. Such a word was, in his Lordship's view,

(b) Copyright Infringement of Computer Software: Non-Literal Copying

(i) Non-literal elements and copying generally

2.34 Under UK copyright law, non-literal[104] expression has been recognised as being within the scope of copyright protection, especially in the context of the plots of a play.[105] A program's written code makes up only one part of the program and programming process.[106] The program's design and structure, "the hierarchical division of tasks into subtasks, the interaction of one module with another, and the way data passes from one part of the program to another"[107] is the other. The latter could be referred to as the non-literal elements of a program.[108]

2.35   The following sub-sections discuss case law developments in the USA in the field of non-literal software copyright protection.[109]

(ii) Protection of non-literal elements in the USA: the broad question of copyrightability

2.36 It has been pointed out that the relevant decisions in the USA have addressed two questions. The first is whether non-literal, non-visual elements of computer programs can be protected by copyright in the first place[110]—what has usefully been referred to as the "broad question of copyrightability".[111] The second

"merely to substitute another term for the statutory concept of substantiality without providing any useful criterion in the process" (para 79).

[104] In the USA, Courts have also recognised the importance of protecting non-literal elements of copyright works. In *Nichols v Universal Pictures Co* 45 F.2d 119 at 121 (2nd Cir 1930) Judge Learned Hand has said: "It is of course essential to any protection of literary property . . . that the right cannot be limited literally to the text, else a plagiarist would escape by immaterial variations". The judge went on to discuss the different levels of abstraction, from text to general theme of a play, and the difficulty in determining where, along this spectrum of abstractions, the boundary between protection and non-protection lay.

[105] See *Rees v Melville* [1911–1916] MacCC 168; *Corelli v Gray* [1913] TLR 570.

[106] See Velasco "The Copyrightability of Non-literal elements of Computer Programs" (1994) 94 Colum LR 242 at 247.

[107] See Daniels "Learned Hand Never Played Nintendo: A Better Way to Think about the Non-literal, Non-visual Software Copyright Cases" (1994) 61 U Chicago 613 at 617.

[108] Some writers also include the user interface of a program—the mechanism through which the user operates a program—as part of a program's non-elements. See eg Brendan Cash "The Last Place in the World—Copyright Protection for Computer Software in New Zealand" (1997) 27 VUWLR 391 at 394. This is undoubtedly true, but this thesis treats the subject of user interface protection as different from other non-literal elements; in no small part due to the *Lotus v Borland* decision in the USA. See Chapter 4.

[109] As this chapter of the work principally deals with infringement methodology and the test for evaluating substantial similarity, and because of the vast jurisprudence which has pervaded this field, the author will confine himself to essential facts of cases, placing greater emphasis on the techniques of determination employed by the courts.

[110] The software developer's case for protecting non-literal, non-visual program elements depends crucially on the assumption that a second programmer who copies the structure of the first can cut the time and cost otherwise required to bring a similar product to market. See Clapes *Software, Copyright and Competition* (Quorum, 1989) at pp 25–27.

[111] See Nicholas, "GUI Wars" (1994) 47 Ark L Rev 139 at 141.

question refers to the applicable test to adopt, having decided that non-literal elements can be protected, for copyright and substantial similarity in individual cases (sometimes referred to as the "narrow question of copyrightability"). The second question is discussed in the next sub-section.

It is well known that *Whelan Associates v Jaslow Dental Laboratory*[112] was   **2.37** one of the first circuit decisions to consider non-literal copyright protection. *Whelan* involved a custom designed record-keeping program for dental laboratories, and the primary issue was whether the "structure (or sequence and organisation) of a program"[113] could receive protection. The court confirmed that "copyrights of computer programs can be infringed even absent copying of the literal elements of the program".[114] Critics have argued that a program's structure is more akin to idea rather than expression, and thus should not be protected.[115]

The broad question of copyright protection for non-literal elements was also   **2.38** subsequently confirmed by Judge Keeton in *Lotus Dev Corp v Paperback Software International*.[116] *Lotus v Paperback* involved the copying of the user interface in Lotus' spreadsheet program 1–2–3. The primary issue was whether Lotus' user interface could be protected by copyright and the Court did not hesitate to decide in the affirmative.[117]

The seminal case to date on the broad question of copyrightability has been   **2.39** *Computer Associates International v Altai*,[118] in which the functionality of the plaintiff's program was allegedly duplicated. Judge Walker defined the issue as the:

> "challenging question of whether and to what extent the non-literal aspects of a computer program, that is, those aspects not reduced to a written code, are protected by copyright".[119]

Whilst the Second Circuit endorsed in principle that as to the broad question, non-literal elements could be protected, it criticised the approach to infringement adopted by the *Whelan* Court, in deciding the narrow question of copyrightability, as wrong. It is to this that the discussion in the next sub-section pertains, the broad question of copyrightability being largely settled in the USA.[120]

---

[112] 797 F.2d 1222 (3rd Cir 1986).

[113] Ibid at 1224.

[114] Ibid at 1234.

[115] See eg Velasco, *supra*, n 106 at 262; Menell "An Analysis of the Scope of Copyright Protection for Application Programs" (1989) Stan Law Rev 1045; England "Idea, Process or Protected Expression?" (1990) Mich L Rev 866.

[116] 740 F.Supp 37 (D Mass 1990).

[117] Ibid at 51.

[118] 982 F.2d 693 (2nd Cir 1992). *Infra*, n 130.

[119] Ibid, at 806.

[120] But in some quarters the academic debate rages on. See eg the views of Professor Wienreb, who argues the position that, against a backdrop of industry standardisation, anything less than literal copying should not constitute copyright infringement; see Wienreb, (1998) 111 Harvard L Rev 1149 at 1249–1250.

(iii)   Protection of non-literal elements in the USA: the narrow question of copyrightability

2.40   *Whelan* and *Paperback* undoubtedly represent the high point of copyright protection for computer software. In *Whelan* the court held that:

> "[T]he purpose or function of a utilitarian work would be the work's idea, and everything that is not necessary to that purpose or function would be part of the expression of that idea".[121]

This formulation is generally thought to be too extensive in its protection of program structure, since it is based on the mistaken assumption that only one idea underlies any computer program.

2.41   In *Paperback*, a three-part test was formulated, which gave more semblance of a prescriptive test, compared with *Whelan*, but was not fundamentally different[122] in effect:

> "FIRST, . . . the decision maker must focus on alternatives . . . along the scale from the most generalised conception to the most particularised, and choose some formulation—some conception or definition of the idea—for the purpose of distinguishing between the idea and its expression . . .
>
> SECOND, the decision maker must focus upon whether an alleged expression of the idea is limited to the elements essential to the expression of that idea. . .or instead includes identifiable elements of expression not essential to the every expression of the idea.
>
> THIRD, having identified elements of expression not essential to the every expression of the idea, the decision maker must focus on whether these elements are a substantial part of the allegedly copyrightable work".[123]

The first stage of the above formulation quite possibly paved the way for the "abstractions" test in *Computer Associates v Altai*. Some writers have taken the view that it would not look out of place with the *Whelan* formulation, since it appears to make the fundamental idea-expression distinction.[124] The *Paperback* formulation is restricted in application since Judge Keeton refused to perform a dissection of the individual elements of the program[125] invariably leading to the overall protection of user interface of Lotus 1–2–3.[126] Both the *Paperback* and *Whelan* formulations indicate that a judge can compare both program struc-

---

[121] *Supra*, n 112 at 1236.

[122] See Nicholas, *supra*, n 111 at 146; Velasco, *supra*, n 106 at 275.

[123] *Lotus v Paperback, supra*, n 116 at 60–61.

[124] eg see Velasco, *supra*, n 106 at 275–276.

[125] *Supra*, n 116 at 67.

[126] The decision was thought a departure from the reality of computer practice. See Stern, "Legal Protection of Screen Displays and other user interfaces for computers: A problem in balancing incentives for creation against need for free access to the utilitarian" (1990) 15 Colum VLA J.L & Art s 283 at 338 ("[t]he Paperback opinion and the industry reaction to it reveal a clash in hierarchies of values . . . The court's underlying attitude fundamentally contrasts with that of those in the technological community; in a nutshell, the judge is no hacker").

tures at any level, including the works as a whole.[127] As such they represent the "high point" in non-literal copyright protection of computer software.[128]

As mentioned earlier, *Whelan* came under criticism by the Second Circuit in **2.42** *Computer Associates v Altai,*[129] for its primary failure to appreciate the nuances of computer technology, leading to consequent over-protection. *Computer Associates* involved the defendants' replication of the functionality and interfaces of the plaintiff's job-scheduling program.[130] Writing for the court, Judge Walker laid down a three-step "successive filtration" method for non-literal copying; the abstraction-filtration-comparison test[131] ("the *Altai* test") which took three stages; (i) *abstraction*—examining the program in terms of its structure rather than its specific sequence of code, and identifying its various modules, routines and sub-routines so that the functions of each may be ascertained; (ii) *filtration*—sifting out from the core of protectable expression, unprotectable elements which are dictated by efficiency (doctrine of merger), dictated by external conditions (doctrine of *scènes à faire*) or otherwise resides in the public domain, resulting in a reduction to a "core of protectable expression" or the "golden nugget" of the program; and (iii) *comparison*—of the remaining protectable expression between the competing works for substantial similarity.

The *Altai* test directs that a trial court should break down the allegedly **2.43** infringing program into its constituent structural parts, sift out all non-protectable material, so as to confine the comparison to the core of protectable expression which remains after such a process of elimination.[132] Applying this test the Second Circuit found that only a few elements of the plaintiff's scheduling program could survive such scrutiny and be protected by copyright.[133] As such they could not succeed in their claim of infringement.

---

[127] In *Whelan* the court stated that it was "concerned with overall similarities between programs" (*supra*, n 112 at 1246). See further Daniels "Learned Hand Never Played Nintendo: A Better Way to the Think about the Non-literal, Non-visual Software Copyright Cases" (1994) 61 U Chicago L Rev 613 at 629.

[128] See Nicholas, *supra* n 111 at 145.

[129] *Supra*, n 118.

[130] The plaintiff developed a program, CA-SCHEDULER, which contained a sub-program entitled ADAPTER (an operating system compatibility component), which translated the language of a given computer program into the specific language that the compiler's own operating system could decipher. Having illicitly obtained 30 per cent of the source code for ADAPTER, the defendant developed its own version, OSCAR 3.4. When this was found to infringe the copyright in the plaintiff's program, the defendants developed a new version OSCAR 3.5, which the plaintiff later alleged amounted to non-literal infringement. It failed in its action.

[131] *Supra*, n 118 at 707–712. Such a methodology first featured in an article by Nimmer, *et al* "A Structured Approach to Analyzing the Substantial Similarity of Computer Software in Copyright Infringement Cases" (1988) 20 Ariz St LJ 625.

[132] The presence of unprotectable elements is probative of copying, but must be excluded when the trier of fact reaches the ultimate infringement determination as to whether there is substantial similarity in expressive aspects of the plaintiff's work. See Alan Latman "Probative Similarity as proof of copying: toward dispelling some myths of copyright infringement" (1990) 90 Colum LR 1187.

[133] *Supra*, n 118 at 714.

2.44   The *Altai* test has found favour,[134] and has been applied in subsequent decisions,[135] to the extent that it is recognised in the USA,[136] and elsewhere,[137] as the accepted standard regarding whether non-literal elements in a computer program constitute protectable expression. Critics (typically ultra-protectionists) have identified the case as a "legal Chernobyl"[138] due to the drastic reduction in protection it provides.[139] The principal criticism is that by "dissecting" a program and removing individually unprotected items before comparing it to the allegedly infringing program the court may in fact miss or eliminate protectable elements, such as the way in which various elements are organised or combined.[140] As such the net effect of the *Altai* test is to render much of the structure of a program unprotectable.[141] *Altai* itself fails to make clear whether the court must only apply filtration to each element within a program; and also

---

[134] David Bender has praised *Altai* as "a significant advance in establishing, for software copyright cases, a method for determining infringement that is both consistent with traditional copyright law and workable". See Bender "*Computer Associates v Altai*: Rationality Prevails" [1992] *The Computer Lawyer* 1. See also 4 *Nimmer on Copyright* §13.03[F] at 13–118; 13–147.

[135] See *Sega v Accolade* 977 F.2d 1510 (9th Cir 1993); *Atari v Nintendo of America* 975 F.2d 832 (Fed Cir 1992); and more recently, *Gates v Bando Chemical Industries* 9 F.3d 823 (10th Cir 1993) (the Tenth Circuit endorsed the *Altai* test as a way of determining whether menus and sorting criteria are copyrightable; *Engineering Dynamics v Structural Software* 26 F.3d 1335 at 1342 (5th Cir 1994); and *Apple Computer v Microsoft Corp* 35 F.3d 1435 at 1445 (9th Cir 1994) cert denied, 15 S.Ct 1176 (1995) (recognising in dictum that other courts have accepted and utilised the *Altai* test). See also the First Circuit's decision in *Lotus v Borland* 49 F.3d 807 (1st Cir 1995). While the court did not find *Altai* useful in deciding whether the "literal copying of a menu command hierarchy constitutes copyright infringement", the "*Altai* test may provide a useful framework for assessing the alleged non-literal copying of computer code" (ibid at 814). See also *Softel v Dragon Medical & Scientific Communications Inc.* 118 F.3d 955 (2d Cir 1997), cert denied, 118 S.Ct 1300 (1998). cf *Avtec Sys v Peoffer* 21 F.3d 569 at 571(4th Cir 1994) (where the Fourth Circuit had an opportunity to adopt the test but declined, explaining that the facts were not conducive to that type of conclusion); *Maclean Assoc v Wm M Mercer-Meidinger-Hansen* 952 F.2d 769 at 777n.6 (3rd Cir 1991) (the 3rd Circuit apparently still applies the *Whelan* test).

[136] See Jonathan Retsky "Computer Software Protection in 1996: A Practitioner's Nightmare" (1996) 29 John Marshall L Rev 853 at 868.

[137] Courts in Canada seem to have no difficulty in applying *Altai*. See *Delrina Corp v Triolet Systems Inc* [1993] 47 CPR (3d) and *Matrox Electronic Systems v Gaudreau* [1994] 6 EIPR D–138. In *Delrina*, O'Leary J applied the Altai test to deny copyright protection to the plaintiff's user interface, based on the limitations to the layout and content of screen displays. See Handa, Buchan, "Copyright as it applies to the Protection of Computer Programs in Canada" (1995) 26 IIC 48 at 68–72 (Addendum (1995) 26 IIC 527 at 534). For the United Kingdom, see Band, Schwartz, Vinje, "Computer Associates Crosses the Atlantic and Lake Ontario: Richardson v Flanders and Delrina v Triolet" *International Computer Lawyer* (June 1993) at 2.

[138] See Clapes, *et al* "Revenge of the Luddites: A Closer Look at Computer Associates v Altai" [1992] *The Computer Lawyer* 11.

[139] The result of *Altai* has prompted the comment that the process of abstraction is so thorough that little or no kernel of protectable expression remains for comparison; see Goodman and Willes "US Case sets precedent for software copyright" (1992) 5 AIPLB 92.

[140] Fitzgerald "Square Pegs and Round Holes" (1993) 4 J Law and Information Science 142 at 147.

[141] See Karjala "Recent US and International Developments in Software Protection (Part 2)" [1994] EIPR 58 at 59–60; Karjala (1997) 66 U. Cinn L Rev 53 at 80–81; Gary Rinck "Maturing US Law on Copyright Protection for Computer Programs" [1992] 10 EIPR 361. *Altai* has been criticised because each layer peeled from a program makes the program less recognisable to its intended consumer. See Coulter, (1995) XIV J of Computer and Information Law 47 at 66.

consider the *combination* of elements as a whole, which may constitute an expressive choice.[142]

The US Ninth Circuit has developed a similar test for substantial similarity, **2.45** the bifurcated test of "analytic dissection",[143] comprising "extrinsic"[144] and "intrinsic"[145] stages. As such, "analytic dissection" is not fundamentally different from the *Altai* test. Both tests dissect, filter the elements of a program, and compare the "kernels" of remaining original expression.

The principal US decisions discussed above resolve the narrow question of pro- **2.46** tecting non-literal elements in favour of a limiting analysis. With a trend emerging where the *Altai* approach is also being applied to literal copying,[146] it is unlikely that US courts will ever return to the *Whelan* and *Lotus* high points of protection.

(iv) Protection of non-literal elements in the United Kingdom

The broad question as to the copyrightabilty of non-literal elements is now well **2.47** settled in the United Kingdom.[147] In *John Richardson v Flanders*,[148] Ferris J acknowledged that UK copyright law protected a program's structure,[149] before

---

[142] *Softel v Dragon Medical, supra,* n 135. The plaintiff sued the defendant for non-literal copyright infringement in respect of the structure of its software program which reads/displays video medical images. The plaintiff argued that it had combined in an expressive way four individual features, (i) hierarchy of menus; (ii) functional modules; (iii) external files and (iv) English language commands; which had been filtered by the lower court (applying the *Altai* test (*supra,* n 135 at 963). The Second Circuit accepted the plaintiff's argument by reference to traditional works of authorship, such as the compilation of individually unprotected elements (including abstract paintings comprised of individually unprotected geometric forms) (ibid at 964). The case was remanded to the district court to determine whether the combinations of the above elements (i) to (iv) were expressive, and if so whether the defendant had substantially copied those expressive characteristics (ibid at 967). For criticisms of this "compilations" approach, see Karjala "Copyright Protection of Computer Program Structure" 64(2) *Brooklyn Law Review* 519 at 539 *et seq.*

[143] *Brown Bag Software v Symantec Corporation* 960 F.2d 1465(9th Cir 1992). An independent programmer developed an out-lining program which was sold to the Brown Bag Software. The programmer then developed a competing product which was sold to the Symantec. Brown Bag sued for copyright infringement, the key issue being whether copyright in the program's non-literal elements had been infringed. See *infra,* paras 4.17–4.18. Such an approach was applied by the Californian District Court to dissect Apple's Graphical User Interface in *Apple Computer v Microsoft Corp.* 799 F.Supp 1106 at 1023 (ND Cal 1992), aff'd 35 F.3d 1435 (9th Cir 1994).

[144] Objective analysis of expression, where a program is analytically dissected and unprotected elements eliminated.

[145] A subjective appraisal of substantial similarity.

[146] *Infra,* para 2.55–2.58.

[147] Several interlocutory decisions in the late 1980s indicated some willingness to protect against non-literal copying. See *CIS v Forward Trust* (judgment of Aldous J, dated 19 February 1987, unreported); *MS Associates v Power* and *Missing Link Software v Magee* [1989] FSR 361. See also *Computer Aided Design v Bolwell* 23 August 1989, unreported, digested in IPD, April 1990 at 15.

[148] [1993] FSR 497. See generally, Arnold "Infringement of Copyright in Computer Software by Non-textual Copying: First Decision at Trial by an English Court" [1993] EIPR 250; Hogan "John Richardson Computers v Flanders—a Commentary" (1993) 9 *Computer Law and Practice* 70–73; Horton "John Richardson Computers v Flanders" (1993) 8 *Computer Digest* 133; Bainbridge (1993) 2 Law, Computers and Artificial Intelligence 269.

[149] Ibid, at 519 *et seq.* See *Cantor Fitzgerald (supra,* n 92), where it was observed by Pumfrey J that the "architecture" of a computer program is capable of protection if a substantial part of the programmer's skill, labour and judgment went into it (para 77 and Appendix of the judgment).

proceeding to decide the best approach to resolve the narrow question. Even in *Ibcos*, Jacob J readily acknowledged that overall program structure is protectable by copyright.[150]

2.48   At present, UK judicial opinion varies when addressing the narrow question of copyrightability; specifically, deciding the correct approach towards evaluating the substantiality of non-literal similarities between two programs. The question is whether it is appropriate to apply US infringement methodology into this area of UK law.[151]

2.49   In *Richardson v Flanders*, the plaintiffs commenced infringement proceedings alleging that the defendants had copied the "look and feel" of their computer software which was developed to enable pharmacists to label prescription drugs and to track inventory. The judgment of Ferris J is significant in that it specifically endorsed the utility of the *Altai* test in assisting a UK Court to determine substantial similarity.[152] When considering the question of substantiality, Ferris J stated that the similarities between the two programs should be considered individually and then it should be considered whether the entirety of what was compared represented a substantial part of the plaintiff's program.[153] Undertaking such an exercise, his Lordship evaluated the similarities between both programs, feature by feature, and divided them into four categories:[154] (i) similarities which were the result of copying a substantial part of the plaintiff's program;[155] (ii) similarities which were the result of copying but which do not by themselves involve the copying of a substantial part of the plaintiff's program;[156] (iii) similarities which the judge was not satisfied might have been the result of copying, but even if they were, they did not by themselves involve substantial copying of the plaintiff's program;[157] and finally (iv) the similarities which were not the result of copying.[158]

2.50   Ferris J then adopted a curious overall assessment of the degree of copying—whether the similarities in category (ii), when taken as a whole, would indicate copying of a substantial part of the plaintiff's program to a greater extent than

---

[150] *Supra*, n 96 at 302. The judge distinguished between "literal similarities" and "program structure" and "design features".

[151] *Richardson v Flanders*, cf *Ibcos*, *supra*, n 96.

[152] *Supra*, n 148 at 526–527. "There is thus nothing in any English decision which conflicts with the general approach adopted in the *Computer Associates* case". cf Jacob J in *Ibcos*, *supra* n 96 at 302 ("For myself I do not find the route of going via United States case law particularly helpful").

[153] Ibid at 548–549.

[154] Ibid at 558.

[155] Namely, the Line Editor, Amendment Routines (ibid at 553–554) and the Dose Codes (ibid 557–558).

[156] These features included the Date Option (ibid at 549–550), "Operation Successful" (550), "Quantity First" (relating to the position of the quantity prompt and the figure entered) (551–552), Pre-printing options (554), "Best day's use stock control" (554–555) and the Daily Figures Reset (555).

[157] The "vertical arrangement" (549) and "Entry label routine" (551) features.

[158] These features included the Date Entry (ibid at 549), escape key use (ibid 550) position of the label on the screen (551), "Quantity First" (in so far as it relates to the entry of quantity before the drug)(551–552), Drug entry (552–553); Secondary Access (553) and the Label Entry Sequence (553).

taking only the similarities in category (i).[159] His Lordship concluded that placing the similarities in (ii) alongside those in (i) did not reveal any more substantial copying than established by similarities in (i). In the circumstances he did not accept that what was established amounted to a multitude of similarities, as argued by the plaintiff. Only some infringement occurred.[160]

The *Flanders* judgment of Ferris J is not beyond criticism. First, Ferris J was **2.51** influenced by a "compilations" analysis,[161] and this resulted in his performance of comparing similarities of category (ii) with category (i). If the *Altai* test was applied in totality, the similarities in category (ii) should have been discounted, at the very outset, from the evaluation of substantial similarity, after the application of a filtration analysis. Critics of *Richardson v Flanders* have pressed the point that by relying on the speech of Lord Pearce in *Ladbroke v Hill*,[162] Ferris J did not believe that the *Altai* test should be applied directly in an English case.[163]

Secondly, while endorsing the utility of *Altai*, Ferris J chose not to apply the **2.52** "abstractions" stage. There are undoubtedly clear traces of applying merger doctrine (a key feature of the "filtration stage")[164] to various elements in his judgment,[165] but no actual definition of abstraction levels. This is a striking omission, which perhaps also resulted in the protection of "relatively trivial and mundane parts"[166] of the program.

Thirdly, much of the evidential analysis was shrouded in and restricted to the **2.53** screen comparison, which suggests that for the purpose of this book, *Richardson v Flanders* should be strictly addressed as a case concerning "user interface protection".[167]

Notwithstanding these reservations, this book argues that the judgment in **2.54** *Richardson v Flanders* should be commended for introducing the beginnings of a limiting analysis to assessing the substantiality of copying non-literal elements of a computer program. Specifically, US infringement methodology carries resonance in this determination, as the following chapters will show. By contemplating and applying limiting doctrines such as *scènes à faire* and merger in the United Kingdom, it is argued that the scope of software copyright can be better

---

[159] Ibid at 558.

[160] Ibid at 559.

[161] Ibid at 548. Heavy reliance was also place on *Ladbroke v William Hill* [1964] 1 WLR 273, particularly the judgment of Lord Pearce (at 291).

[162] Ibid. Lord Pearce sets out the following steps determining the substantial taking of a copyrightable compilation; (i) decide whether copyright subsists in a plaintiff's work, (ii) if so, decide whether there is a derivation and (iii) if so, decide whether a substantial part had been reproduced. If the part copied carries no originality, then it is not substantial. It has been pointed out by Arnold that step (iii) does not quadrate with the filtration stage as described by the Second Circuit in *Computer Associates v Altai*: see Arnold [1993] EIPR 250 at 253.

[163] See Rowland, MacDonald, *Information Technology Law* (1997) at p 49.

[164] But other parts of the "filtration stage" were also not applied, eg public domain routines.

[165] *Infra*, para 3.15.

[166] See Bainbridge *Intellectual Property*, 3rd edn (1996) at p188, in which the author criticises the judgment for not applying the second stage of the *Altai* test, especially to the line editor function.

[167] See my discussion *infra* in paras 4.41–4.44.

defined, where, in determining substantial similarity, a UK judge is able to direct his or her mind to the following questions with appropriate reference to expert opinion:[168]

- Is the plaintiff's program as a whole entitled to copyright protection?
- Are there similarities between the plaintiff's and defendant's programs?
- Are these similarities due to copying?
- Do such similarities constitute a substantial reproduction, assessed by reference to the originality of the material (or otherwise), the processes of abstraction, filtration and comparison?

It is argued that this approach is more prescriptive, when compared to a test of "overborrowing" of a plaintiff's skill, labour and judgment.[169] The latter test is an ill-tasting recipe for over-protection,[170] and may not be applied with any degree of consistency.

V.   SUMMARY OF TRENDS IN US INFRINGEMENT METHODOLOGY

(a) Adoption of the Altai test by Other Courts

2.55   As mentioned earlier, the *Altai* test has found acceptance in other Circuits and District Courts in the USA,[171] with significant modifications in two cases.

---

[168] On expert opinion generally see *infra*, paras 2.61–2.63.

[169] Per Jacob J in *Ibcos* [1994] FSR 275 at 302.

[170] Coupled with a rejection of a dichotomy which, according to Jacob J is a fundamental distinction between US and UK laws, the effect of *Ibcos* would be to place at risk the traditional concept of the non-protectability of ideas, which is symbolic of the policy goal of maximising knowledge in the public domain. This heavily creates the risk of non-standardisation. See Sean Gordon "The very idea—why copyright law is an inappropriate way to protect computer programs" [1998] 1 EIPR 10 at 13; Longdin "Copyright Protection for Computerised Compilations: A Cautionary Tale from New Zealand" 5(3) Int J of Law and Tech 249 at 262–263.

[171] See the District Court decision in *Softel v Dragon Medical & Scientific Communications* 1992 WL 108190 (SDNY, 1992) (a case of "total filtration" of stock elements that were neither commonly used nor mandated by efficiency considerations), rev'd on appeal, *supra*, n 142 (lower court failed to address combination of unprotected elements); *Autoskill v NESS* 793 F.Supp 157 at 158 (DNM, 1992) aff'd 994 F.2d 1476 (10th Cir 1993); *Engineering Dynamics v Structural Software* 26 F.3d 1335 at 1339, 1343–46 (5th Cir 1994) (applying the test and concluding that the input and output formats of the plaintiff's structural analysis program constituted protectable expression); *MiTek Holdings v Arce Engineering* 864 F.Supp 1568 at 1579–84 (MD Fla 1994), appeal pending No. 94–262 (11th Cir) (investigating the non-literal elements of a "wood truss layout program", the court in applying the *Altai* test, limited its abstractions inquiry to 18 non-literal elements which were identified by the plaintiff to be protected by copyright. After applying "successive filtration", it concluded that 13 of these elements were not protectable, being drawn from the public domain, or excluded by merger or *scènes à faire*); *Productivity Software International v Healthcare Technologies* 37 USPQ 2.d (BNA) 1036 at 1038–42 (SDNY, 1995) (where, inter alia, the arrangement of "Short Form" and "Long Form" lists from plaintiff's abbreviations-expanding program were found to be dictated by necessity, so as to form the basis for comparison); *CMAX/Cleveland v NCR* 804 F.Supp 337 at 352–355 (MD Ga 1992) (Court held that the plaintiff's file structures, screens and reports and transaction codes were protectable after applying the *Altai* test. See also the 9th Circuit's analysis in *Apple v Microsoft*, *infra*, paras 4.21–4.23.

In *Gates Rubber Co. v Bando Chemical Industries*,[172] the Tenth Circuit **2.56**
vacated and remanded the district court's judgment that the defendant infringed
the copyright of the plaintiff's computer program (Gate's "Design Flex" aids in
the selection of replacement belts for industrial belt customers). The Court
adopted the *Altai* test in "substantial part",[173] holding that in the first stage, "a
court should dissect the program according to its varying levels of generality as
proved in the abstractions test". The Court usefully observed that programs can
generally be reduced into:

> "six levels of generally declining abstraction: (i) the main purpose; (ii) the program
> structure or architecture; (iii) modules; (iv) algorithms and data structures; (v) source
> code and (vi) object code."[174]

In the filtration stage, the Court had to filter elements not protected by copyright, including ideas, processes, facts and public domain material, applying
merger and *scènes à faire* doctrines. According to the Court, the *scènes à faire*
doctrine excluded from protection aspects of the program dictated by external
factors, which may include hardware standards and mechanical specifications,
software standards and compatibility requirements, computer manufacturer
design standards, target industry practices and demands and computer industry
programming practices.[175] The Court concluded its infringement analysis by
stating that the comparison between the two programs was "primarily a qualitative rather than a purely quantitative analysis . . . and must be performed on
a case by case basis".[176]

The Tenth Circuit took the view that the District Court failed to apply a **2.57**
proper filtration analysis, relying on similarities in unprotectable facts. With
features like menus and sorting criteria,[177] control and data flow, engineering
calculation and design modules, it concluded that the District Court was unclear
in its analysis on what were protectable aspects of the program. By suggesting
that menus and sorting criteria were also subject to a filtration analysis, the

---

[172] 9 F.3d 823 (10th Cir 1993).

[173] Ibid at 834. Significantly the Court also suggested an initial holistic comparison of protected
and unprotected elements to precede the *Altai* test, in order to "reveal a pattern of copying that is
not obvious when only certain components are examined" (ibid at 841).

[174] Ibid at 835.

[175] Ibid at 838. The Court recognised that it was not required to determine the scope of protection for "interfacing" which was a sensitive topic with broad ramifications.

[176] Ibid at 839.

[177] Ibid at 843. Menus were understood to mean the "visual screen displays that present a computer operator with limited number of commands available at a given stage in the computer program's operation". According to the court, sorting criteria "would ordinarily mean the factors that
determine how the data in the program is organised" (ibid). This part of the opinion is slightly suspect, as it relied heavily on the District Court's opinion in *Lotus v Borland* 799 F.Supp 203 at 206
(D.Mass 1992). It is always raised as a direct conflict to the First Circuit's position that a menu command hierarchy was an unprotectable "method of operation". See *Bateman v Mnemonics, infra* n
179 at 1545.

Tenth Circuit may have been suggesting that filtration should equally be applied to the literal similarities as well.[178]

2.58   Another significant decision is *Bateman v Mnemonics*.[179] The plaintiffs developed computer hardware and an operating system for a single board computer for use in automated parking systems. It instituted proceedings against the defendant, who reverse engineered the plaintiff's software and hardware to develop its own single board computer. At trial the jury returned a verdict for the plaintiffs. One of the issues on appeal was the jury instruction pertaining to the *Altai* test; specifically the following words:

> "substantial similarity of the *non literal elements* is determined by comparing with the defendant's program, that protectable expression of the copyrighted work which remains after filtering out any portion of the copyrighted work, which represents only ideas, elements dictated solely by logic and efficiency, elements dictated by hardware or software standards, computer industry programming and practices or elements which are taken from the public domain"[180] (emphasis added).

The defendant objected to the above instructions being limited to apply the filtration step only to the non-literal elements of computer programs. The Court observed that whilst other circuits disagreed on whether the *Altai* test should only be limited to the non-literal copying or whether it was equally applicable to the literal copying cases,[181] the Court saw this disagreement as being more a matter of semantics than of substance,[182] taking the view that challenges to the copying of literal elements also had to be considered, whether as part of the *Altai* filtration process,[183] or as a separate parallel analysis. Since the jury instructions implied that the *Altai* filtration step was limited only to the non-literal copying, the jury must have concluded that any instances of literal copying of Bateman's code by the defendant were by definition acts of copyright infringement. According to the Court, "this conclusion is a manifest distortion and misstatement of the law".[184] This is an extreme application of *Altai*, and arguably has limited relevance for the United Kingdom, save for user interface protection.

---

[178] cf *Lotus v Borland* 49 F.3d at 815, where the First Circuit noted that "the Altai test may provide a useful framework for assessing the alleged non-literal copying of computer code, we find it to be of little help in assessing whether the literal copying of a menu command hierarchy constitutes copyright infringement". In the subsequent case of *Bateman, infra*, n 179 at 1545, the apparent disagreement was viewed as more a matter of semantics than substance.

[179] 79 F.3d 1532 (11th Cir 1996)

[180] Ibid at 1544.

[181] Notably the courts in *Gates, supra*, n 172 and *Lotus v Borland, supra*, n 178.

[182] Ibid at 1545.

[183] cf *Data General Corp v Grismman Sys Support Corp* 803 F.Supp 487 (D.Mass 1992)—the *Altai* test was held to be inapplicable to a situation in which the defendant admitted taking, reproducing and using copies of the plaintiff's program, without modification.

[184] Ibid.

(b) Other Tests of Substantial Similarity

Other tests which were operational prior to *Altai* were the "iterative test",[185]   **2.59**
"structure, sequence and organisation"[186] test and "total concept and feel"[187]
(or "look and feel")[188] test.

It is argued that these tests are inferior to the more comprehensive *Altai* test,   **2.60**
or its equivalent,[189] and as such are poor candidates for application in the
United Kingdom. They all lack a proper abstractions framework from which
each specified feature of programming may be identified and subsequently filtered.[190] This invariably leads to an abdication of analysis[191] and vagueness[192]
as to their scope of application, not unlike a test of "overborrowing".

---

[185] See *EF Johnson v Uniden Corp of America* 623 F.Supp 1485 (D.Minn 1985). The "iterative
test" is in two stages; first, whether "the defendant "used" the copyrighted work in preparing the
alleged copy, which may be established by proof of access and similarity sufficient to reasonably
infer use of the copyrighted work"(at 1493); and secondly, whether "the defendant's work is an iterative reproduction, that is, one produced by iterative or exact duplication of substantial portions of
the copyrighted work" (ibid). In *Uniden* the Court interpreted the second stage as a prohibition
against literal copyright or literal translation of code (ibid. at 1497–1498) The test divides programs
into protected literal code, protected literal translations of code and the unprotected remainder of
the program.

[186] See *Whelan v Jaslow Dental Laboratories* 797 F.2d 1222 (3rd Cir 1986), see *supra*, n 146 *et seq*
and accompanying text. The Court stated that "the purpose or function of a utilitarian work would
be the work's idea, and everything that is not necessary to that purpose or function would be part
of the expression of the idea" (at 1236). Protection is available to every part of a program except its
single overriding purpose (at 1238) This formulation has been criticised for failing to distinguish
between different levels of abstraction within a program's structure, and prior to *Altai* courts have
been compelled to define abstraction levels; see *Healthcare Affiliated Services v Lippany* 701 F.Supp
1142 at 1152 (WD Pa. 1988).

[187] A vague test (sometimes referred to as "look and feel"), emerging from a case about greeting
cards: *Roth Greeting Cards v United Card Co.* 429 F.2d 1106 (9th Cir 1970); subsequently applied
in *Reyher v Children's Television Workshop* 533 F.2d 87 (2d Cir), cert denied 429 US 908 (1976); *Sid
& Marty Kroft Television Productions v McDonald's Corp* 562 F.2d 1157 (9th Cir 1977). It came to
feature in "video game" cases; *Atari v North American Philips Consumer Electronics* 672 F.2d 607
at 619–620 (7th Cir) cert denied 459 US 880 (1982); *Atari v Amusement World* 547 F.SUPP 222 at
228–230 (D.Md 1981). Featuring mostly in "user interface" cases, the test does not define any program parts, finding substantial similarity if the allegedly infringing work captures the copyrighted
work's "total concept and feel". See further *Broderbund Software v Unison World* 648 F.Supp 1127
at 1134, 1137 (NC Cal 1988); and *Lotus v Paperback* 740 F.Supp 37 at 62–63 (D.Mass 1990) (where
Keeton J discusses the history and application of the test).

[188] Discussed in the next chapter.

[189] See *Brown Bag v Symantec Corp* 960 F.2d 1465 at 1475 (9th Cir 1992).

[190] Comprehensively explained by John Ogilvie "Defining Computer Program Parts under
Learned Hand's Abstractive Test in Software Copyright Infringement Cases" 91 Michigan Law Rev
526 at 545, 550–559.

[191] 4 *Nimmer* §13.03[A][1][c]–[d].

[192] See Samuelson, "Reflections on the State of American Software Copyright Law and the Perils
of Teaching it" (1988) 13 Colum VLA J.L. & Arts 61 at 69.

(c) Proper Definition of Abstraction Levels

2.61 To implement the limiting doctrines at the filtration stage, much still turns on a proper application of the "abstractions" stage of the *Altai* test.[193] The comment has been made that this adjudication lacks technical sophistication,[194] since it is too far removed from the original conception in *Nichols v Universal Pictures*, but not defined to any precise degree.[195] With respect this is where the role of the court-appointed expert becomes definitive.[196] Stephen Kahn (counsel for Computer Associates) has acknowledged that a full application of the "abstractions" stage of the *Altai* test could only practically be performed by software experts.[197]

2.62 What is apparent is that Courts should seek to distinguish program elements which display the exercise of a programmer's art from those elements which are the objectives of his art.[198] It is suggested that a *sine qua non* for a proper application of the *Altai* test must be that the first stage of the test should be conducted with reference to a universally accepted list of "abstraction levels", which are recognised in computing practice.[199] Thus far this has not been apparent from the decided cases,[200] including *Altai*.[201] The result is a lack of consistency, with each case being decided according to its own factual and technical idiosyncrasies.

2.63 In relation to "top-down programming",[202] technical writers disagree on standardising the levels of abstraction,[203] but as a general guide, the following model may be suggested for the future:

---

[193] A deficiency in *Flanders*, *supra*, para 2.52.

[194] Ogilvie, *supra*, n 190 at 533.

[195] Although 14 characteristics or levels of abstractions that may be used as the basis for comparison were identified by Randall Davis, "The nature of software and its consequences for establishing and evaluating similarity" (1992) 5 Software LJ 299 at 317–325.

[196] See generally Conley and Peterson "The Role of Experts in Software Infringement Cases" (1988) 22 Ga L Rev 425 at 453–468; Anthony Clapes, *et al* "Silicon Epics and Binary Boards" (1987) 34 UCLA L Rev 1493 at 1574 ("Expert opinion is particularly helpful in differentiating independent development from copying in cases of comprehensive non-literal similarity of computer programs").

[197] *Seminar on Computer Associates v Altai*, 6th Annual Computer and Information Technology Law Institute (17 September 1992); discussed in Effoss "Assaying Computer Associates v Altai: How will the Golden Nugget Test pan out?" (1993) 19(1) Rutgers Computer & Technology LJ 1 at 52–55 (highlighting the dangers of expert testimony)

[198] Daniels, *supra* n 107 at 638.

[199] The need to import fundamental programming concepts into software copyright law has been noted; Richard Bentel "Software Engineering Practices and the Idea/Expression dichotomy: can structured design methodologies define the scope of software copyright?" (1991) 32 Jurimetrics J 1 at 3.

[200] Arguably, this stage of the *Altai* test contributed to Ferris J's difficulties of application in *Richardson v Flanders*, *supra* n 147 at 527, 549.

[201] The abstraction definitions used in *Computer Associates v Altai* were tailored too closely to a specific type of program. The District Court recognised levels of abstraction such as "parameter lists" and "services required" (775 F.Supp 544 at 560 (EDNY 1991)).

[202] A process that starts with a concept and culminates in a particular computer program. See Appendix, at A.2.

[203] For example, compare Alfred Aho, *et al Data Structures and Algorithms* (1983) at 1 (listing problem formulation and specification, design, implementation, testing and documentation as

- The Program's Main Purpose;
- System Architecture;
- Abstract Data Types;
- Algorithms and Data Structures;
- Source Code;
- Object Code.[204]

Such an explicit framework clearly divides a computer program into an intellectually manageable test of discrete abstraction parts, covering the entire range, from a program's main purpose to its object code, and if implemented will bring about a desirable decrease in the case-by-case proliferation of new protectable program parts.

(d) Observations

Certain trends may be observed from the above discussion of recent US decisions. The broad question of copyright protection for the non-literal elements of software has been answered in the affirmative, with the *Altai* test recognised as the prescriptive answer to the narrow question in all cases. There remains the question whether the *Altai* test should be applied to the literal and non-literal infringements, as held by the Eleventh Circuit.[205]   **2.64**

From the perspective of UK law, there may be some cognisance of an *Altai*-type approach. Even in *Ibcos*, despite his rejection of the applicability of US tests, and in the face of literal similarities in coding, Jacob J refused to find infringement in the copying of the following features of the plaintiff's software; (i) nine levels of security, (ii) ability to create difference invoice types, (iii) internal sales system within the ordinary sales ledger package, (iv) month end sales audit combined with VAT, (v) 22 character points description, (vi) use of three separate programs for stock ordering, (vii) 12 labour rates, (viii) five levels of sub-totalling, (ix) audit report by posting in identical form, (x) automatic check on depreciation, (xi) holiday stamp facility. His Lordship took the following view of the above features: **2.65**

> "But I do not regard these matters as themselves constituting a copyright compilation. They are features of the package of interest to the customers and no more. We are here at a level of generality where there is little of the programmer's skill, labour and judgment. Even if the set were copyright, the mere taking of those functions would not be an infringement—it would be the taking of a mere general idea or scheme".[206]

---

programming steps) with Conley and Peterson "The Role of Experts in Software Infringement Cases" (1988) 22 Ga L Rev 425 at 442–449, 453–468.

[204] Each of these features represent a programmer's view; thoroughly discussed by Ogilvie, *supra*, n 190 at 533–543.

[205] *Supra*, para 2.58.

[206] *Supra*, n 96 at 304–305.

Evidently Jacob J applied a filtration process for non-originality, but also went on to mention the taking of a "general idea or scheme", which may be akin to the "abstractions" stage of the *Altai* test.

VI. CONCLUSION

2.66 It is hoped that this chapter has set out a basis for applying US infringement methodology into UK copyright jurisprudence. The discussion of *Altai* and its progeny has shown that its test has gained sufficient acceptance amongst the majority of courts in the USA, and arguably presents a credible formula for application by a UK judge, as acknowledged by Ferris J in *Richardson v Flanders*. The next chapter further develops this theme, demonstrating how limiting doctrines like merger and *scènes à faire* are sufficiently well grounded in UK law for application, in relation to both program internals and externals.

3

Limiting Doctrines of Merger and Scènes à Faire

One of the many challenges to UK software copyright law lies in the extent to **3.1**
which tolerance is or should be shown by English Courts towards the doctrines
of "merger" and *scènes à faire*. The former states that when the underlying idea
of a given work can only be expressed in a limited number of ways, the idea and
expression are said to merge, thus rendering the latter unprotectable by copyright.[1] The latter doctrine discounts from protection elements which are standard and inevitably arise in the treatment of a given topic.[2]

In the realm of software copyright, as apparent from the previous chapter, **3.2**
both limiting doctrines have acquired prominence, by featuring in the "filtration" stage of the *Altai* test. For the purposes of this book, it is in this particular
context that they will be studied.

Comparisons will primarily be made between the laws of the USA and the **3.3**
United Kingdom, with the ultimate object of arguing that the doctrines of
merger and *scènes à faire* may be seen as credible prescriptive guides to English
Courts in ascertaining what constitutes the "idea" behind a computer program
over which copyright is asserted.

II. MERGER DOCTRINE

(a) US Origins

In the USA the idea/expression inquiry has been directed towards the preserva- **3.4**
tion of the "balance between competition and protection reflected in the patent
and copyright laws".[3] The merger doctrine embodies this view. Under the doctrine, courts will not protect the expression of an idea that can be expressed in

---

[1] A creature of US case law. See *Herbert Rosenthal Jewellery Corpn v Kalpakian* 446 F 2d 738
(9th Cir 1971); *Sid & Marty Kroft Television Productions v McDonald's Production* 562 F.2d1157
(9th Cir 1977); *Financial Control Associates v Equity Builders* 799 F Supp 1103 (D Kan 1992). See
Paul Goldstein, *Copyright Principles, Law and Practice* (Vol 1) §2.152 at 209–210 (1989).

[2] Judge Yankwich, a California Federal District Court Judge, first introduced this phrase into US
copyright law; see *Cain v Universal Pictures Co.* 47 F.Supp 1013 at 1017 (SD Cal 1942). See also
Alexander v Haley 460 F.Supp 40 at 45 (SDNY 1978).

[3] *Herbert Rosenthal Jewelry Corp v Kalpakian* 446 F 2d 738 at 742 (9th Cir 1971).

one or only a few ways, because doing so would confer a monopoly on the idea itself. The basic principle of the doctrine is derived from *Baker v Selden*,[4] in which the Supreme Court held that in so far as the book expression of a book-keeping system is *separable* from the system itself, it is copyrightable.[5]

3.5   One of the earliest US cases on the doctrine is the oft-cited *Herbert Rosenthal Jewelry Corp v Kalpakian*,[6] in which the Ninth Circuit invoked the merger doctrine to deny copyright protection for a jewelled bee pin.[7] The merger doctrine is not truly a separate element of copyright theory. In reality it is merely one aspect of the requirement that copyright protection extend only to an author's *original expression*. A copyright defendant who argues the merger doctrine is really claiming that despite factual similarities between his work and the plaintiff's, the similarities are due entirely to the fact that both works deal with unprotectable ideas or concepts that lie closer to the "surface" of the work than the ideas which are embodied in the typical novel.[8] The US courts have recognised several categories of cases in which the merger doctrine applies.

(i) Merger where the idea dictates the form of expression

3.6   As originally defined in *Baker v Selden*,[9] for merger the underlying idea must be such that only a near verbatim copy of the author's expression can capture it. If the copyright law granted protection to the author's expression, he would receive an inadvertent monopoly upon the idea as well, since by definition no other expression could illustrate the idea. Works that fall under this category are characterised by simple ideas with a single central concept that is not protectable by copyright.[10] In *Kalpakian*,[11] the central feature of the jewellery pin was the naturally occurring form of a bee, held to be uncopyrightable.

---

[4]   101 US 99 (1879).

[5]   Ibid at 107. Prominent US writers differ in their interpretation of *Baker v Selden*. Nimmer tends to the principle as stated (viewing it as a "merger" case): *Nimmer on Copyright* (1997) §2.18[B][2], §2.18[C][1]. cf Wienreb (1998) 111 Harv L Rev 1149, where *Baker v Selden* is seen to represent the straightforward proposition that a system or "art" of practical utility canot be the subject of copyright, no matter what its manner of representation (ibid at 1173–1176). It does not follow that copyright protection is available only if there exists diversity in expression (so-called "reverse merger"). See Isao Noishiki (1993) 24 IIC 200 at 209.

[6]   *Supra*, n 3.

[7]   Ibid at 742.

[8]   See Stephen R Mick, "Applying the Merger Doctrine to the Copyright of Computer Software" 37 *Copyright Law Symposium* 173 at 184.

[9]   *Baker v Selden, supra,* n 4 at 102–103 (distinguishing between a copyrighted book and the bookkeeping system it expounded). See also *Sid & Marty Kroft v McDonald's Corp* 562 F.2d 1157 at 1168 (9th Cir 1977) ("[T]he scope of copyright protection increases with the extent expression differs from the idea").

[10]   In *Baker v Selden*, the accounting scheme was an unprotectable "system".

[11]   *Supra*, n 3.

(ii) Merger where the idea permits very little variation in expression

This category differs from (i) above in that unlike Selden's bookkeeping charts, **3.7** the plaintiff's work in these cases adds some minimal amount of original expression. The courts will consequently protect the plaintiff in instances where the entire expression has been appropriated, under the theory of "wholesale usurpation".[12] In other works, where small variations occur between the works, courts have relied upon the rule enunciated in *Dorsey v Old Surety Life Ins Co.*,[13] that when the subject-matter in question allows very little variation by way of expression, the plaintiff must demonstrate nearly verbatim copying in order to prove infringement.[14]

(b) Difficulties in Application

In the post-*Feist* "compilations" case of *Kregos v The Associated Press*,[15] the **3.8** court recognised that determining merger is a task requiring considerable care, especially in relation to selections of factual information.[16] If applied too readily, available alternative forms of expression will be precluded; if applied too sparingly, protection will be accorded for ideas.[17]

Mick has expressed the view that another category of merger cases involves **3.9** the use of *scènes à faire*.[18] It is submitted that *scènes à faire* and merger have developed as separate doctrines through judicial efforts which have been devoted to articulating and applying the idea-expression distinction to different cases. This is particularly evident in the software sphere. In the case of merger, idea and expression have fused so as to exclude protection. With *scènes à faire*, expression "follows" the idea, to the same effect of denying protection.

Critics of merger have indicated their suspicion of the doctrine since its "inde- **3.10** terminacy overwhelms its logic".[19] Detractors have taken the view that the

---

[12] See Francione, "Facing the Nation: The Standards for Copyright, Infringement, and Fair Use of Factual Works" (1986) 134 U Pa L Rev 519 at 579–597.

[13] 98 F.2d 872 (10th Cir 1938).

[14] See also *Morrisey v Proctor & Gamble* 379 F.2d 675 (1st Cir 1967). For a modern application of this aspect of the merger doctrine, see *Apple Computer v Microsoft Corporation* 35 F.3d 1435 (9th Cir 1994) (discussed in paras 4.19–4.23), where the Ninth Circuit refers to this form of protection as "thin". See further Nicholas P Terry, "GUI wars: The Windows Litigation and the Continuing Decline of 'Look and Feel'" (1994) 47 Ark L Rev. 93 at 113.

[15] 937 F.2d 700 (2d Cir 1991).

[16] Ibid at 706. See further Miller "Life after Feist: Facts, the First Amendment and the Copyright Status of Automated Databases" (1991–92) 60 Fordham L Rev 507 at 516.

[17] *Supra*, n 15 at 705. In *Kregos*, the Court took the view that the underlying idea was "an outcome predicting pitching form", an idea which allowed alternative expressions. Hence merger did not apply.

[18] See Mick, *supra*, n 8, at 187–188. See *infra*.

[19] eg John Shepard Wiley Jr, "Copyright at the School of Patent" (1991) 58 U Chi L Rev 119 at 127

merger inquiry necessarily depends upon how the Court defines "idea".[20] Since the "idea" of any given work can be defined in an infinite number of ways, it has been argued that the merger doctrine illuminates nothing.[21] Others, in apparently sensing the same logical indeterminacy, have denounced the doctrine as "bogus".[22]

3.11   Nimmer recognises that the distinction between idea and expression is particularly important in the field of computer science, where growth and development depend on free access to existing ideas.[23] If the test is correctly construed the doctrine requires the Courts to consider carefully on a case by case basis, how one balances competition with copyright protection. Courts have successfully used the merger doctrine to maintain the balance in cases covering a broad range of subjects, including contest rules,[24] life-size concrete animal statues,[25] maps,[26] stuffed dinosaurs,[27] "You are Special Today" plates[28] and animal nose masks.[29]

(c) Traces of Merger in the United Kingdom

3.12   Under UK copyright, in determining whether that which has been taken is qualitatively significant, it is permissible to take into account the relative simplicity of the work's expression. This was illustrated in the case of *Kenrick v Lawrence*,[30] where a simple line drawing of a hand marking a cross (artistic work) was very closely related to the idea of using a drawing of a hand marking a cross to help illiterate voters understand how to fill out voting cards. Any two drawings of hands marking a cross were bound to share many similar features simply because of the nature of the subject-matter.[31] It is arguable that *Kenrick* is a "merger" case.

3.13   In the software context, *Total Information Processing Systems Limited v Daman Limited*[32] generated considerable interest, since it was the first decision in the United Kingdom to consider whether an interface file (part of a costing

---

[20] This was also the view taken by Jacob J in *Ibcos Computers v Barclays Mercantile Finance* [1994] FSR 275, *infra* at para 3.16.

[21] Wiley Jr, *supra*, n 19, at 127–129.

[22] See Thomas MS Hemnes, "Three Common Fallacies in the User Interface Copyright Debate" *Computer Law* (February 1990) 14 at 17.

[23] 4 *Nimmer* §13.03[F][1] at 13–119. See also Note, "Copyright Infringement of Computer Programs: A Modification of the Substantial Similarity Test" (1984) 68 Minn L Rev 1264 at 1291.

[24] See *Morrissey v Procter & Gamble* 379 F. 2d 675 (1st Cir 1967), in which the First Circuit refused to protect a set of contest rules (at 678–679).

[25] *Concrete Mach Co v Classic Lawn Ornaments* 843 F.2d 600 (1st Cir 1988).

[26] *Kern River Gas Transmission Co v Coastal Corp* 899 F.2d 1458 (5th Cir) cert denied 111 S.Ct 374 (1990).

[27] *Aliotti v R Dakin & Co* 831 F.2d 898 (9th Cir 1987).

[28] *McCulloch v Albert E Price Inc* 823 F.2d 316 (9th Cir 1987).

[29] *Masquerade Novelty Inc v Unique Indus Inc* 912 F.2d 663 (3rd Cir 1990).

[30] (1890) 25 QBD 99 (Wills J).

[31] Ibid at 103.

[32] [1992] FSR 171.

program specifically designed to perform calculations relating to costing of contracts using data which was fed into it from other programs, and in particular
from a payroll program) was protected by copyright.

Judge Paul Baker, in denying copyright to the interface file, held that if the   **3.14**
idea was to write such a program file to ensure that the program could be linked
to other programs, and, if there was only one way of expressing that idea, then
the way chosen would not be protected by copyright since it merges into the
idea. His Honour was quite content to accept that it was a part of UK law (in
the "line of authorities commencing with *Kenrick & Company v Lawrence &
Company*") that if there is only one way of expressing an idea that way is not
the subject of copyright.[33]

The merger doctrine was most recently recognised by the High Court in *John*   **3.15**
Richardson v Flanders.[34] It will be recalled that the plaintiff complained that the
defendant had taken the general scheme of a pharmaceutical listings program
(designed to operate on BBC micro-computers) including the details of "certain
routines of an idiosyncratic nature", especially, but not exclusively, the reproduction in the defendant's program of a feature called "Best day's use of Stock
Control". The language of merger was evident from the judgment of Ferris J:

> "If displaying the minimum stock figure on screen or printing it on the label is expres-
> sion rather than idea it is, in my view, the adoption of the *only practicable means by
> which the idea can be expressed*"[35] (emphasis added).

It is a matter of some regret that the applicability of merger has recently been   **3.16**
doubted by Jacob J in *Ibcos Computers v Barclays Mercantile Finance*.[36]
Commenting on the merger doctrine, his Lordship took the view that its application in the United Kingdom was "dangerous". In his Lordship's view, *Kenrick*
was not considered to be a case which set out the merger doctrine—it merely
stood for the proposition that the taking of an idea from another work would
not be infringement.[37] His Lordship expressed discontent in the proposition
that "If there is only one way of expressing an idea that way is not the subject of
copyright". Referring to Lord Hailsham's dictum,[38] Jacob J was content to
reduce the inquiry to an investigation of the specificity of the idea behind the

---

[33] Ibid at 180–181.
[34] [1993] FSR 497. It will be recalled that the famed *Altai* test was expressly endorsed by Ferris J
(ibid, at 526–527).
[35] Ibid, at 555–557. Ferris J also made similar references to the label entry sequence—in holding
that there was no copying, given the commonsense choice between very restricted alternatives (ibid,
at 553). See also Sterling, "Testing for subsistence and infringement of copyright in computer programs: some US and UK cases" [1995] 11 CLSR 119 at 124.
[36] [1994] FSR 275.
[37] Ibid at 290–291.
[38] *LB Plastics v Swish* [1997] RPC 551 at 629. ("Of course, it is trite law that there is no copyright
in ideas. But of course, as the late Professor Joad used to observe, it all depends on what you mean
by ideas.") In Laddie, *et al Modern Law of Copyright and Designs*, 2nd edn. Vol 1, it is pointed out
that Professor Joad, who was a member of the Second World War radio programme "Brains Trust"
was unrelenting "in his determination not to be bound by ill-defined questions" (p 61).

work, and that it was a "question of degree" as to what was meant by the "idea" behind a work.[39]

3.17   It is quite clear from the above discussion that merger doctrine, as applied by Baker J in *Daman*, has been spurned by Jacob J. The United Kingdom is now faced with two High Court decisions, each of which is opposed to the other on the applicability of merger in the United Kingdom. The English position has been described as "currently very confused",[40] and the issue awaits appellate guidance.

III.   MERGER AND SOFTWARE COPYRIGHT PROTECTION

(a) The Operation of the Doctrine in the USA

3.18   In the now unpopular *Whelan v Jaslow*,[41] the Third Circuit defined structural protection of software in extravagant terms, in defining as an "idea", the ultimate purpose of the program, the efficient organisation of a dental laboratory. Given the narrow interpretation, the undesirable consequence was that every part of the program's structure had to be "expression" as long as it originated from the author. Prior to *Altai*, other US Courts narrowed the range of protectable expression in computer programs, by interpreting "ideas" more broadly, for example by declining to find original expression in technical specifications, such as input and output formats that are highly constrained or determined by the functions they must perform.[42]

3.19   In *Computer Associates v Altai*[43] the Second Circuit offered a revised test as an alternative to the *Whelan* formulation for "idea" as regards program structure. Under *Altai* the use of the efficiency filter has effectively made merger a necessary part of the infringement exercise. The Court took the view that where efficiency considerations limited the design choices available, then the merger doctrine should apply. It said:

[39] *Supra*, n 36 at 291. Jacob J again refers at (p303) to "a question of degree" in deciding whether there has been a substantial taking of a work, for the purposes of establishing copyright infringement. (disputing Judge Baker's observations in *Total Information Processing v Daman* (above) that it would be very unusual for a table of contents to constitute a substantial part of a book).

[40] See Christopher Arnold "Copying Ideas in Computer Programs" (1995) 9 *International Yearbook of Law, Computers and Technology* 187 at 188. A contrast may be provided by Commonwealth countries. In Canada, despite earlier doubts (*Apple Computer Inc v Mackintosh Computers Ltd & Others* (1986) 10 CPR (3d) 1 at 24, aff'd 18 CPR (3d) 129 (Fed. CA), aff'd 30 CPR (3d) 257 (SCC)) the doctrine has gained acceptance: *Delrina v Triolet Systems Inc* (1993) 47 CPR (3d) 1 at 41 (Ont GD). The doctrine has also been applied in Australia: see *Autodesk v Dyason* (1992) 22 IPR 163 at 172 (High Court of Australia); and more recently, *Powerflex v Data Access* (1997) 37 IPR 436 at 452 (Full Federal Court). See further Sookman "International Differences in Copyright Protection for Software" [1995] 5 CTLR 142 at 145–146.

[41] 797 F.2d 1222 (3rd Cir 1986).

[42] See *Plains Cotton Co-op Association v Goodpasture Computer Serv Inc* 807 F.2d 1256 (5th Cir 1987), where the Fifth Circuit held that many of the non-literal aspects of a computer program were not original expression, but ideas "dictated by the externalities of the cotton market" (ibid, 1262).

[43] 982 F.2d 693 (2nd Cir 1992), see earlier discussion, *supra*, paras 2.63, 2.66–2.69.

"While, hypothetically there might be a myriad of ways in which a programmer may effectuate certain functions within a program—ie express the idea embodied in a given subroutine, efficiency concerns may so narrow the practical range of choice as to make only one or two forms of expression workable options".[44]

The merger doctrine has not always enjoyed such prominence in US software copyright law. Earlier US cases revealed the tendency to treat merger as an isolated issue.[45] Through such isolation, the doctrine was narrowed to such an extent that it broadened the copyrightability of software.[46]   **3.20**

Merger has been widely applied in other Circuits[47] and other tests of copyright infringement. For example, in *Apple Computer v Microsoft*[48] the Ninth Circuit affirmed that merger is a well-recognised precept which guides the process of "analytic dissection".[49] The Court recognised that the idea of an icon[50] in a desktop metaphor representing a document stored in a computer program can only be expressed in so many ways. An iconic image shaped like a page is an obvious, but not the only example.[51] The application of merger to screen elements, as seen in *Apple v Microsoft,* shows how the the doctrine is traversing new ground in software cases. For example, merger has been applied as a means of preserving the public domain so as to assist future thinkers,[52] and more recently, the Massachussets District Court held that data file names were unprotected because of merger with the functions to which they related.[53]   **3.21**

---

[44] Ibid, at 708. An early recognition of the applicability of merger to the software field may be seen in the Final Report of CONTU at p 20.

[45] See Mick, *supra*, n 8.

[46] See eg *Apple v Franklin* 714 F.2d 1240 at 1253 (3rd Cir 1983); *Apple Computer v Formula Int'l* 725 F.2d 521 at 525 (9th Cir 1984).

[47] *Supra*, paras 2.83–2.87 and references therein.

[48] 35 F. 3d 1435 (9th Cir 1994).

[49] The test, evolved in the Ninth Circuit, was originally conceived in *Sid & Marty Krofft Television Productions v McDonald's Corp* 562 F.2d 1157 (9th Cir 1977). For further discussion, see *supra*, para 2.70.

[50] Perhaps an expansion of the doctrine to cover screen elements, quite apart from the underlying coding.

[51] *Supra*, n 72 at 1444 (only the exact reproduction of the icon would constitute infringement). In the USA, merger has also gained significance as a limiting requirement for the copyright protection of graphical user interfaces. See Doug Neville, "Thermal Windows: How Well-insulated are Software Developers from Copying of their Program's Visual Displays?" (1996) 61 Missouri Law Rev 203 at 207.

[52] See *CCC Information Services v Maclean Hunter Market Reports* 44 F.3d 61 at 71 (2d Cir 1994), where it was said that the merger doctrine should be applied to "those ideas that undertake to advance the understanding of phenomena or the solution of problems, such as the identification of the symptoms that are most useful in identifying the presence of a particular disease" (hard ideas), but not to those "that do not undertake to explain phenomena or furnish solutions, but are infused with the author's taste and opinion" (soft ideas). The Court was of the view that it was much more important to keep ideas in the former class "free from private ownership" than those "that merely represent the author's taste or opinion and therefore do not materially assist the understanding of future thinkers". See further Ginsburg (1997) 66 U Cinn L Rev 151 at 153–157.

[53] See *Baystate Technologies v Bentley Systems* 946 F.Supp 1079 at 1088 (D.Mass 1996). Appeal to the First Circuit is pending (at the time of writing).

(b)   Possibility of Applying Merger in the United Kingdom?

3.22   The United Kingdom stands at a vital crossroad for the future development of both the nature and extent of protection of structural features of computer programs itself and of the idea/expression dichotomy. Under the Software Directive, protection is required for "expression" in programs, but not "ideas and principles which underlie any element of a computer program, including that which underlie its interfaces".[54]

3.23   Whilst recognising the existence of the dichotomy, the Directive is silent on how it is to be applied,[55] and the accompanying recitals do not provide more assistance.[56] This is not surprising, as the dichotomy is "easier to assert than to apply".[57] Writers have sought to interpret Artcle 1(2) Software Directive in the light of its legislative history,[58] and to suggest that the US debate over the scope of copyright protection for interfaces may inform the interpretation of Article 1(2).[59]

---

[54] Ibid, Art 1(2). The Explanatory Memorandum accompanying the Proposed Software Directive is instructive; para 3.13 states: "If similarities in the code which implements the ideas, rules or principles occur as between interoperative programs, . . . where the constraints of the interface are such that in the circumstances no different implementation is possible, then no copyright infringement will normally occur, because in these circumstances it is generally said that idea and expression have merged". See also the references in Reed [1991] 2 EIPR at 52.

[55] When the United Kingdom implemented the directive, the Department of Trade and Industry, in drafting the Statutory Instrument, did not include Art 1(2) language, on the grounds that the idea/expression dichotomy was one of the basic principles of UK copyright law. See Vanessa Marsland, "Trial Court Clarifies Software Infringement Test" *International Computer Lawyer* (May 1994) at 37, 38. In a Parliamentary speech, Commission Vice-President Bangemann set forth the Commission's view that there was no need to adopt a Parliamentary Amendment on the merger doctrine: "the 'merger doctrine', according to which there is no copyright protection where an idea and its expression cannot be separated . . . is a permanent feature of copyright [and] we do not need to mention it in the directive". See Bangemann, Eur Parl Deb. (3–404)56.37 (16 April 1991).

[56] Recitals 13–15, Software Directive.

[57] *Warner Brothers Inc v American Broadcasting* Co 720 F.2d 231 at 239 (2nd Cir 1983).

[58] Article 1(3) of the Initial Proposal for the Directive, issued by the EC Commission in January 1989 provided: "Protection in accordance with this Directive will apply to the expression in any form of a computer program but shall not extend to the ideas, principles, logic, algorithms or programming languages underlying the program. Where the specification of interfaces constitutes ideas and principles which underlie the program, those ideas and principles are not copyrightable subject matter".

The last sentence of Art 1(3) threatened the ability to create interoperable computer products, hence spurring the establishment of the European Committee of Interoperable Systems ("ECIS") in September 1989. The ECIS position was that the above wording could be read to imply that interface specifications which did not constitute "ideas and principles" could be protected under the proposal. It argued that interface specifications, as opposed to the implementation of program code, were by their very nature unprotected ideas and principles. This was subsequently amended (see Working Doc No.2/90, 28 February 1990).

[59] See Band, Steinberg, Vinje "The US decision in Computer Associates v Altai compared to the EC Software Directive: translatlantic convergence of copyright standards favouring software interoperability" (1992) 8(5) *Computer Law & Practice* 137 at 141–142. In addition, the writers make the valid technical observation that small portions of expression (in the form of program code) are required to make an unprotectable interface work. Recognising that this raises an opportunity for divergence between Member States, the writers argue that small portions of code necessary to implementing the interface in question should be held unprotected by copyright, under a *de minimis* doctrine, a lack of sufficient originality or under the merger doctrine (ibid).

It follows that the possibility of applying a doctrine of merger in the United **3.24**
Kingdom is not one without legal foundation.[60] In *John Richardson v
Flanders*,[61] Ferris J sanctioned the application of US infringement methodology (the *Altai* test) to software infringement cases in the United Kingdom.[62] It
is submitted that the application of the *Altai* test necessarily imports the need
to apply a criterion approximating to the merger doctrine, as a means of deciding substantial similarity. Although Ferris J did not refer to the doctrine of
merger specifically, his Lordship observed that the "very limited choice of
available alternatives" to the date entry procedures, and with respect to the
date option, "once the idea of giving the option has been adopted, there is
really nothing of substance left in the expression of that idea".[63] As mentioned
above, Ferris J observed that the similarity of label entry sequences between
the two programs were the result of a "common sense choice . . . between very
restricted alternatives".[64] Further the display of minimum stock figures on
screen or printed on labels was regarded to be "the adoption of the only practical means by which the idea can be expressed".[65] It is submitted that this is
the language of merger.

The potentially successful application of this approach faces the immediate **3.25**
resistance presented by Jacob J, who was quick to spurn this approach in
Ibcos.[66] Due to the absence of a prescriptive test/criterion, UK software copyright law will be placed in a more invidious position than US, if *Ibcos* is followed. Arguably, the scope of software copyright protection is presently greater
in the United Kingdom than in the USA. *Whelan*-type fears of broad protection
are there to be realised for the future.

(c) Case Against the Application of the Doctrine of Merger

Perhaps the strongest objection to the application of merger doctrine to the **3.26**
United Kingdom lies in the argument that merger has been regarded by the USA
as part of its policy to keep copyright out of the functional field,[67] and the
United Kingdom is not adverse to protecting functional works, eg the unregistered design right, which is capable of protecting designs that are solely dictated
by function.[68] Laddie, Prescott and Vitoria argue this point strongly,[69]

---

[60] See the above discussion on *Total Information Processing System v Daman; Kenrick v
Lawrence, supra*, paras 3.12–3.15.
[61] *Supra*, n 34.
[62] Ibid at 526–527.
[63] Ibid, 550.
[64] Ibid, 553.
[65] Ibid, 555–557.
[66] [1994] FSR 275 at 290–291, 301–302.
[67] The seminal case for this being *Baker v Selden* 101 US 99 (Sup Ct 1879) (a case which Jacob J
in *Ibcos* thought would have been decided differently by a UK court).
[68] See s 213, CDPA. cf ss 1(1)(a) and 1(b)(i) Registered Designs Act 1949 (as amended).
[69] Laddie, *et al, Modern Law of Copyright and Designs*, 2nd edn, Vol 1 at p 838.

emphasising Ferris J's admission that he found the *Altai* test difficult to apply, despite having endorsed it.[70]

3.27   Moreover it may be argued that the history, development and statute law in the USA are markedly different and are unlikely to be of any real assistance in the United Kingdom.[71] The application of merger is inextricably linked to the suitability infringement test of which it forms a part. The *Altai* test, together with its counterparts (eg the Ninth Circuit's intrinsic/extrinsic test of "analytic dissection") and forerunners, are regarded by Laddie, *et al* as being "irrelevant or exotic tests" for the purposes of UK law.[72]

3.28   Arguments against merger can also be found in the USA. Warnings have been issued to the effect that merger will "discourage innovative programming techniques and leave non-literal elements of computer programs unprotected".[73] There is some validity for this view, given that programming is starting out with finite choices, and because so many elements of software may be regarded as functional, merger theoretically prevents a programmer from securing copyright protection for his efforts, which are ultimately aimed at achieving efficiency.[74]

3.29   Another legitimate concern is that the *Altai* Court's treatment of merger would permit programmers to introduce moderately inefficient structures into their programs as "traps" for potential infringers.[75]

3.30   A more resounding challenge to the "soundness" of the merger doctrine is that its absence may give rise to the inference that the work is creative and copyrightable by the number of alternative but strictly functional expressions which exist. Merger doctrine has been criticised as flawed because it fails to take into account the policies which underlie the exclusions from copyright protection. Karjala has strongly argued that when dealing with functional subject-matter other than program code, it is imperative that Courts consider the exclusions from copyright protection as provided by section 102(b) USCA.[76]

---

[70] Ibid, referring to *Flanders, supra*, n 34 at 527, 549.

[71] This is the nub of Jacob J's objection in *Ibcos*.

[72] Ibid at 837.

[73] See Note in (1992) 106 Harv L Rev 510 at 511, 514.

[74] See Menell "An Analysis of the Scope of Copyright Protection for Application Programs" (1989) 42 Stanford L Rev 1045 at 1056 ("Though some programmers have distinctive programming styles, what matters in the end . . . is the accuracy, efficiency, and reliability of the resulting program").

[75] Miller "Copyright Protection for Computer Programs, Databases and Computer-Generated works: Is Anything New Since CONTU?" (1993) 106 Harv L Rev 977 at 1004; Duncan Davidson "Common law, uncommon software" (1986) 47 U Pitt L Rev 1037 at 1086–1087 (discussing, inter alia, the arrangements of subroutines and optimal implimentations that may provide evidence of copying).

[76] See Karjala "Copyright Protection of Computer Program Structure" 64(2) Brooklyn L Rev 519 at 539 *et seq*; Cohen "Reverse Engineering and the Rise of Electronic Vigilantism: Intellectual Property Implications of "Lock-out" Programs" (1995) 68 S Cal L Rev 1091 at 1147.

(d) Case for the Application of the Doctrine of Merger

Yet it may not be wise to be too dismissive of merger. It is submitted that the **3.31**
doctrine of merger offers a calculated judicial exercise which lends efficacy to
the effective application of the dichotomy in the software field. The concerns
expressed about the over-citation of US authority in UK courts[77] are unfounded,
for there is little harm if the US decisions have been properly analysed and their
principles distilled, as this work has sought to accomplish. Under-efficiency
fears can be overcome by applying the doctrine only when a programming routine is "the only and essential means of accomplishing a given task".[78]

As mentioned earlier,[79] the functionality of a product is irrelevant for the pur- **3.32**
poses of securing unregistered protection under section 213 CDPA. Yet the section contains a "must fit" exception so as to exclude features of shape or
configuration of an article which enable the article to be connected to, or placed
in, around and against, another article so that either article may perform its
respective function.[80] With designs which are solely dictated by function, there
may be very little scope for adopting any other physical shape or form. Though
it lies outside the ambit of this work, there may be an argument that any proposed changes to design law should be accompanied by a move towards a general doctrine of merger.[81] Implicit support for this justification may be found in
Laddie J's lecture of November 1995,[82] in which he questioned whether the "full
armoury of copyright protection" should be available to protect the "trite, the
commonplace and the valueless".[83]

The apparent divergence between US and UK laws may, to a large extent, **3.33**
have been removed by the TRIPS Agreement, which opted for the explicit rule;
"copyright protection shall extend to expressions and not to ideas, procedures,
methods of operation or mathematical concepts as such".[84] It is obvious that
this provision is partially based on section 102(b) USCA[85]—thus forging the

[77] *Ibcos, supra*, n 36 at 302 (per Jacob J).
[78] A narrow interpretation in CONTU given to the application of merger for previously copyrighted computer languages (at p20).
[79] *Supra*, para 3.26.
[80] See s 213(3)(b)(i) CDPA.
[81] Especially when viewed in its historical context; how s 213 CDPA was enacted to *remove* functional designs from copyright protection. This addressed the serious anomaly created by the combined effect of the Copyright Act 1956 and Design Copyright Act 1968, where functional articles
(excluded from registered design protection) received greater protection through artistic copyright
(drawings) in the 1970s. See *LB Plastics* [1979] RPC 551; *British Northrop v Texteam Blackburn*
[1974] RPC 57.
[82] The Stephen Stewart Memorial Lecture "Copyright: Over-strength, Over-regulated, Over-
rated?", delivered at the Common Law Institute of Intellectual Property, reproduced in [1996] 5
EIPR 253.
[83] Ibid at 260.
[84] Article 9(2) TRIPS, a phrase that also features in Art 2 WIPO Copyright Treaty (1996); see Lai
"The Impact of the Recent WIPO Copyright Treaty and Other Initatives on Software Copyright in
the United Kingdom" [1999] 1 IPQ 35 at 36–39.
[85] See Correa, "TRIPS Agreement: Copyright and Related Rights" (1994) 25 IIC 543 at 545.

dichotomy as a necessary tenet of copyright law.[86] Can future UK Courts afford to ignore this provision? The harmonisation of copyright methodology may become a necessary feature of a future intellectual property world order.[87]

3.34   In the next substantive part of this chapter, I shall analyse the *scènes à faire* doctrine—another prescriptive filter in the *Altai* test that merits consideration.

IV. THE SCENES À FAIRE DOCTRINE

(a) The Origin and Development of *Scènes à Faire*

3.35   The phrase *"scènes à faire"* probably originated from the nineteenth century drama critic Francisque Sarcey. Although Sarcey never provided a strict definition, he used the phrase to mean an "obligatory scene",[88] one the public "has been permitted to foresee and to desire from the progress of the action; and such a scene can never be omitted without a consequent dissatisfaction".[89]

3.36   In 1942, Judge Yankwich introduced this phrase in *Cain v Universal Pictures Co.*[90] Judge Yankwich took the view that the small details from events that took place in a church in scenes from two works (a motion picture and novel), such as playing the piano, prayer and hunger, were inherent in the situation itself:

> "They are what the French call "scènes à faire". Once having placed two persons in a church during a big storm, it was inevitable that incidents like these . . . should force themselves upon the writer in developing the theme. Courts have held repeatedly that such similarities and incidental details necessary to the environment or setting of an action are not the material of which copyrightable originality consists".[91]

3.37   The doctrine developed with underpinnings of necessity,[92] indispensability and

---

[86]   Together with Art 1(2) Software Directive.

[87]   For the case in favour of international standards for limiting doctrines like merger, and *scènes à faire*, see Zimmerman "Global Limits on 'Look and Feel': Defining the Scope of Software Copyright Protection by International Agreement" (1996) 34 Colum J Transnat'l L. 503 at 522, where it is argued that the merger doctrine seems the most logical choice for elevating to an international standard. Unlike some other notions used to limit copyright, such as the allowance of limited copying to achieve compatibility, the merger doctrine does not reflect any particular policy considerations. Rather the doctrine only seeks to ensure that Courts do not inadvertently protect the idea within a work, by forcing Courts to enforce the idea/expression distinction rigorously.

[88]   Archer, *Play-Making, A Manual of Craftsmanship* (1960), p 147.

[89]   Hamilton, *Problems of the Playwright* (1917), p 56; Archer, *supra*, n 88 p 148 (the obligatory scene, according to Sarcey, is one which for one reason or another, an audience expects and ardently desires).

[90]   47 F.Supp 1013 (SD Cal. 1942).

[91]   Ibid, at 1017. See further Yankwich, "Originality in the Law of Intellectual Property" (1951) 11 FRD 457, 462. For a comprehensive account of the doctrine, see Kurtz, "Copyright: The Scenes A Faire Doctrine" (1989) 41 Florida L Rev 79 at 80 *et seq*.

[92]   The notion that the subject-matter represented can be expressed in no other way than through the particular scene. Thus granting a copyright "would give the first author a monopoly on the commonplace ideas behind the scènes à faire". See *Whelan v Jaslow* 797 F.2d 1222 at 1236 (3d Cir 1986), quoting from *Landsberg v Scrabble Crossword Game Players Inc.* 736 F.2d 485 at 489 (9th Cir) cert denied, 469 US 1037, cert denied, 479 US 1031 (1987).

commonality.[93] In *Reyher v Children's Television Workshop*,[94] the Court described as *scènes à faire* "sequences of events which necessarily follow from a common theme", taking the view that "similarity of expression . . . which necessarily results from the fact that the common idea is only capable of expression in more or less stereotyped form will preclude a finding of actionable similarity".[95] The primary strands of the doctrine are; first, that there are scenes which "must" be included in a given context, because such situations call for identical scenes and secondly, that certain scenes are standard or "stock"—the common stock of literary composition.[96] In either context, *scènes à faire* are considered unprotected by US copyright, generally, for three reasons; (i) they may not originate with the author;[97] (ii) not every similarity between a plaintiff's and a defendant's work necessarily constitutes evidence of copying;[98] and (iii) even the copying of some material that is original to a plaintiff should be tolerated.

(b) The Idea/Expression Dichotomy

An understanding of *scènes à faire*, particularly its unprotectability, is best pre-   **3.38**
cipitated against the background of the dichotomy. As remarked by Brandeis J, "the noblest of human productions—knowledge, truths ascertained, conceptions and ideas—become, after voluntary communication to others, free as air to common use".[99] For this reason, a playwright cannot, for example, obtain exclusive rights to the idea of feuding Irish and Jewish families whose children marry and produce grandchildren, leading to reconciliation.[100] Nor will

[93] Certain scenes appear almost inevitably in every genre. See *Hoehling v Universal Studios* 618 F.2d 972, 979 (2d Cir), cert denied 449 US 841 (1980) (scenes such as a German beer hall, in which the Hindenberg aircrew engaged in revelry prior to the tragic voyage, greetings of the period or songs such as the German national anthem, were all considered to be *scènes à faire*, forming "incidents, characters or settings which are as a practical matter indispensable, or at least standard, in the treatment of a given topic").

[94] 533 F.2d 87 (2d Cir), cert denied, 429 US 980 (1976). Both the plaintiff's and defendant's stories involved a lost child who identifies his or her mother as the most beautiful woman in the world. The scenario develops where the village leader gathers beautiful women from the surrounding area, but none is the child's mother, until she appears, to the delight of the child.

[95] Ibid, at 91. See *Alexander v Haley* 460 F.Supp 40 at 45 (SDNY 1978). The author of the novel *Jubilee* claimed that the book *Roots* infringed her copyright. The *scènes à faire* included attempted escapes, flights though the woods pursued by dogs, sex between a slave owner and his female slave, and the sale of slave child away from her family.

[96] A very helpful classification of cases falling under these two lists has been provided by Professor Kurtz , *supra*, n 91 at 81 *et seq*.

[97] If two works are based on a common source, many of the events in each of them are likely to be unoriginal; see *Emeson v Davies* 8 F.Cas 615 at 619 (D.Mass 1845); *London v Biograph* 231 F.696 (3d Cir 1916). In particular, Yankwich has related the doctrine of *scènes à faire* to originality, suggesting that stock themes and incidental elaborations which inevitably flow from them do not contain sufficient originality for the purposes of copyright: Yankwich, *supra*, n 91 at 464–465.

[98] Based on the proposition that independent creation is a plausible explanation for recurring similarities between two works that flow from stock scenes: *Warshawsky v Carter* 132 F.Supp 758 (DDC 1955); *Bachman v Belasco* 24 F. 817 (2d Cir 1915).

[99] *International News Service v Associated Press* 248 US 215 at 250.

[100] *Nichols v Universal Pictures Corp* 45 F.2d 119 (2d Cir 1930).

copyright confer on an artist the exclusive right to paint two cardinals on the branches of a blossoming apple tree.[101]

3.39   The distinction between ideas and expression provides the way of reconciling two competing interests—the interests in rewarding ingenuity and the interest in allowing the public to benefit from new works by other authors on the same subject.[102] The doctrine of *scènes à faire* has developed as a "sophistication" in the law's quest to maintain this balance.

3.40   An idea ordinarily encompasses many means of expression, but if an author could gain control over an idea simply by expressing it in one form, then the stock of raw materials available to other authors would be diminished. All authors build on the work of their predecessors. "No man writes exclusively from his own thoughts, unaided and uninstructed by the thoughts of others."[103] It is the *raison d'être* of *scènes à faire* that when similarities naturally or necessarily result from an idea common to both works, protection, even of expression, may harm the very interests copyright seeks to advance.[104]

V. THE POSITION OF *SCENES À FAIRE* IN ENGLISH LAW

3.41   The *scènes à faire* doctrine had never been expressly endorsed by a UK Court, until the judgment of Ferris J in *John Richardson v Flanders*,[105] which accepted the utility and applicability of *Altai*.[106] Looking to whether there was any prior trace which may point to the presence of an operative *scènes à faire* doctrine in UK copyright law, it is useful to study cases concerning works that draw on common sources, eg historical events and facts; as well as certain literary and dramatic works which draw from common plots, themes and characters. The only reservation with the cases relating to works based on historical sources,[107] common plots and characters is that the lattitude (of the kind seen in the operation of the *scènes à faire* doctrine) shown by the Courts has mostly supported

[101] *Franklin Mint Corp v National Wildlife Art* 575 F.2d 62 (3d Cir) cert denied 439 US 880 (1978).
[102] *Steinberg v Columbia Pictures Indus* 663 F.Supp 706, 712 (SDNY 1987) (the rationale for copyright protection must reconcile two competing social interests, namely "rewarding individual ingenuity, and nevertheless allowing progress and improvements based on the same subject matter by others than the original author"): *Durham Indus v Tomy Corp* 630 F.2d 905, 912 (2d Cir 1980); *Reyher v Children's Television Workshop* 533 F.2d 87, 90 (2d) cert denied 429 US 980 (1976).
[103] *Emerson v Davies* 8 F.Cas 615 at 619. See also *Berkie v Crichton* 761 F.2d 1289, 1294 (9th Cir) cert denied 474 US 82 (1985) ("there is nothing original or new under the sun"); *Bachman v Belasco* 224 F 817 (2d Cir 1915) ("there is rarely anything that is physically new that does not contain something from a previous publication"); *Simonton v Gordon* 297 F. 625, 627 (SDNY 1924) ("works inevitably contain something found in previous publications").
[104] This is especially apparent in the software field. *Infra*, para 3.49 *et seq*.
[105] *Supra*, n 34.
[106] Ibid, at 526.
[107] *Infra*, para 3.42 and references therein.

a defendant's denial of copying; rather than a determination of substantial similarity.[108]

(a) Historical Accounts and Incidents

In most cases involving news stories and historical accounts it is the "proof of **3.42** similarity in literary embellishments and treatment of incidents and situations which may establish a prima facie case of copyright infringement".[109] Similarities in incidents and situations, whilst affording prima facie evidence of copying, may not be sufficient to override a denial of copying especially when accompanied by an explanation of the similarities by reference to common historical sources.[110] In the same vein, UK copyright law generally extends more latitude to the copying of historical works.[111]

It could be argued that under English law, the existence of common historical **3.43** sources and characters makes it necessary for the courts to establish a *closer pattern of similarity* between the two works to disprove coincidence than would possibly be necessary in a work of pure imagination. By contrast, US law is clearly tolerant of similarities between two works which are "necessitated by the use of the same historical setting".[112] Such scenes are considered by US courts to be "inherent in the situation".

(b) Plots, Themes, Characters and Dramatic Ideas

The situation relating to the copyright protection of plots, themes and charac- **3.44** ters under English law is less clear from the point of view of *scènes à faire*. Whilst the doctrine has never been recognised under English law, the Courts are prepared to acknowledge that generalised basic plots or themes are not protected by copyright, and may be more usefully categorised as "ideas". In *Rees v Melville*,[113] it was held that the similarity between two plays was only of the

---

[108] See however *Ravenscroft v Herbert & New English Library* [1980] RPC 193, where Brightman J stated that the law of copyright would allow a wider use to be made of a historical work than a novel so that knowledge could be built upon knowledge, but a person could not appropriate the skill and labour employed by an author in selecting and putting together the compilation of material or the author's literary labour (ibid at 204–207).

[109] See Lahore *Copyright Law* at 4.11.185.

[110] *Poznanski v London Film Production Ltd* [1936–45] MacCC 107 at 108, where the court recognised that there was an "inevitable similarity" arising from a common historical subject, on which there was considerable literature.

[111] *Harman Pictures v Osborne* [1967] 1 WLR 723 at 728, where Goff J made the observation that in the case of literature about historical characters, one must be careful not to jump to the conclusion that there had been copying merely because of similarity of stock or historical incidents.

[112] *Bevan v Columbia Broadcasting Sys* 329 F.Supp 601,607 (SDNY 1971). For example, similar details such as burning Jewish books and students rioting against their Jewish teacher, drawn from the historical backdrop of Nazi Germany: *Rosen v Loew's Inc.* 162 F.2d 785 at 788 (2d Cir 1947).

[113] [1911–16] MacCC 168.

most superficial character and there was no substantial copying of the plaintiff's play.[114] However Courts have also found infringement where the copying of a play's "non-literal" elements has been sufficiently detailed to justify copyright's intervention.[115] Equally the taking of a combination of incidents in a copyright novel for the purposes of producing a dramatic work has been held to be infringement, even if no actual words were copied.[116]

(c) Case for the Direct Application of the *Scènes à Faire* Doctrine

3.45 It is only in the recent past, that the *scènes à faire* doctrine has actually emerged in UK copyright law, in the field of software copyright.[117] It is anticipated that it remains only a question of time before a UK Court will have to examine the utility of such a doctrine. The doctrine itself should gain explicit recognition, categorising stock scenes and stock characterisation as unprotectable "ideas" in a substantial similarity analysis. This is the treatment which has thus far been accorded to the most general themes and ideas of a literary or dramatic work.[118]

3.46   Perhaps an analogy may be drawn with the scope of copyright protection that is accorded to fictional characters. The basic idea of a character cannot be the subject-matter of copyright protection as such, but there is a point where what is taken from the plaintiff's work may constitute an infringement of copyright if it comprises more than the simple idea of a character. In *Kelly v Cinema Houses Ltd,*[119] Maugham J doubted if it would be an infringement if a modern playwright created a distinctive and remarkable character, such as a Falstaff, a Tattuffe or a Sherlock Holmes, and his character was copied by another playwright. It is the use which the author makes of these well-known characters in composing his dramatic scenes that the Court must consider in a case of alleged infringement.[120]

3.47   Of course such a doctrine can only hinge upon the existence of idea-expression dichotomy, and UK writers have more recently disputed[121] its existence, thus forming the basis for not applying limiting doctrines such as *scènes à faire*. As justified elsewhere in this work, case law, various international and

---

[114] However, Pickford LJ considered that copyright in a play could be infringed by copying the idea and arrangement of the incidents and stock characters (ibid at 174–175).

[115] *Holland v Vivian van Damm Productions* [1936–45] MacCC 69.

[116] *Correlli v Gray* (1913) 29 TLR 570, affirmed 30 TLR 116.

[117] In the United Kingdom "*scènes à faire*" has never been described as such. But in *Computer Associates v Altai*, the doctrine was expressly included in the "filtration" stage of the test (para 2.42), which was adopted by Ferris J in *Flanders, supra*, n 34 at 526.

[118] *Supra*, n 113 and accompanying text.

[119] [1928–35] MacCC 362 at 368.

[120] Ibid at 368.

[121] Laddie *et al, Modern Law of Copyright and Designs* (1995) Vol 1 at para 2.73.

regional initiatives confirm and reiterate the dichotomy's existence and importance.[122]

Scènes à faire may also achieve more acceptance in the United Kingdom, if the **3.48**
Continental definition of "originality" is to be adopted for the purposes of copyright subsistence.[123] Applying this criterion (possibly beyond the province of computer software copyright), it is arguable that standard programming devices, programming features that are dictated by industry and manufacturers, may all fall to be unprotected since they do not form part of the author's intellectual creation.[124] This could see the possible inception of *scènes à faire* in the United Kingdom.

VI. SOFTWARE COPYRIGHT: THE RELEVANCE OF SCENES À FAIRE

In the field of software copyright law, the relevance of *scènes à faire* is even more **3.49**
apparent. Designers of computer programs will often use standard or "stock" programming devices to make their programs easy to use, and easy for the user to learn, so as to enhance marketability, catering for user attachment[125] and the so-called "lock-in effect".[126] When used by the programmer, such devices, even though fully expressed in a specific manner, are not part of the copyrightable subject-matter created by the programmer, are necessarily "filtered out" as unprotectable expression. It is imperative to identify the material for such exclusion.

(a) **Material for Exclusion**

Professor Nimmer has noted that the doctrine of *scènes à faire* and the lack of **3.50**
originality apply particularly to computer programs, because in many instances it is virtually "impossible to write a program to perform particular functions in a specific computing environment without employing the standard techniques".[127] As another step in its analysis, a Court should examine the allegedly infringed computer after eliminating from consideration elements that are not original, or flow naturally from considerations external to the author's creativity.[128]

---

[122] See paras 2.25–2.28. For interaction between Art 2 WIPO Copyright Treaty and *scènes à faire*, see Lai [1998] 1 IPQ 35 at 36–38.
[123] *Supra*, paras 2.11–2.14.
[124] See Lai, *supra*, n 122, at 33–34.
[125] User attachment to the particular way a popular program functions has spawned a segment of the software industry devoted almost exclusively to "cloning" programs—the production of less expensive look-alike and work-alike versions of popular software. See eg *Digital v Softklone* 659 F.Supp 449 at 452–453 (ND Ga 1987).
[126] See Vinje in Lehmann and Tapper (eds) *A Handbook of European Software Law* at p 47. This is particularly evident with user interface production; *infra*, para 4.59 *et seq*.
[127] 4 Nimmer §13.03[F][3] at 13–130.
[128] Programmers will often "reuse" computer code that performs a well-defined function, or implements a standard user interface device. Code is reused, so as to improve the reliability of the

3.51   Whilst acknowledging that the *scènes à faire* doctrine can operate through external programming constraints, many writers are unable to offer a comprehensive and not necessarily exhaustive list of external factors.[129] Professor Nimmer has usefully identified five external constraints which dictate how a programmer implements certain elements of a computer program.[130] They are: (i) hardware standards;[131] (ii) software standardisation;[132] (iii) manufacturing design standards;[133] (iv) requirements of the target audience;[134] and (v) industry programming practices.[135] To a certain extent programming languages may

program, being by its very nature error-free. Arguably such reused code cannot be protected by copyright, since it is not original expression. See Ronald A Radie and Richard W Phillips, *Software Engineering: An Industrial Approach* (1988) Vol 1, pp 15–18; Roger Pressman, *Software Engineering: A Practitioner's Approach* (1987) at p 88.

[129]   See for example, the reference to "interoperability standards", which may be technical standards or market standards by Wald and Kirby "Standards for interoperability and the Copyright Protection of Computer Programs" (1996) 449 PLI/Pat 73 at 107.

[130]   See 4 Nimmer §13.03[F][3][a]–[e].

[131]   Ibid at 13–66. A further example is how the IBM PC generates a video display. See L Scanlon *IBM PC & XT Assembly Language: A Guide for Programmers* (1983), pp 245–265. In *Apple v Microsoft* 35 F.3d 1435 (9th Cir 1994), the 9th Circuit noted that the processing power of computers limits the choices that programmers have in depicting functions in the graphical user interface. The fact that the Macintosh Operating System used a moving outline of a window to represent the change in position of the entire window could be explained by the inability of the computer to move all of the contents of the window at once (ibid at 1445).

[132]   eg compatibility with the operating system will dictate the numerous aspects of program design, such as the way in which the program accesses data files on disk, or the way in which they are called up by the user.

[133]   An example of such a standard is the set of "BIOS service routines" which were found in earlier IBM computers (eg PC, XT, Pcgr, PC, AT, etc). Since programmers clearly used these routines, the result was that many aesthetic elements of software designed to work on IBM PCs were identical. See Norton, *Programmer's Guide to the IBM PC* at 17 (1985), discussed in McGahn II "Copyright Infringement of Protected Computer Software: an Analytical Method to Determine Substantial Similarity" (1995) Rutgers Computer & Technology Law J 88 at 136–139. Norton lists three reasons for the use of BIOS routines: (i) it encourages good programming practice, (ii) it increases the chance of programs working in every computer in the PC family; and (iii) it gives IBM more flexibility in making improvements and additions to its line of PCs.

[134]   The business and technical requirements of the end user also constitute a significant external factor which influences program design. Nimmer describes how programs used on the New York Stock Exchange must be designed to comply with the rules and practices of the exchange. See 4 Nimmer §13.03[F][3][d]. In *Plains Cotton v Goodpasture Computer Services* 807 F.2d 1256 at 1262 (5th Cir 1987), the 5th Circuit held that the similarities between two cotton marketing programs which were "dictated by the externalities of the cotton market" should not play any role in determining whether the structure and organisation of the two programs were substantially similar. See also *Business Trends Analysts v Freedonia Group* 650 F.Supp 1452 (SDNY 1987).

[135]   Certain programming practices and techniques have become widely used and accepted in the software industry, and so form another source of consistency between programs. See *Autoskill v NESS* 793 F.Supp 1557 at 1569 (D.NM 1992) aff'd 994 F.2d 1476 (10th Cir 1993). Pascal programmers also developed the "linked list" data structure to cope with sorting and retrieving large quantities of data, where the maximum amount of data is not known in advance. See Schneifer and Bruell *Advanced Programming and Problem Solving with Pascal* (1981) at pp 309–334. Recently the doctrine was applied to exclude the organisation of data files within a mechanical computer-aided design program from protection, because it was the practice of the industry to copy such file structures for reasons of interoperability: *Baystate Technologies v Bentley Systems* 946 F.Supp 1079 at 1088 (D.Mass 1996). The decision has been correctly criticised because of the misapplication of the *scènes à faire* doctrine. Data structures do not become an "industry standard" merely through their popularity with copyists. See Zimmerman 14(4) *Computer Lawyer* (April 1997) 9 at 17–18.

also dictate how certain codes will appear.[136] Moreover programmers will often "reuse" computer code that performs a well-defined function, or implements a standard user interface device.[137]

As such, standard programming techniques are as much the "stock" elements **3.52** of computer programming as are the common themes, incidents and plot elements referred to in the literary *scènes à faire* cases above.[138]

(b) De Facto Standardisation

Numerous de facto standards have been established by software developers[139] **3.53** and should be contrasted with "interface standards" established by international bodies such as the International Standards Organization (in the case of Open Systems Interconnect interfaces) and X-Open (in the case of UNIX application program interfaces). The latter is established so that interface specifications are beyond the control of a particular vendor. Much of the debate surrounding the accessibility of program interfaces (through decompilation and testing) leading to the implementation of the Software Directive concerned the "lock in effect" which ties certain companies into compliance with de facto standards set up by developers.[140]

Any lines of programming which are in accordance with a de facto standard, **3.54** whether from IBM or the ISO, that are subsequently copied by a competitor, will be necessarily excluded from an infringement analysis. They constitute *scènes à faire*.[141]

---

[136] Richard L Bernacchi *et al*, 1 *Bernacchi on Computer Law* (1992) §3.12.2 at 3–108.

[137] See Radie and Phillips *Software Engineering: An Industrial Approach* (1998) Vol 1, pp 15–18; also Roger Pressman, *Software Engineering: A Practitioner's Approach* (1987), p 88. Code is reused, simply to improve reliability of the program, since reused code is error-free.

[138] *Supra*, para 3.44.

[139] For example IBM's Systems Network Architecture (for ma*infr*ames) and its PC-BIOS (for personal computers). See also IBM's Systems Application Architecture (SAA), a standard developed by IBM to ensure compatibility between IBM PS/2 personal computers, microcomputers and mainframes. As a result, many of the aesthetic elements of any software that is designed to run under IBM's SAA Manual will appear always identical. See Fisher, "IBM Manual Explains How SAA User Interface Should Look" *Infoworld*, 9 November 1987 at 6.

[140] ECIS's position translated into an interest in ensuring that no single company could monopolise any interface specifications, and that reverse analysis was permissible when necessary to ascertain such specifications. The converse position was argued by the SAGE, who had a clear economic interest in securing broad protection for interface specifications and tight restrictions on reverse analysis, so that even if competitors were entitled to use interface specifications, the copyright holder could control access to those specifications. See further Vinje, "The History of the EC Software Directive" in *Handbook of European Software Law* at pp 46–47.

[141] Although some US writers suggest that the merger doctrine can be invoked to exclude market standards from protection. See eg Menell "An Analysis of the Scope of Copyright Protection for Application Programs" (1989) 41 Stan L Rev 1045 at 1101; John Pilarski "User Interfaces and the Idea-Expression Dichotomy, or, Are the Copyright Laws User Friendly?" (1987) 15 AIPLA QJ 325 at 348–349. Teter has suggested that this be described as "dynamic merger", which is to be invoked only where elements of functional works have become de facto standards, and should only be used to allow copying of elements that are essential to compatibility. See Teter (1993) 45 Stanford L Rev 1061 at 1088.

(c) Video Games

3.55 The relevance of *scènes à faire* in software copyright can be further seen in video games cases[142]—whether a standard gaming configuration should be available to all, rather than remain in the province of one software developer.

3.56   In *Atari v Amusement World Inc*[143] the defendants based their video game on the plaintiff's. Both games involved spaceships combatting rocks and other spaceships, and had many common characteristics as well as differences. The Court concluded that the many detailed similarities in expression between the two games were dictated by the requirements of any version of the basic idea of a video game involving space rocks.[144]

3.57   Despite the Court's conclusion, were these similarities inevitable? Both games had three sizes of rocks which appeared in waves. The large rock, when hit, split into two medium rocks, a medium rock into two smaller ones and a small rock disappeared.[145] One could argue that the similarities were not "inevitable" or "necessary".[146] Presumably these rocks could have come in four sizes and not three, and could have broken into three parts rather than two. Nevertheless, the view was quite possibly taken by the Court that the first comer should not acquire a monopoly on what might well have been the most convenient configuration of rocks in the game.

3.58   In *Data East USA v Epyx,*[147] in comparing two home computer karate games, the Ninth Circuit took the view that similarities relating to, inter alia, how the figures as depicted in both games each used identical moves, were supervised by the referee, and were each given the opportunity to accumulate bonus points, were "inherent" in the sport of karate, or in its home-computer version.[148] These similarities were held not to warrant a finding of "substantial similarity" for the purposes of copyright infringement.

VII. CONCLUSION

3.59 The above discussion shows that the underlying process of computer software, or its "idea" is always an intellectual distraction to the unwary judge who is engaged in copyright analysis. "[I]t is not so much the expression of the program which involves ingenuity and creativity as the perception and formulation of the problem to be solved and the function to be realised followed by the selection

---

[142] Discussed in Chapter 5.
[143] 547 F.Supp 222 (D Md 1981).
[144] Ibid at 229.
[145] Ibid at 224
[146] *Supra*, para 3.36.
[147] 862 F.2d 204 (9th Cir 1988)
[148] Ibid at 209. These features were considered by the Court to "follow from the *idea* of a martial arts karate combat game, or are inseparable from, indispensable to, or even standard treatment of the *idea* of the karate sport. As such they are not protectable".

and relation of components designed to achieve this aim".[149] This chapter has examined the limiting doctrines of merger and *scènes à faire* and their future relevance to software copyright in the United Kingdom.[150]

---

[149] See Christopher Arup, *Innovation, Policy and Law* (Cambrige University Press, 1993), p 102. See also Kindermann, "The International Copyright of Computer Software: History, Status and Developments" *Monthly Review of the World Intellectual Property Organisation*, April 1988, at 201.

[150] Or some other international agreeement; see Zimmerman 34 Colum J.Transnat'l L. 503 at 522 *et seq*. From the viewpoint of international standardisation, the author is less optimistic about efficiency concerns (ibid at 524).

Part 2

The Scope of Copyright Protection of User Interfaces

4

The Copyright Protection for
User Interfaces

I. INTRODUCTION

This chapter presents an analysis on the scope of copyright protection that **4.1**
should be accorded to "user interfaces", ie screen displays and key configuration
(as reflected on the screen), the medium through which computer and user communicate. The importance of this discussion should not be underestimated, for
it is the user interface which first confronts every user, and every judge. It is
therefore most influential in the impression which it makes upon both physical
and temporal perception and interaction.

At the very outset it is necessary to resolve the semantic difficulties which **4.2**
accompany this subject. A user interface is often equated with the "look and
feel" of a computer program, but whether "user interface" and "look and feel"
are identical notions is essentially an issue of definition.[1] Very often the notion
of "look and feel" is used to describe all non-literal elements of a work,[2] and in
this broader context "look and feel" not only includes the user interface, but
also the overall structure, sequence and organisation of a program.[3]

(a) Report of the Australian Copyright Law Review Committee

Perhaps the clearest attempt at articulating a definition has been made by the **4.3**
Australian Copyright Law Review Committee (CLRC).[4] The CLRC recognised

---

[1] cf Brian Johnson, "An Analysis of the Copyrightability of the 'Look and Feel' of a Computer
Program: *Lotus v Paperback Software*" (1991) 52 Ohio St LJ 947 at 955 *et seq*.
[2] cf Judge Keeton in *Lotus Development Corporation v Paperback Software International* 740
F.Supp 37 (D. Mass 1990)
[3] Writers vary in their approach; eg David Hayes, in his article "A Comprehensive Current
Analysis of Software Look and Feel Protection (Part I)" [1995] 11 CLSR 304 divides his analysis into
"look" cases and "feel" cases. The "look" cases focus on copyright infringement claims based primarily on the appearance of various screen display elements of the computer program user interfaces at issue. The "feel" cases by contrast focus on infringement claims based on non-visible or less
visible "non-literal" aspects of computer programs—such as the structure of the code itself, the
structure of the menu command system or "menu tree" of the program, and the overall dynamic
behaviour or flow of the program and the underlying methodologies and program features. See also
Russo and Derwin, "Copyright in the "Look and Feel" of Computer Software" 2 *The Computer
Lawyer*, 1 February 1985.
[4] *Computer Software Protection*, Report of the Copyright Law Review Committee (Canberra,
1995).

that owners of copyright in computer programs have long sought to protect various aspects of the text and behaviour of a program, often referred to by such descriptions as "look and feel", "user interface", "non-literal elements" and "structure, sequence and organisation". In its final report CLRC considered the meanings of these terms and examined the question of protection in some detail.[5] It correctly made a distinction between the structure, sequence and organisation of the literal or textual elements of a program and the program's behavioural elements which possess their own structure, sequence and organisation.[6] CLRC observed that while the former may be dealt with by the application of traditional copyright concepts, that is not possible with the latter. After considering the arguments for and against protection CLRC ultimately concluded that "look and feel" amounted to behaviour and as such should not be protected by copyright in the computer program,[7] and did not recommend any additional form of protection for screen displays.[8]

(b) Definitions

4.4   For the purposes of this chapter, the terms "look" and "feel", in so far as they are applied to user interfaces, refer only to screen displays and key configuration, and should, in the author's view, exclude the structure, sequence and organisation of interface specifications and literal coding which lie within the domain of the underlying program.[9] "Look" refers to the screen outputs or sequence of screen outputs displayed on the video display unit. "Feel" concentrates on the operation of the program by the user, eg the sequence of the required keystrokes and general command structure of a software product.[10] The "feel" of a program includes the dynamic, operational flow of the program, its keystrokes and other means for invoking functions, and the general recognisable "style" of operation the program presents to the user. A useful analogy has been made with describing the "feel" of a motor vehicle when being driven; that is, how the designers of a motor vehicle have fashioned the steering and

---

[5] *Computer Software Protection*, Report of the Copyright Law Review Committee (Canberra, 1995) paras 9.06–9.50.

[6] Ibid, paras 9.09–9.12, 9.23.

[7] Ibid, paras 9.42–9.43.

[8] Ibid, para 9.48.

[9] Although there may be scope for overlap, for example where features such as input formats, when stored, also become part of the technical interface in so far as they are used and can be read by other programs. See further Zimmerman "Baystate: Technical Interfaces not copyrightable—on to the First Circuit" 14(4) *Computer Lawyer* (April 1997) 9 at 13–14.

[10] See Carr and Arnold, *Computer Software: Legal Protection in the United Kingdom*, 2nd edn (Sweet & Maxwell, 1992) at p 88. A helpful description of "user interfaces" is given by Pilarski, "User Interfaces and the Idea-Expression Dichotomy, or are Copyright Laws User-friendly?" ASCAP Copyright Law Symposium (Vol 37) 45 at 48–49; in which a distinction is drawn between the audiovisual components and functional components of a user interface (the "look" and "feel"). See further Bandey, *International Copyright in Computer Program Technology* (CLT, 1996) at pp 87–89.

suspension geometries and how the ergonomics of the instrument panel have been contrived are features which lend themselves to how a vehicle "feels" to a driver.[11]

It should at once be recognised that there is an immediate divergence between **4.5** the USA and United Kingdom in their treatment of this subject, with much more of the litigation taking place in the former. The discussion in this chapter first attempts to provide a brief historical perspective of user interface copyright protection in the USA, with a focus on recent developments, especially such notable cases as *Apple v Microsoft*[12] and *Lotus v Borland*.[13] The discussion then turns to United Kingdom copyright law, in particular whether screen displays can be protected under the CDPA, with appropriate comparisons being made with US law. A section is also devoted to the economic and policy considerations which fetter the protection of user interfaces, particularly the speeches of Boudin and Stahl JJ in *Lotus v Borland*.

The chapter concludes with the observation that what has come to be known **4.6** as the "look and feel" (or the "total concept and feel") approach in the copyright protection of user interfaces is on the decline, with the emergence of standardisation, interoperability, a more sophisticated infringement methodology aimed at the rigorous dissection of screen elements, and a shift of fundamental copyright paradigms.

II. COPYRIGHT PROTECTION OF USER INTERFACES IN THE USA: A SURVEY OF RECENT CASES AND DETERMINATION OF PROTECTABLE ELEMENTS

The earliest cases to protect screen displays produced by computer programs **4.7** were the video games cases brought in the late 1970s and early 1980s, which treated the fanciful screen displays of the games produced by the computer program as "audiovisual works",[14] quite separate from the "literary work" comprising the computer code itself.[15] In the mid-1980s software developers began to attempt to protect the look and feel of the user interfaces and other aspects of screen displays through copyright. The challenge is to distill and determine protectable expression or otherwise from the elements of a program's user interface.[16]

---

[11] See Bandey, ibid at p89.
[12] 35 F.3d 1435 (9th Cir 1994).
[13] 49 F.3d 907 (1st Cir 1995), subsequently affirmed by the US Supreme Court.
[14] Defined as "works that consist of a series of related images which are intrinsically intended to be shown by the use of machines or devices constitutes a copyrightable work separate from the "literary work" comprising the computer code itself" (s 101 USCA).
[15] eg see *Stern Electronics Inc. v Kaufman* 669 F.2d 852 (2nd Cir 1982); *Williams Electronics v Arctic Int'l* 685 F.2d 870 (3rd Cir 1982); *Midway Mfg v Strohon* 564 F.Supp 741 (ND Ill 1983).
[16] See Drexl "What is Protected in a Computer Program?" Vol 15 IIC Studies at p 27 *et seq*.

(a) The Early Cases

4.8 Early controversy surrounded the question of whether the copyright of an underlying program extended to its audio-visual display. In *Broderbund v Unison World*,[17] by adopting an approach protecting the "total concept and feel"[18] of the plaintiff's program, the Court extended the copyright in the underlying program to extend to its overall structure, including its screen display.[19]

4.9   Subsequently, in *Digital Communications Associates v Softklone*,[20] the Court denounced this approach.[21] Beyond showing screen replication it was held that the plaintiff was required to show substantial similarities in the source or object codes of both works.[22] This decision marked the beginnings of a more methodical analysis towards the protection of user interface elements.[23]

(b) The High-water Mark for User Interface Protection: *Lotus v Paperback*

4.10 The decline of "look and feel" analyses was steadily exemplified by decisions in the early 1990s, where as the following discussion will show, Courts increasingly began to dissect specific elements of a user interface to determine general protectability. The highwater mark for the copyright protection of a user interface was perhaps reached in 1990, with Judge Keeton's opinion in *Lotus v Paperback*.

4.11   The case of *Lotus Development Corporation v Paperback Software*[24] is one of two important copyright infringement cases brought by Lotus Development

---

[17] 648 F.Supp 1127 (ND Cal 1986). The plaintiff in this case alleged that the defendant had infringed its audiovisual copyright in its Apple II+-compatible PRINTSHOP program, by developing an IBM-compatible PRINTMASTER.

[18] On the "total concept and feel" test generally, see *supra*, para 2.59 and references therein.

[19] *Supra*, n 17 at 1133, 1137. This was arguably a misapplication of *Whelan v Jaslow*, the prevailing authority for non-literal copyright infringement at the time.

[20] 659 F.Supp 449 (ND Ga, 1987). The plaintiff developed a command driven status screen for its CROSSTALK IV program. It proceeded against the defendant, who developed a clone, MIRROR, which included, inter alia, a precise copy of the CROSSTALK screen display (ibid at 453). See generally Middleton, "A thousand clones: The scope of copyright protection in the 'look and feel' of computer programs—Digital Communications Associates v Softklone Distributing Corp" (1988) 63 Wash L Rev 195.

[21] Ibid at 455. See further Kaplan, "Screen Displays are proper subject matter for copyright protection" (1988) 3 U Ill L Rev 757 at 771–774.

[22] Ibid at 455–456. In the event the plaintiff had registered a separate copyright for its status screen, and this was enforced against the defendant. The US Copyright Office subsequently ruled that a program and its screen displays could only be protected by a single copyright; see Notice of Registration Decision: Registration and Deposit of Computer Screen Displays 53 Fed Reg 21 (1988). See further Daubert "Copyright potential markets and the user interface: defining the scope of the limited monopoly" (1992) 55(2) *Law and Contemporary Problems* 355 at 364–365 (1992).

[23] Ibid at 458–459, where the the Court identified as unprotectable "ideas" the use of a screen to display the program's status, and the activation of commands by the typing of two symbols. It took the view that these elements related to how the computer program received and reflected its instructions. See similarly, *Manufacturers Technologies v CAMS* 706 F.Supp 984 at 966 (D.Conn 1987).

[24] 740 F.Supp 37 (D.Mass 1990).

Corporation in respect of copyrights existing in its spreadsheet program, LOTUS 1–2–3.[25] Judge Keeton concluded that the user interface of the Lotus 1–2–3, by which he meant "the menus (and their structure and organisation), the long prompts, the screens on which they appear, the function key assignments, and the macro commands and language",[26] were protected by copyright.[27] He went on to conclude that the similarities found in the defendant's rival spreadsheet were "overwhelming and persuasive",[28] and the differences were not sufficient to keep the two interfaces from looking "substantially, indeed strikingly similar".[29]

Lotus v Paperback represents the high-water mark of copyright protection for user interfaces in the USA. Many writers have considered that the decision can be interpreted as giving an overly broad copyright monopoly for user interfaces,[30] and for this reason the decision has attracted heavy criticism.[31] **4.12**

Judge Keeton did not give proper consideration to the prescriptive "abstractions" test to determine where the line should be drawn between idea and expression, in relation to individual elements.[32] Crucially he failed to articulate how limiting doctrines like merger and *scènes à faire* may be employed to limit copyright protection of *individual* elements. In relation to true dissection, the *Lotus v Paperback* opinion is to be found wanting, when compared with later decisions. **4.13**

Further, in the broader scheme of this discussion, the Lotus interface was protected as part of the underlying program's copyright,[33] Judge Keeton taking the view that the conceptualisation of the program and the user interface required significantly more intellectual effort than the encoding.[34] In this respect, the earlier case of *Broderbund* was followed.[35] However, in his formulation of the **4.14**

---

[25] The other being *Lotus v Borland*, discussed, *infra*, at para 4.24 *et seq.*

[26] Ibid, at 65.

[27] At the same time certain elements were excluded from protection, for example, the two-line moving cursor menu format itself, the "rotated L" screen display that formed the basic spreadsheet cell grid, the use of the "/" key to invoke the menu command system, and other obvious keys like "+" and "–". Ibid, at 66.

[28] Ibid, at 66. The two products used the same menu structure and functioned in the same way, keystroke for keystroke.

[29] Ibid, at 70.

[30] Daubert, *supra*, n 22 at 366.

[31] See generally, Abrahmson, "Why Lotus-Paperback uses the wrong test and what the new software protection legislation should look like" (1990) 7 Computer L 6; Anton and Hoffman, "The Impact of Lotus Development v Paperback Software" (1990) 7 Computer L 1; Stern, "Legal Protection of Screen Displays and other User Interfaces for Computers: A Problem in Balancing Incentives for Creation against the Need for Free Access to the Utilitarian" (1990) 14 Colum-VLA J L & Arts 283; Lewis "Note: Lotus Development Corp v Paperback Software International: Broad Copyright Protection for User Interfaces Ignores the Software Industry's Trend Toward Standardisation" (1991) 52 U Pitt L Rev 689. For a valuable critqe, see Pamela Samuelson, "Computer Programs, User Interfaces and section 102(b) of the Copyright Act of 1976: a critique of Lotus v Paperback" (1992) 55 *Law and Contemporary Problems* 311.

[32] Beyond identifying the "electronic spreadsheet" as the highest level of abstraction. *Supra*, n 24 at 65.

[33] Contrary to the approach taken in *Digital v Softklone*, *infra*, para 4.9.

[34] Ibid at 55.

[35] See *supra*, n 17.

three-step test,[36] the judge correctly rejected the imprecise "total concept and feel" test applied in *Broderbund*.[37]

4.15   Turning to the issue of infringement methodology, his Honour held, as did the Third Circuit in *Whelan*, that a computer program embodies only one idea and that all other elements of a program are expressions of that idea.[38] As discussed elsewhere in this work, this approach was subsequently rejected by the Second Circuit in *Computer Associates v Altai*.[39] Whilst *Altai* did not concern the copyright of a user interface as such, in an important dictum, the Second Circuit rejected the concept of protecting screen displays as part of their underlying program.[40]

4.16   For the future, it has been speculated that in the Second Circuit, protection will not be accorded to screen displays as part of the copyrighted underlying program, and it is likely that the *Altai* test will be applied to filter out the unprotected ideas of an audiovisual screen display.[41] For the purpose of UK law, this would be the correct approach.[42]

(c) Contributions of the Ninth Circuit to User Interface Protection

(i) *Brown Bag Software v Symantec Corp*

4.17   To this end the Ninth Circuit's contribution to "look and feel" cases has been influential, and this began two years before it heard *Apple v Microsoft*, in *Brown Bag Software v Symantec Corp*,[43] a case noted for transforming the legal test which had previously been applied to computer program "look and feel" claims.[44] The groundwork for this transformation was laid two years earlier, in *Shaw v Lindheim*.[45] In *Shaw* the Ninth Circuit transformed the "extrinsic-intrinsic" test into an "objective-subjective" analysis of expression.[46] Although

---

[36] Outlined *supra*, in para 2.41.

[37] *Supra*, n 24 at 62.

[38] See *Whelan v Jaslow* 797 F.2d 122 at 1238 (3d Cir 1986) (the court noting that the purpose of the Whelan program was to assist in the daily operations of a dental laboratory); *Lotus v Paperback supra*, n 24 at 65 (Judge Keeton stating that the "idea" embodied in the Lotus program was that of an electronic spreadsheet).

[39] 982 F.2d 693 (2nd Cir 1992). Although in *Lotus v Borland*, Judge Keeton went to great lengths to try and show that his three-part "essential elements" test was consistent with the test developed in *Altai*, 799 F.Supp 203 at 211–212 (D.Mass 1992).

[40] Ibid at 703.

[41] See Drexl, "What is Protected in a Computer Program?" Vol 15 IIC Studies at 32.

[42] See *infra*, para 4.39 *et seq*.

[43] 960 F2d 1465 (9th Cir), cert denied 113 S.Ct 198 (1992).

[44] See generally Zimmerman, "Substantial Similarity of Computer Programs After Brown Bag" (1992) 9 *The Computer Lawyer* 6.

[45] 919 F2d 1353 (9th Cir 1990).

[46] Ibid at 1357. "Because the criteria incorporated into the extrinsic test encompass all objective manifestations of creativity, the two tests are more sensibly described as objective and subjective analyses of expression".

the Court expressly limited its new test in *Shaw* to works of literature, in *Brown Bag* this reformulation was applied to computer programs.[47]

In *Brown Bag*, the Ninth Circuit, in rejecting an "overall look and feel" **4.18** approach in favour of a limiting analysis,[48] affirmed the District Court's finding that the presence of four options in the main menu screen (including pull-down menus, the use of a main editing screen) for accessing existing files, editing existing files, and printing; were "fundamental to a host of computer programs" and therefore not protectable.[49]

(ii) Apple v Microsoft

One of the most closely watched "user interface" cases in the industry during the **4.19** last several years has been *Apple v Microsoft*.[50] When Microsoft first released Windows 1.0, a Graphical User Interface ("GUI") for IBM/IBM-compatible computers, Apple objected on the basis of the similarity between Windows and the Lisa[51] and Macintosh GUIs. The dispute resulted in Apple granting a licence giving Microsoft the right to use and sublicense derivative works of Windows 1.0 in present and future products. Subsequently Microsoft released Windows 2.03 and Windows 3.0. In addition, Microsoft's licensee, Hewlett-Packard ("HP") released New Wave 1.0 and 3.0, both of which ran in conjunction with Windows. Apple alleged that Microsoft had made subsequent versions of Windows too "mac-like", thus exceeding the terms of the original licence.

A series of opinions were issued by the Californian District Court in response **4.20** to numerous motions filed by the parties.[52] Entering judgment in favour of Microsoft, the District Court construed the licence agreement to cover the visual displays in respect of Windows version 1.0, and not the Windows interface simpliciter.[53] Applying the limiting doctrines, the District Court determined that with the exception of a few elements (including the "zooming rectangle", the dimming folder and a trash can icon), there were no individual elements which were both unlicensed and protectable.[54] It held that the similarities between both works were not great enough to warrant a breach of copyright.

[47] "Computer programs are subject to a Shaw-type analytic dissection of various standard components, eg screens, menus, dissection of various standard components, eg screens, menus and keystrokes." *Supra*, n 43.
[48] *Supra*, n 43 at 1476–1477.
[49] *Supra*, n 43 at 1475.
[50] 35 F3d 1435 (9th Cir,1994), preceded by numerous District Court opinions, *infra*, n 52.
[51] Lisa was the predecessor of the Mackintosh, which was discontinued in 1985.
[52] 709 F.Supp 925 (ND Cal 1989); 717 F.Supp 1428 (ND Cal 1989); 759 F.Supp 1444 (ND Cal 1991); 779 F.Supp 133 (ND Cal 1991); 799 F.Supp 1006 (ND Cal 1992); 821 F. Supp 616 (ND Cal 1993). For comprehensive accounts of these decisions, see Sue Ann Mota "Apple Computer v Microsoft: The Ninth Circuit finds no copyright infringement of Apple's Graphical User Interface" (1995) 23 *Western State University Law Review* 39 at 41–46; Hayes, "A Comprehensive Current Analysis of Software 'Look and Feel' Protection—Part I" [1995] 11 CLSR 304 at 308–315.
[53] *Apple v Microsoft* 799 F.Supp 1006 (ND Cal 1992). For detailed comments, see Moutsatsos, Cumming "Apple v Microsoft: has the pendulum swung too far?" (1993) 9(5) *Computer Law & Practice* 162.
[54] Ibid at 1021–1024. For a useful "*scènes à faire* table", see 1024.

4.21   The Ninth Circuit took the view that the District Court was correct in dissecting the works to determine which similarities "lack originality, flow naturally from basic ideas, or are one of the few ways in which a particular idea can be expressed, given the constraints of the computer environment".[55] Numerous aspects of Apple's GUI failed to meet the requisite standard of originality, since they were first developed by Xerox and later used by Apple.[56] Other limits to protection included hardware constraints, environmental and ergonomic factors.[57]

4.22   The Ninth Circuit confirmed that "thin" copyright protection should be accorded to Apple's GUI, that "virtual identity" formed the basis for comparison between the two works.[58]

4.23   The *Apple* decision may also be noted for its readiness to affirm that Apple's graphical user interface was subject to the same process of analytic dissection as other works, even if GUIs were "thought of as the 'look and feel' of a computer".[59]

(d) A New Dawn: *Lotus Development Corp v Borland*

4.24 To date the only "user interface" case to have gone before the US Supreme Court is *Lotus v Borland*.[60] It is also significant since it was the first US case dealing with the copyrightability of Lotus' "menu command hierarchy" (which Borland replicated in the "emulation interface"[61] of its Quattro products)[62] standing on its own.[63]

---

[55] *Supra*, n 50 at 1439. Numerous similarities were excluded under merger or *scènes à faire*. These included, inter alia, an icon depicting a document file, which in the Court's view was the obvious choice for an icon-graphic image of a piece of paper. Further, in a windows environment, there are only two possible ways to position multiple windows on the screen simultaneously—either overlapping or tiled. This significantly narrowed the range of possible expression of the windows concept. See further Neville (1996) 61 Missouri LR 203 at 210–212.

[56] *Supra*, n 50 at 1446.

[57] *Supra*, n 50 at 1445.

[58] *Supra* n 50 at 1446.

[59] *Supra*, n 50 at 1439, 1445.

[60] 49 F3d 807 (1st Cir 1995) aff'd by an equally divided Supreme Court; 133 L.Ed 2d 610 (1996).

[61] The emulation interface contained all the commands of Lotus 1-2-3, which were presented visually in a screen display generated by Borland's native interface. Lotus-users could accordingly use Quattro products with ease, since they could generate Lotus macros and commands.

[62] In the District Court Judge Keeton noted: "In this case, Borland has appropriated to a great extent the 'look' of 1-2-3. Indeed, Borland has designed an interface that in many respects looks substantially different from the 1-2-3 user interface . . . The 'feel', on the other hand of the emulation modes of the Quattro programs depends in large part on the keystroke sequences one enters to perform spreadsheet operations. One enters the same keystroke sequence to perform the same spreadsheet operations in both 1-2-3 and Quattro Pro's emulation mode. They *feel the same*" (emphasis added) 799 F.Supp 203 at 220.

[63] So stated by the First Circuit; *supra* n 60 at 813.

(i) District Court

In a series of lengthy opinions,[64] Judge Keeton sitting in the District Court found **4.25**
in favour of Lotus, holding that its menu command hierarchy and other elements in the emulation interface were copyrightable[65] and were copied by
Borland.[66]

(ii) Appeal to the First Circuit

On appeal the First Circuit reversed Judge Keeton's decisions, holding that the **4.26**
Lotus menu command hierarchy was a "method of operation" under section
102(b) USC and not protectable by copyright.[67] The *Altai* test was not considered appropriate in this situation, given that the Court was not faced with an
issue of non-literal copy-ring in respect of program code.[68] The Court noted
that the *Altai* test, if applied, would be misleading since "abstracting menu command hierarchies down to their individual word and menu levels and then filtering idea from expression at that stage . . . obscures the fundamental question
of whether a menu command hierarchy can be protected at all".[69]

(iii) The menu command hierarchy as a "method of operation"

The Court concluded that the menu command hierarchy was a "method of **4.27**
operation", given that it "provides the means by which users control and operate Lotus 1–2–3".[70] Lotus had argued strongly and successfully in the District
Court that the hierarchy contained expression because it communicated to the
user the choices which were available to accomplish spreadsheet tasks. The First
Circuit rejected this argument, taking the view that:

---

[64] 788 F.Supp 78 (D.Mass 1992); 799 F.Supp 203 (D.Mass 1992); 831 F.Supp 202 (D.Mass 1993);
831 F.Supp 223 at 226–227(D.Mass 1993) (supplementary complaint alleging infringement based on
the "Key Reader" feature in Borland's spreadsheet features). For a comprehensive discussion of
these opinions, see Hayes "A Comprehensive Current analysis of Software Look and feel
Protection—Part III" 12 CLSR 66 at 70–73.

[65] Notwithstanding that in *Lotus v Paperback*, Judge Keeton held that Lotus' user interface was
protectable as a whole (*supra*, para 4.11), his Honour did recognise this finding did not resolve the
copyright question in respect of individual elements of a user interface, like the menu command hierarchy (788 F.Supp at 81). Judge Keeton's opinions were widely criticised. See Amicus Briefs filed in
the First Circuit, Computer Industry Litigation Reporter, 6 January 1994 at 17957. For further criticisms, see Dennis Charleton, "Lotus Development v Borland International: Determining Software
Copyright Infringement is not as easy as 1–2–3" (1995) 56 U Pitts L Rev 919.

[66] See in particular 788 F.Supp 78 at 84; 799 F.Supp 203 at 209, 212–213, 221; 831 F.Supp 223 at
226–227 (D.Mass 1992); The approach adopted by Judge Keeton was criticised as overly broad. See
Linder, "A recommended copyright test for Computer Program User Interfaces" (1993) 66 Temple
Law Rev 969 at 992–993.

[67] *Supra*, n 60 at 815–818.

[68] *Supra*, n 60 at 814.

[69] *Supra*, n 60 at 815.

[70] Ibid.

> "The Lotus menu command hierarchy does not merely explain and present Lotus 1–2–3's functional capabilities to the user; it also serves as the method by which the program is operated and controlled."[71]

4.28 The fact that the Lotus menu command hierarchy "serves as the basis for Lotus 1–2–3 macros, supported the conclusion that the menu command hierarchy constituted an uncopyrightable method of operation".[72] What is even more conceptually significant, is how the Court held that word commands (even if they were the result of expressive choice) can constitute a method of operation where such words are the direct mechanism for invoking operations,[73] drawing an analogy with the buttons used to operate a video cassette recorder.[74] In reaching this finding the Court was also moved by considerations of interoperability, noting the implications for cross-product compatibility if the appeal was dismissed.[75]

(iv) Affirmation by the Supreme Court

4.29 The Supreme Court granted a petition for certiorari by Lotus. On 16 January 1996 (one week after oral argument of the case), the Supreme Court affirmed the First Circuit's decision by an equally divided Court.[76] No written grounds were given.

(v) Importance of Lotus v Borland

4.30 The following observations may be made of the First Circuit decision. First, its logic suggests that computer program menu command structures may not be copyrightable in any instance. Secondly, it now appears that a threshold question must be asked, before commencing analytic dissection or an *Altai*-type infringement analysis of a user interface—whether the allegedly copied elements

---

[71] *Supra*, n 60 at 816. By contrast, the Court held that the long prompts could potentially constitute protectable expression "for the long prompts are not necessary to the operation of the program; users could operate Lotus 1–2–3 even if there were no long prompts" although a strong argument could also be made that the brief explanations which the long prompts provided could merge with their underlying idea. The Lotus screen displays were also potentially copyrightable expression, since users need not "use" any expressive aspects of the screen displays in order to operate Lotus 1–2–3 (ibid).

[72] *Supra*, n 60 at 818.

[73] *Supra*, n 60 at 816. This ruling may prove to be extremely important, with the onset of a new generation of voice recognition user interfaces and software. The Court however noted that its holding that methods of operation are not limited to abstractions is contrary to the Tenth Circuit decision of *Autoskill v National Educational Support Sys* 994 F.2d 1476 (10th Cir) cert denied 114 S.Ct 307 (1993), in which the keying procedure used by the plaintiff's program (the user selected responses to the program's queries by pressing keys), was held to be sufficiently original to be protectable (ibid, at 819).

[74] *Supra*, n 60 at 817.

[75] *Supra*, n 60 at 817–818.

[76] 133 L Ed.2d 610 (1996) (4–4 decision, with Justice Stevens taking no part in the consideration of the case).

of a computer program even constitute copyrightable subject-matter. If not, no further analysis need be made.[77] Thirdly, it rejects the approach taken by many US courts in software copyright cases, where they proceed by looking principally at whether there were other ways a particular element could have been designed or implemented, rather than by looking at the inherent characteristics or nature of the element itself. If the element is not even copyrightable subject-matter, the inquiry ends there.

Finally, the First Circuit in *Lotus v Borland* was largely motivated by policy **4.31** considerations, displaying a sensitivity to the implications of a decision that would impede cross-product compatibility in functional areas such as menu commands, particularly where such commands have become the basis for independently created works such as macros. This is perhaps consistent with the increasing trend of US Appellate Courts to be more sensitive to the risks of over-protection of the elements of computer programs that are directly related to a program's functionality.

It remains to be seen how future US Courts are likely to extend the "method **4.32** of operation" philosophy, or otherwise. An extension could be made to interpret simple programming code as a "method of operation". While the First Circuit in *Lotus v Borland* distinguished between code and hierarchy, the next court might see no distinction. If the extreme position is taken, that programming instructions constitute an unprotectable "method of operation", the entire notion of affording copyright protection to computer programs could be in jeopardy.[78]

(e) Other Courts: Clash of Circuits

This section discusses the various judicial pronouncements in the USA over the **4.33** protection of particular features of the user interface, and it will be apparent that there is considerable divergence of views shared by different circuits.

(i) *Keying procedures*

In *Autoskill v NESS*,[79] the plaintiffs alleged, inter alia, that the keying procedure **4.34** deployed in the user interface of its reading disorder software was also copied by the defendants. The Tenth Circuit rejected the defendants' argument that keying procedures were unprotectable procedures or methods of operation under section 102(b) USCA. The program in question required users to select responses to the program's queries by pressing "1", "2" or "3" keys, and the

---

[77] Ibid. Equally original expression can be foreclosed from protection when it is a method of operation.
[78] See David Bender "Lotus v Borland Appeal—on-screen program menus not copyright-protected" (1995) 11(3) *Computer Law & Practice* 71 at 72; Swatz [1995] 7 EIPR 337.
[79] 994 F.2d 1476 (10th Cir 1993).

Court took the view that the procedure reflected at least a minimal degree of creativity for protection.[80]

4.35   This part of the *Autoskill* decision was subsequently criticised by the First Circuit in *Lotus v Borland*,[81] which questioned whether a programmer's decision to have users select a response by pressing relevant keys was "original". It failed to see how "a student selecting a response by pressing the '1', '2' or '3' keys can be anything but an unprotectable method of operation".[82]

(ii) Menus and sorting criteria

4.36   It will be recalled that in *Gates Rubber v Bando*,[83] the Tenth Circuit held, inter alia, that in relation to the menu and sorting criteria from the plaintiff's program, the District Court had failed to conduct a proper filtration analysis.[84] This part of the *Gates* decision is arguably suspect, since it relied heavily on the District Court's opinion in *Lotus v Borland*,[85] and as such is in direct conflict with the First Circuit's holding that a menu command hierarchy is an unprotectable "method of operation".[86] Further, by suggesting that menus and sorting criteria were also subject to a filtration analysis, the Tenth Circuit may have indirectly suggested that filtration should be equally applied to literal similarities as well.[87]

---

[80]   Ibid at 1495 n 3.

[81]   *Supra*, n 73.

[82]   49 F.3d 807 at 819. The Ninth Circuit has also indicated, albeit in dicta, that "menus" and "keystrokes" may be protected by copyright: *Brown Bag v Symantec*, *supra*, n 43 at 1477. See also *Lotus v Paperback*, discussed *supra*, para 4.11 *et seq*.

[83]   9 F.3d 823 (10th Cir 1993). *Supra*, paras 2.56–2.57.

[84]   Ibid at 843. Menus were understood to mean the "visual screen displays that present a computer operator with limited number of commands available at a given stage in the computer program's operation" and sorting criteria "would ordinarily mean the factors that determine how the data in the program is organised" (ibid).

[85]   799 F.Supp 203 at 206 (D.Mass 1992).

[86]   See discussion in *Bateman v Mnemonics* 79 F.3d 1532 (11th Cir 1996). By contrast in *MiTek Holdings v Arce Engineering* 864 F.Supp 1568 (MD Fla 1994), the District Court examined the main menu and submenu command structure of the plaintiff's "wood truss layout program", and whilst recognising similarities in the defendant's program, nevertheless held them to be unprotected, since they "mimic the steps a draftsman would follow in designing a roof truss by hand" (ibid at 1580). The approach taken in *Mitek* is more akin to that taken by the First Circuit in *Lotus v Borland*. cf *Productivity Software International v Healthcare Technologies* 37 USPQ 2.d (BNA) 1036 at 1041–42 (SDNY 1995) (excluding menu bar from protection since it was largely dictated by efficiency concerns)

[87]   cf *Lotus v Borland* 49 F.3d at 815, where the First Circuit noted that "the Altai test may provide a useful framework for assessing the alleged non-literal copying of computer code, we find it to be of little help in assessing whether the literal copying of a menu command hierarchy constitutes copyright infringement". In *Bateman v Mnemonics*, this apparent disagreement was viewed as more a matter of semantics than substance (ibid at 1545).

(iii) Input/output formats

Rather exceptionally, the Fifth Circuit recently held in *Engineering Dynamics v* **4.37**
Structural Software[88] that the overall structure of input and output formats in
respect of a structural analysis program was protected by copyright, after applying the *Altai* test. In considering the "abstractions" stage, the Court formed the
view that the formats, as part of the user interface, were "analytically distinct
from other parts of the program",[89] and their communicative features justified
protection.[90] The decision is arguably broad, and ironically may be contrasted
with the conservative approach of another Court in finding that the sequence
and arrangement of the same formats were not protected by copyright, when
Engineering Dynamics was then at the receiving end of litigation.[91]

The approach adopted in *Engineering Dynamics* has been followed by some **4.38**
Courts,[92] and will in time generate a line of authority in conflict with *Lotus v
Borland*.

III. GENERAL CONCLUSIONS ON USER INTERFACE PROTECTION IN THE USA AND
ITS IMPACT ON UK SOFTWARE COPYRIGHT LAW

(a) **Ramifications for UK Software Copyright Law: Infringement Analysis**

It is evident from the above discussion that in the last few years a number of new **4.39**
tests have emerged in the USA for judging what constitutes copyright "expression", and how one determines "substantial similarity"; corresponding to the
decline of the ill-defined "look and feel" approach to software protection.[93] In
relation to user interface elements, it is argued that UK judges should, in future,
adhere to the following framework for determining substantial similarity:

---

[88] 26 F.3d 1335 (5th Cir 1994).

[89] Ibid at 1344. The Court added that difficulties were raised when considering the abstractions
of user interfaces, because of their functional qualities, cautioning that "[n]ot all user interfaces will
so easily passes that test" (ibid).

[90] Ibid at 1346.

[91] In 1975 Engineering Dynamics' first version of its program copied exactly the input formats
and their sequence from a third party, Synercom, so as to reduce training time for users familiar with
Synercom's formats. Ironically, Synercom was unsuccessful in its suit. See *Synercom Technology v
University Computing* 462 F.Supp 1003 at 1012, 1014 (ND Texas 1978), where the Court held that
the arrangement of input formats was unprotected by copyright. Such arrangement was largely
intrinsic to the idea, allegorically demonstrated by Judge Higginbottom's famous "H" pattern
gearshift example.

[92] See eg *Interactive Network v NTN Communications* 875 F.Supp 1398 (ND Cal 1995) (opinion
issued a month before *Lotus v Borland*, protecting data feed structures, following the reasoning in
Engineering Dynamics); discussed in Linda Skon, Comment "Copyright Protection of Computer
User Interfaces: "Creative Ferment' in the Courts" (1995) 27 Ariz St LJ 1063 at 1080–1082.

[93] See *supra*, paras 4.8–4.29.

- identify the common elements of a user interface (as manifested in the screen displays, and the coding that generates them);[94]
- exclude "ideas" (eg methods of operation) from overall expression;[95]
- apply the *Altai* test directly both to user interface elements, and non-literal similarities in the coding of both works.

4.40   The last of these steps is perhaps the most controversial, since it is questionable whether the *Altai* test is applicable to screen displays simpliciter. There appears to be a lack of consensus between the First, Fifth and Ninth Circuits on this crucial question.[96] However, as shown by the Ninth Circuit in *Apple v Microsoft*, some form of limiting analysis [97] should be applied to user interface elements, quite apart from that performed on the coding that generates such elements.[98]

(b) *John Richardson v Flanders*: a User Interface Case

4.41   One UK decision[99] has applied the *Altai* test without hesitation, and it remains to be seen whether this approach will be followed with consistency in the future, especially in view of Jacob J's judgment in *Ibcos v Barclays Mercantile*.[100] The latter suggests that elements of the user interface, such as the menu command hierarchy in *Lotus v Borland* could be protected under UK copyright law, being analogous to a detailed table of contents.[101] It has been suggested by Professor Karjala[102] that *Richardson* could be considered to be a user interface rather than a scope-of-protection type case, since the court *declined* to compare actual program code and structure.[103] All the features relied on by the Court to determine

---

[94] As to the latter, similarities between screen displays should only lead to an inference of non-literal or literal copying of program code.

[95] See analysis in *Lotus v Borland*, which forecloses otherwise protectable expression.

[96] *Supra*, paras 4.33–4.38.

[97] Filtration subject to hardware constraints, environmental and ergonomic factors. *Supra* at paras 4.19–4.23.

[98] See *Bateman v Nmemonics*, *supra*, para 2.58, in which the *Altai* test was held to apply to literal elements of computer software. cf the caution in *Lotus v Borland* against the application of the "abstractions" test to every visible element of the user interface, to the point of ignoring the protectability of the whole (*supra*, at n 87).

[99] *John Richardson v Flanders* [1993] FSR 497.

[100] [1994] FSR 275

[101] The most notable feature of Jacob J's decision was the statement that the table of contents in a book, if representative of a reasonably detailed arrangement of topics, could be protected by copyright. Clearly, according to his Lordship, "ideas" were protectable if expressed in sufficient detail. One writer has said that this places at risk the traditional concept of non-protectability of ideas, creating a risk of non-standardisation: Gordon "The very idea—why copyright law is an inappropriate way to protect computer programs" [1998] 1 EIPR 10 at 13.

[102] Karjala, "Recent US and International Developments in Software Protection" [1994] 2 EIPR 58 at 63–64.

[103] *Supra*, n 99 at 533–534. The Court appears to have been under the impression that it was disadvantaging the plaintiff in adopting this approach of not comparing code in the two programs; giving the reason that the plaintiff's counsel did not avail himself of the opportunity to explain the expert comparison in more detail. It is not clear why the defendant's counsel did not make stronger effort to keep the Court focused on the programs rather on what the programs did.

infringement were either collections of keystroke sequences (the "dose codes") or screen display aspects (line editor and amendment routines). Professor Karjala comments that Ferris J's admitted difficulties of applying aspects of the *Altai* test[104] resulted from his refusal to consider such program elements.[105] Evidently Ferris J placed much emphasis on screen displays, to the extent that they "demonstrate the contents of the underlying program in which the relevant copyright subsists".[106]

While the Court accepted the general principle of the idea/expression **4.42** dichotomy[107], it was also prepared to protect "systems", provided that such systems were original to the plaintiff. Ferris J envisaged that other systems could be protectable by copyright if there were equally good alternative ways to perform the same function.[108] But by what standard does a judge know that a particular way is the "best" way of doing something? It is submitted that this is a determination which has to be made with reference to habits and/or human psychology. If a particular way of doing something is determined to be the "best", and is therefore unprotected, but later a better way emerges—does the earlier system then become protected?

This is where Article 9(2) TRIPS and Article 2 WIPO Copyright Treaty can **4.43** strongly assist a UK court.[109] It is based on the definition provided by section 102(b) USCA. In relation to user interfaces, as defined in this chapter, it is argued that a UK court will in future be able usefully to rule a system, procedure, method of operation, etc as uncopyrightable subject-matter, regardless of creative merit, at the very outset, following the approach of the First Circuit in *Lotus v Borland*.[110]

In *Richardson v Flanders*, the infringing items were in fact part of the user **4.44** interface, and while distinguishing the screen display from underlying program code,[111] the Court made no effort to relate them to the underlying programs. The net result was that auspices of the plaintiff's program copyright may have inadvertently been extended to functional or systemic features of the program's user interface,[112] a result that goes even further than *Altai* (which concentrated

---

[104] *Supra*, n 99 at 549.
[105] *Supra*, n 102 at 64, n 64 and the explanation given in n 103 *supra*.
[106] *Supra*, n 99 at 527.
[107] *Supra*, n 99 at 522–527.
[108] *Supra*, n 99 at 555.
[109] In the absence of strong assurance that Article 1(2) Software Directive applies to user interfaces, Samuelson takes the view that nothing in the Software Directive extends protection to user interfaces, keystroke sequences, macro systems or program behaviour: (1994) 13 J. L&Com 279 at 297–98. On interfaces generally, see Appendix, A.28.
[110] A parallel may be drawn with *Amp v Utilux* [1972] RPC 103, where the House of Lords considered the exclusion from registered design protection of features of shape or configuration which are dictated solely by function. The relevant exclusion was construed as covering any features of shape which were adopted for purely functional reasons, and was not limited to cases where only one possible shape was capable of fulfilling the function.
[111] *Supra*, n 99 at 527.
[112] Ultimately the Court found infringement based on similarities of line editor and label amendment routines that the pharmacist would use in writing labels for drugs, and on similarities in the

on program structure and parameter lists). A more acceptable approach would have been to consider the protectability of screen elements separately from the non-literal elements of program coding, as suggested above.[113]

(c) Two Avenues of Protection

4.45 There currently appears to be two main avenues for the protection of user interfaces in the United Kingdom; first, from the above discussion—a differentiated analysis and respective comparisons of the program elements which generate the user interface, as well as elements of the user interface itself (where separable); secondly, if there has been a total or substantial replication or emulation of the screen display itself, it may be possible to pursue direct copyright infringement of the screen display as a separate category of copyright work.

IV. PROTECTION OF SCREEN DISPLAYS UNDER UK COPYRIGHT LAW

4.46 In *Richardson v Flanders*, Ferris J rightly said:

> "The screen display is not itself the literary work which is entitled to copyright protection. A particular display may enjoy a separate copyright protection as an artistic work in the form of a photograph, or as a film, or as being reproduction of an artistic work in the form of a drawing the copying of which will be for copyright purposes the copying of the drawing".[114]

Heeding these words, it is submitted that under UK law screen displays are not altogether excluded from copyright protection. The following discussion will be divided into two parts; the protection of static displays and a sequence of displays.

(a) The Protection of Static Displays

(i) Preparatory design materials

4.47 It is argued that the clearest route to protection of individual screen displays is now through preparatory materials. Preparatory design materials will presumably include layouts for text to be displayed, drawings for graphics screens, etc. On inspection section 3(1) CDPA may add little to the already existing protection of screen displays through the copyright protection of antecedent

---

default collection of "dose codes'; appearing as "macros" supplied by both programs (enabling the pharmacist to enter commonly used dosage instructions with fewer strokes); *supra*, n 99 at 553–557.

[113] *Supra*, para 4.39.
[114] *Supra*, n 99 at 527.

works.[115] The copying of a screen display would be an infringement of the copyright that subsisted in any preparatory drawings. Even if individual screens are not drawn, the individual characters appearing in the game may be drawn, thus conferring indirect protection upon the screen display.[116]

What is less clear is whether antecedent drawings would actually be protected **4.48** under section 3(1) CDPA as "literary works" (being preparatory design material), or as "artistic works". This was not addressed by the implementing Regulations, but Laddie J offered the following guidance in *Electronic Techniques (Anglia) v Critchley Components*,[117] that "anything which was appreciated simply with the eye" had to be excluded from the ambit of literary copyright.[118] It is however by no means clear whether the test for "eye appreciation" is objective or subjective.

(ii) A photograph?

A "photograph", as a form of artistic work, is defined as "a recording of light or **4.49** other radiation on any medium on which an image is produced or from which an image may by any means be produced, and which is not part of a film".[119] This could arguably include a static screen display. Code that represents the display which is stored on a magnetic disk or a JPEG card could be deemed to be recording from which an image may be produced. The decisive factor is whether the screen display can be regarded as a recording of light or other radiation.[120]

(iii) Protection of the screen display as a literary work or artistic work in its own right

It is arguable that a text screen shown in a screen display may itself represent a **4.50** literary work, given that the definition of "writing" in section 178 CDPA gives copyright to any work "regardless of the *medium* in or on which it is recorded" (emphasis added). If this is so, then a reproduction of the text screen would constitute infringement of copyright in the text itself, quite apart from any question

[115] Lloyd has made the general observation that protecting the result achieved by a computer program rather than the manner in which it is produced offers a potentially significant extension in protection. See Lloyd, *Information Technology Law*, 2nd edn (1997) at para 20.79.
[116] See video game cases, eg *Atari v Phillips* [1988] FSR 416 at 417; also *Sega Enterprises v Richards* [1983] FSR 73.
[117] [1997] FSR 401.
[118] Ibid at 413. cf *Anacon Corp v Environmental Research Technology* [1994] FSR 659, where Jacob J held that engineering drawings and functional charts were protected both as literary and artistic works.
[119] See s 4(2) CDPA. Contrast s 48 Copyright Act 1956, which defined "photograph" as "any product of photography or of any process akin to photography". For consideration of "photographs" under the Protection of Children Act 1978, see *R v Fellows* [1997] 2 All ER 548 at 556 (Evans LJ).
[120] See Lloyd, *Information Technology Law*, 2nd edn (1996) at para 20.76. With the advent of digital cameras it is quite possible for images to be recorded directly onto a computer disk and viewed on a computer monitor.

of whether the copyright of the underlying program is infringed in this process. A novel aspect is that moral rights would subsist in the screen-displayed text, allowing the author of the text to claim rights under sections 77 and 80 CDPA, even though such rights are not available to the author of a computer program![121]

4.51   If the actual display is protectable as an artistic work (typically a graphic work),[122] the reproduction of the display on its own would not infringe the copyright in the underlying computer program, since it is not an infringement of copyright in a literary work to make an artistic work of it.[123]

(b) A Running Sequence of Displays: Protection as Films or Computer-Generated Works under the CDPA

(i) Films

4.52   The CDPA defines a "film" as "a recording on which any medium from which a moving image may by any means be produced".[124] This definition is wider than that which applied under the Copyright Act 1956.[125] It is arguable that the form of words used in the CDPA are wide enough to cover the storage of moving images on a computer hard disk, floppy disk or tape.[126]

4.53   In *Richardson v Flanders*, Ferris J did not rule out the possibility of protecting screen displays as films.[127] The question turns on the effectiveness of scope of protection that is offered by film copyright that should determine its utility as a vehicle of protection. In particular, the scope of protection in respect of films is limited to direct reproduction of the work (which includes taking a photograph of a substantial part of the images of the film).[128] As such it is likely that film copyright could be pleaded as an alternative action, over and above the primary cause of action in the infringement of copyright in relation to the antecedent artistic work, or any preparatory design material.

---

[121] See s 79 CDPA. See further Sterling, "Testing for subsistence and infringement of copyright in computer programs: some US and UK cases" [1995] 11 CLSR 119 at 125.

[122] See s 4(2)(a) CDPA, including any painting, drawing, diagram, chart or plan.

[123] See further, Bainbridge *Software Copyright Law*, 2nd edn (1996) at p131 *et seq*.

[124] See s 5(1) CDPA.

[125] See s 13(1) Copyright Act 1956. It should be noted that copyright was explicitly claimed for screen displays associated with a video game as an artistic work and as a film in addition to a claim for the underlying program under the provisions of the Copyright Act 1956 in *Sega Enterprises v Richards* [1983] FSR 73. It was however unnecessary for the Court to consider these claims since it was satisfied that a sufficient case had been shown of infringement in the underlying program.

[126] The difference in wording between the 1956 and 1988 provisions reflects technological advance, and covers interactivity such as computer games and other multimedia works; see Cornish *Intellectual Property*, 3rd edn (1996) at para 10–25.

[127] *Supra*, n 114.

[128] See s 17(4) CDPA.

(ii) Computer-generated works

A difficult question is whether a screen display is a computer-generated work— **4.54**
defined in the CDPA as a work that is created by computer "in circumstances
such that there is no human author of the work".[129] Bainbridge takes a strict
view on this type of subject-matter, especially in situations where the
programmed computer is used merely as a tool. A word-processed document
or a table of accounts that is created using a spreadsheet are not thought to be
computer-generated works.[130] It is suggested that a similar argument exists in
relation to screen displays.

The sceptical response towards the argument that a screen display is a "com- **4.55**
puter-generated work" may be seen from the judgment of Whitford J in *Express
Newspapers plc v Liverpool Daily Post*,[131] where his Lordship said, in response
to an argument that there was no human author in respect of a computer which
generated random sequences of winning numbers for a newspaper competition,
that such a submission was as unrealistic as saying that a pen was the author of
a work of literature.[132] Evidently the case law before the CDPA contradicted the
very existence of computer-generated works.[133]

The better view is to acknowledge that the CDPA recognises the existence of **4.56**
a "computer-generated computer program", by reason of section 3(1) CDPA in
classifying computer programs as original works of literary authorship. There
are computer programs which generate code, eg to produce a screen display
designed by the process of "screen painting".[134] In practice the shorter duration
of protection for computer-generated works from the end of the calendar year
in which the work was made would be of primary concern to the person seeking protection for screen displays.[135]

V. POLICY/ECONOMIC JUSTIFICATIONS

This final section examines the impact of economic and policy arguments which **4.57**
have also informed the scope of protection of user interfaces in the USA. It is by

[129] Ibid s 178. Ibid s 9(3) provides that "In the case of a literary, dramatic, musical or artistic work
which is computer-generated, the author shall be taken to be the person by whom the arrangements
necessary for the creation of the work are undertaken". The consequence of classification is a
shorter term of protection (s 12 CDPA).
[130] See Bainbridge, *Software Copyright Law*, 3rd edn (1997) at p 67 and ch 9.
[131] [1985] 1 WLR 1089.
[132] Ibid at 1093G. See the earlier unreported case of *The Jockey Club v Rahim*, 22 July 1983,
where the same argument met a similar judicial response.
[133] And this is difficult to reconcile. It has been suggested that there is actually no inconsistency,
because in *Express Newspapers* a human author was responsible for defining the basic format and
content of the output produced. In other words he partly determined the resulting work (Bainbridge,
supra, n 130 at p 224). On this analysis, the argument that a screen display is a computer-generated
work will generally fail.
[134] Bainbridge, *supra*, n 130 at p 223.
[135] See s 12 CDPA.

no means clear as to how influential such arguments will be on a UK Court. The following sections discuss some of the more prominent arguments which featured in the *Apple* and *Lotus* cases.

(a) Menell's Economic Analysis

4.58 Policy and economic justifications cannot be excluded from the copyright protection of user interfaces. In *Apple v Microsoft*,[136] the District Court recognised the difficulty of balancing monopoly interests (for the benefit of Apple) against promoting competition for a more efficient and user friendly system.[137] The Court in *Apple* was impressed by Menell's economic analysis,[138] which argues that once a computer program is on the market it is a public good because its use by additional persons would not decrease its availability. Competitors may free-ride at the expense of the manufacturer by unauthorised copying. Copyright law internalises this externality by limiting the availability of the program through the creation of a property right.[139] On the other hand, Menell argues that overly inclusive copyright protection can produce its own negative effects by inhibiting the adoption of compatible standards (and reducing so-called "network externalities"—the technical term describing a class of goods for which the utility or satisfaction derived from the good's consumption increases with the number of other persons consuming the good).[140] At the same time Menell cautions that whilst a widely adopted computer-human interface can offer important benefits to computer users, it can also "trap" the industry in an obsolete or inferior standard.[141]

(b) Policy and Economic Considerations in *Lotus v Borland*

(i) *Judge Stahl's policy grounds*

4.59 In *Lotus v Borland*,[142] Stahl J articulated three "fallible" policy concerns which justified identifying Lotus' command hierarchy to be an unprotectable idea: first, because Lotus wrote its menu hierarchy so that people could learn and use it, the command structure must be denied protection;[143] secondly, once a user has learned to use the Lotus command structure, he or she will be reluctant to

---

[136] 799 F.Supp 1006 (ND Cal 1993).
[137] Ibid, at 1025.
[138] Menell, "An analysis of the scope of protection for applications programs" (1989) 41 Stan L Rev 1045.
[139] Ibid at 1059.
[140] See Katz and Shapiro "Network Externalities, Competition and Compatibility" 75 Am Econ Rev 424 (June 1985). See generally Hemenway, *Industrywide Voluntary Product Standards* (1975).
[141] Menell, *supra*, n 138 at 1070. Menell explains that in this way, network externalities can retard innovation and slow or prevent adoption of improved interfaces.
[142] 49 F3d 807 (1st Cir 1995).
[143] Ibid at 817.

switch to some other electronic spreadsheet because of the retraining costs involved;[144] thirdly, progress in computer programming depends more heavily on building on the work of others. To ensure progress in the computer programming field, copyright should limit its protection for programs so as to allow later authors with a degree of copying leeway with respect to programs, more so than the more traditional works.[145]

(ii) Judge Boudin's views

Boudin J wrote a concurring opinion that was overtly policy-based. Given the obvious benefits to the user resulting from withholding copyright protection from the menu command hierarchy, his Honour identified another ground upon which Borland should prevail—as a "privileged use",[146] justified on grounds of interoperability.[147] Evidently his Honour was influenced by monopolisation arguments, aware of the "lock-in" effect on Lotus users, and recognising that the Lotus spreadsheet had become a de facto standard in the spreadsheet industry.[148] Boudin J's views on the fair use doctrine may set a trend for its deployment outside the software reverse engineering context.[149]

4.60

---

[144] Ibid at 818. These have been challenged by Professor Lunney as unpersuasive. See Glynn Lunney Jr "*Lotus v Borland*: Copyright and Computer Programs" (1996) 70 *Tulane Law Review* 2397 (a comprehensive analysis of the policy and economic underpinnings of the *Lotus v Borland* decision). He concludes that while the 1st Circuit reached the correct decision, its reasoning does not justify or explain its conclusion. Two further questions should be asked, (i) whether denying protection to the "lock-in" element would lead to the under-protection of such works and (ii) if it would, whether given a choice between protecting or denying protection to the "lock-in" element, under-protection or overprotection would come closer to providing the optimal level of copyright protection (ibid at 2422). Professor Lunney perceives the question as one-copying advantage—whether the copying at issue would give the copyist an undue copying advantage in creating a competing work (ibid at 2432–2435). From available evidence, he concludes that by the time a competitor has purchased a copy of Lotus 1–2–3; taken time to learn and understand the command structure and rewrite the coding in order to replicate functionality, any copying advantage reaped by the copyist is insufficient to justify legal intervention (ibid at 2434).

[145] Ibid.

[146] 49 F.3d at 821. The concept is analogous to fair use, and has been argued to be a viable means of copyright protection for non-literal elements of software. See further David Maiorana, "Privileged Use: Has Judge Boudin Suggested a Viable Means of Protection for the Non-Literal Aspects of Computer Software in Lotus Development v Borland International?" (1996) 46 Am U L Rev 149 at 175–188.

[147] 49 F.3d at 821–822. Jonathan Band describes Boudin J's reasoning as "unabashedly results-oriented". See Band, "Lotus v Borland viewed through the lens of interoperability" (1995) 11 *Computer Law and Practice* 135 at 138. An interesting alternative to similar reliance on copyright law was seen in the *Magill* case by the ECJ, which allowed the European Commission to force the holder of intellectual property rights to grant licences to competitors in circumstances where to do otherwise would create a monopoly working against the public interest.

[148] There have also been broad domestic (UK) endorsements for these principles. For example the DTI paper *Intellectual Property and Innovation* (1986) stated that: "The overall objectives of intellectual property laws are to protect and reward, and thus provide an incentive to, innovation and creation, while ensuring that the resulting rights and obligations strike a fair balance between the originator, his competitors and the users" (para 3.1).

[149] Discussed *infra*, para 6.42 *et seq*. On the use of the Fair Use doctrine to evaluate issues of interoperability, see further David Owen, "Interfaces and Interoperability in Lotus v Borland: A Market-Oriented Approach to the Fair Use Doctrine" (1996) 64 Fordham L Rev 2381 at 2411–2418.

4.61   It is not inconceivable that in UK software copyright cases to come, one might see the emergence of these policy considerations which will be considered by judges, ultimately preventing a judicial stance in favour of over-protectionism.

VI. CONCLUSION

4.62   This chapter has consolidated the approaches adopted by various circuits in the USA towards user interface protection, arguing that a limiting analysis is not inappropriate for user interface elements in the United Kingdom. The crucial distinction between the user interface and the code that generates it should always be made.

4.63   The significance of *Lotus v Borland* cannot be overstated, and it is suggested that UK courts should also conduct a preliminary test of whether an interface component may be excluded altogether from protection, even foreclosing any original expression which may be present.

4.64   The chapter has also traversed the CDPA, highlighting the various possibilities for screen display protection in the United Kingdom, and concludes by raising policy and economic arguments which may be relevant to a UK court in a future determination.

4.65   This chapter has focused on copyright issues. Other mechanisms for the protection of user interface elements include database protection of collections of screen elements,[150] passing off,[151] trade mark and trade dress protection in the USA.[152] Technological developments such as voice activated or virtual reality user interfaces also challenge courts for the future.[153]

[150] See discussion *infra*, paras 9.11–9.15.

[151] Lea, "Passing off and the Protection of Program Look and Feel" (1994) 10 CLSR 82.

[152] See Note "Dressing up Software Interface Protection: The Application of Two Pesos to Look and Feel" (1994) 80 Cornell L Rev 159; Kellner "Computer User Interfaces: Trade Dress Protection for 'Look and Feel' " (1993) 84 Trademark Rep 337; Oratz "User Interfaces: Copyright v Trade Dress Protection" 13 *Computer Law* 1 (January 1996); Zimmerman "Trade Dress Protection for User Interfaces Revisited" 13 *Computer Law* 4 (February 1996); Likorezos "Trademark Law in the Computer Age: Applying Trademark Principles to the 'Look and Feel' of Software" J. Pat Off Society (June 1995) at 451.

[153] See *Engineering Dynamics v Structural Software* 26 F.3d 1335 at 1342 (5th Cir 1994).

5

Copyright Protection of Video Games

I. INTRODUCTION

This short chapter investigates the protection of video games,[1] and discusses **5.1**
some of the relevant cases in the USA and United Kingdom. Again it is observed,
that a limiting analysis should also narrow the scope of copyright protection in
this area.

II. PROTECTION OF VIDEO GAMES IN THE USA

In the USA it has been held that the visual elements of computer game, though **5.2**
changing, may well justify its copyrightability as an audiovisual work.[2] US
Courts have consistently held that a game screen and the computer program
that generated it are separately protected by copyright.[3] They have found that
screen displays possess original authorship independent of the copyright of the
program.[4]

It was consistent with the emergence and subsequent decline of "look and **5.3**
feel" that until the 1990s generally broad protection was given to video game
displays.[5] Even when a defendant's game varied significantly in detail from
the plaintiff's, Courts have been persuaded where two games shared a similar

---

[1] Described as a "strange and idiosyncratic subset operating to the fringe of the main software
sector", raising issues barely considered in UK copyright law. See Gurnsey, *Copyright Theft* (1995)
at pp 127–130.

[2] See Rich, "When Technology and the Law Collide—Look and Feel Copyright Evolves" (1998)
16 Western State U L. Rev 183 at 188–190.

[3] *Midway Mfg v Strohon* 564 F.Supp 741 at 749; and *Stern Electronics v Kaufman* 669 F.2d 852
at 857 (2nd Cir 1982) (where it was held that in "assessing the entire effect of the electronic video
game as it appears and sounds . . . its repetitive sequence of images is copyrightable as an audiovisual display"). Also *M Kramer Mfg v Andrews* 783 F2d 421 at 436 (4th Cir 1986); *Atari v North
American Philips Consumer Elecs Corp* 672 F2d 607 at 615 (7th Cir 1982) cert denied 459 US 880
(1982); *Atari v Amusement World* 547 F.Supp 222 at 226 (D.Md 1981); *Midway Mfg v Dirkenhead*
643 FSupp 466 at 479 (D Neb 1981).

[4] In the USA the originality of video screen displays has been challenged on two grounds; first,
the original content is contained in the programs, not the display, and secondly, the game screens
are too much the product of the individual player's interactive input to be original to the copyright
holder. These arguments have been rejected, the Courts taking the view that there is sufficient independent authorship in both program and screen for copyright to vest in each as an original work.
See *Stern Electronics*, 699 F.2d at 856.

[5] Benson, "Copyright protection for computer screen displays" (1988) 72 Minnesota L Rev
1123.

concept and feel.[6] This initial broad standard of protection may be attributed to the highly creative visual impact made by computer games on its players.

5.4   It is observed that with the onset of a more differentiated approach towards testing for software copyright subsistence and infringement, the scope of copyright protection for video games has simultaneously diminished. This is overwhelmingly evident from the Ninth Circuit decision of *Data East v Epx*,[7] which laid the foundation for the analytic dissection of user interfaces of business software to remove uncopyrightable elements that the Ninth Circuit would later establish in *Brown Bag v Symantec*.[8] The plaintiff was the owner of the copyright in a video game called "Karate Champ". The defendant distributed its own karate game called "World Karate Championship", which the plaintiff alleged was infringing its copyright. The District Court found for the plaintiffs, citing numerous similarities between the two games. This was reversed by the Ninth Circuit, which found, after analytic dissection[9] that all the similarities cited by the District Court related to unprotected elements of the plaintiffs' karate game. Each game had 14 moves, a two player option, a one-player option, forward and backward somersault moves and about-face moves, a squatting reverse punch in which the heel is not on the ground, an upper-lunge punch, a backfoot sweep, a jumping side-kick, changing background scenes, 30 seconds countdown rounds and a single referee.[10] These similarities were found by the Ninth Circuit to "necessarily follow from the idea of a martial arts karate combat game, or are inseparable from, indispensable to, or even standard treatment of the idea of the karate sport. As such they are not protectable [even if copied]".[11]

5.5   More recently, in *Interactive Network v NTN Communications*,[12] in relation to an interactive football game, the District Court held that even if certain individual elements of the football game were standard and as such unprotectable (following *Apple v Microsoft*),[13] copyright protection would be accorded to the original combination of elements.[14] The Court went on to find that the scoring system, including the "consecutive" and "clutch pick" bonus features were protected.[15]

---

[6] Benson, "Copyright protection for computer screen displays" (1988) 72 Minnesota L Rev 1123 at 1138, where the author cites the case of *Atari v North American Philips*—the "PAC MAN" game in which many were found to be unprotectable because of *scènes à faire;* nevertheless the defendant's portrayal of the central figures as "ghost monsters" was an infringement of copyrightable expression.

[7] 862 F.2d 204 (9th Cir 1988).

[8] 960 F.2d 1465 (9th Cir), cert denied 113 S.Ct 198 (1992).

[9] *Supra*, n 7 at 208.

[10] *Supra*, n 7 at 209.

[11] Ibid. The Court found that the only protectable expression in the plaintiff's game related to the scoreboard and the background scenes, and these elements were in fact dissimilar in the defendant's game.

[12] 875 F.Supp 1398 at 1403–05 (ND Cal 1995), where the Court reasoned that it must exclude all unprotectable elements of NTN's original game before comparing the works for substantial similarity.

[13] 35 F.3d 1435 at 1444 (9th Cir 1994), discussed *supra*, paras 4.19–4.23.

[14] Ibid at 1404.

[15] Ibid at 1405.

III. PROTECTION OF VIDEO GAMES IN THE UNITED KINGDOM

(a) **Play Mode/Attract Mode: Film Protection of Screen Images**

Lloyd[16] has argued that a computer game should not be classified as a film,[17] **5.6**
because its user plays an active rather than a passive role (eg with multiple image
screen savers) in procuring the moving images. Computer games generally have
two modes.[18] First, *"play mode"*, where the sequence of images that is reproduced on a video display unit is determined within the limits placed on it by the
program, and by the specific intervention of the player. It may be difficult to
argue that such a sequence of images qualifies as a "film" as defined.
"Recording" implies that the sequence of moving images should be the same
each time it is shown; whereas in this mode the sequence is different on each
occasion, although stock visual images may be employed.[19] On the other hand,
the definition of "film" in the CDPA may be viewed by a Court as broad enough
to accommodate such interactivity.[20] Secondly, *"attract mode"* refers to portions of a computer game appearing in a pre-ordained sequence, eg the introductory segments which show the name of the game, explain its operation to the
player, and perhaps contain previous game scores; which remain the same each
occasion the game is played. Such a sequence of moving images may be classified as a "film".[21]

The only nuance is to ensure that copyright attaches to every existing copy, **5.7**
either in magnetic media, primary memory or during electronic processing,
when an animated sequence is generated. As such the recording on which the
moving images are stored should be construed as the computer program.[22]

In either mode, there will be short animated sequences which are generated **5.8**
regardless of play, and the question arises as to whether these short pieces of

---

[16] See Lloyd, *Information Technology*, 2nd edn (1997) at paras 20.80–20.81.
[17] Contrast, however, the position in South Africa, where a video game has been held to fall
within the definition of "cinematograph film" under the South Africa Copyright Act; see *Nintendo
Co Ltd v Golden China TV-Game Centre and Others*, noted by David Webber "Video Games protected as cinematograph films" [1994] 10(4) *Computer Law & Practice* 137 (upheld on appeal, see
Bulletin of Legal Developments, 23 March 1998 at 55). See similarly, Australia, *Sega Enterprises v
Galaxy Electronics* (1996) 35 IPR 161, noted in Fitzgerald [1997] 5 Ent LR 182.
[18] See *Williams Electronics v Arctic International* 685 F.2d 870 (3rd Cir 1982).
[19] See *Williams*, ibid at 872 n 3. However, it may be arguable that such images are protectable as
"computer-generated" works (s 9(3) CDPA)—provided that they are classifiable as literary, dramatic, musical or artistic works. See discussion in previous chapter.
[20] See Cornish *Intellectual Property*, 3rd edn (1996) at para 10–25.
[21] See Bandey *International Copyright in Computer Program Technology* (CLT, 1996) at pp
75–76; Carr, *Computer Software-Legal Protection in the United Kingdom*, 2nd edn (1992) at
124–125; and *Williams*, supra, n 18 at 872 n 3. On the film protection of screen displays, see discussion in previous chapter.
[22] Bandey, supra, n 21, at 74 *et seq*; contrast Bainbridge, who argues that a screen display could
constitute a "film" under s 5(1) CDPA, in that "the display is a moving image and a magnetic disk
or other computer storage must come within the definition of 'any medium' and 'any means' must
include computer technology" (*Software Copyright law*, 3rd edn (1997) at p 127).

animation, which may last no longer than a second in length when played, are protected by copyright. A tentative submission may be advanced that although the single frame of the computer animation cannot be protected as a photograph[23] it may be protected as part of a film.[24]

(b) Other Products of Execution

5.9   Ferris J in *Richardson v Flanders* alluded to a screen display existing as a separate copyright (whether in the form of a photograph, film or artistic work), notwithstanding its generation by a computer program.[25]

5.10   Other products, apart from screen displays, which should be discussed are music, sound effects, visual backgrounds, characters, game icons and game plots. Preludes to games and introductory sequence music are clearly protected as "musical works" under the CDPA. Sound effects may arguably be protected "sound recordings" under section 5(1) CDPA, recorded in the medium of a computer program, rather than a specific magnetic medium or disk.[26]

5.11   Visual backgrounds that remain static, are not moving images (or sprites), and thus may be protected as artistic works. As for characters, copyright has traditionally protected drawings of cartoon characters, against the substantial reproduction of their "salient features" in the same medium, or otherwise.[27] It is also a feature of many computer games that characters pick up, acquire and use certain icons. Icons by nature are small symbolic drawings that are "simple in design but suggestive of their function"[28] so that the player can easily assimilate their action and purpose within the game. Like characters, game icons may be protected as drawings.

5.12   A significant question arises about the copyright protection of "game plots". In *Ibcos*, Jacob J said:

> "most literary copyright works involve both literal matter (the exact words of a novel or computer program) and varying levels of abstraction (plot, more or less detailed of a novel, general structure of a computer program)".[29]

Bandey has speculated that it may be possible to argue, from the above passage, that the plot in a computer game is protected as a copyright work.[30] This is

---

[23] Since s 4(2) CDPA excludes a single frame of a film from being protected as a photograph.
[24] *Spelling Goldberg Productions v BPC Publishing* [1981] RPC 283 (albeit the short track of film in this case lasted longer than a few seconds).
[25] *Richardson v Flanders* [1993] FSR 497 at 527.
[26] Bandey, *supra*, n 21, at pp 73–74.
[27] eg, the "Popeye" character in *King Features Syndicate v Kleeman* [1941] AC 417. In determining infringement of these characters, one investigates whether "there is such a degree of similarity as would lead one to say that the alleged infringement is a copy or reproduction of the original or the design—having adopted its essential features and substance". See *Hansfstaengl v Baines & Co* [1895] AC 20 at 31 (per Lord Shand).
[28] Described by Bandey, *supra*, n 21, at p79.
[29] [1994] FSR 275 at 302.
[30] Bandey, *supra*, n 21, at pp 80–82.

particularly true where a substantial amount of the detail of a plot or a scenario are copied.[31] At the same time it is recognised that hackneyed themes in games programs such as "Defender" and "Space Invaders", should not receive protection in new games.[32] In this latter observation, few reasons are offered for a narrow or no scope of copyright protection.

A limiting analysis, through deploying doctrines like merger and *scènes à faire*, leads one to this type of conclusion. This was particularly evident from the *Data East v Epx* decision in the USA, in that many of the similarities in both games were held to be unprotected by copyright since they necessarily followed from the idea of a martial arts game.[33]   **5.13**

IV. CONCLUSION

The nuances of screen display protection are very much accentuated in video   **5.14**
games, and for this reason the subject has been separately treated. Consistent with previous chapters, a limiting analysis features in much of the US case law, and in tandem with the previous discussion on user interfaces, may be similarly applied in the United Kingdom, alongside the provisions of the CDPA.

---

[31] Ibid, citing cases like *Holland v Vivian Van Damm Productions* [1936–45] MacCC 69; *Sutton Vane v Famous Players* [1923–28] MacCC 374 and [1928–35] MacCC 62; *Corelli v Gray* [1911–16] MacCC 107. See earlier discussion, *infra*, paras 3.43; 3.54–3.57.
[32] Ibid.
[33] *Supra*, paras 5.5–5.6.

Part 3

Reverse Engineering and Defences

6

Reverse Engineering

I. INTRODUCTION

(a) Structure

The first two parts of this book have concentrated on infringement method- **6.1**
ology applicable both to underlying program specifications, user interface elements and screen displays. A considerable emphasis has also been placed, in
recent years, on the extent to which users may gain access to the underlying coding of software, through the process known as reverse engineering.[1] To this end,
in 1992 the CDPA was amended[2] to incorporate the provisions of the Software
Directive[3]—the most influential legislation permitting the practice of reverse
engineering in circumscribed situations.

This chapter focuses on (i) the provisions of the Software Directive which are **6.2**
concerned with reverse engineering; (ii) the implementation by the United
Kingdom of these provisions; in contrast to (iii) the US approach to reverse engineering; (iv) comparisons which may be drawn between the two systems; and
finally (v) a brief discussion of relevant developments in the Commonwealth,
notably in Singapore and Australia. Through this study of various selected jurisdictions one hopes to draw lessons for future UK software litigation practice.

(b) Reverse Engineering[4] Defined

Commonly employed reverse engineering techniques include the following: **6.3**
studying available manuals and documentation; using intermediate empirical

---

[1] *Infra*, para 6.3 and Appendix, A.42–A.76 for a technical explanation.

[2] See the Copyright (Computer Programs) Regulations 1992 (SI 1992 No 3233); introducing, inter
alia, ss 50A-C CDPA.

[3] Council Directive on the Legal Protection of Computer Programs, 91/250/EEC of 14 May 1991.

[4] Also known as "reverse analysis", described by Bainbridge as the process by which ideas and
principles contained and expressed in a computer program (in whatever form), are made transpar-
ent and available by means of an operation such as disassembly of the object code program.
(Bainbridge, *Software Copyright Law*, 3rd edn (1998) at 155). Some US programmers prefer a more
general definition: "The process of analysing an existing system to identify its components and their
interrelationships and create representations of the system in another form or at a higher level of
abstraction". See further Kaner, Falk and Nguyen, *Testing Computer Software*, 2nd edn (VNR).
The difficulty with this definition is that it can potentially include the publication of the results of
such observation, eg any person who observes the Windows NT system and writes a manual may
arguably have "reverse engineered" Microsoft Press' tutorial books and Microsoft's Online
Windows Help Files.

processes such as observing the program in operation through the use of test inputs and monitoring inputs and outputs from a program (the so called "black-box" technique) or displaying on a computer screen or in a printout contents of the computer memory; and the more complex techniques of disassembly and decompilation.[5] The basic technique of studying available manuals and documentation does not pose any copyright problems as such. On the other hand the more "intermediate" techniques involve the reproduction[6] and adaptation[7] rights, and as such are subject to authorisation.[8]

(c) Implications of the Adaptation Right: Section 21 CDPA

6.4 Although a distinction exists between the concepts of disassembly and decompilation, under the CDPA, the distinction is not apparent. Section 21 CDPA provides that the restricted act of making an adaptation for computer programs involves making an "arrangement" or "altered version"[9] of the program or a "translation" which includes:

> "a version of the program in which it is *converted* into or out of a computer language or code or into a different computer language or code"[10] (emphasis added).

---

[5] See Appendix, A.62–A.73.

[6] Section 17(6) CDPA contemplates copying by temporary storage. The position has not changed with the Copyright Treaty emanating from the WIPO Diplomatic Conference held in Geneva (2 to 20 December 1996).

[7] *Infra*, para 6.4.

[8] To date the only software reverse engineering case in the United Kingdom is *Hycontrol v Milltronics* (Harman J, 20 December 1988, unreported), discussed in *Milltronics v Hycontrol* [1990] FSR 273 (appealed on other grounds). In this decision Milltronics disassembled Hycontrol's Multi-Ranger System by disassembling object code and substantially reassembled lines of code in a very similar order but with sections transposed. Harman J ordered an injunction, inclined to the view that Hycontrol had a serious arguable case of copyright infringement ([1990] FSR 273 at 275–276). See further discussion in Davey 'Reverse Engineering of Computer Programs" [1993] 4 AIPJ 59 at 74–75.

[9] A program may be an "arrangement" if the original software was written for a different platform (eg mainframe software for use on a personal computer). It is likely that an "altered version" of a computer program would not cover translation, but some other process, such as porting (describing the process where a computer program is adapted so that it will execute within a different hardware or operating system environment, where new code is always added to existing programs). See further Bandey, *International Copyright in Computer Program Technology* (CLT, 1996) at pp 60, 178.

[10] See s 21(4) CDPA. It is not clear whether "conversion" includes only line-by-line conversion, or covers situations where a compiled version of object code has several lines corresponding to a single line of source code. The former construction would be too restrictive.

II.   THE SOFTWARE DIRECTIVE AND REVERSE ENGINEERING

(a) Origins of the Software Directive

The Software Directive has emerged amidst debate and controversy[11] amongst   **6.5**
interoperable developers, ultraprotectionists and users never before witnessed
in the European copyright sphere.[12] This was a battle over the protectability of
interface specifications and the permissibility of reverse engineering.[13] Authors
have written at length about the history and genesis of the Directive,[14] and the
document trail leading to its actual adoption has been well reported.[15]

(b) Protection of Interfaces

The reverse engineering provisions contained in the Software Directive, can   **6.6**
only be understood against the larger scheme for interface[16] protection within
the Directive. Article 1(2) *implicitly* excludes interface specifications from copyright protection.[17] Through it the EC endorses the distinction between interface

---

[11] Principally following the Commission's investigation into IBM's refusal to disclose interface information and consequent violation of Article 86 EC Treaty, and IBM's subsequent undertaking, [1984] 3 CMLR 147, Bulletin of the European Communities (10–1984) at 96.

[12] The two main competing interest groups which emerged were the European Committee for Interoperable Systems (ECIS) (comprising most notably, Bull, Olivetti, NCR, Unisys, Fujitsu Espona, Sun Microsystems, etc) and the Software Action Group of Europe (SAGE) (comprising IBM, DEC, Apple, Microsoft and Lotus). The former strongly argued in favour of a "pro-competition" approach towards interface specifications and reverse engineering; the latter comprised ultra-protectionists arguing for extensions to their copyright monopoly. For other organisations and interest groups, see Vinje, *Handbook of European Software Law* (1993) at p 46. See further Conniff, "World Watches as EC Mulls Software Copyright Directive" *Computerworld*, 30 October 1989.

[13] See eg the debate between Cornish, Lake *et al*, and Colombe and Meyer [1989] 11 EIPR 391; [1989] 12 EIPR 431; [1990] 3 EIPR 79; [1990] 4 EIPR 129 and [1990] 9 EIPR 325; Miller [1990] 10 EIPR 47; Staines [1989] 6 EIPR 183.

[14] For comprehensive accounts, see Vinje, Palmer, "The EC Directive on the Legal Protection of Computer Software: New Law Governing Software Development" (1992) 2 Duke J. Comp & Int'l Law 65; see also Vinje, "The Legislative History of the EC Software Directive" in *A Handbook of European Software law* (1993) at p 39 *et seq*; largely followed by Band, Katoh *Interfaces on Trial* (1995) at pp 228–241.

[15] For a comprehensive chronology of drafts (1988–91) see Drier, "The Council Directive of 14 May 1991 on the Legal Protection of Computer Programs" [1991] 9 EIPR 319.

[16] Recital 11 defines interfaces as "the parts of the program which provide for such interconnection *and* interaction between elements of software and hardware". This definition is significant, because "interface" does not carry any real meaning in programming. See further, definitions in Appendix A.28.

[17] Article 1(2) states that "Protection . . . shall apply to the expression in any form of a computer program. Ideas and principles which underlie any element of a computer program, including those which underlie its interfaces are not protected by copyright". Earlier drafts were more equivocal, eg Art 1(3) Proposed Directive OJ C91/4 of 12 April 1989 ("Where the specification of interfaces constitutes ideas and principles which underlie the program, those ideas and principles are not copyrightable sugject matter"), which implied that in certain circumstances interface specifications might constitute protected expression. See further Band, Katoh *supra*, n 14 at pp 242–243; Hart

specifications (the ideas and principles underlying the interface) and their implementations (ie the expression underlying the interface).

6.7   The presence of Article 6 also supports the construction that interface specifications remain unprotected. Through limiting the permitted use of the information to achieving interoperability,[18] Article 6 prohibits the use of all information obtained from the act of decompilation, save for interface specifications, and assumes that no other provision of the Directive, including Article 1(2), restricts the use of interface specifications.[19]

6.8   The following sections discuss the provisions permitting reverse engineering techniques other than decompilation (Article 5(3)) and decompilation (Article 6).

(c) Reverse Engineering Techniques other than Decompilation

6.9   Techniques of reverse engineering generally involve the performance of acts mentioned in Article 4 of the Software Directive. For example, the studying of object code requires displaying the code on the screen or on paper. It has been observed that Article 4(a) does not state that all acts of "loading, displaying, running, [and] storage" constitute "reproductions", and from the wording of this provision it is by no means clear when particular acts of this nature are to be considered "reproductions".[20] Some of the Continental literature consider that an appropriate guideline for interpreting the term "reproduction" would be the examination of the interest of the rightholder in participating in the legitimate economic benefits which result from the use of his program.[21] Thus an act which might technically be considered to be a reproduction , but which would not lead to an increased use of the program, in the sense of using a multiplicity of copies, would not be considered a reproduction for the purposes of copyright law.[22] This is a novel suggestion, which perhaps lacks efficacy owing to its arbitrary nature. The making of reproductions is an exclusive right under Article 4, and covers any act of loading, displaying, running, transmission or storage which "necessitates such reproduction".[23]

"Interfaces, Interoperability and Maintenance" [1991] 4 EIPR 111 at 111–113. For US comparisons, see Band, Steinberg and Vinje "The US decision in Computer Associates v Altai compared to the EC Software Directive: transatlantic convergence of copyright standards favouring software interoperability" (1992) 8(5) *Computer Law & Practice* 137 at 140–142.

[18]   Articles 6(1),(2) Software Directive. The recitals also reflect a commitment to the ideal of interoperability which is inconsistent with the protection of interface specifications: Recitals 10, 23.

[19]   See Pamela Samuelson, "Comparing US and EC Copyright Protection for Computer Programs: Are they More Different than They Seem?" (1994) 13 J.L & Com. 279 at 286.

[20]   See Band, Katoh , *supra*, n 17 at p 244.

[21]   See Michael Lehmann "Die Europaische Richtlinie über den Schultz von Computerprogrammen" 5 GRUR Int'l 327 (May 1991); also Michael Lehmann, "Der neue Europaische Rechtsschutz von Computerprogrammen" 34 Neue Juristische Wochenschrift 2112 (August 1991).

[22]   A similar formula of economic significance has been proposed by the EU for the treatment of temporary copies made in the course of Internet browsing and caching. See Proposed Directive discussed *infra*, in paras 8.21–8.22.

[23]   Article 4(a) Software Directive.

Acts of observation, testing and "black-box"[24] analyses are governed by **6.10** Article 5(3):

> "The person having a right to use a copy of a computer program shall be entitled, without the authorization of the rightholder, to observe, study or test the functioning of the program in order to determine the ideas and principles which underlie any element of the program if he does so while performing any of the acts of loading, displaying, running, transmitting or storing the program which he is *entitled* to do" (emphasis added).

By stipulating that a developer must have "a right to use a copy of the computer program" he seeks to analyse, Article 5(3) prevents the use of an illicit copy of the program.

Article 5(3) is correctly viewed as a stringent condition,[25] since a lawful user **6.11** is entitled to do that which is dictated by the terms of his software licence, subject to Article 9(1) which prohibits a contractual exclusion of the Article 5(3) right. A term that confines a licensee only to a certain use would not permit the user to subject the software to testing.[26] For this reason, Article 5(3) has been described as a "tame provision", since the rightholder is at liberty to license the use of his program for a limited purpose.[27]

The provision refers to observation, study or testing of the "functioning" of **6.12** the program and not of the "program" itself. If the analysis goes beyond the search for ideas and principles behind the functionality of the program, and the objective is to derive specific information or protected expression in the form of code, then it is Article 6 and not Article 5 which provides the platform for such further re-examination.[28]

(d) Decompilation

Article 6 addresses the issue of decompilation, and the following discussion is **6.13** divided into three sub-sections, (i) permissible purposes; (ii) permissible circumstances and (iii) permissible use.

---

[24] Where an engineer observes and studies screen displays of the object code of a program to determine how it functions, without any invasions into the program itself. "Black-Box" observation, for the purposes of Art 5(3), may not extend to the running of line traces (an engineer causes messages to be transmitted from the analysed program to another program or device and uses a line tracer to determine how the program interacts or functions with other programs or devices). See *infra*, n 28 and Appendix A.54.

[25] Laddie, *et al*, *Modern Law of Copyright and Designs* Vol 1 at para 20.46. The wording is said to bear the hallmark of a successful attempt by one sector of the industry to frustrate the drive to interoperability.

[26] Further corroboration for this view is provided by Art 19, which states that a person having a right to use a computer program should not be prevented from performing acts necessary to observe, study or test the functioning of the program, provided that these acts do not infringe the copyright in the program.

[27] Laddie *et al*, *supra*, n 25.

[28] The exception provided by Art 5(3) prevents a licensee from controlling the running of a program, for example in conjunction with line tracing equipment. See Czarnota, Hart, *Legal Protection of Computer Programs in Europe—A Guide to the EC Directive* (1991) at p 71.

(i) Permissible purposes

6.14   Article 6 permits decompilation for the purposes of developing "competing" as well as "attaching" programs. The Commission stated in its *Twentieth Report on Competition Policy* that a program developed through decompilation "may compete with the decompiled program and in such cases will not normally connect to it".[29] Sucker has noted that "it would be permissible to decompile the interfaces of an operating program that allowed the interoperation with application programs in order to market an independently created substitute program that could replace the target program".[30]

6.15   Crucially, the Software Directive does not permit a person to decompile a program for purposes unrelated to interoperability—in practice this means that a developer may not decompile a program solely to research its functionality and underlying ideas, such as a novel algorithm, and then implement those ideas in a different program.[31]

6.16   Czarnota and Hart have suggested that Article 6 does not permit decompilation of a computer program to achieve interoperability between hardware and software, because the Software Directive does not explicitly mention hardware interoperability as a permissible purpose of decompilation.[32] The authors argue that software decompilation is unnecessary to achieve hardware interoperability. With hardware devices, a physical link is always provided between a hardware device and the hardware device(s) storing and executing the program to be interfaced with. The functions of the interface can therefore be observed by monitoring the signals communicated across the physical interface when executing the program interfacing with the hardware.[33]

6.17   However hardware interoperability is clearly an objective that is contemplated by the implementation of Article 6,[34] the basic intention of which is to permit competition at all levels.[35] It is a fallacy to suggest that software decompilation is never necessary to achieve hardware interoperability.[36] Indeed drawing a distinction between software-to-software compatibility and software-to-hardware compatibility has been rightly described as "perverse";[37]

[29] Commission of the European Communities, *Twentieth Report on Competition Policy* (1991).

[30] Michael Sucker, *Handbook of European Software Law* (1993) at p 17 ("The Software Directive—Between the Combat against Piracy and the Preservation of Undistorted Competition").

[31] Jean-Francois Verstrynge, "Protecting Intellectual Property Rights within the New Pan-European Framework—Computer Software" 5 Int'l Computer L. Adviser (June 1991) at 7.

[32] Czarnota and Hart, *supra*, n 28 at pp 84–86.

[33] Ibid, at 85.

[34] See Recitals 10, 23, which have not been uninfluential on Member States. The French National Assembly in its report on the implementation of the Software Directive stated that it would permit decompilation to achieve interoperability between hardware and software: Assemblée Nationale Rapport No 724 (1993) at 31–32.

[35] Lehmann, *Handbook of European Software Law* (1993) at p 178 ("The European Directive on the Protection of Computer Programs").

[36] Czarnota and Hart, *supra*, n 28 at 85; see also examples of CPU and operating system interaction in Sucker, *supra*, n 30 at p 17.

[37] Band, Katoh, *supra*, n 17 at p 249.

and does not appear to be a realistic distinction to make in the software world.[38]

It should also be mentioned that the Software Directive does not actually con- **6.18** fine decompilation to the purpose of interoperability pursuant to Article 6. Decompilation may also be conducted under Article 5(1), for the purposes of error-correction.[39]

(ii) Permissible circumstances

Pursuant to Article 6, decompilation must be "indispensable to obtain the infor- **6.19** mation necessary to achieve . . . interoperability" and satisfy the conditions in subsections (1)(a)–(c). One notable omission from the Directive is a definition of "indispensable". It has been suggested that while it was clearly meant to impose a strict requirement of technical necessity, it must be assumed that the Courts will strike a reasonable balance and interpret the term in the light of existing practice.[40] One questions whether the "indispensability" requirement is even necessary in the first place. The practice of software reverse engineering already renders decompilation a measure of last resort, not least because of the difficulties inherent in the practice.[41]

Subsection (1)(a) requires first that a developer be a licensee of the program **6.20** or be authorised to use the program by a licensee or by any other person who is entitled to use the program. Subsection (1)(b) requires that the necessary interface information "has not previously been made available" to the developer.[42] The issue arises as to whether it is necessary for a developer to request interface information from the rightholder, or offer to pay a licence fee before engaging in decompilation.[43] Several formulations imposing such a requirement were considered by all three EC institutions, and each was rejected.[44]

---

[38] Sucker, *supra*, n 30 at 18.
[39] Keustermans and Arckens, *International Computer Law* §7.13[E] at 7–34.7; Vinje, "Licensing Software in Europe: EC Competition Law Considerations" 1 Int'l Computer Lawyer (November 1982) 1 at 8. See discussion, *infra* at paras 7.44–7.45.
[40] See Band, Katoh, *supra*, n 17 at p 250.
[41] See Appendix A.76. The Commission recognised this in its Explanatory Memorandum to the Proposed Directive, OJ C91/7 at para 3.41 (describing decompilation as a "lengthy, costly and inefficient procedure").
[42] Band, Katoh, *supra*, n 17 at p 250. The authors take the view that this condition is unlikely to impose an unreasonable burden on developers.
[43] It is not clear whether payment can be demanded for the provision of interface information. For opposing views; see Czarnota and Hart, *supra*, n 28 at p 80 and Dreier [1991] 13 EIPR 319 at 324.
[44] eg the proposal made by the Irish delegation to the Council Working Group dated 2 May 1990 (SN/2382/90) (PI), which would have required, as a precondition to decompilation, "a request to the copyright holder [for] transmission of the relevant information". See further Band, Katoh, *supra*, n 17 at 251–252; Keustermans and Arkens, *supra*, n 39 §7.13[E] at 7–34.9 (several delegations to the Council Working Group proposed that the developer has to ask the rightholder for the necessary information before decompiling the program).

6.21   Michael Sucker has addressed the rationale[45] behind this rejection, supporting the view that interface information has "previously been made available" only if it has been published in an easily accessible manner. Dreier usefully observes that, (i) this condition leaves the rightholder with some possibility of control over some acts of decompilation. Insofar as he publishes information on interfaces, third parties will be restrained from decompilation without his consent; (ii) since such information must be "readily" available, third parties would have no duty to ask for information if it is not contained in general program documentation; (iii) nor can it be said that interface information is "readily available" if the rightholder is only willing to disclose it upon payment of a licence fee—since this would undermine the very purpose of limited but reliable access to interface information; and (iv) in inviting rightholders to disclose interface information, Article 6(1)(b) furthers the formation of open standards.[46]

6.22   Under subsection (1)(c), a developer must confine his decompilation to those parts of the analysed program that contain the interface information he requires to make his own independently created, interoperable program. As with the issue about "indispensability"[47] the actual utility of this provision is questionable, in that in practice it seems difficult if not impossible to impose meaningful limits on the extent to which a program may be decompiled.[48] The inherent difficulty and expense of decompilation is such that this particular technique of reverse engineering will not be used to analyse more of a program than necessary.[49] It is also clear that an engineer is not limited to decompiling portions of the program "intended" by the program author to constitute interfaces.[50] Professors Huet and Ginsburg observe that "because the Directive does not specify only interfaces envisioned by the original programmer, . . . the decompiler may seek information concerning any kind of interoperability to which the program may lend itself".[51]

---

[45] Sucker, *supra*, n 30 at pp 19–20.

[46] Dreier "The Council Directive of 14 May 1991 on the Legal Protection of Computer Programs" [1991] 9 EIPR 319 at 324.

[47] *Supra*, para 6.19.

[48] Jerome Huet and Jane Ginsburg "Computer Programs in Europe: a Comparative Analysis of the 1991 EC Software Directive" (1992) 30 Colum. J. Transnat'l Law 327 at 363–364. The authors also add that limiting decompilation to those portions of the program relating to interoperability is unrealistic because the decompiler "may not know where in the program the elements concerning interfaces are located; she therefore may be obliged to decompile the entire program in order to find the pertinent sections".

[49] See further Keustermans and Arckens, *supra*, n 39 §7.13[E] at 7–34.10 ("As decompilation is very expensive and difficult, the developer will in fact never decompile more parts of the program than is really necessary").

[50] Suggestions to the contrary were rejected by the EC institutions; see Vinje, *Handbook of European Software Law* at pp 61, 64, 67, 80–81.

[51] *Supra*, n 48 at 363.

(iii) Permissible use

Another three conditions are imposed[52] on the use which may be made of the **6.23**
results of decompilation. Article 6(2)(a) restricts the use of information resulting from decompilation only for purposes relating to the interoperability of the
newly created program. It has been suggested that such limitation on Article
6(2)(a) is inconsistent with traditional copyright law, since the preclusion of
access to ideas which are irrelevant or unrelated to interoperability results in the
de facto protection of such ideas.[53] This is a basic fallacy, as elements which fall
outside a statutory exception to infringement are not automatically protected by
copyright law; they still remain subject to the limiting doctrines within the
infringement methodology that is argued elsewhere in this book.[54]

Article 6(2)(b) retains the interoperability objective, by providing that a **6.24**
developer may not give any of the interface information derived from decompilation to others except where necessary for the interoperability of his independently created program.[55]

Article 6(2)(c) provides that the information obtained through decompilation **6.25**
may not be used for "the development, production or marketing of a computer
program *substantially similar in its expression*, or for *any other act* which
infringes copyright"[56] (emphasis added). This provision is broad, since expression extends beyond literal code, but much depends on the constraints which
affect the form of expression from the decompiled program which is required
for the making of the second program.[57] If the decompiler is unable to find alternate expression, he will be constrained to use the same form of coding from the
first program, which for the purposes of Article 6(2)(c) will not constitute
"expression" because of merger.[58]

III. IMPLEMENTATION OF THE SOFTWARE DIRECTIVE IN THE CDPA

The provisions of the Software Directive, described above, were incorporated **6.26**
into the CDPA[59] by the Copyright (Computer Programs) Regulations

[52] Article 6(2) Software Directive.
[53] See Band, Katoh, *supra*, n 17 at p 253, n 105.
[54] Recitals 13–15, Art 1(2) Software Directive. Chapters 2–4.
[55] If the decompilation has satisfied the requirements of Article 6, it is thought unlikely that disclosure of interface information would be harmful to the original developer. See Czarnota & Hart,
supra, n 28 at p 81.
[56] There is a slight discrepancy raised in the UK implementation of this particular provision; see
infra, at para 6.31.
[57] Czarnota, Hart, *supra*, n 28 at p 81.
[58] Ibid at p 82.
[59] For a comparison of pre–1992 CDPA provisions governing the copyright protection of software and the provisions of the Software Directive, see Colin Tapper, "The European Software
Directive: The Perspective from the United Kingdom" in *The Handbook of European Software
Law*, p 143 *et seq*. Professor Tapper concludes that the most dramatic changes required to the law
of the United Kingdom to accommodate the Software Directive lie in, inter alia, the amplification of

1992.[60] This part will ascertain the extent to which the relevant sections[61] of the CDPA can be said to have incorporated *all* the principles of the Software Directive which pertain to reverse engineering.

(a) Decompilation under the CDPA

(i) The absence of definition

6.27 Like the Software Directive, the CDPA does not specifically define "decompilation", but this is to be inferred from section 50B(1), which contemplates the conversion of a program expressed in a low level language into a program expressed in a higher level language,[62] or incidentally in the course of such conversion, to make a copy thereof. Although the permitted act may be referred to as "decompilation" under section 50B, the conversion between low-level and high-level languages manifestly covers a broad range of activity; including disassembly. It has been observed by Professor Cornish that section 50B(1) by its wording may not apply to a "hex dump", which entails a conversion from object to hexadecimal code, since the latter is not itself a higher language.[63] However it is argued that a hex dump is a part of the disassembly process, one which, as argued above, is equally brought under the rubric of section 50B CDPA.

(ii) The "permitted objective"

6.28 Section 50B(2)(a) defines the "permitted objective" as the creation of "an *independent* program which *can be operated with* the program *decompiled or with another program*" (emphasis added). Conspicuously absent is any reference to "interoperabilty" in the UK amendments, the draftsman preferring "can be operated with". This wording, whilst carrying the merit of simplicity, does not immediately convey "functional interconnection and interaction",[64] and between what elements.[65]

---

the fair dealing exception to cope with Art 5(3), and the creation of means of implementing the requirements of Art 6 to foster interoperability.

[60] Copyright (Computer Programs) Regulations 1992 (SI 1992 No 3233), which came into force on 1 January 1993.

[61] See ss 50B–C CDPA.

[62] eg covering manual conversion from assembly language (such as Z80) to a high level language (such as PASCAL, C++, COBOL), or decompilation from machine language to a high level language.

[63] Cornish, *Intellectual Property*, 3rd edn at p453 n 52. See further Appendix, A.60–A.61.

[64] See Recital 12, Software Directive.

[65] Leading some to take the view that s 50B(2)(a) is actually broader in application. See Christopher Millard in Jongen, Meijboom (eds) *Copyright Software Protection in the EC* ch 13 (United Kingdom) at p 242; cf Sherwood-Edwards "Seven degrees of separation: the Software Directive and UK implementation" (1993) 9(5) *Computer Law & Practice* 169 at 172. Section 50B(2)(a) allows decompilation not only for the creation of a program which will complement the target program, but also one that would compete with it, provided that the resulting program does

Whilst it is settled that decompilation may be employed under section 50B **6.29** CDPA to produce competing programs, section 50B states that information obtained must be that which is necessary to create an independent program. If the reverse engineer's program already exists, and he wishes to make use of such obtained information to adapt, correct or maintain the interoperability of his program, on a literal construction of section 50B, he will not be creating an independent program. When confronted with this awkward scenario, a UK Court may either have to interpret section 50B against its literal meaning,[66] or apply section 50C. The latter may be the preferable option.

(iii) Software-to-hardware interoperability

It is unfortunate that the UK implementation of the Software Directive in sec- **6.30** tion 50B(2)(a) does not appear to cover software-to-hardware interoperability. From the above discussion,[67] it is clear from the wording of Recital 23 in the Software Directive, and in technical reality such an exclusion under section 50B is unrealistic.[68]

(iv) Creation of a pirate copy from decompilation

Section 50B(3)(d) CDPA states that the lawful user of a computer program must **6.31** not use such information obtained from its decompilation to "to *do any act restricted by copyright*" (emphasis added). Article 6(2)(c) of the Software Directive prohibits information resulting from decompilation "to be used . . . for *any other act which infringes copyright*"(emphasis added). Surprisingly it is suggested by Laddie, *et al* that subsection (3)(d) has been inadequately drafted, for it does not stipulate an "ultimate and only" test of copyright infringement, which, they argue was contemplated by Article 6(2)(c).[69] Dreier takes the view that the only test contemplated in Article 6(2)(c) is the classic copyright infringement test, that the second program must not be substantially similar in code.[70] It is argued that the better view must be that section 50B(3)(d) clearly extends beyond a straightforward test of copying to other infringing acts such as transmission, translation or storage.[71]

not infringe copyright in the target program. See Laddie, *et al, supra,* n 25 at para 20.44; Dreier [1991] 9 EIPR 319 at 325 n 57. Whilst Art 6 Software Directive cannot be used for the purpose of creating a competing product, a program that is developed by decompilation under Art 6 may compete with other programs provided that the decompilation is done for the purposes of interoperability: Czarnota and Hart, *supra,* n 28 at p 83.

[66] Following *Litser v Forth Dry Dock* [1989] 2 WLR 634. See further Sherwood-Edwards, *supra,* n 65 at 172; Rowland, MacDonald *Information Technology Law* (Cavendish, 1997) at p 62.

[67] *Supra,* paras 6.16–6.17.

[68] The contrary view would nevertheless find sympathy with writers like Hart [1991] 4 EIPR 111 at 114.

[69] *Supra,* n 25 at para 20.42 n 2. It is not clear why the authors have taken this view of Art 6(2)(c), which obviously goes further than a basic test of substantial similarity.

[70] See Dreier [1991] 9 EIPR 319 at 325.

[71] See Czarnota and Hart, *supra,* n 28 at p 82. The second proviso to Art 6(2)(c) is by no means superfluous.

(b) Reverse Engineering Techniques other than Decompilation under the CDPA

6.32 There is curiously no express provision in the CDPA catering for "observation, study and testing", as provided by Article 5(3) Software Directive.[72] The view has been taken that the acts permitted by Article 5(3) are not expressly permitted by any amendment to the CDPA, presumably because the act of observation, study and testing would not per se infringe copyright in a computer program.[73] This is perhaps an over-simplification, and one is more inclined to share the view of Laddie, *et al*, who state that whilst the United Kingdom has made no distinct attempt to implement Article 5(3), the point is formally within the scope of the fair dealing provisions of section 29 CDPA.[74]

IV. REVERSE ENGINEERING IN THE USA

6.33 The next substantive part of this chapter examines how the US courts have approached software reverse engineering, through applying the pertinent provisions of the USCA.

(a) Attitude of the US Supreme Court Towards Reverse Engineering Generally

6.34 The US Supreme Court has long realised that there is nothing inherently wrong with studying a competitor's product to understand how it works and to determine how a better product may be created. In *Kewanee Oil v Bicron Corporation*[75] it was said in relation to trade secret protection:

> "trade secret law . . . does not offer protection against discovery by fair and honest means such as . . . by so-called reverse engineering, that is by starting with the known product and working backward to divine the process which aided in its development or manufacture".[76]

6.35 The Supreme Court has also stated in the patent context that "the competitive reality of reverse engineering may act as a spur to the inventor, creating an incentive to develop inventions that meet the requirements of patentability".[77]

---

[72] See however s 296A(1) CDPA, which prohibits a contractual exclusion of Art 5(3).

[73] Millard, *supra*, n 65 at 241. For this reason, Art 5(3) Software Directive has been labelled as "tame" (Laddie, *et al*, *supra*, n 25 at para 20.46)—since it purports to state an exception to the restricted acts, while claiming not to operate where there would be copyright infringement. See further Cornish, *supra*, n 20 at para 13–36 n 56.

[74] Laddie, *et al*, *supra*, n 25 at para 20.46. See also para 20.40, where the authors question the basis underlying the possible application of s 29 CDPA to techniques of observation and testing, but not to acts decompilation. On the expansion of the fair dealing concept, see Tapper, *supra*, n 59; and further discussion in ch 7.

[75] 416 US 470 (1974).

[76] Ibid at 476.

[77] See *Bonito Boats v Thunder Craft* 489 US 141 (1989).

Significantly there has been no decision from the Supreme Court examining the **6.36** copyright implications of software reverse engineering to date. The following discussion will examine the various sections[78] of the USCA that have been considered by various Courts to exempt reverse engineering techniques from the scope of copyright infringement.

(b) Permissibility of Reverse Engineering under Section 117 USCA

Section 117 USCA provides that: **6.37**

> "it is not an infringement for the owner of a copy of a computer program to make or authorise the making of another copy or adaptation of that computer program provided that such a new copy or adaptation of that computer program is created as an essential step in the utilization of the computer program in conjunction with a machine that it is used in no other manner".

This provision was the result of Congressional implementation of the Final Report of CONTU, which recommended, inter alia, the amendment of US copyright law to permit the making of a copy of a computer program when "it is created as an essential step in the utilization of the computer program".[79] Apart from section 107 USCA (Fair Use Doctrine), it is the only provision which may *potentially* admit reverse engineering as an excepted practice within US copyright law.

(i) *"Black-box" reverse engineering and section 117(1):* Vault v Quaid

In *Vault v Quaid*,[80] the Fifth Circuit held that the copying of the plaintiff's **6.38** program ("PROLOK") by the defendant into a computer's memory in order to circumvent its anti-copying software features constituted "an essential step in the utilization" of the program under section 117 USCA.[81] The defendant's circumvention program ("RAMKEY") was developed in three stages. The first version of RAMKEY was developed by analysing the PROLOK program using DISK EXPLORER an IBM DEBUG. The second version was developed with information gained through the disassembly of PROLOK, but this version was

---

[78] In particular, ss 107 and 117 USCA. cf the Semiconductor Chip Protection Act of 1984 (17 USC §§ 901–906), where the US Congress explicitly embraced the concept of reverse engineering. §906 authorises reverse engineering of a semiconductor chip "solely for the purpose of teaching, analysing or evaluating the concepts or techniques embodied in the mask work or circuitry, logic flow, or organisation of components used in the mask work". To date it remains the most explicit reverse engineering provision under US law. See further Christie *Integrated Circuits and their Contents: International Protection* (1995), ch 9.

[79] CONTU Report, p 13. See generally Kreiss "Section 117 of the Copyright Act" (1991) Brigham Young U LR 1497 at 1527–1528.

[80] *Vault v Quaid* 847 F. 2d 255 (5th Cir 1988).

[81] Ibid at 261.

discontinued. A new version was developed which allowed the defendants to analyse PROLOK without disassembling it.[82]

6.39   The *Vault* case has controversially[83] paved the way for some US District Courts to endorse the practice of "black-box" reverse engineering under US copyright law.[84] The more conventional analysis of section 117 is that it should apply to merely "inputting" a program to use it.[85] One possible reason for the decision was that the defendant's RAMKEY program made it possible for PRO-LOCK purchasers to make back-up copies—a lawful use under section 117(2) USCA. Arguably the Fifth Circuit gave a broad construction to subsection (1) in order to give effect to subsection (2).[86]

(ii)   Decompilation and disassembly: application of section 117(1) USCA

6.40   The facts of *Vault* do not support any proposition that section 117(1) USCA authorises program adaptation.[87] The Ninth Circuit in *Sega v Accolade*[88] has taken the view that section 117(1) USCA does not apply to disassembly. With very little discussion, the Court took the view that section 117 "does not purport to protect a user who disassembles object code, converts it from assembly into source code, and makes printouts and photocopies of the refined source code version".[89]

---

[82]   See District Court's analysis, 655 F.Supp 750 at 755 (ED La. 1987).

[83]   For criticisms see Miller "Copyright Protection of Computer Programs, Databases and Computer-generated Works: is Anything New Since CONTU?" (1993) 106 Harv L Rev 978 at 1016 n 185 (*Vault* construction of s 117(1) described as "questionable"); Conley and Brown "Revisiting s.117 of the Copyright Act: An Economic Approach" *Computer Lawyer* (November 1990) 1 at 9.

[84]   See eg *EF Johnson v Uniden Corp of America* 623 F.Supp 1485 (D.Minn 1986); where it was said: "the mere fact that the defendant's engineers dumped, flow-charted and analysed the plaintiff's code was not, in and of itself, established pirating. As both parties' witnesses admitted, dumping and analysing competitors' codes is standard practice in the industry" (ibid at 1501 n 17). At least one writer has also argued for the application of s117 (or its equivalent) to legitimise the practice of black-box reverse engineering; see Ng-Loy Wee Loon, "Legitimizing Reverse Engineering of Computer Programs in Copyright Law—How Far Have We Gone in Singapore?" [1996] 4 Int J of Law and Information Technology (No 1) 48 at 61–62; US Congress, Office of Technology Assessment, Computer Software and Intellectual Property (March 1990) at 20; McManis "Intellectual Property Protection and Reverse Engineering of Computer Programs in the United States and the European Community" (1993) 8 High Technology LJ 25 at 87 (supporting the *Vault* conclusion).

[85]   See *Micros-Sparc v Amtype Corporation* 592 F.Supp 33 at 34–35 (1984); *Apple Computer v Formula* 594 F.Supp 617 at 621 (CD Cal 1984); *Allen-Myland v IBM* 746 F.Supp 520 at 536 (ED Pa 1990); *Atari v JS & A Group* 597 F.Supp 5 at 9–10 (ND Ill. 1983). For criticisms of this restricted approach, see Stern, "Section 117 of the Copyright Act: Charter of the Software Users' Rights or an Illusory Promise?" (1985) 7 W New Eng L Rev 459 at 476.

[86]   See *Creative v Aztech* [1997] 1 SLR 621 at 641.

[87]   See Miller, *supra*, n 83 at 1017 (where it is said that the case is often misconstrued as supporting this proposition, because of the common failure to distinguish between permissible observation and storage of the same object code).

[88]   977 F.2d 1510 (9th Cir 1992)

[89]   Ibid, at 1512 n 6. The issue could, ironically, have been settled four years earlier, by the 5th Circuit in the *Vault* case (*supra*, n 80). Although Quaid appeared to have disassembled PROLOK, Vault did not challenge, in the District Court, the legality of the process "by which a machine language is placed in another programming language which is more readily understood by human

It is submitted that for the purposes of US law, this approach applies equally **6.41** to the practice of decompilation.

(c) Reverse Engineering and Fair Use: Section 107 USCA

(i) Fair use generally

Section 107 USCA contains the Fair Use doctrine, which has pervasively become **6.42** increasingly relevant to software reverse engineering in the USA. Often described as the "equitable rule of reason"[90] the doctine permits Courts to avoid rigid application of the copyright statute when, on occasion, it would "stifle the very creativity which the law is designed to foster".[91] Section 107 provides, in part:

> "In determining whether the use made of a work in any particular case is a fair use the factors to be considered shall include—
> (1) the purpose and character of the use, including whether such use is of a commercial nature or is for nonprofit educational purposes;
> (2) the nature of the copyright work;
> (3) the amount and substantiality of the portion used in relation to the copyrighted work as a whole; and
> (4) the effect of the use upon the potential market for or value of the copyrighted work".

Courts have developed guidelines for applying the four factors. In respect of the **6.43** first factor, for a 10-year period the US Supreme Court held that commercial uses are presumptively unfair.[92] For the second factor, Courts are more likely to find fair use of factual as opposed to non-factual works.[93] At the same time they are more inclined to find fair use of published rather than unpublished

beings" (635 F.Supp 750 at 754 (ED La 1987). It challenged only the practice of loading machine language into the computer before the disassembly process. Had Vault challenged the issue of disassembly head-on, and the 5th Circuit ruled on it directly, the subsequent controversy concerning disassembly may have been avoided altogether.

[90] See William W Fisher III "Reconstructing the Fair Use Doctrine" (1988) 101 Harv L Rev 1659, 1668–1669, 1692–1695 (describing the equitable nature of the Fair Use doctrine, but concluding that the doctrine as it stands is incoherent).

[91] *Stewart v Abend* 495 US 207 at 237 (1990).

[92] The US Supreme Court established the presumption in 1984 in *Sony Corporation America v Universal City Studios* 464 US 417 at 449 (1984), and subsequenlty revised this 10 years later, in *Campbell v Acuff-Rose* 114 S.Ct 1164 (1994). Acuff Rose (owner of the copyright in "Oh Pretty Woman" sued Campbell (the lead vocalist and song writer of the group "2 Live Crew") for writing and releasing a parody rap of "Pretty Woman". The Supreme Court held that Campbell's parody could be fair use, notwithstanding its commercial purpose (ibid, at 1179). In reaching this finding the Supreme Court distinguished between "potentially remediable displacement and unremediable disparagement" in the form of criticism. The defendant's parody of the plaintiff's song fell into the latter category and so was potentially fair (ibid at 1178). *Campbell* has to be read in the light of the high intellectual and First Amendment values placed on criticism in its various forms.

[93] eg *Consumers Union v General Signal Corp* 724 F.2d 1044 at 1049 (2nd Cir 1983) cert denied 469 US 823 (1984).

works.[94] In respect of the third factor, Courts have emphasised qualitative rather than quantitative substantiality.[95] The fourth factor is particularly important, the Courts generally applying a presumption of harm to the market of the copyright work in cases where copying involves a commercial use.[96]

(ii) Sega v Accolade; Atari v Nintendo

6.44   US case law developments in the area of decompilation and section 107 USCA have been considerable. In *Atari Games Corp v Nintendo of America Inc*[97] (*Atari*) and *Sega Enterprises v Accolade Inc*[98] (*Sega*), the US Courts of Appeal for the Federal Circuit and Ninth Circuits, respectively introduced a limited decompilation privilege under the Fair Use doctrine.[99]

6.45   Both *Sega* and *Atari* involved defendants who reverse engineered[100] the plaintiff's game cartridges so as to create their own compatible cartridges which circumvented the technical protection measures housed in the plaintiffs' game consoles.[101] On the application of fair use to intermediate copying[102] (which occurs in the course of disassembly), *Sega* provides a more comprehensive analysis of the doctrine.[103]

---

[94] Traditionally the Fair Use doctrine was applied more narrowly to unpublished works than published works; see *Harper & Row Publishers* 471 US 539 at 554–55 (1985). Subsequent decisions excluded the operation of the fair use defence in respect of unpublished works altogether. See *Salinger v Random House, Inc.* 811 F.2d 90 (2nd Cir) cert denied 484 US 890 (1987) and *New Era Publications Int'l v Henry Holt* 84 F.2d 659 (2nd Cir 1989) cert denied, 493 US 1094 (1990). This position was subsequently altered by the insertion of the following words to the end of s 107: "The fact that a work is unpublished shall not itself bar a finding of fair use if such finding is made upon consideration of all the above factors" (HR 4412, 1992). In the stages leading to the passing of this amendment, computer interest groups tainted the draft bill with a "disassembly colouration", concerned that source codes might be jeopardised by this legislation. See *Interfaces on Trial*, at pp 172–183. In *Sega v Accolade*, Sega tried to argue that its object code was unpublished, thus tipping the scales against a finding of fair use. The 9th Circuit dismissed this argument, stating that "computer game cartridges that are held out to the public for sale are published works for purposes of copyright" (977 F.2d at 1526, n 8).

[95] See eg the case of *Harper & Row Publishers, supra*, n 94 at 566.

[96] Ibid. In *Campbell v Acuff-Rose, supra*, n 92 at 1167, the Supreme Court stated that this presumption applies only in cases which involved "mere duplication for commercial purposes", and not transformative uses.

[97] 975 F.2d 832 (Fed. Cir 1992).

[98] 977 F.2d 1510 (9th Cir 1992).

[99] *Atari, supra*, n 97 at 842–844; *Sega, supra*, n 98 at 1527–1528.

[100] In *Sega*, Accolade reverse engineered Sega's game cartridges by disassembling and copying the coding for Sega's "Trademark Security System" into its own software as a standardised header file; *supra*, n 98 at 1514–1516. In *Atari*, the reverse engineering involved a breakdown of Nintendo's 10NES semconductor chip design; *supra*, n 97 at 842. See further McManis, *supra*, n 84 at 38–39.

[101] *Sega, supra*, n 98 at 1514–1516; *Atari, supra*, n 97 at 815–836.

[102] The 9th Circuit in *Sega* presumed that intermediate copying is infringement, whether or not the original work and the end prouct of the copying are substantially similar (*supra*, n 98 at 1518–1519).

[103] *Atari* being consistent with it in most respects, albeit in dictum. *Supra*, n 97 at 836 n 1. The *Atari* judgment was complicated by the fact that Atari had illegally obtained a copy of the program source code from the Copyright Office, thus precluding the reliance on fair use (ibid at 843).

In conducting its fair use analysis,[104] in relation to the first factor, the Ninth **6.46**
Circuit took the view that although the purpose of intermediate copying may be
commercial, this characteristic will operate against a finding of fair use *only* as
the commerciality grows.[105] In other words, commercial use is not per se
"unfair" use.[106] The Court noted that Accolade's intermediate copy of Sega's
code to secure compatibility[107] with Sega's game console created a commercial
impact of "minimal significance", and the copying resulted in a "growth in the
creative expression" from which the public benefited.[108] Accordingly, the first
fair use factor operated in favour of disassembly.

When considering section 107(4)USCA, the Court noted that although any **6.47**
use which "effectively usurp[s] the market for the copyrighted work" is dispositively unfair,[109] this principle was inapplicable in the context of an intermediate copy which enabled a "copier to enter the market for works of the same type
as the copied work".[110] Whilst recognising that Sega's market would undoubtedly be affected by Accolade's presence, the Court held that this "minor economic loss" to Sega was outweighed by public policy which favoured such
competition.[111] It is argued that the Court did not give convincing treatment to
this ground, and did not consider the potential harm caused to Sega's existing
licensing market, despite its knowledge that other developers had already purchased Sega licences.[112] The Ninth Circuit's definition of market was moreover
confined to game cartridges, rather than home entertainments systems (game
consoles), where Sega and Nintendo compete fiercely.[113]

---

[104] *Supra*, n 98 at 1521–1528.

[105] Ibid, at 1522. US copyright scholars have long criticised this commercial/non-commercial dis-
tinction as being both simplistic and inherently ambiguous. See Fisher III, *supra*, n 90 at 1673–1674;
Leval "Toward a Fair Use Standard" (1990) 103 Harv L Rev 1105 at 1111–1116; William Patry, Shira
Perlmutter "Fair Use misconstrued: Profit, Presumption and Parody" (1993) 11 Cardozo Arts and
Ent LJ 667 at 676–687.

[106] Ibid.

[107] Ibid. The Court stated that Sega's program code was copied "solely in order to discover the
functional requirements for compatibility with the Genesis Console".

[108] Ibid, at 1523. Clearly the characterisation of this narrow question enabled the Court to gloss
over the blatant commercial motives behind the defendant's activities. Critics have argued that the
9th Circuit effectively ignored the presumption against commercial use. See eg Miller, *supra*, n 83 at
1019. cf discussion by Julie Cohen in "Reverse Engineering and the Rise of Electronic Vigilantism:
Intellectual Property Implications of 'Lock Out' Programs" (1995) 68 South California L Rev 1091
at 1116–1124, in which she argues that the *Sega* Court's approach to the first statutory factor was
one that was vindicated by the US Supreme Court in *Cambell v Acuff Rose*.

[109] Quoting *Harper & Row*, *supra*, n 94 at 567–569.

[110] *Supra*, n 98 at 1523.

[111] *Sega*, ibid, at 1524. This conclusion is largely based on a presumption that video game consumers are likely to purchase multiple cartridges.

[112] Ibid, at 1514–1516. See *Atari*, where the Court's emphasis on the role of the first and fourth
factors in preventing commercial exploitation in other instances implies that the Court did not think
that it existed in the present case. *Supra*, n 97 at 843.

[113] See Miller, *supra*, n 83 at 1019–1020. Clapes relates that Sega was at the time it sued Accolade,
attempting to compete with a stronger Nintendo in the console market, and trying to induce game
developers, many of whom had already surrendered a certain freedom of action in order to become
Nintendo licensees, to develop games for the Sega Genesis console. See Clapes *Softwars: The Legal
Battles for Control of the Global Software Industry* (1993) at p 8.

6.48   Under section 107(2), the Court stated that works with qualitatively disparate copyrightable elements will receive differing degrees of protection.[114] In order to discern the protectable expression in this case, the Court employed the *Altai* analysis to break down Sega's program into its constituent elements.[115] It took the view that object code is generally not so accessible, and Accolade's disassembly of Sega's program was a necessary step to discern its functional aspects.[116]

6.49   The third fair use factor clearly weighed against decompilation, since the process involved a whole intermediate copy,[117] and the *Sega* court admitted as much.[118] However it minimised its significance by noting that not all of the copied work had been used in creating the final product.[119]

6.50   The *ratio* of the *Sega* decision was thus stated: "where disassembly is the only way to gain access to the ideas and functional elements embodied in a copyrighted computer program and where there is *a legitimate reason* for seeking such access, disassembly is a fair use of the copyrighted work, as a matter of law"[120] (emphasis added). Together with *Atari*, the *Sega* case is generally viewed by writers as a major setback to the use of copyright law to enforce software "lock and key schemes".[121]

(iii) Section 107 and software clones

6.51   A question which was not addressed by the Ninth Circuit on the facts of *Sega* is whether it is permissible to make and use intermediate copies to reverse engineer

[114] See Miller, *supra*, n 83 at 1524–1525.

[115] Ibid, at 1525. See further Teter, "Merger and Machines: An Analysis of the Pro-compatibility Trend in Computer Software Copyright cases" (1993) 45 Stanford L.Rev 1061 at 1086, where the author advances the concept of "static merger" as a defence to the unauthorised "copying of elements necessary to achieve compatibility".

[116] Ibid, at 1525–1526. The *Atari* Court attempted to preserve some of the rights of copyright owners, stipulating that decompilers may copy only as much of the protected expression as is necessary to understand the program's unprotected aspects. *Supra*, n 97 at 843. This restraint on decompilers has been described as unenforceable (Miller, *supra*, n 83 at 1021–1022) and parallels may be drawn with the equivalent restraint in the Software Directive, *supra* at paras 6.14–6.18.

[117] Hence the qualitative unfairness of s 107(3): see Walker, *et al* "Copyright Protection: Has Look and Feel Crashed?" (1993) 11 Cardozo Arts & Ent LJ 721 at 747. It has been argued that the requirement of "substantiality of the amount copied" under s 107(3) renders the Fair Use doctrine incompatible with reverse engineering. See Roskind, "Reverse Engineering, Unfair Competition and Fair Use" (1985) 70 Minn L Rev 385 at 395.

[118] Ibid, at 1526–1527.

[119] Ibid. Professor Miller strongly criticises the focus on the final product as contradicting the initial finding that an intermediate copy is an infringement. In his view the Court's finding also encourages decompilers to engage in hunting expeditions, careful to limit what is eventually used for the creation of the final program. See Miller, *supra*, n 83 at 1018. Another criticism has been made that since disassembly involved a 100 per cent taking, this factor should have weighed heavily against Accolade: Victor de Cyarfus "Sega v Accolade: A Step Forward For Reverse Engineering?" (1994) 23 SW U L Rev 571 at 588.

[120] Ibid, at 1527–1528.

[121] See eg Stern, "Reverse Engineering of Software as Copyright Infringement—an Update: Sega Enterprises v Accolade" [1993] 1 EIPR 34–35. See however the onset of legislation safeguarding technical protection systems, *infra*, para 8.39 *et seq*.

software so as to develop "clone" products, ie "substituting" or "work-alike" programs.[122] In this situation, unlike *Sega* and *Atari*, a fair use analysis may operate against the clone producer for the following reasons.

The clone product will not represent a significant growth in creative expres- **6.52** sion to justify a finding of fair use under the first factor.[123] A clone product is moreover in direct competition with the decompiled software, and in "usurping the market" for the copyright work, will be dispositively unfair under the fourth factor.[124] As in *Sega*, the third factor (amount of work copied) is inherently inconsistent with fair use, although the Ninth Circuit minimised its significance by the finding that not all of the intermediate copy had been used in the final product.[125] This is not the case when a clone is produced, there are bound to be overwhelming similarities in the final product. Even if the clone producer asserts that he used a "clean room" procedure,[126] it may be difficult to rebut any infer- ence of copying in the face of glaring similarity.[127]

The only conceivable factor which may operate to the benefit of the clone **6.53** producer is section 107(2). The utilitarian nature of computer software necessi- tates the discovery of unprotected ideas only through copying, disassembly and decompilation.[128] As such they should be given a lower degree of protection than traditional literary works.[129] Overall, it is argued that a fair use defence would not avail a clone producer under US law.[130]

(iv) A suggested alternative approach for the future: transformative use[131]

Critics will continue to argue that the application of the Fair Use doctrine **6.54** to software reverse engineering undermines the creation incentive[132] of pro- grammers by exposing their work to "compatibility pirates".[133] The *ratio* in *Sega* stands in the midst of a glaringly obvious commercial purpose behind the

[122] A situation which, in the EU will contravene Art 6(2)(c) Software Directive. Discussed *supra* at para 6.25.
[123] cf *Sega*, *supra*, n 98 at 1523. There is arguably little public benefit to be derived from the mar- keting of a similar product. Compare discussion in para 6.46.
[124] See *Harper & Row*, *supra*, n 94 at 567–569. Compare discussion in para 6.47.
[125] See *supra*, para 6.49.
[126] See explanation in Appendix A.77–A.79.
[127] See Clapes *Software, Copyright and Competition: The "Look and Feel" of the Law* (1989) at p 153. See also Judge Reinhardt's remarks in *Sega*, *supra*, n 94 at 1526.
[128] *Supra*, para 6.48.
[129] *Sega*, *supra*, n 98 at 1526; *Atari*, *supra*, n 97 at 843.
[130] See Grogan "Decompilation and Disassembly: undoing Software Protection" 1 *Computer Law* 1 at 10 (February 1984) (where it is argued that the practice of reverse enginering an interme- diate copy for financial gain should never be fair use, where this results in a competitive software product).
[131] A concept derived from the writings of Judge Pierre Leval, one of the Fair Use doctrine's most thoughtful critics. See Leval, "Toward a Fair Use Standard" 103 Harv L Rev 1105 at 1171 ("the more transformative the new work, the less will be the significance of other factors like commercialism that may weigh against a finding of fair use").
[132] For a discussion of this and other criticisms, see Miller, *supra*, n 83 at 1026–1033.
[133] Hager "Apples & Oranges" (1994) 20 Rutgers Computer & Technology Law J 259 at 319.

disassembly,[134] which a Court in a given case may choose to trivialise, since fair use is an "equitable rule of reason".[135]

6.55   A viable suggestion may be to re-orientate the Fair Use doctrine around the end-product; and despite a clear commercial purpose tainting the intermediate copy, examine whether such exploitation has resulted in a transformative use of the copyrighted work. Such a use justified the invocation of fair use in the US Supreme Court decision of *Campbell v Acuff Rose*.[136] The Supreme Court was prepared to accept that an infringement is transformative if it "adds something new, with a further purpose or different character, altering the original with new expression, meaning or message so that the infringement avoids superseding or supplanting the original's expression or purpose".[137] Transformative use effectively renders the commercial purpose behind a work less significant (under the first statutory factor),[138] in furtherance of maintaining the difficult balance between innovation and competition. A strong likelihood of transformative use can also rebut the presumption that an infringement having a commercial purpose caused unfair market harm.[139]

6.56   This is not to say that a transformative use precludes or overrides each of the four fair use factors. Being an affirmative defence, as a matter of principle, the infringer must still argue that an inquiry under each of the four statutory factors satisfies the finding of fair use.[140]

6.57   This could prove to be a most useful device to copyright defendants like Accolade. For example the Sega Court tried to minimise the commercial purpose of an infringement which clearly had a commercial motive. A "transformative use" of the copyrighted work may liberate a Court to reconcile this true commercial character with the utilisation of uncopyrightable but otherwise inaccessible material. When reverse engineers disassemble copyrighted software only to allow independently created programs to enter the market, or merely to develop new software programs that build upon the uncopyrightable elements of existing software, any resulting market harm may be excusable, because allowing a transformative use justifiably promotes the dis-

---

[134] In *Sega* the inquiry into the work's functionality was cloaked under an illusive concern for "compatibility" (*supra*, n 98 at 1522). This ideal may only be putative at best, and US writers have argued that the true objectives of the defendants in *Sega* and *Atari* were to "cash in" on the commercial markets created by the plaintiffs' game consoles. See Hagar, *supra*, n 133 at 320; Clapes *Softwars: The Legal Battles for Control of the Global Software Industry* (1993) at pp 12–13.

[135] See the first US case to allude to the fair use defence; *Folsom v Marsh* 9 F.Cas 342 (CCD Mass 1841) (No. 4901).

[136] *Supra*, n 92.

[137] *Supra*, n 92 at 1171.

[138] *Supra*, n 92 at 1179.

[139] The Supreme Court stated that "no 'presumption' or inference of market harm . . . is applicable to a case involving something beyond mere duplication for commercial purposes" (*supra*, n 92 at 1177).

[140] *Supra*, n 92 at 1177. The Court also said: "Nor may the four statutory factors be treated in isolation; one from another. All are to be explored, and the results weighed together, in the light of the purposes of copyright" (ibid at 1171).

semination of creative expression, and this ultimately promotes software development.[141]

For the future it is suggested that "transformative use" analysis, when taken   **6.58**
out of the parody context, may perhaps be suited to disassembly cases,[142] since
the resulting work is non-infringing,[143] if not copyrightable in its own right.[144]

V. REVERSE ENGINEERING UNDER US AND UK COPYRIGHT LAWS:
POINTS OF CONTRAST

This section highlights the major differences between the two copyright regimes   **6.59**
in their respective treatment of software reverse engineering.

The debate and controversy leading up to the implementation of the Software   **6.60**
Directive introduced Europeans to American-style lobbying on a massive
scale.[145] It is notable that the USA finally supported the Directive as enacted,[146]
in contrast to their earlier attitudes of opposition to particular provisions of various
drafts of the Directive.[147]

(a) Differences Between the Two Regimes

(i) *Protectability of interface specifications*

In its final form, the Software Directive eliminated the implication in earlier   **6.61**
drafts that copyright protects interface specifications, as opposed to their

---

[141] *Supra*, n 92 at 1177–1179.

[142] This has been argued by Williams, "Can Reverse Engineering of Software ever be Fair Use? Application of Campbell's 'Transformative Use" Concept" (1996) 71 Washington L Rev 255. See also William Patry "The Fair Use Privilege in Copyright Law", 2nd edn at 469–470. There has been an even broader conception of fair use suggested by Professor Cohen, *supra*, n 108 at 1120–1121, 1133, where it is said that under the language of s 107 USCA a use that simply *enables* understanding of the copied material may also qualify as fair use. This approach is arguably too broad.

[143] Of course if both end products are substantially similar there can be no question of the doctrine of fair use operating to excuse wholesale, outright as opposed to intermediate copying: see *DSC v DGI* 898 F.Supp 1183 at 1194 (ND Texas 1995). See also analysis in relation to clones, *supra*, paras 6.51–6.53.

[144] There is nothing to suggest that the Supreme Court's approach in *Campbell* cannot be transplanted to a non-parody application. More recently the 2nd Circuit expressly utilised the "transformative use" concept in a dispute solely involving the photocopying of copyrighted material: *American Geophysical Union v Texaco* 60 F.3d 913 (2nd Cir 1994).

[145] See Alan Crane, "Computer users fight EC Software Directive" *Financial Times*, 10 September 1990, p 4; Barry James "Europe's software markets fear backlash from piracy law" *International Herald Tribune*, 10 November 1990.

[146] See accounts in Band and Katoh, *Interfaces on Trial* (1995) at p 255; Jean Francois Verstrynge "Protecting Intellectual Property Rights within the New Pan-European Framework—Computer Software" *International Computer Law Adviser* (June 1991) at 12.

[147] For a full historical account, see *Interfaces on Trial*, ibid at pp 238–239.

implementations.[148] US law arguably goes further; in excluding from copyright protection any internal elements which are dictated by "(i) mechanical specifications of the computer on which a particular program is intended to run; (ii) compatibility requirements of other programs with which a program is designed to operate in conjunction, (iii) computer manufacturer's design standards, (iv) demands of the industry being serviced; and (v) widely accepted programming practices within the computer industry".[149] This distillation process assists in separating underlying ideas and principles from expression under Article 1(2) Software Directive.[150]

(ii) Reverse engineering other than decompilation/disassembly

6.62 Reverse engineering through testing and observation receives more decisive protection from Article 5(3)[151] of the Software Directive; whereas in the USA, the permissibility of "black box" reverse engineering largely derives from the application section 117 USCA in the *Vault* case,[152] where the Fifth Circuit employed a controversial analysis.[153] Section 117(1) is also limited by its application to owners, not licensees.[154]

(iii) Decompilation/disassembly: Article 6 Software Directive versus Fair Use

6.63 The Software Directive may appear stronger in its protection of the rights of decompilation and disassembly, not only in the express exception in Article 6, or section 50B CDPA, but also in its provisions which prohibit contractual restrictions in these practices.[155] However decompilation under the Directive is

---

[148] See earlier discussion on Art 1(2), paras 6.6–6.8. The UK implementation of the Software Directive contains no reference to the exclusion of ideas, and in particular interface specifications, from protection. This is unfortunate, as recent judicial pronouncements in *Ibcos* have doubted the very existence of the idea-expression dichotomy.

[149] See *Computer Associates v Altai* 982 F.2d at 709–710 (admittedly infringement-based).

[150] This may be a more satisfactory explanation, especially when *Whelan v Jaslow* was the prevailing case of reference at the time when the Directive was being prepared. The ethos of US infringement methodology has since changed.

[151] Under the CDPA, the acts permitted by Art 5(3) are not expressly permitted, but from ss 296(1)(c) and 29(4) CDPA it is to be presumed that the acts of observation, study and testing would not constitute an infringement of UK copyright. Under s 50C, such acts may also be held to constitute "lawful use".

[152] *Supra*, n.80.

[153] *Supra*, paras 6.38–6.39.

[154] The 5th Circuit did not appear to have recognised the crucial distinction in *Vault v Quaid* (the defendant was a licensee). See similarly *Foresight Resources Corp v Pfortmiller* 719 F.Supp 1006 (D.Kan, 1989); cf *MAI Systems v Peak Computer* 991 F.2d 511 (9th Cir 1995), where the distinction was applied. In this situation licensees can arguably rely on the Fair Use doctrine to permit reverse engineering other than decompilation.

[155] Article 9(1) Software Directive. Although it is unlikely that mass-market licence restrictions on decompilation would be given any legal effect in the USA (see however *ProCD v Zeidenberg*, discussed at para 10.34), there is a greater likelihood that negotiated restrictions on decompilation would be enforced in the USA. See Samuelson "Symposium on US–EC legal relations: comparing US and EC Copyright Protection for Computer Programs: Are they more different than they

restricted by the requirements of achieving interoperability, under prescribed conditions and circumstances.[156]

Even though the Ninth Circuit in *Sega* emphasised disassembly for the purpose of acquiring information for promoting software-hardware (key-lock) compatibility, it did not only limit the scope of fair use to this context. As stated by the Court: **6.64**

> "The need to disassemble object code arises, if at all, only in connection with operations systems, system interface procedures, and other programs that are not visible to the user when operating—and then only when non alternative means of gaining an understanding of the ideas and functional concepts exists".[157]

It is arguable that the decompilation of a program to obtain access to an unpatentable algorithm may also be regarded as fair use.[158] By contrast the Software Directive would regard decompilation for this purpose to be infringing in the absence of fulfilling an objective of interoperability, even if this carried the secondary consequence of allowing program developers to use copyright to protect "ideas".[159] The Software Directive may also not permit the use of decompilation as a means of investigating infringement, unlike the USA.[160]

Anthony Clapes has commented that the decompilation privilege in Article 6 Software Directive "is a heavily circumscribed right, far more limited than the "fair use" privilege granted in Sega and Nintendo".[161] A practical example may illustrate the contrast between the two approaches. The word-processing program, Wordperfect, contains, in addition to the word processing elements with which the user interacts, elements that link the program to printer functions, and which connect word processing to auxiliary applications such as spell-checkers, thesauruses and graphics editors. Under the Software Directive, a programmer wishing to create a spell-checker that would work with Wordperfect would be permitted to exploit the information derived from decompiling the **6.65**

---

seem?" (1994) 13 J. L&Com 279 at 288. Some US commentators have suggested that the copyright misuse doctrine might be used as an equivalent public policy limitation on the ability of copyright owners to forbid decompilation to get access to interface information. See Charles McManis "Intellectual Property Protection and Reverse Engineering of Computer Programs in the US and the European Community" (1993) 8 High Tech LJ 25.

[156] See above discussion, paras 6.14–6.25.

[157] *Supra*, n 98 at 1520. The last category of programs which are invisible to users may extend well beyond "interfaces".

[158] Ibid at 1525–1526.

[159] See Samuelson, *supra* n 155, at 289–290.

[160] *EF Johnson v Uniden Corp of Am* 623 F.Supp 1480 (D.Minn 1985)—a fair use claim under similar circumstances may succeed.

[161] See Clapes, Book Note, (1994) 20 Rutgers Computer & Technology LJ 329 at 335; Huet, Ginsburg "Computer Programs in Europe: A comparative Analysis of the 1991 EC Software Directive" (1992) 30 Colum J Transnational Law 327 at 358–359 ("To the extent that the Directive truncates the user's right to study the program, it appears inconsistent with the general copyright approach"). The differences between the Software Directive and the operation of the Fair Use doctrine in governing reverse engineering have been attributed to the contrast between civilian and common law systems. See Band and Katoh, *supra*, n 146 at p 257.

Wordperfect program, but only insofar as that information relates to the interaction of the word processing and spell-checking programs. Under US law, it appears that all information obtained from reverse engineering and the making of an intermediate high-level language copy of Wordperfect could be exploited to create not only a Wordperfect-compatible spell checker, but a rival to Wordperfect itself (subject to the resulting program not infringing the protected expression of the original work).[162]

(b) Similarities between the Two Regimes

6.66   Through two different routes, both systems have permitted copying which is incidental to disassembly, and have also excluded interface specifications from copyright protection.[163] The permissibility of reverse engineering, has not extended to the appropriation of protected expression in relation to end-products[164] under both systems. The Ninth Circuit has emphasised that disassembly will only qualify as a fair use if there are no other means of access to the unprotected programming information.[165] This correlates to the requirement

---

[162] For a more detailed comparative study, based on nine hypothetical situations surrounding a Legal Dictionary and Word-processor, see Soma, Winfield and Friesan "Software Interoperablity and Reverse Engineering" (1994) 20 Rutgers Computer & Technology Law J 189 at 242–257. After applying the provisions of US law and the Software Directive to each of the nine situations ((1) dictionary program-reading disk filed; (2) competing but non-infringing product; (3) invoking software in a companion program; (4) redirecting a companion program; (5) temporary run-time copying; (6) redirecting a companion program to new display code; (7) modifying display software in a companion application; (8) reverse engineering demo keys and (9) reverse engineering commercial keys) the authors conclude that both systems agree on seven of the nine situations, the exceptions being items (5) and (8), which are contrary to Art 4(a) and 6(3) of the Software Directive respectively. This study is extremely useful, and it is hoped that software enthusiasts will in future undertake similar studies in respect of a spectrum of application programs. From this lawyers will be able to broaden the base for legal comparisons.

[163] Assumptions have been made that the circumstances under which the Software Directive allows reverse engineering would similarly be held a fair use by a US or UK Court. See Jean Francois Verstrynge, "Protecting Intellectual Property Rights within the new Pan-European Framework— Computer Software" Int'l Computer L Adviser (June 1991) at 12; see also Connors, Westphal, "The European Community Directive on the Legal Protection of Computer Programs: A Comparison between European and US Copyright Law" *Communications and the Law* (March 1992), 25 at 54.

[164] *Atari, supra,* n 97 at 847. See also the following cases, which remain unaffected by *Sega* or *Atari,* since they are also based on infringing end products; *EF Johnson v Uniden* 623 F.Supp 1485 (D.Minn 1985); *Telerate Systems v Caro* 689 F.Supp 221 (SDNY 1988); *Williams v Arndt* 626 F.Supp 571 (D Mass 1985); *Midway Mfg v Arctic* 547 F.Supp 999 (ND Ill 1982) aff'd 704 F.2d 1009 (7th Cir) cert denied 464 US 823 (1983). At the same time the prohibition on copying a whole or substantial part of a program is not all encompassing. Copying and exploitation may nevertheless occur when the decompiled program's instructions or specifications are banal or standard, or if the form of the program is dictated by the function it performs.

[165] *Supra,* n 108 at 1527–1528. Czarnota and Hart in *Legal Protection of Computer Programs in Europe: A Guide to the EC Directive* (1991) have stated that one major difference between Art 6 and fair dealing or fair use defences is that acts covered under Art 6 are permitted only if alternative, non-infringing means are not available; whereas the fair use defence may excuse the conduct regardless of whether such alternative means are available (at p 77). This is an overstatement. The availability of alternative means of obtaining access to the ideas of a work would be highly relevant to consideration of the first factor under s 107 USCA: see *Sega, supra,* n 108 at 1522–1523.

under the Directive that interface information must not previously have been made available to the decompiler.[166] The Software Directive can be interpreted to cover software-hardware interoperability.[167] This is also consistent with the US position, with the *Sega* case as prime illustration.[168]

(c) Future Compatibility

In an addendum[169] to the *Atari v Nintendo* litigation, a US District Court **6.67** decided that Atari had no right to copy any more than the interface specifications necessary to secure *present* interoperability between its cartridge and the Nintendo system, and did not extend to elements of cartridges that were necessary to achieve compatibility with Nintendo's console in the event of a design change. The Court rejected this "future compatibility defence".[170] In the light of the European Commission's investigation into IBM's refusal to disclose interface information,[171] which gave rise to discussions implementing the Software Directive, a "future compatibility" argument may find greater sympathy in the EU.[172]

VI. COMMONWEALTH DEVELOPMENTS

A study on software reverse engineering would be incomplete without a discus- **6.68** sion of jurisprudence from the Commonwealth which has directly considered the subject, namely the Courts of Australia and Singapore.

(a) Australia

(i) Autodesk v Dyason

In *Autodesk v Dyason*[173] it will be recalled that Autodesk's complaint was that **6.69** the respondent broke a code and produced a device which could be used to allow the Autodesk's computer program, AutoCAD, to run on any suitable computer, without using a lock device which is normally necessary for AutoCAD to run (the AutoCAD lock). A certain part of the AutoCAD program,

---

[166] Art 6(1)(b) Software Directive, discussed *supra*, at paras 6.20–6.21.
[167] *Supra*, at paras 6.16–6.18.
[168] Involving software to hardware interoperability on the facts; *supra*, n 98 at 1510.
[169] Nos C–88–4805 FMS, C–89–0027 FMS, 1993 WL 214886 (ND Cal 15 April 1993).
[170] Ibid.
[171] *Supra*, para 1.18.
[172] Samuelson, *supra*, n 155 at 287.
[173] *Autodesk v Dyason* (1989) 15 IPR 1 (Northrop J), (1990) 18 IPR 109 (Full Federal Court), (1992) 22 IPR 163 (High Court of Australia); *Autodesk v Dyason (No 2)* (1993) 25 IPR 33 (High Court of Australia).

"Widget C" contained instructions (from a 127-bit look-up table) to the computer on which it was run, requiring the latter to send "challenges" to the AutoCAD lock.[174]

6.70   The respondents invented an "AutoKey" lock which enabled AutoCAD to run without its hardware lock, producing in EPROM a look-up table similar to that found in Widget C from which to send responses. The values were derived by means of an oscilloscope, allowing a reverse engineer to observe electronic signals passing from computer to lock and vice versa.[175] From this each of the 127 bits were derived over a number of weeks and sequentially stored in an EPROM chip, which was incorporated into the AutoKey lock and operated as a look-up table which produced the same readings as the look-up table in Widget C when read in a manner adopted by Widget C.[176]

6.71   A central issue of *Autodesk* was whether the AutoKey was a reproduction in material form or an adaptation of the AutoCAD program. This turned on whether the 127-bit look-up table which was produced in AutoKey constituted a substantial reproduction of Widget C or the AutoCAD program. Dawson J, delivering the judgment of the High Court, took the view that the respondents had infringed copyright, in creating a device which reproduced a substantial part of Widget C (ie the look-up table).[177]

6.72   The respondents subsequently applied to the High Court to vacate its prior judgment, on the basis, inter alia, that the respondents had not been heard on the substantiality of the look-up table in their software.[178] The application was dismissed, the majority taking the view that either the submissions were made by the respondents (however briefly); or that in any event the arguments of the respondents would carry little prospects of success.

6.73   A significant dissent was led by Mason CJ, who held reservations about the substantiality of the reproduction of Widget C.[179] His Honour took the view that it was arguable that the 127-bit look-up table was simply "data or information which is accessed and used by the instructions that constitute the program Widget C",[180] may not have formed a "substantial" part of the protected copyright work for the purposes of determining infringement. The majority did

---

[174] For details on the working of the AutoCAD lock, see the exposition by Dawson J in (1992) 22 IPR 163 at 168–169; and Appendix at A.40.

[175] Ibid at 165, 169 esp lines 20–50. Arguably this form of testing would fall under Art 5 Software Directive. The High Court identified the infringing act of the reverse engineer (third respondent): "The third respondent copied the look-up table in Widget C indirectly only by copying the sequence of numbers put out by the AutoCAD lock. But copyright may be infringed by copying something which is a copy of the copyright work; indeed, that is the most common form of infringement" (ibid at 173).

[176] Ibid.

[177] (1992) 22 IPR 163 at 173. His Honour also considered the look-up table to be a "table or compilation" (ibid at 174).

[178] *Autodesk v Dyason (No 2)* (1993) 25 IPR 33 (Brennan, Dawson and Gaudron JJ; Mason CJ and Deane J dissenting). The primary question was whether the copying of data in a computer program can constitute a reproduction of a substantial part of a computer program (ibid at 46).

[179] Ibid at 37.

[180] Ibid at 38.

not agree with this view,[181] and the High Court's conclusions on substantiality in relation to the look-up table have given the Australian Copyright Law Reform Committee (CLRC) some cause for concern.[182]

Whether a look-up table forms an essential part of a computer program so as **6.74** to constitute a substantial reproduction,[183] if copied, is germane to the present discussion, and sets *Autodesk* against Anglo-American reverse engineering traditions.[184] It cannot be doubted that reverse engineering in the *Autodesk* litigation was strictly for the purposes of interoperability—to allow the interaction between the AutoCAD program and any computer system through a circumvention of a hardware lock—yet the High Court decisions offer a subtle mechanism for maximising intellectual property protection. Hunter correctly observes that rather than code a random number generator in the form of a state machine table, manufacturers may simply include a look-up table in their programs as part of a security system.[185] With this "security system" in place it would mean that only licensed peripherals would lawfully work with these systems or programs. This is a severe limitation for reverse engineering, a trend which is unlikely to change following the recent decision of *Powerflex v Data Access*.[186]

(ii) Powerflex v Data Access

Data Access produced "Dataflex", an application development system which **6.75** provides the tools to develop customised database applications. Powerflex created another application development system, called "PFXPlus", which was

---

[181] The majority relied on the "essentiality" or "criticality" of the look-up table to determine substantiality, which is absurd, given that every line of code is "essential", given the precise nature of programming. See Kremer "Copyright and Computer Programs: Data Access v Powerflex Before the High Court" [1998] 20 Sydney L Rev 296 at 306–307.

[182] See CLRC's Final Report on *Computer Software Protection* (1995) at para 5.25. In an effort to bring Australian law more in line with the European model, CLRC recommended, inter alia, decompilation provisions similar to Art 6 Software Directive; and that the modification of locked computer program for the purpose of circumventing the lock should be prohibited. Ibid, at ch 10; esp paras 10.70–10.73. Autodesk has been at the forefront of this campaign; see further Stewart McKeough, *Intellectual Property in Australia*, 2nd edn (1997) at para 9.19.

[183] According to Peter Prescott QC, this confuses two very different concepts. The presence of a thing in a work may be essential, in the sense that without it the production will fall flat or be inoperable; but this does not necessarily imply that the thing constitutes a substantial reproduction. A computer program will not work if one digit is altered. It is therefore essential, but it would be startling to hold that not even a single digit from a computer program may be copied, *a fortiori* 127 (unless this creation results from skill and labour). In his view the High Court's reasoning is flawed. See Prescott "Was AutoCAD wrongly decided?" [1992] 6 EIPR 191 at 193–194.

[184] Not least for the reason that if the facts of *Autodesk* were to recur in the United Kingdom, AutoKey would have constituted a device designed to circumvent copy protection and as such be proscribed under s 296 CDPA. See *infra*, para 8.50.

[185] Dan Hunter "Reverse engineering computer software—Australia parts company with the world" (1993) 9(4) *Computer Law and Practice* 122 at 126.

[186] *Data Access Corporation v Powerflex Services* (1996) 33 IPR 194 (Jenkinson J); *Powerflex Services v Data Access Corporation* (1997) 37 IPR 436 (Full Federal Court, Black CJ, Hill and Sundberg JJ). At the time of writing, the appeal is before the High Court of Australia.

intended to be highly compatible, and shared many common features[187] with Dataflex.

6.76   The Full Federal Court considered that the word commands used, being mere ciphers, were not "computer programs" as defined under the Australian Copyright Act.[188] For the purposes of the present discussion, it was not disputed that in developing PFXplus, Powerflex's programmer, by a process of reverse engineering and study of the documentation and operation of the DataFlex program, created PFXplus intending that the program would be compatible with the Dataflex program,[189] for example by use of the same commands. He determined the Huffman Compression Table (HCT) found in Dataflex "by a process of observing the behaviour of the Dataflex system and not by decompiling or looking inside the Dataflex runtime".[190]

6.77   The Full Court agreed with the trial judge in finding that the table was capable of being the subject of copyright, not as a computer program itself, but as a table or compilation,[191] and ordered that the appellants (Powerflex *et al*) be restrained from reproducing in a material form or making an adaptation of the Dataflex HCT or a substantial part of that table in Powerflex programs or adaptations of the same.[192]

(iii) Observations on Autodesk and Powerflex

6.78   There appears to be a close parallel between the derivations of the HCT in *Powerflex,* and the look-up table in *Autodesk*. Both decisions recorded how, inter alia, the tables were respectively derived; in *Autodesk*, by close observation and the use of an oscilloscope which read pulses being sent from the AutoCAD key to the program in order to derive the contents of the look-up table;[193] in *Powerflex*, by "the process of observing the behaviour of the DataFlex system, and not by decompiling or looking inside the DataFlex runtime".[194]

6.79   In neither case was mention made of the infringing acts that occurred during the process of reverse engineering described; and from this one may be entitled to infer that the afore-discussed techniques are permitted under Australian law. However, when these tasks can be carried out, the reverse engineer runs aground when he substantially reproduces a look-up table or HCT that is held to be a "table or compilation" protected by copyright.[195] Thus there appears to

---

[187] Including use of the same word commands, function keys, identical macros, file structure, Huffman Compression Table and Error Text Table.
[188] (1997) 37 IPR 436 at 450. For further discussion, see Kremer, *supra*, n 181 at 298–305.
[189] Ibid at 439.
[190] Ibid. For further details of the HCT, see Appendix at A.41.
[191] Ibid at 457. Compare treatment of the "look-up" table in *Autodesk, supra,* n 177 and accompanying text.
[192] Ibid at 460.
[193] *Supra*, n 175 and accompanying text.
[194] *Supra*, n 186 at 439.
[195] Given that both tables had to be reproduced in a particular form to fulfil their respective functions , perhaps the doctrine of merger should have been applied. For a concurring view, see Kremer, *supra*, n 181 at 308, 312.

be no legitimate way for a reverse engineer to derive these tables, unless he can prove he derived them independently.[196] Hence under Australian copyright law it is presently unclear as to what extent a competitor may decompile or disassemble a rival's program with a view to identifying its underlying ideas and structure, so as to construct a functionally equivalent program or one that will interface with it.[197]

Both these Australian cases illustrate how a far-reaching scope of copyright **6.80** protection can severely cripple reverse analysis. It is also unfortunate that the defence of fair dealing for research and private study was not considered in either case—a possibility which should have been explored.[198] From 12 August 1999 the Australian Copyright Act has now been amended to include exceptions for testing and decompilations in certain situations (Copyright Amendment (Computer Programs) Act 1999). The Australian Copyright Act now allows reproduction of non-infringing copies of computer programs that are made, *inter alia,* in the course of running the program for the purposes of studying the ideas behind the program and the way in which it functions (s. 47B(3)); and to obtain information necessary to make independently another program to interoperate with the original program or any other program, but only to the extent (a) reasonably necessary to obtain such information and to achieve such interoperability and (b) that the information was not readily available to the other licensee. (Section 47D). Comparison with the EU Software Directive and its agenda as "interoperability" are indeed compelling.

(b) Singapore

In *Creative Technology v Aztech Systems*[199] the Court of Appeal in Singapore **6.81** considered the legality of disassembly under the Singapore Copyright Act 1987—pursuant to the production of a competing sound card. The Court was faced with the issues of (i) the alleged disassembly of Creative's Sound Blaster firmware, (ii) the admitted intermediate copying by Aztech of Creative's

---

[196] See FitzSimons "Powerflex v Data Access Corporation (Reverse Engineers Beware!)" (1998) 14 *Computer Law & Security Report* 45 at 47; Dan Hunter [1998] 3 EIPR 98 at 105–106. As a matter of policy , allowing copyright in respect of the HCT would grant an undesirable monopoly over the use created with the table; the effect would be that no other Dataflex-compatible program could be written, short of infringing copyright or negotiating a licence. See Kremer, *supra*, n 181 at 313.

[197] See Sam Ricketson *Intellectual Property—Cases, Materials and Commentary* (Butterworths, 1994) at p259 for legal and policy questions related to this subject.

[198] See s 40 Australian Copyright Act 1968. Whether this will provide a reverse engineering defence has been discussed elsewhere. See further Davey "Reverse Engineering of Computer Programs" [1993] 4 *Australian Intellectual Property Journal* 59; Dworkin "The Concept of Reverse Engineering in Intellectual Property Law and Application to Computer Programs" [1990] 1 *Australian Intellectual Property Journal* 164.

[199] *Creative Technologies v Aztech Systems* [1997] 1 SLR 621; also reported in [1997] FSR 491. For a full discussion of the decision, see Stanley Lai "Recent Developments in Copyright Protection and Software Reverse Engineering in Singapore—a Triumph for the Ultra-protectionists?"[1997] 9 EIPR 525.

auxiliary program, TEST-SBC and whether this copying constituted fair dealing for the purposes of research and private study under section 35 Singapore Copyright Act and (iii) other defences.[200] On the first issue the Court of Appeal held that Aztech had "the means, motive and opportunity" to disassemble Creative's firmware, especially in relation to features that were not "intuitively apparent" but yet appeared, and design flaws which appeared in the firmware of both parties.[201]

On the second issue, the Court of Appeal took the view that a fair dealing defence under section 35 Singapore Copyright Act was not available to Aztech in the light of the limited exclusion of "commercial research" from the definition of "research" under the Act.[202]

6.83   For the purpose of the present discussion, *Creative v Aztech* may also be noted for the clear distinction in terms of liability drawn by the Court between the infringing product and infringing process, the latter involving the intermediate copy. It is a distinction that is not commonly made, and was certainly not recognised by the Courts in the *Autodesk* and *Powerflex* decisions noted above.[203] Creative argued that the similarities which were found in Aztech's end-product formed an independent cause of action in copyright infringement. After making a literal comparison between the two end-products, the Court took the view that since up to 4 per cent of Aztech's code was actually identical to Creative's coding, this did not amount to a substantial reproduction. The Court was however quick to state:

> "This, in no way, prejudices our finding of disassembly, which involves a degree of reproduction and adaptation having a greater impact in terms of revealing the ideas and interfaces of a copyright holder's program, insights which would not otherwise have been obtained by independent development or empirical observation within a given time frame".[204]

VII. CONCLUSION

6.84   It is hoped that the above chapter has provided a comparative insight into the laws of two major copyright systems which govern the practice of reverse engineering. At the same time, significant Commonwealth developments were discussed to provide another contrast. The following conclusions are offered.

6.85   The EC/UK system has been acknowledged by some writers to be the most systematic tailoring of copyright to meet the technological and economic needs

---

[200] See discussion on implied licences, *infra*, paras 10.66–10.70.
[201] [1997] 1 SLR at 633–634. Lai Kew Chai J, delivering the judgment of the Court, stressed the significance of similarities in non-essentials and errors in forming proof of copying.
[202] Formerly s 35(5) Singapore Copyright Act, which following the decision, has been repealed.
[203] But recognised in *Sega v Accolade, supra*, n 98 at 1518–1519.
[204] [1997] 1 SLR at 634.

of software protection.[205] It is likely that the Software Directive will continue to set the agenda for software copyright protection, especially in matters of reverse engineering, for the foreseeable future.[206]

In an effort to reach certain uniformity of treatment between the two systems **6.86** towards what constitutes legally acceptable reverse engineering practice, it is hoped that evolving case law in the USA will in future replicate the tenets of the Software Directive.[207]

Against the Anglo-American tradition, developments in Australia provide the **6.87** most direct contrast, in the *Autodesk* and *Powerflex* decisions which cumulatively exhibit little scope for the permissibility of reverse engineering (either through observation, testing or *a fortiori*, disassembly/decompilation) as long as Courts show willingness to confer copyright protection on essential interoperable requirements (eg look-up tables and compression tables). The status quo may be altered with future judicial consideration of the scope of copyright defences which may apply to the subject, for example, fair dealing for research and private study. By contrast, the fair dealing defence was considered by the Singapore Court of Appeal in *Creative v Aztech*, only to be declared inapplicable to the conduct in question, *a verbis legis non recedendum est*.

---

[205] eg see Paul Goldstein, "The EC Software Directive: A View from the USA" in *The Handbook of European Software Law*, p 203 at p 214.

[206] Thus refining the pattern started by the USA through case law and legislation which set the software copyright agenda for the decade just past. See Goldstein, ibid at 215.

[207] There is some emerging evidence of this; see the recent "interoperability" provisions put forward by the US Digital Millenium Copyright Bill, discussed *infra*, at para 8.46.

7

Defences and Other Permitted Acts

I. INTRODUCTION

This chapter addresses the scope and continued relevance of the section 29 **7.1**
CDPA (fair dealing) defence in the wake of the Copyright (Computer Programs)
Regulations (1992) which implemented the Software Directive; other defences
(eg the *British Leyland* "spare parts" exception) and permitted acts (eg back up
copies and software maintenance) which arise in software copyright litigation.

II. SECTION 29 CDPA: FAIR DEALING FOR RESEARCH AND PRIVATE STUDY AND ITS CONTINUED RELEVANCE FOR UK SOFTWARE COPYRIGHT LAW

(a) Section 29(4) CDPA

Section 29(4) CDPA[1] states that it is not fair dealing to convert a low level lan- **7.2**
guage program to a higher language version, or to copy the program in the
course of such conversion, the matter being governed by section 50B CDPA. The
question arises as to whether the fair dealing defence in section 29 CDPA in relation to research and private study[2] will have a continued relevance for software
copyright under the CDPA.

   Ultimately it is argued that the fair dealing defence not only has a continued **7.3**
role to play in the protection of users' interests, but forms a useful complement
to the decompilation provisions of section 50B CDPA. The underlying question
is whether a traditional analysis, under which a dealing may be adjudged "fair",
is equally applicable to software reverse engineering cases, which often involve
line-by-line intermediate copying, leaving no room for any analysis on "substantial similarity".[3]

---

[1] As amended by the Copyright (Computer Programs) Regulations 1992, subject to reg 12(2)
(agreements entered into before 1 January 1993 to remain unaffected).
[2] Although s 30 CDPA covers fair dealing for news reporting, criticism and review, it is suggested
that "research and private study" under s 29 would be most applicable to software copyright
infringements.
[3] See Cornish, *Intellectual Property*, 3rd edn (1996) at p 452.

(b) Continued Relevance of the Fair Dealing Defence

7.4 Several writers have stated, without further analysis, that section 29 readily applies to acts other than the decompilation of computer programs, such as those falling under Article 5(3) Software Directive.[4] This is an unfortunate oversimplification, if the issue is even discussed at all.[5] Laddie, *et al*[6] have considered the matter more carefully, dividing the operation of section 29 in terms of time periods[7] and permitted acts[8] under the formal text of the CDPA.

7.5   Professor Cornish orientates the discussion around section 296A CDPA[9] (in the absence of any mention of acts covered by Article 5(3) in the formal text), stating that it covers acts which fall outside decompilation, for which fair dealing is in any case a defence[10] and should be regarded "both as defining one form of fair dealing and ensuring that it is not displaced by exclusory contract".[11]

7.6   The Software Directive, in defining "interoperability" and "interfaces",[12] wisely avoided language conversions and Article 6(1) makes specific reference to "reproduction of code" and "translation of form". By contrast, section 50B(1) CDPA defines "decompilation" to cover, inter alia, low-to-high level translations. As discussed elsewhere,[13] on one construction s50B(1) does not apply to "hex dumps".[14] It is submitted that in this situation, if the act complained of is so-called "dumping", the software developer will have recourse to section 29(1) CDPA. But he should advisedly proceed with caution, since "dumping" is often

---

[4] See eg Bainbridge, *Software Copyright Law*, 2nd edn at p26; Christopher Millard, "Implementation of the EC Directive" in Jorgen, Meihboom (eds) *Copyright Software Protection in the EC* at p 238 *et seq*.

[5] There is a conspicuous absence of any discussion in recent works like Bandey, *International Copyright in Computer Program Technology* (CLT, 1996); Lloyd, *Information Technology Law*, 2nd edn (1997) at para 20.27; and Reed (ed) *Computer Law*, 3rd edn (1996).

[6] Laddie, Prescott and Vitoria, *Modern Law of Copyright and Designs*, 2nd edn, Vol 1.

[7] Ibid at para 20.40. Section 29 will govern decompilation prior to 1 January 1993. For decompilation, taking place before 1 August 1989, s 6(1) Copyright Act 1956 will apply.

[8] Governing the circumstances to which Art 5(3) Software Directive is applicable (ibid at 20.46); and pre-Directive decompilation activity (ibid, at para 20.40). As to the latter the authors argue that if it is reasonable to imply a right to manufacture replica spare parts for cars, it would not be stretching the fair dealing concept to say that software designers should be at liberty to carry out research on a computer program in private with a view to designing a non-infringing interoperable program (ibid).

[9] Section 296A(1) provides, in relation to software usage, that "any term or condition in the agreement shall be void in so far as it purports to prohibit or restrict . . . (c) the use of an device or means to observe, study or test the functioning of the program in order to understand the ideas and principles which underlie any element of the program".

[10] See Cornish, *Intellectual Property Law*, 3rd edn, at para 13–36.

[11] Ibid.

[12] See Recitals 10–12, Software Directive.

[13] *Supra*, para 6.27. See Cornish, *supra*, n 3 at p 453 n 52.

[14] Which comprises nothing more than a horizontal conversion of binary code into hexadecimal code. This process can be effected by use of a program like DEBUG (*Creative Technology v Aztech Systems* [1997] FSR 491). For further explanation of this process, see Hawksley and White *Assembly Language Programming on the IBM PC* (1987) at p211. See also Appendix, A.60–A.61. "Dumping" is a technique which has been recognised in US courts to be a standard practice in the software industry; see *EF Johnson v Uniden* 623 F.Supp 1485 at 1501 n 17 (D.Minn 1985).

the precursor to disassembly and the exclusion of the fair dealing defence by section 29(4).

By way of summary, section 29(1) will continue to apply in the following sit- **7.7**
uations:

- decompilation occurring before 1 January 1993—the enactment of section 29(4) CDPA;
- decompilation occurring before the enactment of the Software Directive (14 May 1991);
- where "black-box"[15] testing is used to discover a program's underlying ideas and functionality, to which Article 5(3) Software Directive applies;
- where the act complained of is "dumping" or "iterative testing".[16]

(c) Meaning of "Research and Private Study"

(i) Historical background

The phrase "research and private study" was introduced in the Copyright Act **7.8**
1911,[17] and reused in sections 6(1) and 9(1) Copyright Act 1956.[18] The most influential committee which has reported on fair dealing to date is the Whitford Committee,[19] established in 1973 to consider appropriate changes to copyright law as provided by the Copyright Act 1956 and Design Copyright Act 1968.[20] In its recommendation of the fair dealing exception, the Committee concluded that if specific reference to "research or private study" was to be retained, it should be in the form "private research or private study".[21] Such a qualification to "research" was interpreted to exclude research carried out for commercial purposes,[22] although

---

[15] See Appendix, A.54.

[16] See para 7.6. On iterative testing, see *infra*, paras 7.21–7.22.

[17] See s 2(1) Copyright Act 1911 (1 & 2 Geo 5, c13) ("the 1911 Act"). The 1911 Act was largely due to the work of the Gorrell Committee, the success of which can be judged by the fact that its basic principles still underpin the law of copyright in the United Kingdom. See further John Feather, *Publishing, Piracy and Politics—A Historical Study of Copyright in Britain* (Mansell, 1994), ch 7 at 204.

[18] The Copyright Act 1956 ("the 1956 Act") resulted from the work of the Gregory Committee (which eventually produced the *Report of the Copyright Committee,* 1951 (Cmd 8862)). The Gregory Committee had to contend with, inter alia, the vagaries of photocopying (first developed in the late 1930s), and moral rights. Pressed by conflicting interests between publishers and librarians, the Committee suggested that the law should allow reproduction by mechanical or photographic means of extracts up to a certain length for private study, and these extracts could be made either by the person who required the material or by a librarian acting on that person's behalf—an ingenious compromise well received by publishers: Gregory Report, at pp 17–21, 117.

[19] The Whitford Committee eventually produced the Report *Copyright and Designs Law: Report of the Committee to Consider the Law on Copyright and Designs,* 1977 (Cmd 6732).

[20] Ibid, p 1.

[21] Ibid, ch 14, paras 676–677.

[22] See Green Paper on *Reform of the Law Relating to Copyright Designs and Performers Protection: A Consultative Document* (Cmnd 8302) at pp 9–11, 45–46; and subsequently, *Intellectual Property and Innovation* (Cmnd 9712) at para 8.13, where it was indicated that s 6 Copyright Act 1956 would be amended to exclude commercial research.

the Whitford Committee made no reference to such an exclusion,[23] and it is not apparent why the above phrase "private research or private study" should necessarily be so interpreted. At its Bill stage, before intervention by the House of Lords, the defence was limited to research "other than commercial research".[24] An amendment removing the exclusion of commercial research was tabled in the House of Lords,[25] resulting in the present wording of section 29.[26] A fair dealing defence which does not distinguish between commercial and non-commercial research is probably sound, given that such a distinction has proved unworkable elsewhere.[27]

(ii)   "Research" and "study"

7.9   "Research" has been defined by the Federal Court of Australia[28] to mean the "diligent and systematic enquiry or investigation into a subject in order to discover facts or principles".[29] "Study" has been defined by the same Court to mean

---

[23] See generally the Whitford Committee Report, *supra*, n 18 at paras 204–291; 657–696; 927, 941–942.

[24] Clause 29, Copyright Designs and Patents Bill 1987. Clause 161 defined "commercial research" as "research done for the benefit of a trade or business carried on for profit".

[25] See Parliamentary Debates, House of Lords, Hansard 23 February 1988, Cols 1153–1157. Lord Beaverbrook moved the amendment to include commercial research. At Committee stage concerns were expressed that (i) the necessary consent from copyright owners for commercial research might not be forthcoming; (ii) there was thought to be considerable overlap between commercial and non-commercial research (the Government wished to encourage collaborative research between academic and industrial communities); and (iii) it was essential that small and large businesses alike should be afforded every opportunity to develop their research potential, without additional burden (ibid at 1153–1154).

[26] In fact the fair dealing defence goes further by actually affirming that "copying by a person other than the researcher or student himself" can constitute a fair dealing if "the person doing the copying does not know or has no reason to believe that it will result in copies of substantially the same material being provided to more than one person at substantially the same time for substantially the same purpose" (s 29(3)(b) CDPA). On s.29(3)(b) see Skone James, Mummery, Rayner James and Garnett, *Copinger and Skone James on Copyright*, 13th edn (1991), para 10–7 at pp 250–251. See further Cornish, *supra*, n 3 at para 13-11: "Since after substantial debate, the government agreed that those in commerce and industry who undertake research and private study should *not* be excluded, it must be their view that the exception is of rather broad scope. But it remains for the courts to decide how far business, and for that matter government, should be able to take single copies without licence by claiming to need for these purposes" (emphasis added).

[27] Such a distinction used to exist in Singapore (s 35(5) Singapore Copyright Act 1987, repealed) until *Creative Technologies v Aztech* [1997] 1 SLR 621 at 637, where the Court of Appeal considered such a distinction unworkable; cf *Aztech v Creative Technologies* [1996] 1 SLR 683.

[28] *De Garis v Neville Jeffress Pideler Pty Ltd* (1990) 18 IPR 291 (Federal Court of Australia)—a case in which Beaumont J held that the provision of a media monitoring service for a fee was not "research" within the meaning of the Australian Copyright Act. For the relevant extracts of this decision, see Sam Ricketson, *Intellectual Property—Cases, Materials and Commentary* (Butterworths, 1994) at pp 301–304. See also the recent New Zealand case of *Television New Zealand v Newsmonitor Services Ltd* (1993) 27 IPR 441 (High Court of New Zealand)), where the High Court stated that "research means searching into a matter or subject, or the investigation or close study of it, including written materials or those captured in electronic form", while private study "connotes a form of study which is personal to the person undertaking it" (ibid at 463).

[29] Ibid at 298 (according to the Macquarie Dictionary). The defendants in the *De Garis* case could not rely on the fair dealing defence because their object was purely commercial, in supplying a

the "application of the mind to the acquisition of knowledge, as by reading, investigation or reflection; . . . a particular course of effort to acquire knowledge; a thorough examination and analysis of a particular subject".[30]

The relationship between research and study is undoubtedly a close one. **7.10** "Study" may lead to "research", since the acquisition of existing knowledge can lead the student to discover new and as yet undiscovered knowledge; or even knowledge which is hitherto unknown to him, but known to others.[31] It has been suggested that in order to remove this element of subjectivity from any test which seeks to distinguish between the two, an objective test similar to that applied to the test of "novelty" for patents should be adopted.[32] Thus the clearest indication of "research" is whether the acquisition is of any information not yet made available to the public anywhere in the world, whether by use, description or any other method.[33]

(iii) Qualifying "study": "private study"

Under the 1956 Act, "private study" was held to apply to the actual student, and **7.11** that others such as the publishers of study notes were not entitled to the benefit of the fair dealing defence.[34] The CDPA now provides that someone other than the student or researcher may make a copy on his or her behalf.[35] It is questionable whether the word "private" still serves any meaningful role within section 29(1) CDPA.[36]

(iv) An immaterial distinction

From the above discussion, it is clear that the fair dealing defence under UK **7.12** copyright law does not distinguish between the reverse engineering of popular

photocopy of material already published in return for a key. As such it was not " a diligent and systematic enquiry or investigation into a subject in order to discover facts or principles."

[30] Ibid at 298–299 (according to the Macquarie Dictionary).

[31] Hence the reservation expressed by Laddie *et al*, about the correctness of the *De Garis* definition of "research" (*supra*, n 28) in *Modern Law of Copyright and Designs*, 2nd edn (1995) at para 2.155, n 6 ("There may be research in finding a needle in a haystack").

[32] See Daniel Seng, "Reviewing the Defence of Fair Dealing for Research or Private Study" [1996] SJLS 136 at 159.

[33] Ibid. However the author was writing in respect of Singapore's fair dealing defence, where the distinction between "research" and "private study" was at the time material, given that s 35(5) (now repealed) excluded industrial or commercial research save in the case of bodies corporate owned or controlled by the Government. His suggestions should be read in this context.

[34] See *Sillitoe v McGraw Hill Book Company* [1983] FSR 545.

[35] See s 29(3)(b) CDPA, *supra*, n 26.

[36] In Australia, following the recommendations of the Franki Committee on *Reprographic Reproduction* (Canberra, 1976), the Australian Copyright Amendment Act 1980 was passed, to remove all references to the word "private" in s 40. The Franki Committee took the view that the original provision was so drafted to exclude use for classroom instruction by educational institutions, as opposed to private study, from the fair dealing defence (ibid at para 2.64). In its view the absence of the qualifier was not material, since the defendant still had to satisfy the requirements for "fairness" under s 40(2) (conspicuously absent from s 29 CDPA). A similar move by the New Zealand legislature would also be welcome; Puri "Fair Dealing with Copyright Material in Australia and New Zealand" (1983) 13 VUWLR 277 at 284 n 30.

software (of a kind to which section 29(1) potentially applies)[37] which is undertaken by a software engineer working for a software company on the one hand, and that undertaken by an independent contractor who wishes to sell his end-product, on the other. It is submitted that it is unnecessary to make a distinction between "research" and "study". With this simplified approach, the Court is then able to focus its determination on the substantive question of whether the dealing in question is "fair".

(d) Whether the Dealing is "Fair" in a Reverse Engineering Situation to which Section 29(1) CDPA Applies

(i) Underlying principles

7.13 UK copyright law fails to lay down any bright-line definition of what constitutes "fair dealing".[38] Being a matter of fact, degree and impression,[39] it involves both a quantitative and qualitative appraisal.

7.14   The underlying principle behind fair dealing is the dissemination and advancement of learning—that to promote the progress of knowledge, the rewards to the copyright owner for his creativity must occasionally be subordinated to the greater public interest of developing science, art and industry.[40] It was once said, "a dwarf standing on the shoulders of a giant can see further than the giant himself",[41] revealing a strong social interest in advancing the frontiers of knowledge and encouraging further research in all fields.[42]

---

[37] *Supra*, paras 7.4–7.7.

[38] Contrast some jurisdictions which legislate the "Fair Use" factors; see s 35 Singapore Copyright Act; s 40(2) Australia Copyright Act.

[39] *Hubbard v Vosper* [1972] 2 QB 84 at 94–95, 98. See also *Time Warner v Channel 4* [1994] EMLR 1.

[40] For recognition of the "public interest" foundation to fair dealing, see Sir Anthony Mason "The Australian Library and Information Association Library Week Oration, State Library of New South Wales" (1996) *The Australian Library Journal* 81 at 89.

[41] See Newton's declaration: "If I have seen further it is by standing on ye shoulders of Giants"; Sir Isaac Newton, *Letter to Robert Hooke*, 5 February 1675/1676; quoted in Merton, *On the Shoulders of Giants: A Shandean Postscript* (1965) 31. Newton's phrase, "on ye shoulders of Giants" may have been copied from Bernard of Chartes who, according to Merton, authored the aphorism in the early twelfth century when he taught: "we are like dwarfs standing upon the shoulders of giants, and so able to see more and see farther than the ancients" (ibid at pp 178–192). The two possible applications of this "on the shoulders of giants" principle are first; innovation in computer programing is advanced as each programmer builds upon the ideas of previous programmers; and secondly, some of the innovative ideas may be expressed in a particular way that is so effective or efficient that the expression becomes standardised throughout the field even though the idea is capable of being expressed in other ways, that is even though the particular expression is not an essential to every expression of the idea. The principle was considered by Judge Keeton in *Lotus v Paperback* 740 F.Supp 37 at 77–79 (D.Mass 1990).

[42] *Sayers v Moore* (1785) 102 ER 139, 140 (Lord Mansfield).

(ii) Adjudication of what is "fair"

The most important factor in determining what is "fair" is arguably whether the **7.15**
dealing in question is commercially competing with the copyrighted work, and
forms a market substitute for the latter.[43]

Another consideration is whether the work has already been published or not; **7.16**
and the means used to obtain the work.[44] In the software context, the obtaining
of program source code by deception,[45] or the testing of illegitimate copies of
the plaintiff's computer program, would arguably preclude any finding of fair
dealing. With other works, it is at times necessary to make use of "leaked information" to air a controversy or ventilate a grievance,[46] but this is unlikely to
occur in the software context, save for the situation where, for example, one
wishes to expose a hardware and software defect (or "bug") caused by a particular program which is on sale to the public; or to expose cyber-terrorism spread-
ing through the sale of commercial software.

Another determination is the substantiality of the taking.[47] Whilst it is often **7.17**
said that taking a substantial part of a work can never be fair dealing,[48] in certain circumstances it is proper to quote an entire work[49]—a window of opportunity for software engineers who are automatically given to making entire
copies of the copyright owner's software for "black-box" testing and other

---

[43] Numerous English cases point to this, eg see *Hubbard v Vosper, supra*, n 40 at 93–94;
Johnstone v Bernard Jones Publications Ltd [1938] Ch 599 at 607; *Associated Newspapers Group
plc v New Group Newspapers Ltd* [1986] RPC 515 (rival newspaper lifting extracts of the corre-
spondence between the Duke and Duchess of Windsor); *Independent Television Publications Ltd v
Time Out Ltd* [1984] FSR 64 at 75 (defendant's use of the plaintiff's programme listings so as to provide an alternative listings service). For Commonwealth decisions, see *Moorhouse v University of
New South Wales* [1975] RPC 454 (Australia) (students photocopying books instead of buying
them—reversed on appeal [1976] RPC 151, albeit on different grounds); and *Longman Group Ltd v
Carrington Technical Institute Board of Governors* (1990) 20 IPR 264 at 279–280 (New Zealand).

[44] If the material is obtained by unscrupulous or underhand means, Courts will be reluctant to
find in favour of a fair dealing: see *British Oxygen v Liquid Air Ltd* [1925] Ch 383; *Beloff v Pressdram*
[1973] RPC 765; *Commonwealth of Australia v John Fairfax & Sons Ltd* (1980) 32 ALR 485;
Wiggington v Brisbane TV Ltd (1992) 25 IPR 58; *Distillers Co (Biochemicals) Ltd v Times
Newspapers* [1975] QB 613 (copying of documents disclosed on discovery during litigation—admittedly a special case). However if the work was already in the public domain, a dealing may not be
rendered unfair simply because of the method by which the copyright material has been obtained.
See *Time Warner v Channel 4* [1994] EMLR 1 at 9–10 (in relation to s 30(1) CDPA).

[45] A US example would be *Atari v Nintendo*, where a copy of the plaintiff's computer program
was obtained from the Copyright Office through misrepresentation.

[46] Breach of confidence cases may apply by way of analogy; eg *Schering Chemicals v Falkman*
[1982] QB 1; *Stephens v Avery* [1988] Ch 449; *AG v Guardian Ltd (No 2)* [1990] 1 AC 109; see also
Beloff v Presdram [1973] RPC 765; *Fraser v Evans* [1969] 1 QB 349; *Hubbard v Vosper, supra*, n 40.
See further Cripps, *Legal Implication of Disclosure in the Public Interest: an analysis of prohibitions
and protections with particular reference to employers and employees* (Sweet & Maxwell, 1994).

[47] See *Hubbard v Vosper, supra* n 39 at 94, 98; and *Johnstone v Bernard Jones Publications Ltd*
[1938] Ch 599 at 603.

[48] *Independent Television Publications v Time Out Ltd* [1984] FSR 64 at 75; where it was said
that once the conclusion is reached that a substantial part of the copyright work has been taken, a
fair dealing defence is unlikely to succeed. Criticised by Laddie, *et al, supra*, n 31 at para 2.158 n 9.

[49] *Hubbard v Vosper, supra*, n 39 at 98 (per Megaw LJ); see also *Beloff v Pressdram* [1973] RPC
at 786. Laddie, *et al* cite the example of a bona fide criticism of a poem; *supra*, n 31 at para 2.158.

analytical techniques which fall within the rubric of Article 5(3) Software Directive.

7.18 In adjudicating whether an intermediate copy of software that is made for purposes of *permissible* reverse engineering is fair, it is submitted that Lord Denning MR's famous words in *Hubbard v Vosper*[50] cease to be applicable. With computer software, it is argued that a judgement cannot be made simply by deciding a question of degree based on impression—a test that is aptly suited to criticism and review, and by parity of reasoning, to copying some subject-matter for research and private study.

(iii) Importing "fair use" considerations: the relevance of US cases and section 107 USCA

7.19 The UK fair dealing defence differs from the US doctrine of "fair use" (provided under section 107 USCA) in that the former comprises "specified statutory limitations", whereas the latter possesses a scope that is "general and central".[51] As discussed elsewhere in this work,[52] section 107 USCA contains statutory factors which have to be considered in deciding whether a use is fair, and the flexibility of the doctrine is viewed as the "safety valve" of copyright law.[53]

7.20 There is some suggestion that a UK judge will also consider the fairness of a dealing by having regard to factors similar to those contained in section 107 USCA.[54] In the USA, two notable decisions have seen the Courts apply the doctrine of fair use to software reverse engineering[55] and it will be recalled that the principle to emerge from a questionable analysis was that:

> "where disassembly is the only way to gain access to the ideas and functional elements embodied in a copyrighted computer program and where there is a legitimate reason for seeking such access, disassembly is a fair use of the copyrighted work, as a matter of law".[56]

---

[50] *Supra*, n 39.

[51] See Cornish, *supra*, n 3 at pp 378–379. Sir Hugh Laddie in his lecture "Copyright: Over-strength, Over-regulated, Over-rated" [1996] 5 EIPR 253, observed that whilst s 107 USCA gives US courts the flexibility to prevent copyright from being abused the absence of precision is a disadvantage. However he goes on to say that a comparison between the USA and the United Kingdom is not flattering to the latter, where "Rigidity is the rule" (ibid at 258).

[52] *Supra*, para 6.42 *et seq.*

[53] US Congress, Office of Technology Assessment, *Finding a Balance: Computer Software, Intellectual Property and the Challenge of Technological Change*, OTA-TCT–527 (Washington DC, US Government Printing Office, 1992) at 62.

[54] See Vanessa Marsland, "Copyright Protection and Reverse Engineering of Software—an EC/UK Perspective" (1994) 19(3) U Dayton L Rev 1021 at 1024. See also considerations of Judge Mervyn Davies in *Sillitoe v McGraw-Hill Book* [1983] FSR 545 at 563–564.

[55] See *Atari v Nintendo* 975 F.2nd 832 (Fed Cir 1992); *Sega v Accolade* 977 F.2nd 1510 (9th Cir 1993). Discussed *supra*, paras 6.44–6.50.

[56] A bright-lined approach which effectively creates a "disassembly" exception in US copyright law: see *Sega* 977 F.2nd 1510 at 1527–1528 (9th Cir 1992).

In the UK context, in relation to section 29 CDPA, the *Sega* and *Atari* cases have to be approached with a deliberate caution.[57] From 1 January 1993, the above principle is excluded from section 29 by subsection (4), since disassembly contemplates a low-to-high level language conversion, with the incidental reproduction of the software taking place amidst such conversion. As for pre-Software Directive decompilation, the two cases carry at best persuasive effect.

(iv) A new principle

The cases from the Ninth and Federal Circuits do not address the question of 7.21 "black-box" reverse engineering as such (including activities like "dumping"),[58] and it is to this type of reverse engineering that section 29 CDPA is particularly suited, in the absence of any explicit implementation of Article 5(3) Software Directive. The following proposition is advanced:

> *Where the "iterative" process of changing inputs and observing the corresponding outputs is the only means to gain access to the ideas and functional elements within a copyrighted computer program, and where there is a legitimate reason for seeking such access, such a process constitutes fair dealing for the purposes of research or private study within section 29 CDPA.*

Such a formulation is feasible, given that mere observation of a computer program is a recognised practice in the software industry.[59] It is not an expeditious technique, and far less invasive than disassembly or decompilation. As such the practice "does not conflict with a normal exploitation of the work and does not unreasonably prejudice the legitimate interests of the author".[60]

The greatest obstacle to the "fairness" of iterative testing lies in the making of 7.22 at least one whole copy of the copyrighted software. But this is a matter of technical necessity. As discussed above, in certain circumstances, the taking of an entire literary work (albeit one that is short in length, eg a poem) could still constitute fair dealing.[61] Different considerations have been stated to apply to computer software. Ian Lloyd writes, first, while it is a simple task to copy portions of a book, the reverse is the case with a computer program. Secondly, "[s]oftware is a much more fragile creature and, especially if research is being conducted as to its make-up, terminal damage may easily result. In such an event the making of a back-up copy might appear a reasonable precaution".[62] A more

---

[57] Although a "transformative use" analysis may be feasible: paras 6.54–6.58.

[58] *Supra*, para 7.6.

[59] *EF Johnson v Uniden, supra*, n 14.

[60] Article 9(2) Berne Convention; see also the Preamble to the WIPO Copyright Treaty 1996. Such a proposition is also necessary for the advancement of technological innovation and dissemination in a manner conducive to social and economic welfare, principles underwritten by Art 7 TRIPs.

[61] See the discussion in *Sega v Accolade, supra*, para 6.49 (where the end use is limited the intermediate copy carries little weight). See also *Sony Corp v Universal Studios* 64 US at 449–450.

[62] See Lloyd, *Information Technology Law* (Butterworths, 1997) at para 20.26. Surprisingly the author does not adhere to the right to make back-up copies under s 50A(1) CDPA, but brings it under s29.

general argument can also be made that section 29(1)'s tolerance of incidental copies of computer software made in the course of the iterative testing has also increased in the wake of Directive implementation,[63] without prejudice to section 17(6) CDPA.

III. BACK-UP COPIES

7.23 Section 50A(1) CDPA (implementing Article 5(2) Software Directive) permits a lawful user of a computer program to make any back-up copy which is *"necessary for him to have for the purposes of his lawful use"*[64] (emphasis added). There is no stipulation as to the number of copies which can be made, but if a lawful user made more than one back-up copy, he would have difficulty in justifying the necessity of each additional copy for his lawful use.[65]

7.24 The right to make back-ups cannot be excluded by contract.[66] However this does not extend to other materials provided with the computer program, such as a database, thesaurus and documents such as user materials, and it is likely that the making of back-up copies of "non-program" items will be governed by implied licence.[67] In relation to "non-program" items, what is or is not a "computer program" also determines the scope of the right under section 50A(1).[68] Under UK law, there is at present no statutory right to make back-up copies of preparatory design material, and the matter will most likely be determined by implied licence.

7.25 Generally speaking section 50A(1) is not a controversial provision. It has been observed that the software community has always been at ease with the notion of reasonable number of back-up copies made by a licensed end-user,[69] and it may be said that the provision simply mirrors good computing practice.[70] Section 50A(1) may be a very narrow provision, since the making of back-ups is

[63] eg see s 50C(1) CDPA, implementing Art 4 Software Directive, which provides that in the absence of any contrary contractual provision, any reproduction necessary for the "loading, displaying, running, transmission or storage of the computer program" may lawfully be conducted. cf Sir Hugh Laddie's view that the "detailed and pedantic" exceptions to copyright protection "reinforce the perception that virtually all reproductions of copyright works, no matter how innocuous, are infringements", *supra* n 51 at 259.

[64] "lawful user" is defined in s 50B(2) as any person having the right to use the program (whether under licence or otherwise).

[65] Czarnota and Hart take the strict view that it is "a" copy which is permitted and not "copies", and that the purpose may not be other than as a "back-up", which the authors take to mean "for security reasons". See *Legal Protection of Computer Programs in Europe—A guide to the EC Directive* at p 68.

[66] See s 296A CDPA and Art 9(1) Software Directive, discussed *infra*, para 10.10–10.12.

[67] See Bainbridge, *Software Copyright Law*, 3rd ed (1997, Butterworths) at p 110.

[68] A discrepancy lies with the protection of preparatory design material as a separate literary work (s 3(1) CDPA), and not as a computer program (Recital 7 Software Directive). *Supra*, at paras 2.2–2.5.

[69] See Bandey, *International Copyright in Computer Program Technology* (1996, CLT Professional Publishing) at pp 135–136.

[70] Bainbridge, *supra*, n 67.

often desirable, but rarely strictly necessary for use.[71] Furthermore, in a situation where a software producer distributes an "object code version" back-up, it is arguable that it is no longer necessary for normal use to make a back-up copy.[72]

IV. ERROR-CORRECTION AND MAINTENANCE

Section 50C(2) states: **7.26**

"It may, in particular, be *necessary for the lawful use* of a computer program to *copy it or adapt* it for the purpose of correcting errors in it" (emphasis added).

It has been argued that section 50C(2) does not give effect to Article 5(1) Software Directive.[73] Under section 50C(2) the legality of the error correction in question is determined by considering its necessity in relation to the lawful use of the program, whereas under the Directive error correction is treated as an "intended purpose" in its own right,[74] and hence not affected by contract. Another point of difference between the two regimes lies in the stipulation of otherwise infringing acts which are required to effect correction.[75]

On first inspection section 50C(2) may appear to give a user a *carte blanche* **7.27** to copy with impunity, in a quest to discover program "bugs". A preferred view is that "the right will extend only in respect of particular errors which have been discovered by the user in the course of running the program in a normal manner".[76] The scope of section 50C(2) is arguably limited by (a) how "error correction" is defined; (b) whether "lawful use" extends to correcting positive (discovered in the course of program running) as well as "normative" errors (anticipated upgrading that is necessary); and (c) whether a user may decompile software in effecting such correction. The error correction exception is more restricted in some countries. For example section 47E of the Australian Copyright Act (as amended by the Copyright Amendment (Computer Programs) Act 1999, which was executed on 12 August 1999) permits the reproduction of a non-infringing copy of a computer program for the purpose of correcting an error which prevents the program from operating as intended by the author, or in accordance with the user documentation, but only to the extent reasonably necessary to correct such an error and provided that a functioning copy is not available within a reasonable time at an ordinary commercial price.

---

[71] This is also the view of Laddie, *et al*, *Modern Law of Copyright and Designs* at para 20.47.

[72] Czarnota and Hart, *supra*, n 65 at p69.

[73] See Sherwood-Edwards "Seven degrees of separation: the Software Directive and UK implementation" (1993) 9(5) *Computer Law & Practice* 169 at 171.

[74] Ibid.

[75] Art 4 Software Directive, compared with s 50C(2) CDPA (which covers copying or adaptation rights).

[76] See Lloyd, *Information Technology Law*, 3rd edn (1997, Butterworths) at para 20.34.

(a) "Error Correction" Defined

7.28 Error correction is not defined, but may be understood as including the detection and location of the error as well as the measures taken to correct it.[77] Section 50C(2) pertains only to "errors", and may not be interpreted to cover "improvements" and "modifications" to software packages. The Court will in all likelihood have to consider (i) whether to look at the function or purpose of a particular program as intended by its creator, or by the user; (ii) if the latter is the correct view, whether the user has sufficiently specified what is required of the program.[78] This turns on the type of contract negotiated between user and supplier, and the terms which may be implied therein,[79] particularly after the determination of a commercial relationship.[80]

(b) Extent of "lawful use"

7.29 As stated above, under section 50C(2) CDPA, the legality of error correction is determined by reference to the "lawful use" of the program. The correction of errors and defects that arise in the ordinary course of running a computer program or "beta-testing" may be deemed necessary for its lawful use. These may be classed as "positive errors".

7.30 In contrast, there are "normative errors"; that is, errors that, although previously unforeseen, are anticipated in the future. One clear example would be the "IT 2000 defect" or "millennium timebomb",[81] and the question remains whether the error-correction right may be relied on by a software user to bring his operating system or any computer package into "millennium compliance". If licence terms do not restrict the correction of errors,[82] it is arguable that section 50C allows a lawful user[83] to correct such errors.[84] However it is more

---

[77] Czarnota and Hart, *supra*, n 65 at p 65. The authors suggest that this construction is logical, since Art 5(3) Software Directive provides that non-infringing means of testing the functioning of a program are always at the disposal of the user.

[78] See Pearson, *et al* "Commercial Implications of the European Software Directive" (1992) 8(1) *Computer Law and Practice* 2 at 7–8.

[79] By way of illustration, see *Saphena Computing Limited v Allied Collection Agencies* [1995] FSR 616, where it was held that the implied right of the defendant to copy the plaintiff's source code for the purposes of effecting error correction (at common law) did not extend to making improvements (ibid at 640).

[80] Laddie, *et al* envisage this as the common situation where s50C is invoked; see *Modern Law of Copyright and Designs*, *supra*, n 31 Vol 1 at para 20.48.

[81] Which may be referred to as the simple failure of programmers to allow for 4-digit dates. On legal ramifications, see generally Singleton, *Year 2000: Law and Liability* (Sweet & Maxwell, 1998).

[82] Exclusory contract provisions are lawful: Art 9(1) Software Directive; s 296A CDPA. However see the inconsistency in Recital 18 Software Directive. Czarnota and Hart suggest that a licence agreement may not prohibit error correction without a corresponding offer by the supplier to provide the facility for correction (*supra*, n 65 at p 65).

[83] See s 50C(1). Third party computer maintenance companies will not be "lawful users", and in the absence of a special licence, will have no right to effect correction.

[84] See Singleton, *supra*, n 81 at para 7.3.

likely that a user will be unable to effect correction without the original source code of the defective program, and since he may not use the decompilation right,[85] a tightly drafted escrow agreement (permitting the release of source code by an escrow agent in specified situations, including breach of contract) appears to be the best solution.[86]

(c) Decompilation for the Purposes of Error Correction

From the above discussion, it follows that the user right of error correction is only effectual if the user also acquires the right to be supplied with a copy of the source code.[87] **7.31**

There is no possibility of performing decompilation to achieve an "adequate working version" of a program's source code in the hope of correcting errors, for two reasons. First, such an act falls outside the "permitted objective" of decompilation, stated as one of the conditions for it to constitute a lawful practice under section 50B(2) CDPA. Secondly, the wording of section 50C(2) addresses copying *or* adapting. As decompilation requires both to occur, on a strict interpretation it is arguably excluded from section 50C(2).[88] **7.32**

V. MISCELLANEOUS EXCEPTIONS: OTHER PERMITTED ACTS

(a) Section 56 CDPA: Transfers of Licensed Software

Section 56 CDPA relates to the transfers of copies of works in electronic form, and provides that certain rights of the first purchaser of a computer program shall run with the program.[89] Where a user has purchased a copy of a computer program, a subsequent transferee (and any further sub-transferee)[90] is also permitted to perform those acts, unless expressly agreed to the contrary.[91] The same applies if the original copy is no longer useable and a back-up is transferred in its place.[92] **7.33**

Laddie, *et al* criticise this provision as being unnecessary, since the extent that **7.34**

---

[85] *Infra*, paras 7.31–7.32; see also Singleton, *supra*, n 81 at para 7.4.

[86] See eg the National Computing Centre's launch of "Escrow 2000" for this scenario; discussed in Singleton, *supra*, n 81 at para 7.11.

[87] Laddie, *et al*, *supra*, n 31 at para 20.48; see Pearson *et al*, *supra*, n 78 at 7–8.

[88] Such an interpretation is underwritten by the numerous restrictions placed on the decompilation right. See further Samuelson "Symposium on US–EC legal relations: comparing US and EC copyright protection for computer programs: Are they more different than they seem?" (1994) 13 J. L & Com 279 at 289.

[89] For a useful flow-chart illustrating the transfer of licensed software, see Bainbridge *Software Copyright Law*, 3rd edn (1997) at p 112.

[90] See s 5(4) CDPA.

[91] Ibid s 56(2). But any copy, adaptation, or copy of an adaptation made by the purchaser which is not also transferred shall be treated as an infringing copy.

[92] Ibid s 56(3).

certain rights would run with transfers and sub-transfers will, but for section 56, be governed by the common law of licences.[93] Two specific problems are identified. First, in relation to software that is owned by and subsequently transferred by a business, the business that keeps its back-up copy at once infringes by under sections 56 and 23(a) CDPA,[94] even if it intends to destroy the back-up. Secondly, if back-up copies are handed to a sub-transferee who then disposes of them by private treaty, the sub-transferee, apart from possibly breaching the terms of a sub-licence, has not committed any primary (no "issue to the public" under section 18 CDPA) or secondary (absence of an "infringing copy") copyright infringement.[95]

(b) Common Law Defence of Non-Derogation of Grant: the Retreat of *British Leyland*

7.35 The defence of "non-derogation of grant" is best understood in the context of repair. This section considers the scope of this defence, with reference to recent Privy Council guidance, and its application in recent software cases.

(i) British Leyland v Armstrong

7.36 The case of *British Leyland v Armstrong*[96] is well known in copyright circles; a decision where the House of Lords held that the owner of a copyright in design drawings for a motor car could not rely on copyright to prevent a competitor from manufacturing spare parts. Using the property-based doctrine of "non-derogation of grant", the sale of the car was held to amount to a grant which could not be frustrated through restricting the manufacture of parts for repair.[97]

7.37 The "right of repair"[98] or "spare parts exception"[99] appears to be a principle that is based on overriding public policy considerations, as opposed to being truly founded on any principle of law of contract or property[100], that to allow copyright owners to enforce their rights in certain situations would be "anti-competitive".

---

[93] Laddie, *et al, supra,* n 31 at para 2.184.

[94] Section 23(a) CDPA provides that it is secondary copyright infringement of copyright to possess an article in the course of a business if the possessor knows or has reason to believe it is an infringing copy. Liability is inevitable, since in these circumstances a person will usually have knowledge of the relevant facts. See *Copinger and Skone James on Copyright* (1991) at paras 10–67 and 9–19.

[95] Laddie *et al, supra,* n 31.

[96] [1986] RPC 279.

[97] Ibid at 349, 361.

[98] Lord Templeman, ibid at 374–376.

[99] Lord Edmund Davies, ibid at 350; Lord Griffiths, ibid at 387.

[100] View of the Privy Council in *Canon v Green Cartridge*, discussed *infra*, n 102 at 824.

(ii) Canon v Green Cartridge

The "repair exception" came under recent scrutiny by the Privy Council on an **7.38**
appeal from Hong Kong, in *Canon Kabushiki Kaisha v Green Cartridge*.[101] The
Canon case involved Green's manufacture of interchangeable toner cartridges
(for laser printers and photocopiers) that were copied from Canon's cartridges
by reverse engineering. Green argued the "repair exception", to justify the
supply of new cartridges whenever the toner in the original cartridge ran
out.[102] Two primary issues confronted the Privy Council: (i) whether Green's
reverse engineering constituted copyright infringement; and (ii) determining the
proper scope of the spare parts exception and *British Leyland*. On the first issue,
their Lordships were reluctant to depart from previous decisions which held
that copying a three-dimension object was an indirect reproduction of the drawings (under the Hong Kong Copyright Act, which at that time was still based on
the UK Copyright Act 1956).[103]

On the second issue, Lord Hoffmann held that where the elements of "unfair- **7.39**
ness to the consumer" and the anti-competitive nature of the monopoly are not
"as plain and obvious as it appeared to the House of Lords in *British Leyland*,
the jurisprudential and economic basis for the doctrine becomes extremely fragile".[104] His Lordship further distinguished the present facts as not disclosing a
situation of repair, because the cartridge is usually replaced at a stage when
nothing in the photocopier requires repair. At best there could be an element of
preventive maintenance inherent in replacing a cartridge, but so little of it could
be described as repair that the analogy was implausible.[105]

Turning to the issue of aftermarket competition, two features distinguished **7.40**
the *British Leyland* case. First, the House of Lords in *British Leyland* had
assumed that the cost of replacing an exhaust pipe was a small proportion of
running costs, that purchasers were unlikely to adopt "lifetime costing". Lord

---

[101] [1997] FSR 817 (Lord Hoffmann delivering the judgment of their Lordships). For further commentary, see Holmes "Spare a Thought: Canon KK v Green Cartridge" [1997] 5 ECLR 319;
Rawkins [1997] 11 EIPR 674; Wei (1998) 114 LQR 39.

[102] The defence failed at trial ([1995] FSR 877), Rogers J holding that replacement of the cartridge
was not done for the purposes of "repair" of the printer. Green successfully appealed to the Court
of Appeal on this issue ([1996] FSR 874).

[103] [1997] FSR 817 at 821. Lord Hoffmann made the significant observation that the earlier cases
decided under the 1956 Act did not sufficiently distinguish between the reproduction of an artistic
work, and the use of information contained in an artistic work such as a drawing or diagram
(together with any additional text) as the instructions for making a three-dimensional object which,
although plainly derived from that information, does not reproduce the artistic work. His Lordship
implicitly recognised the need to separate an infringing product from an "infringing" process,
argued in this work to be a vital distinction to make in relation to software reverse engineering
(*supra*, para 6.81).

[104] Ibid at 826.

[105] Ibid. Such a restrictive "repair-based" interpretaion of the "spare parts" exception was followed by Jacob J in *Mars UK v Tecknowledg*, unreported, 11 June 1999 at para 21 ("the 'spare parts
exception' applied only where it as plain and obvious that the replacement was analogous to a repair
which an ordinary purchaser of an article would assume he could do for himself without infringing
the Manufacurer's rights, or that the exercise of monopoly power by means of copyright would be
against consumers' interests"). See *infra*, para 7.47 *et seq*.

Hoffmann took the view that since the cost of cartridges was a significant pro-portion of the lifetime cost of a copier or printer, a similar assumption could not be made in the present case. Secondly, his Lordship also considered that Canon was already competing with a substantial refiller market (recycling used car-tridges), the latter definitely inhibiting its ability to raise prices. It was doubtful in these circumstances that Canon occupied an anti-competitive position.[106]

(iii) The British Leyland *defence and software repair*

7.41   The non-derogation of grant doctrine (or "repair exception") follows from a line of authority recognising that a person may, under an implied licence, carry out what would otherwise be infringing acts, so as to repair an article (so long as an old article is not rebuilt as new under the guise of repair).[107] This would also include reverse engineering for the purposes of repair.[108]

7.42   However the extent to which the doctrine can be applied to software use remains unclear. Professor Dworkin has written:

> "Thus, even if there was an express statement negativing the right of any purchaser of a computer program from making a back-up copy, the courts are likely to say that the only sensible way of owning and using a computer program is to make a back-up copy and so it would be a derogation from grant for the copyright owner to attempt to prevent it by using copyright. How far this doctrine will be developed remains to be seen".[109]

In the event, it has not been in the area of back-up copies that the *British Leyland* defence has surfaced, due to the intervention of the Software Directive, and sec-tion 50A CDPA now governs this subject. This is not to say that the defence has not been treated in other contexts.

7.43   In *Saphena v Allied Collection Agencies*,[110] the defendants (who made use of source code supplied by the plaintiffs for the limited purpose of repair and main-tenance) were held not to be entitled to copy the source programs in the absence of a licence.[111] The Court did consider that if software supplied by the plaintiffs to the defendants turned out to be unfit for its purpose, and the defendants at the time had licensed access to the source code, then under *British Leyland* the plaintiffs could not restrain reproduction of the source code for error correc-tion. However, the Official Referee said:

> "But that does not mean either that the defendants can retain the source code against that eventuality, or that they are entitled to require the plaintiffs to supply [their source code] to them in that event".[112]

---

[106] Ibid at 827.
[107] See Dworkin, "The Concept of Reverse Engineering in Intellectual Property Law and its Application to Computer Programs" (1990) 1 *Australian Intellectual Property Law Journal* 164 at 173.
[108] *Solar Thompson v Barton* [1977] RPC 537; *Weir Pumps v CML Pumps* [1984] FSR 33; cited in Dworkin, ibid.
[109] See Dworkin, *supra*, n 107 at 174.
[110] [1995] FSR 616.
[111] Ibid at 639–640.
[112] Ibid, at 639.

In *Saphena*, *British Leyland* was further distinguished on the ground that in the **7.44** case of ready-written programs, unlike motor cars, the purchaser is not normally in a position to copy source code either to repair or improve it. The "factual basis for restricting what would otherwise be the plaintiff's rights in their source code does not therefore exist".[113] This is a narrow interpretation which, in the author's view, correctly preserves the sanctity of source code.

(iv) The British Leyland *defence and software reverse engineering*

In as much as this chapter has demonstrated a continued relevance of the section **7.45** 29 defence of fair dealing for research and private study, in relation to matters of disassembly or decompilation that are not defined within section 50B CDPA, the *British Leyland* defence may be argued to justify the performance of these acts. The *Green Cartridge* decision has shown the Privy Council's reluctance to allow the defence to operate in situations other than straightforward repair, quite apart from the second proposition that the exercise of copyright must determined to be anti-competitive.

The restriction of *British Leyland* principles to situations of straight-forward **7.46** repair was also apparent in *CreativeTechnologies v Aztech Systems*.[114] The Singapore Court of Appeal heard Aztech argue that it had an implied right to make an intermediate copy of Creative's TEST-SBC program (in the course of performing disassembly and running DEBUG), which was derived from the principle of *non-derogation of grant*, following *British Leyland*. The Court swiftly dismissed this argument, on the primary ground that the "creation of a compatible and competing sound card is materially distinguishable from a situation of repair".[115] It is argued that this approach accords with that adopted by the Privy Council in *Green*, by the Official Referee in *Saphena*, and more recently, Jacob J in *Mars UK v Tecknowledge Ltd*.[116]

In *Mars v Tecknowledge* the defendant performed reverse engineering on the **7.47** programmable read-only memory (PROM) of the plaintiffs' electronic coin Discriminator (which determined the authencity and denomination of coins which were to be fed into coin-receiving and changing machines). By this process the defendants were able to "re-programme" or "re-calibrate" Mars' Discriminators so that they could accept new coinage, without further reference to the plaintiffs. The Discriminator software comprised a data layout, a serial communications protocol and an encryption. The defendants admitted copyright infringement in respect of, inter alia, the transient copies made of program code and the reproduction of the Discriminator's algorithm and other coin data, in the course of developing its own re-calibration software. Infringement admitted, a key issue at trial was whether a *British Leyland* defence was available for re-calibration of Mars' coin machines by the defendants.

---

[113] Ibid at 640.
[114] [1997] 1 SLR 621, [1997] FSR 491. For a discussion of the facts, see Lai [1997] 9 EIPR 525.
[115] [1997] 1 SLR 621 at 640.
[116] Unreported, 11 June 1999 (Chancery Division).

7.48   The defendants in *Mars* argued that a "spare-parts" or analogous defence was available to a situation of software reverse engineering by reason of section 171(3) CDPA:

> "Nothing in this Part affects any rule of law preventing or restricting the enforcement of copyright, on grounds of public interest or otherwise".

Jacob J rejected that there was any room for such an exception in the context of computer program and database rights, which were strictly governed under Community-wide rules (ie the Software and Database Directive) and implementing legislation in the United Kingdom.[117] His Lordship also offered an alternative analysis, in that even if there was room for such an exception, re-calibration were not within the scope of any such defence.[118] The "spare parts defence" was in his Lordship's view founded on public policy, "namely the need to prevent a manufacturer from using copyright (as opposed to patents or design right) in order to control the aftermarket in spare parts".[119] It was concluded that there was no overwhelming public policy reason entitling those who purchase machines with Discriminators to use Mars' copyright and database rights to convert those machines for new coins. Moreover the analogy with *British Leyland* was not compelling in this case. First the purchasers of Discriminators are not ordinary consumers. Those who buy such devices look to the original manufacturer for repair, maintenance and updating. Updates are expected to come from the manufacturer. Secondly, the alteration of machines to receive and dispense different coins was even further removed from the concept of "repair" than the supply of printer cartridges ("consumables") in *Canon*. Strictly speaking the changes in coinage had nothing to do with the operation of the machine at all.[120]

VI. CONCLUSION

7.49   This chapter has considered the scope of applicable defences and other permitted acts under the CDPA and at common law. In relation to the section 29 defence of fair dealing, this study concludes that fair dealing still continues to have particular relevance in respect of (i) decompilation that is not defined under section 50B CDPA nor excluded by section 29(4) CDPA; (ii) activities falling under the domain of Article 5(3) Software Directive. In respect of the latter, a new principle is advanced. Thereafter a study was been made of the acts which are permitted by statute as a consequence of Directive implementation, including back-up copies and error correction.

[117] Ibid, paras 18 and 19. His Lordship reached the firm view that nothing in the Software Directive and consequently ss 50A–C CDPA provided for any "repair" or update exception, although a whole variety of detailed acts are permitted. It was not for a nation of judge-made laws to override or add to what was clearly intended to be Community-wide rules.

[118] Ibid, paras 22–28.

[119] Ibid at para 22.

[120] Ibid at para 28.

On the scope of the *British Leyland* defence and its exact relevance in soft-   **7.50**
ware litigation, it is hoped that judges in future would heed the Privy Council's
re-interpretation of the "spare parts" defence in *Canon*. This is particularly so
when it is invoked in software infringement cases (whether in the context of
making source programs, or reverse engineering, as in *Mars v Tecknowledge*).
In software litigation, it is anticipated that the influence of *British Leyland* will
diminish, with the Software Directive and CDPA (as amended) providing a
strict, if not always unequivocal, regime of user's rights.

Part 4

Challenges for the Future

8

Software Copyright Protection in Relation to Internet Technology

I. INTRODUCTION

The Geneva WIPO Conference held over December 1996 resulted in two treaties **8.1**
(WIPO Copyright Treaty and Performances and Phonograms Treaty), which
update the Berne Convention to cover the legal demands of the new digital age.[1]
This chapter discusses the application of CDPA provisions to the World Wide
Web[2] (WWW), particularly after *Shetland Times v Wills*,[3] and other concerns
raised by the Internet revolution and the digital agenda.

II. COPYRIGHT ISSUES AND THE WWW: APPLICABLE PROVISIONS OF THE CDPA

In applying various provisions of the CDPA to the WWW, the exercise is, in **8.2**
essence, one of classification; whether categories of traditional works can be
expanded and adapted to address features of the WWW.

(a) Websites as "Computer Programs"

At one level, a website comprises actual words, symbols and numerals of **8.3**
HTML code which justify copyright protection.[4] The interpretation has to be
tested against Article 4 WIPO Copyright Treaty, which protects computer
programs as literary works "whatever may be the mode or form of their expression".[5]

---

[1] See generally Silke von Lewinski "WIPO Diplomatic Conference Results in Two New Treaties"
(1997) 28 IIC 203; Peter Wand "New Rules for Our Global Village" [1997] 5 Ent LR 176; Clive
Davies "WIPO Treaties—the new framework for the protection of digital works" (1997) 2(2)
Communications Law 46. For a study of the ramifications of the Treaties on software copyright protection , see Stanley Lai "The Impact of the Recent WIPO Copyright Treaty and Other Initiatives
on Software Copyright in the United Kingdom" [1998] 1 IPQ 35–55.
[2] For a technical account of Internet technology, see Appendix, A.80 *et seq.*
[3] [1997] FSR 604, discussed *infra*, at para 8.5 *et seq.*
[4] See Gringras *Laws of the Internet* (Butterworths, 1997) at pp 167, 182–183.
[5] cf Art 10 TRIPS, which states that computer programs "whether in source or object code" are
to be protected as literary works, but TRIPS did not incorporate a digital agenda. See Hamilton,
"The TRIPS Agreement: Imperialistic, Outdated and Overprotective" (1996) 29 Vanderbilt J of
Transnat'l Law 613. See further Lai, *supra*, n 1 at 39–40.

(b) Websites as Compilation/Database or Computer-Generated Works

8.4   As the Database Directive[6] was implemented to deal especially with digitisation, and multimedia works, it would not be illogical to argue its application to websites, which may be viewed as "collections of independent works or data arranged systematically or methodically and whose contents are individually accessible by any means".[7] It is possible to argue that if a webpage contains numerous "executable programs" (eg Applets)[8] the page may be protected as a "compilation" of "sub-programs", an approach endorsed by Jacob J in *Ibcos*.[9] It is also arguable that webpages published by "web-publishers"[10] are "computer-generated works".[11]

(c) Is a Website a Cable Programme Service?

(i) Shetland Times v Wills

8.5   The potential for this classification was given credence by the now famous case of *Shetland Times v Wills*.[12] The pursuer operated a website on the Internet on which it made available news items which appeared in the printed editions of its newspapers. Once its website was well-established, the pursuer hoped that it would attract advertisements on the front page of the site. The defender to the action also had a website which included in its pages headlines taken verbatim from the pursuer's website. Persons accessing the headlines on the defender's website could, by clicking on them, access the pursuer's news items in such a way so as to by-pass the pursuer's online front page. He sued the defender for copyright infringement in the headlines.

8.6   Lord Hamilton, in granting an interim interdict against the defenders, accepted that it was at least arguable that the pursuer was operating a "cable programme" service within section 7 CDPA,[13] since his activities constituted a "sending". By copying the pursuer's headlines, the defenders had infringed

---

[6] 96/9/EC OJ L77/20, 27 March 1996, implemented by the Copyright and Rights in Databases Regulations 1997 (which came into force on 1 January 1998). For further discussion, see next chapter.

[7] Article 1(2) Database Directive (*infra*, para 9.3).

[8] See Appendix, A.83.

[9] *Ibcos v Barclays* [1994] FSR 275 at 290.

[10] eg Microsoft Publisher.

[11] Without prejudice to any separate copyright existing in the software generating the webpage.

[12] [1997] FSR 604 (Court of Session, 24 October 1996, Lord Hamilton). The case was settled just before the Full Interdict hearing. See MacQueen [1998] 2 Edinburgh L Rev 241.

[13] Ibid at 608. Section 7(1) states that a "cable programme service" refers to a service "which *consists wholly or mainly* in the sending of visual images, sounds or other information by a telecommunications service other than by wireless telegraphy" (emphasis added). There is the additional requirement of reception, (a) at two or more places (whether for simultaneous reception or at different times in response to requests by different users) or (b) for presentation to members of the public.

copyright by including them in his cable programme service, contrary to section 20 CDPA.[14]

Gringras takes the view that a website is not a cable programme service, since **8.7** material is not "published" as such, but made available on a server for the public to access over the Internet. It is retrieved by the user, and is not "pushed" to him by the site owner, unlike a cable TV programme, which is still conveyed to the viewer even if it is not actually watched.[15]

This view is difficult to appreciate, given that with every "retrieval", there **8.8** must be a corresponding "sending".[16] In reality the Internet should be viewed as both a distribution and retrieval system. Prima facie, a website may be classified as a "cable programme service", the question then turning to operation of the interactive exception.[17]

Indeed Lord Hamilton's understanding of the Internet and his explanation **8.9** may be supported by a recent case involving the transmission of child pornography on the Internet. In *R v Arnolds*; *R v Fellows*[18] it was decided that "publication" within the Obscene Publications Act 1959 and 1964 would apply when A makes the data available to be transferred or downloaded electronically by only providing a password to B so that B can access the materials and copy them. In these circumstances it would still be A who transmitted the data even if the actual acts of performance or downloading[19] were performed by B.

(ii) The applicable exception: section 7(2) CDPA

Section 7(2)(a) CDPA excludes essentially interactive services[20] from the defini- **8.10** tion in section 7(1). Lord Hamilton rejected the argument of the defenders that

[14] Infringement by including in a cable programme service of a protected cable programme. This raises the larger question of whether any item on a website is a "programme", even if the site as a whole was a cable programme service. It has been written that at least "in the case of databases or other interactive information services . . . as a result of the severed tie between a single component and its predefined position in a sequential order, these services no longer constitute "programmes" in the traditional sense". See Dreier "The Cable and Satellite Analogy" in Hugenholtz (ed) *The Future of Copyright* 57 at 58.

[15] Gringras, *Laws of the Internet, supra*, n 4 at pp 169–171. There is some sympathy for this view; see Connelly, *et al* "Fair Dealing in Webbed Links of Shetland Yarns" (1992) JILT <http://elj.war wick.ac.uk/jilt/copyright/98_2conn/connolly.htm>

[16] See Campbell "Copyright on the Internet: the View from Shetland" [1997] 5 EIPR 255 at 256. The author takes the view that the *desiderata* of (i) visual images, sounds or other information; (ii) send by means of a telecommunication system, otherwise than by wireless telegraphy; (iii) for reception at two or more places; and (iv) for presentation to members of the public, are each identifiable in the context of Internet use, and can be covered by section 7(1) CDPA, even though it may be suggested that the concept of a "cable programme service" is being overstretched.

[17] *Infra*, para 8.10.

[18] [1997] 2 All ER 548 at 558 (CA).

[19] The meaning of "downloading" was recently held to be that given by the Oxford Dictionary of Current English, 9th edn (1993), which is the "transfer of data from one storage system to another"; see *R v City of London Magistrates' Court, ex p. Green*, *The Times*, 13 March 1997 (Scott-Baker J). It is arguable that "transfer" conveys a sense of a sending.

[20] On s 7(2) CDPA and summary of Parliamentary debates, see Mark Hafte [1998] Ent LR 95 at 96.

since the *Shetland Times* webpages encouraged e-mail feedback, the website fell within the section 7(2) exception.[21] Professor MacQueen has commented that although the subsection requires interactivity to be an essential feature of the service, it only requires that part of the service be interactive, and that only the potential for interactivity is necessary ("will or may be sent from the place of reception . . . for reception by the person providing the service or other persons receiving it").[22]

8.11   In reality, there is a continuous but latent exchange between the user's PC and website from which information retrieval is made, to justify the operation of the exception. "Cookies" and "Checksums" are sent by the user's PC so as to verify the reception of material.[23] However this verification is arguably necessary for operation or control, and is a broad construction placed on the wording of the exception (by requiring no user input or modification).

(d) Websites as "Broadcasts"?

8.12   Section 6(1) CDPA defines "broadcast" to mean a transmission by wireless telegraphy of visual images, sound or other information which is capable of being lawfully received by members of the public, or is transmitted for presentation to members of the public. Section 178 defines "wireless telegraphy" to mean the "sending of electro-magnetic energy over paths not provided by a material substance constructed or arranged for that purpose, *but does not include the transmission of microwave energy between terrestrial fixed points*".[24] Since the WWW generally works by way of a wired telecommunications system (eg ISDN lines, optical fibres and phone lines) and not a wireless transmission,[25] the view has been formed that websites can never be "broadcasts".[26]

8.13   This assertion is unsafe, for future technological advances may call it into question. For example, consider BreezeNet's latest range of LAN-related wireless hardware which allows ethernet network communications to be made without a physical cable connection.[27] Provided that there is no transmission of "microwave energy between terrestrial fixed points", websites which are accessed through wireless ethernet connections to networks could conceivably be "broadcasts".

---

[21] *Supra*, n 12 at 608.

[22] See Hector MacQueen "Copyright and the Internet" in Edwards and Waelde (eds) *Laws and the Internet—Regulating Cyberspace* (Hart Publishing, 1997) at p 78.

[23] For a full description of "cookies" see Chissick, Kelman "Electronic Commerce" (Sweet & Maxwell 1999) at para 7.24.

[24] Words in italic were added by the 1996 Regulations implementing, inter alia, the Cable and Satellite Directive.

[25] But note that a reception of a broadcast includes relay by means of a telecommunications system (s 6(5) CDPA).

[26] See Gringras, *supra*, n 4 at p 170.

[27] For a write-up of this technology, see Neil Cameron "BreezeNET Wireless LAN" Computers and Law (Oct/Nov 1997) at 27.

(e) The Scourge of WWW Links

In *Shetland Times*, the pursuers argued that their headlines were literary works 8.14
owned by them and the defender's activities (of including them in their webpages by means of hyper-links)[28] constituted infringement by copying under
section 17 CDPA. Lord Hamilton agreed that there was an arguable case of
infringement, since the defenders conceded that headlines (overlying the links)
could be protected as literary works.[29] Even if this was true,[30] the underlying
HTML coding *simpliciter* is surely unprotected by copyright, either under the
de minimis principle, or being akin to facts in the public domain.[31] In contrast,
web-linking is viewed as a more benign activity in the USA, and a copyright
action against linking per se is less likely to succeed.[32]

Shetland Times has illustrated the difficulties of adapting the United 8.15
Kingdom's existing copyright structure to *sui generis* Internet technology. The
settlement of *Shetland Times* deprived the courts of a valuable opportunity to
resolve the section 7 dilemma, and consider defences (eg fair dealing) to the
infringing acts in question.

(f) Other Observations

The CDPA is peppered with provisions which are potentially relevant. For 8.16
example, copyright in a webpage may also be secondarily infringed by transmission, under section 24(2) CDPA.[33] If this section is applied, in theory every

---

[28] For description, see Appendix at A.81.

[29] *Supra*, n 12 at 609.

[30] Bearing in mind that copyright has been denied to slogans in the following cases: *Sinanide v La Maison Kosmeo* (1928) 139 LT 365; *Kirk v Flemming (J&R) Ltd* [1928–35] MacCC 44; *Francis Day Hunter* [1940] AC 112; *Licensed Victualler's Newspaper Co v Bingham* (1888) 38 Ch.D 139; *Noah v Shuba* [1991] FSR 14 (where the Court considered, obiter, that a paragraph could not be a work in its own right if it did not afford sufficient information, instruction or literary enjoyment to the reader). cf *Lamb v Evans* [1893] 1 Ch 218, in which headings were protected, being elaborate and given in four languages. See further MacQueen, *supra*, n 22 at p 74.

[31] Lesia Strangret "The legalities of linking on the World Wide Web" (1997) 2(6) *Communications Law* 202 at 203.

[32] *Gary Bernstein v JC Penny, Elizabeth Arden et al*, Case No. 98–2958 R(Ex) 29 September 1998, US District Court, Central District of Califoria. Bernstein brought an action against Arden and JC Penny for copyright infringement based on a series of hypertext links which connected JC Penny's website to a site containing unauthorised copiesof photographs of Elizabeth Taylor taken by Bernstein. Arden advertised their "Passion" perfume on JC Penny's website. This website contained a hypertext link to a movie database which linked to a Swedish University Network site, where two infringing copies of the photographs resided. Bernstein argued that even though there was no direct link to the photographs, JC Penny had infringed copyright by providing the original link which connected to other links and eventually to the infringing photographs. The Court dismissed the action against Elizabeth Arden without issuing an opinion, prompting Bernstein to withdraw its action against JC Penny. The decision is widely viewed as correct, since a finding of infringement for linking per se would fundamentally militate against the nature of the WWW as an infinite series of interconnected sites.

[33] *Supra*, para 2.18.

service provider could be liable for secondary infringement merely by carrying a webpage without licence (express or implied), knowing or *having reason to know* that it could be copied, or that links to it can be made.[34]

8.17   If a webpage is decided as being a broadcast or a cable programme service, section 72 CDPA provides that the showing or playing in public of a broadcast or cable programme to an audience who have not paid for admission to view the same does not infringe copyright in the broadcast or cable programme. Much will turn on whether making available a free downloadable page is a "showing" in public to an audience, which for the purposes of the Internet, comprises a world-wide collection of persons who are downloading material for free,[35] at different times.[36]

8.18   The role of implied licences will be key to the future of Internet copyright in the United Kingdom. The technical ethos is such that linking and browsing are activities which are part of the Internet, and users must reasonably acquire an implied right to make necessary reproductions in effecting the main purpose of the Internet.[37] An Australian Court has already demonstrated the role of implied licences in relation to "shareware" that is disseminated on the Internet.[38]

III. THE DIGITAL AGENDA

8.19   Whilst the WIPO Geneva Conference may be noted for its failure to reach an agreement over the protection of temporary or ephemeral copies over the Internet, it achieved much by way of control over rights management information,[39] as well as an expanded communication right[40] to cover on-demand digital transmissions. The European Commission has subsequently published a Proposed Directive[41] to implement the provisions of the WIPO treaties ("Proposed Directive"), and this initiative has offered an exception to the reproduction right.[42] Across the Atlantic, the USA has also undertaken similar initiatives for implementation.[43]

[34] See also Wienand "The Legal Implications of Electronic Data Exchange" (1997) 18 *Journal of the Society of Archivists* 83 at 85.
[35] Some payment is made to the service provider, but not the owners of websites from which material is downloaded.
[36] See Art 3 Proposed Directive, *infra*, n 39 (right of "making available to the public . . . works in such a way that members of the public may access them from a place and at a time individually chosen by them").
[37] In the same way that, for example, knitting patterns carry the implied right to reproduce the pattern for domestic purposes: *Roberts v Candiware* [1980] FSR 352.
[38] *Trumpet Software v Ozemail* (discussed in paras 10.70–10.71).
[39] Article 12 WIPO Copyright Treaty.
[40] Article 8 WIPO Copyright Treaty.
[41] Proposal for a European Parliament and Council Directive on the Harmonization of Certain Aspects of Copyright and Related Rights in the Information Society COM(97) 628 final, 21 Jan 1998, 97/0359 (COD); reported in OJ C108/6 (7 April 1998).
[42] See Art 5, discussed *infra*, paras 8.21–8.22.
[43] See the Digital Millennium Copyright Act of 1998 (S.2037, HR.2281),passed by the US Senate on 14 May 1998, and by the House of Representatives on 4 August 1998. President Clinton signed it to law on 28 October 1998.

This section examines the regulation of two particular issues within the digi- **8.20**
tal agenda that bear direct relevance to software protection: temporary reproductions and the circumvention of technical protection systems.

(a) Temporary Reproduction: Articles 2 and 5 Proposed Directive

The controversy during the Geneva Diplomatic Conference 1996 leading to **8.21**
exclusion of the reproduction right (Draft Articles 7(1) and (2))[44] from the
Copyright Treaty has been documented by many writers.[45] In its Proposed
Directive[46] the Commission has attempted to introduce a reproduction right[47]
which extends to permanent and temporary copies, accompanied by an obligatory exception for certain acts of temporary reproduction which are an "integral
part" of a technological process for the sole purpose of enabling use to be made
of a work and having "no independent economic significance".[48]

The purpose of the exception is to exclude from the scope of the reproduction **8.22**
right certain acts of reproduction which are dictated by technology but have no
economic significance of their own.[49] It is still uncertain as to whether objec-
tions will not be raised to the insertion of the words "integral" and "economic
significance".[50] Suggestions have been made that a taxonomy should first be
drawn covering the various situations where in the course of net usage, copying
occurs, from the most to the least worrisome from a copyright policy stand-
point.[51] A narrow interpretation of what is "integral" may rule out caching
being covered by the Article 5 exception, since it facilitates faster access, but is
not essential to the working of the WWW.[52]

---

[44] For a discussion of alternative proposals, see Lai, *supra*, n 1 at 49–51.

[45] See eg Vinje, "The New WIPO Copyright Treaty—A Balanced Result in Geneva" [1997] 5
EIPR at 230–234; Reinbothe, Martin-Prat, Von Lewinski, "The New WIPO Treaties: A First
Resume" [1997] 4 EIPR 171 at 172; Samuelson, "Big Brother Beaten Back" *Wired* (March 1997) at
61 *et seq.*

[46] *Supra*, at n 41.

[47] See Art 2.

[48] See Art 5(1), subject to the troublesome "Berne" wording of Art 5(4).

[49] See also Recital 20 to the Proposed Draft Directive.

[50] See p 28 of the Explanatory Memorandum accompanying the Proposed Draft Directive, where
the example is given of transmitting a video-on-demand from a database in Germany to a home
computer in Portugal. Such a retrieval implies a copy of the video, first of all at the place of the database and afterwards, in average, up to at least a hundred acts of temporary storage along transmission to Portugal.

[51] Raised at the Imprimatur Consensus Forum Report "Rights, Limitations and Exceptions:
Striking a Proper Balance" (30–31 October 1997, Amsterdam) at p 33. It is suggested that computer
scientists and economists are among those who should also be consulted.

[52] See Appendix, A.88–A.91. Caching may also not be covered by s 50A(1) CDPA (back-up copies
of computer software—since the provision also contains a test of necessity).

(b) Technical Protection Systems and Anti-Circumvention Legislation

8.23   Over the last few years software developers have been testing prototype copy protection systems[53] for computer software and digital works. Equally substantial efforts have also gone into the circumvention of these protection systems, to the ultimate detriment of the copyright owner. As a result, various legislative measures have been put forward to prohibit acts and devices that circumvent these technical protection systems,[54] the latest offerings to be found in the Proposed Directive[55] and the US Digital Millennium Copyright Act of 1998.[56]

(i) Threat to software reverse engineering

8.24   There was concern that earlier anti-circumvention proposals were too over-reaching in effect,[57] possibly extending to the prohibition of activities like reverse engineering, which would otherwise be lawful either under the Software Directive, or the Fair Use doctrine in the USA.[58] Invariably, technologies that might be used for indisputably unlawful purposes are also useful for achieving many lawful and socially valuable ones.[59] Article 11 WIPO Copyright Treaty alleviated much of the above concerns,[60] providing that anti-circumvention legislation should apply to acts which facilitate copyright infringement:[61]

> "Contracting Parties shall provide adequate legal protection and effective legal remedies against the circumvention of effective technological measures that are used by rights holders in connection with the exercise of their rights under this Treaty and that restrict acts in respect of their works which are not authorisd by the rights holders concerned or permitted by the law".

---

[53] See Gurnsey, *Copyright Theft* at pp 118–121.

[54] See Samuelson "The US Digital Agenda at WIPO" (1997) 37(2) Virginia J of International Law 369 at 409–415; Lai, *supra*, n 1 at 42–49.

[55] See para 8.25.

[56] See para 8.26.

[57] See WIPO Treaty Draft Art 13 (the US-motivated "primary purpose and effect" test). For criticisms, and alternative proposals, see Vinje "A Brave New World of Technical Protection Systems: Will there Still be Room for Copyright?" [1996] 8 EIPR 431 at 435–436; 438; also summary in Lai, *supra*, n 1 at 45–47.

[58] See Cohen "Some Reflections on Copyright Management Systems and Laws Designed to Protect Them" (1997) 12 (1) Berkeley Technology L J 161 at 173.

[59] Ibid at 172. See also Julie Cohen "Reverse Engineering and the Rise of Electronic Vigilantism: Intellectual Property Implications of "Lock-Out Programs" (1995) 68 S. Cal L Rev 1091 at 1104–1134.

[60] Samuelson "Big Media Beaten Back" *Wired* (March 1997) at 61 *et seq.*

[61] Vinje, "The New WIPO Copyright Treaty: A Happy Result in Geneva" [1997] 5 EIPR 230 at 235. See further Lai, *supra*, n 1 at 47–48.

(ii) The Digital Millennium Copyright Act of 1998

The Digital Millennium Copyright Act 1998 (DMC), which was recently **8.25**
enacted in the USA,[62] contains a significant reverse engineering exclusion[63] in
the regulation of technical protection devices, which addresses the concerns outlined above. In implementing Article 11 WIPO Copyright Treaty, the DMC only
regulates devices which are primarily designed or produced for the pupose of
circumvention, or are marketed for use in circumventing and have a limited
commercial significant purpose or use other than circumvention,[64] and as such
will not threaten dual-use technology and equipment. The exception permitting
circumvention for the purposes of achieving interoperability[65] is very similar to
the restrictions of Article 6 Software Directive, and if enacted, will further bring
US law in line with Europe, not only in relation to reverse engineering for
interoperability; but also in the regulation of anti-circumvention measures.[66]
Other exceptions are for important activities such as encryption research, computer system security testing, law enforcement and privacy protection.[67]
Commentators have remarked on how the DMC still basically favours the content community through its large non-infringement related prohibition of circumvention devices.[68]

(iii) Article 6 Proposed Directive

Article 6(1) Proposed Directive,[69] like its US counterpart,[70] proscribes devices **8.26**
which have only limited commercially significant purposes or use apart from

---

[62] *Supra*, n 43.
[63] The DMC implements §1201(f)–(i) USCA, which provides that "a person who has lawfully
obtained the right to use a copy of a computer program may circumvent a technological protection
measure that effectively controls access to a particular portion of that program for the sole purpose
of identifying and analysing those elements of the program that are necessary to achieve interoperability of an independently created computer program with other programs, and that have not previously been readily available to the person engaging in the circumvention, to the extent that any
such acts of identification and analysis do not constitute infringement" (subs (f)). "Interoperability"
is defined as "the ability of computer programs to exchange information, and for such programs
mutually to use the information which has been exchanged" (subs (i)).
[64] See new §1201(2)(B) USCA.
[65] Leaving decisions like *Sega v Accolade* and *Atari v Nintendo* (paras 6.44–6.50) intact.
[66] The US Senate Judiciary Committee recognised that the purpose of the section was to promote
competition and innovation in the computer and software industry, ensuring that "the effect of current
case law interpreting the Copyright Act is not changed by enactment of this legislation for certain acts
of identification and analysis done in respect of computer programs" (S.Rep 105–190 p 32 (1998)).
[67] §§1201(d)–(j) DMC.
[68] See Band, "The Digital Millennium Copyright Act: A Balanced Result" [1999] EIPR 92; Vinje,
"Copyright Imperilled?" [1999] EIPR 192 at 202. Amidst this broad coverage, even if copyright
exceptions remain intact (§1201(c) DMC) their existence is moot given that copyright defences are
not defences to the prohibition of devices within the DMC.
[69] *Supra*, n 42. Article 6(1) states that "[M]ember States shall provide adequate legal protection
against any activities, including manufacture and distribution of devices . . . which have only limited commercially significant purpose or use other than circumvention, and are carried out knowingly or with reasonable grounds to know, that they will enable or facilitate without authority the

circumvention.[71] Compared to its US counterpart, the European proposal is more copyright infringement-centric[72] compared to its US counterpart, save for the words "which have only limited commercially significant purpose or use other than circumvention"; language which may extend to circumvention to facilitate entirely lawful acts. Depending on the balance of determinative influence by the European Commission or European Parliament, it is speculated that the final version of the EU Directive will contain broad prohibition extending to acts of circumvention *and* devices, peppered with numerous specific exemptions like the DMC.[73]

(iv) Anti-circumvention legislation in the United Kingdom: section 296 CDPA

8.27 To date, the only provision of the CDPA in respect of technological measures and circumvention is section 296. In purporting to implement Article 7(1) Software Directive, section 296 CDPA is a narrower provision in terms since subsection (4) only protects against infringement of the reproduction right (as opposed to all rights in the copyright owner's arsenal). Article 11 Copyright Treaty and Article 6 Proposed Directive also cover technical protection in connection with the exercise of rights under the Treaty or Directive or the Berne Convention. Section 296 applies to "devices or means" that are "specifically designed or adapted" to circumvent a copy-protection system, arguably implementing the "sole intended purpose" test in the Software Directive. For the purposes of Treaty and eventual EU compliance, it is imperative that section 296 CDPA be revised to expand its coverage of rights.[74] Section 296, as presently drafted, only grants remedies to the issuer of copies of the work and not to the copyright owner, hence not providing adequate legal protection for the latter.[75]

circumvention of any effective technological measure designed to protect any copyright or any rights related to copyright". Under Art 6(2), "technological measures" refer to "any device, product or component incorporated into a process, device or product designed to prevent or inhibit the infringement of any copyright or any rights related to copyright". They shall only be "deemed effective where the work or other subject matter is rendered accessible to the user only through application of an access code or process, including by decryption, descrambling or other transformation of the work or other subject matter, with the authority of the rightholder".

[70] *Supra*, para 8.25.

[71] The suggestion has been made that the wording of Art 6(1) be improved to clarify that the devices and services include those which have the sole purpose of circumvention; see Lewinski "A Successful Step towards Copyright and Related Rights in the Information Age: The New EC Proposal for a Harmonisation Directive" [1998] EIPR 135 at 138.

[72] See the Commission's Explanatory Memorandum accompanying the Proposed Directive, COM(97) 628 (1998) p 51.

[73] See Vinje, "Copyright Imperilled?" *supra*, n 68 at 206.

[74] See also s 297A CDPA (criminalising the manufacture, sale, importation or hire of unauthorised decoders of encrypted transmissions), which may be invoked against the circumvention of Internet-based technical protection systems. Subsection (3) defines "transmissions" to mean any programme included in a broadcasting or cable programme service which is provided from a place in the United Kingdom; and is also subject to the definitional limits set by *Shetland Times v Wills*, *supra*, n 12 at 607–608.

[75] For this and other differences, see further Garnett, James, Davies (eds) *Copinger and Skone James on Copyright*, 14th edn (Sweet & Maxwell, 1999) at pp 860–861.

IV. CONCLUSION

This chapter has highlighted the major new challenge brought by the Internet,   **8.28**
discussing how, by accretion, the provisions of the CDPA may be potentially
applicable to Internet technology. As regards the digital agenda, the chapter has
focused on two specific areas because of their particular relevance to software
copyright and reverse engineering; temporary reproduction and the regulation
of protection-defeating devices. In relation to the reproduction right, it is
observed that only the EU has suggested an obligatory exception to the reproduction right exempting browsing and caching facilities, the efficacy of which
remains to be seen. On the subject of anti-circumvention legislation, the apparent threat to reverse engineering from earlier proposals, has largely been
addressed. The latest US Digital Millennium Copyright Act contains an exception in section 130 which will, when enacted, represent a significant move in
favour of trans-Atlantic harmonisation of software reverse engineering.

9

Database Protection in the United Kingdom: the New Deal and its Effects on Software Protection

I. INTRODUCTION

The EC Database Directive[1] seeks to harmonise, in the face of considerable **9.1** divergence between Member States' laws,[2] copyright protection of databases throughout the Community; and also creates a new right, as distinct from copyright, which prevents the unauthorised extraction and re-utilisation of the contents of databases.[3] In the United Kingdom the implementing Regulations came into force on 1 January 1998.[4]

This chapter highlights the statutory provisions of the new database law, **9.2** drawing particular attention to salient features and potential areas of concern in the sphere of software protection.

II. DEFINITIONAL SIGNIFICANCE

A new section 3A CDPA[5] provides the means for protecting multimedia works **9.3** and online interactive databases.[6] A "database" is defined as a "collection of

---

[1] Council Directive 96/9/EC of 11 March 1996 on the Legal Protection of Databases OJ L77/20 ("the Database Directive"). For a summary of the provisions contained in the draft Database Directive at various points during the three-year drafting and deliberation process, see Reichman, "Legal Hybrids Between the Patent and Copyright Paradigms" (1994) 94 Colum L Rev 2432 at 2435–2436; Kaye, "The Proposed EU Directive for the Legal Protection of Databases: A Cornerstone of the Information Society?" [1995] 7 EIPR 583.

[2] The essential difference lies between countries like the United Kingdom and Ireland, which accord copyright protection on the basis of low originality threshold, and countries like the Netherlands, which still preserve the author's personal expression as the touchstone of literary copyright: see *Van Dale v Romme*, judgment of 4 January 1991, translated in Dommering and Hugenholtz, *Protecting Works of Fact*, Appendix I (1991). The latter's US counterpart is the well-known decision of *Feist Publications v Rural Telephone* 499 US 340 (1991).

[3] For a comprehensive critique of the Database Directive, see Cornish, "1996 European Community Directive on Database Protection" (1996) 21 Columbia-VLA J of Law & the Arts (1996), 1.

[4] Copyright and Rights in Database Regulations 1997 (1997, SI 3032) (hereinafter referred to as "the Regulations"). For comments, see Lai [1998] 1 EIPR 32.

[5] See reg 6.

[6] For example, Kaye (*supra*, n 1) hails the Database Directive as rescuing database publishers from the perils of under-protection in the age of "digital warehousing" (ibid at 588). See also Recital

independent works, data and other materials which (a) are arranged in a systematic or methodical way, and (b) are individually accessible by electronic or other means". Given this broad definition,[7] it is argued that for the protection of multimedia products[8] (which combine computer-generated displays and digitised pre-existing information, including copyright works, to form its images), analogies that were previously made with the protection of traditional works like films,[9] and suggestions that they be protected as "computer programs"[10] or by patent;[11] need no longer be made. Collections of digital representations of works, data or other materials which are not literary works will be protected under section 3A CDPA, provided they are part of the author's intellectual creation.[12]

III. COPYRIGHT PROTECTION OF DATABASES

9.4   The Regulations amend section 3(1) CDPA by specifically protecting databases as "original" literary works[13] and defines originality for the first time.[14] However the CDPA (as amended) preserves both originality standards; the

9, where databases are stated to be a vital tool in the development of an information market within the Community.

   [7] It is envisaged that a particular webpage on the Internet, comprising text (literary works), graphics, photographs, sound or video may arguably comprise a collection of "independent works". This may be contrasted with literary compilations under s 3(1) CDPA, which could not extend to collections which are not literary works, eg three-dimensional shapes or physical materials. For a judicial consideration of the nature of "literary compilations", covering such diverse works as telegraph codes, football coupons, railway timetables, street directories, novels, electrical circuit diagrams and poety, see Laddie J's judgment in *Autospin (Oil Seals) Ltd v Beehive Spinning* [1995] RPC 683.

   [8] For a definition of "multimedia products", see Stephen Beutler "The protection of multimedia products under international copyright law" (1997) 13(4) CLSR 253 at 253–254; Douglas, "Too Hot to Handle? Copyright Protection of Multimedia" [1997] 8AIPJ 96 at 96–99. See also Henry, *Publishing and Multimedia Law* (Butterworths, 1994) at pp 303–306.

   [9] See Williams, Calow, Lee *Multimedia—Contracts, Rights and Licensing* (FT Law & Tax, 1996) at pp 70–72; Turner, "Do the Old Legal Categories Fit the New Multimedia Products? A Multimedia CD-ROM as a Film" [1995] 3 EIPR 107. A hindrance to the "film" analogy is that s 5(1) CDPA does not appear to take into account the interactive element of a multimedia work; ie the users of multimedia products to a large extent dictate the sequence in which these images appear.

   [10] Davies, "The developing law of multimedia" [1994] 1 *Computer Law and Practice* at 6. ("The argument runs that the digitised text, images and sounds in a multimedia work are merely data for the computer program which is also stored on that disk and the whole work therefore constitutes a computer program"). See also Thorne, "Copyright and multimedia products—fitting a round peg in a square hole?" (1995) 49 *Copyright World* at 20.

   [11] Not least due to the controversy over Compton's new media patent in the USA. See Bednarek, "Comptons New Media's Patent Saga: Lessons of the Software Industry and Others in Emerging Technology" *Patent World* (February 1995) at 29 *et seq*; Lennon "The controversy over the Compton's multimedia patent" (1994) 3 *Computer Law and Practice* at 66 *et seq*; Davies, *supra*, n 10 at 7 *et seq*.

   [12] Hence there will be no longer be the need to consider whether such collections qualify as copyrightable "compilations". cf Rees, Chalton (eds) *Database Law* (Jordan, 1998) at pp 44–46.

   [13] See reg 5.

   [14] The selection or arrangement of contents must constitute the "author's own intellectual creation": s 3A(2) into the CDPA. For ramifications , see paras 2.11–2.14.

higher in respect of databases as defined in the Database Directive,[15] and the lower in respect of "non-database" compilations (applying "sweat of the brow" copyright). In relation to copyright, the Courts and practitioners alike will be expected to render difficult judgments and opinions distinguishing what is a protectable "database" from a non-protectable database but protectable compilation. It is questionable as to whether different standards of protection which exist for essentially similar works are intellectually, as well as practically satisfactory.[16] In addition, the United Kingdom may be accused of offering three-tier protection: "higher" copyright for "databases", "lower" copyright for "non-database" compilations, and *sui generis* protection for content that is compiled as a result of substantial investment.[17] This arguably goes even further than the Database Directive, which requires the standard implementation of uniform provisions.[18] The consequence of Directive implementation is that in some instances countries will be reducing the scope of their current rights, at least in respect of future material.[19] This does not appear to be the case with the United Kingdom, and its compliance with the Database Directive has been questioned.[20]

IV. THE FUTURE OF COMPUTER-GENERATED WORKS[21]

Whilst an author's creativity necessarily includes skill and labour, the converse   **9.5**
does not hold true. This is reflected in the CDPA's treatment of computer-

---

[15] See *Consultation Paper on United Kingdom Implementation*, issued by the Copyright Directorate, Patent Office, DTI in August 1997 at para 8.3.

[16] See Diane Rowland "The EC Database Directive: An original solution to an unoriginal problem?"[1997] 5 WJCLI <http://webjcli.ucl.ac.uk/1997/issue5/rowlands5.html>

[17] Hence it is no surprise that some writers take the view that "[t]he new law appears to be of no immediate benefit to the UK, as most UK databases already enjoy copyright protection". See Angel, Quinn "The New Database Law" (1993) 14(1) CLSR 34 at 37.

[18] This may in practice result in complaints from the Council of Europe. A question which also arises is whether the Regulations are inter vires the powers of the Department of Trade and Industry; or whether they are tantamount to an unauthorised attempt to enact primary legislation, which is the sole sacred function of Parliament. See Laddie, *et al*, *Modern Law of Copyright and Designs*, 2nd edn, Vol 1 at p15. Conversely Chalton argues that the separate classifications of databases and tables and compilations which are not databases are a necessary consequence of Directive implementation. In his view, to alter the application of that protection to tables or compilations which do not conform to the Directive's definition of a database would require primary legislation. See Chalton "The Copyright and Rights in Databases Regulations 1997: Some Outstanding Issues on Implementation of the Database Directive" [1998] EIPR 178. The author sets great store by the definition of a database being largely determined by the quantity of "dependency" between components to a collection; hence the requirement for a collection of "independent works" (ibid at 179). With due respect, this should not be the sole determinant, since the Directive definition also encapsulates collections of "data or other material . . . accessible by electronic or other means", which is arguably broad enough to cover existing "compilations".

[19] See Cornish, *supra*, n 5 at 1. The Consultation Paper also appears to recognise this consequence: *supra*, n 15 at para 6.1.

[20] Hugenholtz, "Implementing the European Database Directive" in Kabel, Mom (eds) *Intellectual Property and Information Law—Essays in Honour of Herman Cohen Jehoram*, of pp 156–157.

[21] For authorship and ownership of different types of work that are created by or with the aid of a computer, see generally, Bainbridge *Software Copyright Law*, 3rd edn (1997), ch 9, pp 224–236.

generated works.[22] A computer-generated database may not qualify for "database copyright" in the absence of an "author's own intellectual creation".[23] This places numerous Internet search engines and other computer-generated listings at potential risk of not receiving any copyright protection after the implementation of the Regulations. The failure to clarify the scope of copyright protection of computer-generated works either as "databases" or "compilations", is a striking omission. It has been suggested that the opportunity should be seized to withdraw copyright protection from all forms of computer-generated work, extending to them instead a related right akin to the *sui generis* right.[24] Presumably computer-generated collections will in the future be protected under the new *sui generis* "database right",[25] subject to such collections satisfying the definition of a "database" under section 3A CDPA.[26] Otherwise, such collections may be protected as non-database literary compilations, subject to the traditionally lower UK criterion of "originality".[27]

V. THE NEW DATABASE RIGHT

9.6 A new "database right" is now available provided there has been a substantial investment over the obtaining, presentation or verification of contents, which may include, inter alia, copyright works.[28] The mysteries of what qualifies as a "substantial investment" have been well articulated,[29] with little assistance from Directive recitals.[30] The Regulations attempt to define "substantial", suggesting an adjudication based on quantity or quality, or a combination of both.[31] In practice this offers little guidance, beyond showing that, as with copyright protection, a range of protection will develop with case law, dependent upon the intrinsic value and functionality of the relevant content under examination.

9.7   The new database right provides the maker[32] and first owner[33] with the right

[22] See ss 9(3), 178 CDPA.
[23] See further, Chalton, *supra*, n 18 at 280.
[24] Ibid at 281.
[25] Part III of the Regulations. See also Recital 23 Database Directive, which states that the term "database" should not be taken to "extend to computer programs used in the making or operation of a database".
[26] Ibid, reg 12(1).
[27] Chalton, *supra*, n 18 at 179.
[28] See reg 13.
[29] See Cornish, *supra* n 3 at 8.
[30] Going beyond Recital 19 Database Directive, which provides that the compilation of several recordings of musical performances on a CD does not qualify for substantial investment.
[31] See reg 12(1).
[32] The database "maker" is defined in reg 14(1) as the person who takes the initiative and assumes the risk of investing in its making. Subsection (4) defines a joint making of a database "if two or more persons acting together in collaboration take the initiative in making it and assumes the risk of investing in its making". Curiously, it may not envisage a situation where two persons work together to "make" a database, where one takes the initiative and the other assumes the risk. The question then arises as to whether the database will be considered to be jointly made in these circumstances?
[33] See reg 15.

against total or substantial extraction or re-utilisation of database content.[34] "Re-utilisation" covers a broad communication right, including online transmission.[35] "Extraction" refers to the permanent or temporary transfer of contents to "another medium" by any means.[36] The "extraction" right is restrictive since it appears to regulate the search of one item within an electronic or online database (where a temporary copy is made in the user's computer), unless performed by a lawful user of the database.[37] Its potency lies in the direct protection of underlying ideas and information derived from database content.

VI. IMPACT OF DATABASE COPYRIGHT PROVISIONS ON SOFTWARE COPYRIGHT PROTECTION

(a) Originality and Substantial Similarity

The question for UK software copyright protection must now be whether UK **9.8** judges are likely to be persuaded that the standard of "author's own intellectual creation" should be applied to computer software as a rule of interpretation,[38] given Article 1(3) Software Directive, and the prominence of these words in the database provisions.[39] This could in turn be significant for the purposes of adjudicating substantial similarity.[40] Writers[41] have argued the imposition of this standard of originality to software cases in support of Jacob J's rejection of US authorities to this area of law in *Ibcos v Barclays Mercantile Highland Finance*.[42]

---

[34] See reg 16(1).

[35] See reg 12, which defines "re-utilisation" as "making those contents available to the public by any means" and Art 7(2)(b) Database Directive.

[36] Ibid. "Medium" remains undefined, but arguably includes any electronic or non-electronic carrier, including machine memory. See also Recital 44 Database Directive, which provides that when the screen display of the contents of a database necessitates the permanent or temporary transfer of all or a substantial part of such contents to another medium, such a transfer is subject to the authorisation of the rights owner.

[37] See reg 9(1), adding s 50D CDPA, which provides that a lawful user of a database or part of one which has been made available to the public in any manner shall be entitled to extract or re-utilise for any purpose insubstantial parts of the contents of that part of the database of which he is a lawful user.

[38] Arguably this would create difficulties, particularly for the protection of computer-generated computer programs. See discussion of computer-generated works, *supra*, para 9.5.

[39] In particular, reg 6.

[40] eg in *Engineering Dynamics v Structured Software* 26 F.3d 1335 (5th Cir 1994), the Court had to decide whether copyright existed in input formats for the plaintiff's Computer Aided Design program used to design offshore structures. The 5th Circuit concluded that some of the formats were so generic as to lack the minimal degree of creativity required for copyright protection. This was particularly true of highly standardised technical information.

[41] Notably, Holyoak and Torremans, *Intellectual Property Law* (Butterworths, 1995) at p420. The authors argue that a proper application of the originality criterion specified in the Software Directive would result in a core of protectable expression, the same result achieved by US infringement methodology.

[42] [1994] FSR 275 at 302; cf approach of Ferris J in *Richardson v Flanders* [1994] FSR 275 at 302. See further Stone, "Software Law—Lessons from America: Filtration of Functionality from Software Copyright" (1997) CLSR Vol 13 No 1 at pp 15–21.

On the other hand, the view can be formed that "author's own intellectual creation" standard is only applicable to databases as defined, and not for other works such as computer software.[43]

(b) Computer Programs Contained within Databases

9.9   There is considerable scope for overlap between the Software and Database Directives, in relation to the protection of underlying computer software. Under the Database Directive, protection also appears to extend to "the materials necessary for the operation or consultation of certain databases such as thesaurus and indexation systems",[44] implicating computer programs. This may be difficult to apply, since Article 1(3) Database Directive states that computer programs used in the manufacture or operation of databases are protected by the Software Directive.[45] The problem is further compounded by the absence of a definition for computer programs either in the Software or Database Directive.[46]

9.10   Under the UK provisions, if the database is computer-generated (as most databases are) then copyright protection may not avail under section 3A CDPA. Although it is arguable that the contents, including underlying software may still be protected by the *sui generis* database right, Article 1(3) should intervene to exclude database protection of underlying software at this stage.

(c) "Databases" Contained within Computer Programs

9.11   Computer programs may qualify as "databases' under the Regulations, being collections of "independent works" (individual sub-programs), data or other material (eg specifications). One area of particular concern is the protection of software content under the new database right. While the Regulations are silent on this issue, the Database Directive operates without prejudice to the software directive[47] and the term "database" should not be taken to "extend to computer programs used in the making or operation of a database".[48]

9.12   While the Database Directive excludes computer programs (being literary works) *as such* from the definition of a "database",[49] it is arguable that insofar as computer programs incorporate any identifiable database components, these components may be the subject of the new database right. This raises a serious

---

[43] See reg 11.
[44] Recital 20, Database Directive.
[45] See also Recital 23, Database Directive.
[46] See Downing "Online services and the EU Database Directive" (1996) 10(1) *International Review of Law, Computers and Technology* 41 at 46.
[47] Article 2(a) Database Directive.
[48] Recital 23 Database Directive.
[49] Recital 17.

question of *sui generis* protection for program elements which are otherwise unprotected by copyright,[50] especially when many of the most commercially valuable components of computer programs, including program interfaces have been characterised as "industrial compilations of applied know-how".[51]

The US Supreme Court has affirmed the First Circuit decision of *Lotus v* **9.13** *Borland* that the menu command hierarchy of the Lotus 1–2–3 spreadsheet program is an unprotected method of operation.[52] Under the new database right, Lotus would not be precluded from arguing that its menu command hierarchy and other interface command sets are separately identifiable database components incorporated into a computer program.[53] The menu command hierarchy is arguably "a collection . . . of . . . information . . . arranged in a systematic or methodical way". From this perspective the extraction[54] and re-utilisation of a command hierarchy readily transforms into an illicit appropriation of a substantial part of a protected database, rather than a legal act of appropriating material outside the copyright domain.

If the above arguments are feasible, the new database right could, in certain **9.14** circumstances protect software content falling outside copyright, possibly undermining the objectives of the Software Directive.[55] In the USA, the Second Circuit has not been adverse to in-principle protection of express compilations of unprotected/filtered software elements.[56]

(d) Computer Programs as Compilations of Sub-Programs

Another issue is whether sub-programs continue to be protected as "databases" **9.15** under the Regulations. In *Ibcos*[57] it will be recalled that Jacob J considered that the ADS program, as a "work", was determined to be a complicated composite of interrelated programs, routines and sub-routines, comprising 335 program

---

[50] Elements of a computer program achieving software interoperability, or look-up tables and command sets could constitue a collection of "data" or "other material".

[51] See Samuelson, Davis, Kapor, Reichman "A Manifesto Concerning the Legal Protection of Computer Programs" (1994) 94 Colum L Rev 2308 at 2326 and 2401–2444.

[52] *Lotus v Borland* 49 F.3d 807 (1st Cir 1995), aff'd 116 S.Ct 804 (1996); discussed *supra*, paras 4.24–4.32.

[53] For parallel discussions in the USA, see Reichman, Samuelson "Intellectual Property Rights in Data?" Vol 50 Vanderbilt Law Rev 1 at 20 (January 1997).

[54] Subject to a fair dealing defence for non-commercial teaching or research, which is only applicable to the extraction right: see reg 20(1).

[55] The main objective of the Software Directive is, on the one hand, to grant substantial protection of investment and skills in programming, and on the other, to limit the rights of the software developer so that independent production of compatible programs cannot be prevented: see further Cornish, "Interoperable systems and copyright" [1989] 11 EIPR 391; Kroker "The Computer Directive and the Balance of Rights" [1997] 5 EIPR 247 at 249–250.

[56] See *Softel v Dragon Medical & Scientific Communications Inc* 118 F.3d 955 at 963–964, 966–967 (2d Cir 1997), cert denied 118 C.Ct 1300 (1998). Such an over-protective approach has been criticised by Karjala "Copyright Protection of Computer Program Structure" (1998) 64(2) Brooklyn L Rev 519 at 539.

[57] *Supra*, n 42.

files, 171 record layout files and 46 screen layout files. His Lordship accepted that the package of programs as a whole had copyright as a kind of compilation. The amount of skill, labour and judgement which went into its creation was thought to be very substantial, "well above the threshold of originality accepted in other fields of copyright".[58] In his Lordship's view there was no reason why a compilation of computer programs should not acquire a separate copyright, the question of originality being all a question of degree, as with any other compilation.[59]

9.16   Arguably the status of the ADS program package as a protectable compilation remains unchanged under the Regulations. The question remains whether it would also attain "database copyright" status, applying the new originality criterion under section 3A(2) CDPA (which does not quadrate with "work, skill and judgement"). It is most likely that an English court would answer this in the negative, having regard to Recital 17 of the Database Directive.

VII. CONCLUSION

9.17 The *Consultation Paper* states, as a guiding principle to Directive implementation, the intention to disturb the status quo as little as possible.[60] The above discussion raises anomalies created by the implementation, and observes that the the ramifications brought by the new database right are indeed profound, particularly in relation to "database components" which may be found within a computer program.

---

[58] Ibid, at 289.
[59] Ibid at 290. In this connection Jacob J criticised the contrary view held by Judge Paul Baker in *TIPS v Daman*]1992] FSR 171 at 179.
[60] *Consultation Paper, supra,* n 15 at para 7.1.

10

The Copyright–Contract Interface and Software Protection

I. INTRODUCTION

This chapter addresses the interface between copyright and contract—the valid- **10.1** ity of shrink-wrap licences; the possibility of a copyright owner or his licensee restricting end user rights by the vehicle of express or implied contract; and the extent to which it is open to an end user to argue an implied licence to use a computer program in a manner which, as some would consider, is detrimental to the copyright owner's interests.

The chapter is divided into two primary sections; first, licensing issues, **10.2** including the legal status and validity of shrink-wrap licences under English law; and secondly, the implied licence and users' rights in software transactions. I seek to address the following questions: Are shrink-wrap licences valid under English law; and to what extent are a copyright owner's exclusive rights capable of being supplanted by an implied licence?

II. SHRINK-WRAP LICENSING

The CDPA states[1] the principle, as did its predecessor,[2] that copyright is **10.3** infringed by any person who does or authorises another person to do any of the acts restricted by the copyright "without the licence"[3] of the copyright owner.[4] To be more precise, the CDPA deems copying not to constitute infringement if

---

[1] See s 16(2) CDPA.

[2] See s 1(2) Copyright Act 1956.

[3] The expression "without the licence" is thought to be of the same effect as the expression "without the consent" which featured in s 2(1) Copyright Act 1911. See further Copinger and Skone James on Copyright, 13th edn (1991) at para 8–144 and references cited therein.

[4] A copyright owner also has a right to grant licences which allow the licensee to grant sub-licences. Whether the licensee may sub-licence depends on the terms of the agreement but in appropriate circumstances such a right may be implied. Section 49(7) Copyright Act 1956 states that: "Where the doing of anything is authorised by the grantee of a licence, or a person deriving title from the grantee, and it is within the terms (including any implied terms) of the licence for him to authorise it, it shall for the purposes of this Act be taken to be done with the licence of the grantor and of every other person (if any) upon whom the licence is binding". The CDPA is silent on this point, but the view has been taken that the above provision is merely a statement of general law; that he who is sub-licensed clearly acts with "the licence of the copyright owner". See Laddie, *et al*, *Modern Law of Copyright and Designs*, 2nd edn, Vol 1 at para 18.14.

the copyright owner has allowed it (by express or implied terms)[5] or in the event that no specific contractual provision is made.[6] At the very outset it should be stated that a licence can exist independently of a contract (eg a bare permission to use the work), but more often a licence commences with a sale and purchase of computer software. As the following sections will show, a popular but controversial mechanism for rights clearance in software transactions is the "shrink-wrap" licence.

(a) Users' Rights Implied by Law

10.4   This section analyses the "use rights" which are conferred on a customer by the Software Directive and the CDPA (as amended).

(i) Article 5(1) Software Directive

10.5   Together with its recitals,[7] Article 5(1) sets out the framework governing the use of computer software; that in the absence of "specific contractual provisions", the lawful acquirer of software may perform the restricted acts of, inter alia, reproduction and adaptation, where such acts are necessary for the use of the computer in accordance with its intended purpose (including error correction).[8] If a program has been sold, the presumption is created, that all the acts which are restricted by Article 4 Software Directive[9] are permitted by the rightholder in respect of its use in accordance with its intended purpose. Czarnota and Hart claim this is a profound reversal of presumptions, the position prior to the Directive being that the absence of specific terms in a licence precluding the performance of specific acts would not necessarily be construed as permitting those acts.[10]

10.6   The extent of the exception in Article 5(1) is determined by three factors. First, the user must be a "lawful acquirer" of the software in question. Secondly, the acts performed with the computer program must be necessary as opposed to

[5] In the absence of express terms governing a software licence they may be implied: see s 56 CDPA, and *infra*, paras 10.42–10.43.

[6] See also s 50C(1)((a) CDPA.

[7] Recitals 16 and 17 Software Directive.

[8] Subject to the contradiction between Recital 18 and Art 5(1) of the Software Directive, in which the latter provides that error correction may not be prohibited by contract. See further, Smith "EC Software Protection Directive—an Attempt to understand Article 5(1)" (1990–1991) 7 CLSR 148. To the extent that this recital contradicts Art 5, the text of Art 5 should prevail over a mere recital; see Dolmans "Software Licensing in Europe—do we need a block exemption?" in Hugh Hansen (ed) *International Intellectual Property Law & Policy* (Jarvis Publishing, Sweet & Maxwell, 1996) Vol 1 at p 418.

[9] Restricted acts include reproduction (permanent and temporary), loading, displaying, running, transmission or storage, translation, adaptation, arrangement and any other alteration of a computer program.

[10] Czarnota and Hart, *Legal Protection of Computer Programs in Europe—Guide to the EC Directive* (Butterworths, 1991) at p 66.

being more than merely commercially advantageous or expedient in terms of time and effort. "Use" itself is not defined, but the recitals[11] state that loading and running the program are permitted under any licence to use the program. Smith has argued that Article 5(1) confers a general right to load, run and correct errors in software, even if there is an express contrary term, by reference to Recitals 16 and 17.[12] On this interpretation, the Software Directive provides the "lawful acquirer" of software with a basic use right which cannot be excluded by contract.

Thirdly, and most significantly, a limitation is placed on "use"—that it is "in accordance with its intended purpose". This purpose may be defined by contract and may include conditions under which the program is to be used and the functions which it is to perform. In the absence of any licence terms governing the "intended purpose", the view has been taken that such purpose will have to be presumed from circumstantial evidence surrounding the transaction.[13]   **10.7**

(ii) User rights under section 50C CDPA

The previous section discussed how Recital 17 supports an interpretation that the "use rights" conferred by Article 5(1) Software Directive could not be derogated by contract. Section 50C[14] makes *any* copying or adapting by the acquirer subject to contrary contractual "agreement".[15] On one analysis, the implementing provision of section 50C appears less stringent, in that contractual provisions which fetter the right may be implied. This is in contrast to the Directive, which stipulates that they be "specific". Under the CDPA, section 50C stipulates the need for a contrary "term or condition of an agreement", which may be inferred in circumstances where a contract could not.[16] For example in the absence of consideration, there may still be an agreement, but no contract.   **10.8**

---

[11] *Supra*, n 7.

[12] See Smith, *supra* n 8. Recital 17 contains the same wording as Art 5(1), but adds the interesting words "including when a copy has been sold". This suggests that Art 5(1) appears to cover the situation where mass marketed software is sold without a signed licence agreement and suggests that the provision will govern any situations not provided by contractual rights of use, and its rights are not derrogable by contract. cf Rowland and MacDonald *Information Technology Law* (1997) at pp 99–102.

[13] Such as the technical capacity of a program to perform certain tasks, its portability (ie whether it remains unchanged from one environment to another), any limitations which may have been placed on user access, etc. See further Czarnota and Hart, *supra*, n 10 at p 65.

[14] Section 50C CDPA provides that "[i]t is not an infringement of copyright for a lawful user of a copy of a computer program to copy or adapt it provided that [it] . . . is not prohibited under any term or condition of an agreement regulating the circumstances in which his use is lawful". Similar use rights now exist for databases; see s 50D CDPA.

[15] Rowland and MacDonald, *supra*, n 12 at pp 101–102.

[16] Much is made of this difference by Sherwood-Edwards, who argues that s 50C is useful for the enforcement of shrink-wrap licences; see Sherwood-Edwards, "Seven Degrees of Separation" (1993) 9(5) *Computer Law & Practice* 169 at 170. Similarly, if the Software Directive is construed so that there is no right under Art 5(1) because of contrary agreement, then there is no requirement for any such agreement to be contractual: Rowland and MacDonald, *supra*, n 10 at p 101.

10.9   Since section 296A CDPA does not apply to the "use right" provided by section 50C, the consequence is that the supplier/producer of a computer program enjoys considerable discretion to restrict the use of the program as much as he wishes, for example in terms of the number of machines on which it may run and number of users.[17] Commentators have therefore rightly concluded that this provision constitutes a significant diminution of users' rights.[18]

(iii) Provisions against exclusory contract

10.10   This subsection draws attention to relevant provisions of the Software Directive and the CDPA which prohibit the contractual exclusion of certain express terms in a software licence, quite apart from the validity of the licence itself. Article 9(1) Software Directive provides that "[a]ny contractual provisions contrary to Article 6 or to the exceptions provided in Article 5(2) and 5(3) shall be null and void".[19]

10.11   Acts of utilisation (in the study of functionality, or the making of necessary back-up copies) and decompilation for the purpose of achieving interoperability form the "mandatory nucleus" of section 296A(1),[20] and under European law it is most likely a mandatory rule.[21] That said, the effectiveness of a provision against exclusory contract always has to be judged against the real value of the exceptions in question; and doubts remain, as to the effectiveness of Articles 5(3) and 6 of the Software Directive.

10.12   As such the UK/European position on terms which are not subject to exclusory contract, is markedly clearer than US law. The latter sees the invocation of the preemption doctrine, with varied consequences. For example, the Seventh Circuit in *ProCD* has taken a more restricted view of copyright preemption, and has upheld contractual clauses which serve an apparent pro-competitive function, such as contractual prohibitions against disassembly, which are treated as clauses which facilitate the distribution of object code while concealing source code.[22]

---

[17] For a list of restrictive clauses, see Scott "Market Analysis and Software Licensing Restrictions" [1984] 2 *Computer Law & Practice* 48.

[18] See Tapper, "Some Aspects of Contractual Licences for Software" in Rose (ed) *Consensus Ad Idem: Essays in the Law of Contract in Honour of Guenter Treitel* (1996) at p 293; Lehmann and Tapper (eds) *Handbook of European Software Law* (1993 at p 172.

[19] See s 296A CDPA and Recitals 17–24 Software Directive—emphasising the need to constrain the terms of licences to use software.

[20] Such a description has been used in relation to s 29 of the German Copyright Act, which contains the equivalent to s 296A; see further Lehmann (1994) 25 IIC at 46.

[21] Schulte 1992 CR 652; Lehmann 1991 NJW 2115. See also Richard Fentiman, *Intellectual Property and the Conflict of Laws—A Study on Behalf of the European Commission DG XV (Final Report)*.

[22] 86 F.3d 1447 (7th Cir 1996). The 7th Circuit took the view that "whether a particular licence is generous or restrictive, a simple two-party contract is not 'equivalent to any of the exclusive rights within the general scope of copyright'and therefore may be enforced" (ibid at 1455). US writers have commented that the 7th Circuit's decision in *ProCD* implicitly reduces the precedential value of the holding in *Sega v Accolade*; see, for example, Minassian Apik, "The Death of Copyright:

(iv) Non-contractual licence

A licence can exist independently of a contract. In the context of opening a **10.13**
shrink-wrap envelope, it could be argued that the user may not be responding to
the manufacturer's offer of a licence, but rather is exercising a right that is
already acquired, by implied licence.[23]

With a non-contractual licence, by analogy with the law of patents,[24] it may **10.14**
be argued that the user may acquire a basic right to use the software, if one has
not been granted by a copyright holder.[25] This may arise where shrink-wrap
terms are stored in the packaging, thus preventing a user from inspecting them
until he breaks the seal. This begs the question of the extent to which a subsequent discovery of restrictive terms within the packaging revokes the implied
licence which existed prior to discovery. It may be a novel argument to plead
that a licence was created prior to the discovery of restrictive terms, coupled
with the grant of an interest to use the software. In land law, this form of licence
usually combines the grant of an interest with ancillary permission to enter the
land in order to realise or exploit that interest.[26] Crucially it is a general common law principle that a licence coupled with the grant of a proprietary interest
is irrevocable during the subsistence of the proprietary interest to which it pertains.[27] Arguably the same argument cannot be sustained in relation to software, it being more likely that any pre-existing implied licence to use the
software would have been taken to be revoked upon the discovery of overriding
express terms,[28] and in any event, end-users of software can reasonably expect
to be bound by licence conditions.

Enforceability of Shrink-wrap Licensing Agreements" (1997) 45 UCLA L. Rev 569 at 598–601. See
also Maureen O'Rouke "Drawing the Boundary between Copyright and Contract: Copyright
Preemption of Software Licence Terms" (1995) 45 Duke LJ 479, in which the following is said of
ProCD: "[t]he contractual prohibition lessens the provider's need to (1) monitor the market for
decompilation tools to assess the probability that decompilation of its software is technologically
feasible; (2) expend resources on making decompilation of its program more difficult; and (3)
expend resources monitoring legislative efforts to address decompilation" (ibid at 499).

   [23] Implied licences are discussed *infra*, at para 10.42 *et seq.*
   [24] *Betts v Willmott* (1871) LR 6 Ch App 239. See reservations expressed *infra*, at para 10.46 *et seq.*
   [25] Though the point has been made that it is by no means clear whether this analogy still survives
Art 5(1) Software Directive. A non-contractual licence should not provide a means to reduce an
acquirer's rights below that provided for by the Directive. See Rowland and Macdonald, *supra*, n
10 at p 109 *et seq.*
   [26] See *Thomas v Sorrell* (1673) Vaugh 330 at 351; *Wood v Leadbitter* (1845) 13 M&W 838 at 844f.
The types of "interest" do not just include interests in land and chattels: *Hurst v Picture Theatres*
[1915] 1 KB 1; *British Actors Film v Glover* [1918] 1 KB 299; *Winter Garden Theatre v Millennium
Productions Ltd* [1948] AC 173.
   [27] *Wood v Leadbitter* (1845) 13 M & W 838 at 845.
   [28] Consistent with the proposition that such pre-existing licences are gratuitous and as such revo-
cable at will: *Hart v Hayman* [1911–1916] MacG Cop Cas 301.

(b) Description of "Shrink-Wrapping"

10.15   A "shrink-wrap" appears in many guises; a box-top licence, envelope licence or referral licence.[29] In an attempt to constitute a direct contractual relationship between copyright licensor and end-user, these licences try to ensure that a customer has read and agreed to the licence before securing access to the software. For example, the "envelope licence" is printed on the outside of the sealed envelope that contains the software. The "referral licence" has a sticker over the disk or CD-ROM box that states: "Don't open this before reading the licence attached". Certain shrink-wraps are not available for viewing by the customer before purchase. It is after the completion of the transaction with the retailer that customers will discover the shrink-wrap licence inside the box. This is especially true for purchases that are made through mail order, and where a computer is purchased with pre-loaded software. In many "shrink-wrap" situations, consumers may not even see or notice the licence conditions before purchase.

10.16   In determining the validity of shrink-wrap licences, the type of licence used, the way in which its terms and conditions are brought to the notice of users, have to be individually investigated to determine the legal status of the licence under discussion.[30] A general observation is that such a licence involves a chain of supply between producer and user through various third parties such as retailers and wholesalers, the software being supplied is standardised and mass-produced.[31]

10.17   It has been pointed out that in the context of shrink-wrapping, a Court would be reluctant to find there was no contract, and the choice is between treating the transaction either as a licence or a contract of sale.[32] In this situation any attempt to impose restrictive terms subsequent to sale would be regarded as a unilateral attempt to vary the existing terms of a contract.[33] At the same time a

[29] Identified in Clive Gringras, "The Validity of Shrink-Wrap Licences" [1996] Int J of Law and Information Technology 77 at 84.

[30] Although a US commentator has observed: "No major mass market software vendor appears to have a shrink-wrap licence visible on the outside of its packing. Some have a 1 or 2 line licence notice on the outside of the package while others have nothing visible on the outside but do have a licence inside the box . . . Video game companies generally sell units of their software products rather than try to licence them. Many lower priced application software packages are also distributed without any attempt to implement a licence agreement". See Greguras, "Current Developments in Computer Software Licensing Practices in the US" [1993] CLSR 197.

[31] Millard "Shrink-Wrap Licensing" [1987] 3 CLSR 8.

[32] See Tapper "United Kingdom", Part II *Handbook of European Law* at (Oxford, 1992) p 61; Tapper, *supra*, n 18 at pp 284–285.

[33] This is reminiscent of failed attempts in the United Kingdom to impose contractual obligations to maintain retail prices, where producers sought to govern the terms of contracts between purchasers of their products and those selling them on: see eg *Taddy v Sterious* [1904] 2 Ch 354; Treitel *Law of Contract*, 9th edn (1995), p 583, n 8. Tapper takes the view that this position would similarly apply to the imposition of onerous licence terms; *supra*, n 18 at p 287.

right to use the software can also be derived from an implied term in the contract under which the software was acquired.[34]

(c) Shrink-Wraps under English Law

(i) Issues going to the formation of a contractual licence

A common variety of shrink-wrap licence, which will form a basis for the   **10.18**
following discussion, is the "envelope licence". This is the system where a purchaser is able to see though the packaging to read a notice attached to the outside of the box setting out the licence, its terms,[35] accompanied by a warning that by opening the packing he will be taken to have accepted the terms of the licence. The licence may contain a provision requiring the user (potential licensee) to return a reply-paid form confirming his acceptance of the terms of the licence, and at the same time registering as a licensed user.[36]

From the scenario described above, in a clear case where the user knowingly   **10.19**
performs these steps, such a procedure is sufficient to create a contract on the terms of the licence. There is also unlikely to be any difficulty if the package is returned unopened.[37] Professor Tapper has suggested[38] that difficulties arise in the following situation, which falls between the two extremes: the customer intends to purchase the package, does not notice or read the licence, opens the package and uses the program and fails to register as a licensed user.

If the supplier is viewed as the offeror in this instance,[39] silence cannot   **10.20**
constitute acceptance,[40] subject to limited exceptions,[41] and in this situation it

---

[34] See, eg *Saphena Computing v Allied Collection Agencies* [1995] FSR 617. Software was supplied to the defendants for the purposes of their business as a debt collecting agency. The Court regarded it as "perfectly clear" that there had to be an implied term "that the defendants should have a copyright licence to enable them to use the Software for that purpose" (ibid at 637).

[35] Subject to the rules of incorporation. The terms of the licence have to be brought to the notice of the user, particularly if unreasonable. Lord Denning MR has stated that certain terms, particularly unreasonable clauses should be printed "with a red hand pointing to [them] . . . before notice could be held to be sufficient": *Spurling v Bradshaw* [1956] 1 WLR 461 at 466. In the situation where shrink-wrap terms are unavailable to the customer until after a sale, it is arguable that such a licence would not be binding on a consumer.

[36] For a full description, see Tapper, "United Kingdom" *Handbook of European Software Law*, *supra*, n 32 Part II, p 60.

[37] Ibid.

[38] Ibid.

[39] For an analysis of the user as the offeror, see Tapper, *supra*, n 32 at p 61. In the first instance, the user's approach to the salesman constitute an offer, the licence in the package constitutes the first counter-offer, and the user's subsequent conduct that is inconsistent with the terms of the licence, another counter-offer. See *Rust v Abbey Life Insurance* [1979] 2 Lloyd's R 355, where a recipient of a documentary first counteroffer was bound, but had performed to positive act in relation to the subject-matter of the contract.

[40] *Holwell Securities v Hughes* [1974] 1 WLR 155 at 157; more recently see *Allied Marine Transport v Vale do Rio Doce Navegacao* [1985] 1 WLR 925 at 937.

[41] Exceptional circumstances warranting dispensation of the general include instances where the offeror expressly or impliedly waives the requirement of communication, for example an offer

is difficult to see how the user, who has not returned an acknowledgement, is bound to the licence terms.

10.21   In a situation where the shrink-wrap licence is not an "envelope licence", and the exterior of the package does not indicate that the product within is licensed inside the package, a question arises as to whether breaking open the seal amounts to acceptance by conduct. In this situation an objective test is applied by the Courts to interpret the actions of the offeree,[42] and conduct will only be regarded as acceptance if the reasonable person would be induced into believing that the offeree has accepted. The difficulty with this analysis is that at the point of sale most customers may not be aware that software is licensed[43] and only contemplate their transaction with the retailer as a contract of sale. It may be difficult to construe the breaking open of a seal as an act of acceptance.[44]

10.22   Another issue in contractual formation is consideration. The customer's payment supports the contract of sale of the physical copy of the software in question. If a shrink-wrap licence is to be viewed as a separate contractual licence between customer and copyright owner, no payment is directly made to the latter but sufficient consideration takes the form of a licence granted by the copyright owner in return for the promise of the end-user to use software within its terms.[45] It is argued that this is a superior analysis, compared with taking consideration to be a "detriment" or "forbearance" suffered by the end-user in not permitting certain activities to be performed to the software in question.[46]

(ii)   A classification exercise

10.23   Although a licence can be included in a contract, a contract is not required to create a licence. The conditions which attach to a licence can have legal effect outside a contract just as a licence itself can. Thus it may be possible for all "use" provisions to have legal effect even if the shrink-wrap licence itself is not a contract by simply treating the conditions as advance notice of the basis upon which a licence will be revoked.[47]

taking the form of delivery of goods to an offeree may be accepted by the latter's user of them: *Weatherby v Banham* [1832] 5 C&P 228. This could arguably include the situation where a shrink-wrap licence indicates to a customer that they need not inform the publisher if they are accepting the terms therein.

[42] See *Brogden v Metropolitan Ry* [1877] 2 AC 666; also Voster [1987] LQR 274.

[43] The exterior of most software packages does not indicate that the product within is the subject of a copyright licence—this is usually stated inside the package and therefore after the sale.

[44] It is not difficult to envisage that consumers could open a shrink-wrap licence without realising they may be entering into a separate licence with the publisher . Apart from not finding acceptance by conduct in this situation, the ignorance of any offer forms the basis of the argument that there was no *consensus ad idem*, especially this type of case where the effect of a contract, if formed, is to impose liabilities: see *Tracomin SA v Anton C Nielson* [1984] 2 Lloyd's Rep 195 at 203.

[45] Consideration is founded on the exchange of mutual promises in the context of a retail sale; see Tapper, *supra*, n 18 at 287.

[46] See further Clive Gringras [1997] Int J of Law and Information Technology 77 at 89.

[47] See Gary Lea "The impossible intangible: shrink-wrap software revisited" (1996) 1(6) *Communications Law* 238 at 241.

Hence the preferred approach in English law is that when software is supplied   **10.24**
by way of licence on a physical medium (disk) and title to that medium passes,
there is both a sale/supply and a licence. As such there are effectively two
contracts—a sale/supply of goods[48] and a licence (subject to incorporation of
licence terms).[49]

A contrast is provided by *Beta Computers (Europe) v Adobe Systems*   **10.25**
(Europe) Limited,[50] the first shrink-wrap case in the United Kingdom, heard by
a Scottish Court. Briefly, the buyer (Adobe) placed a telephone order for software with the seller (Beta); and subsequently sought to return the product, arguing that there was no agreement since the seal had not been broken. Lord
Penrose agreed with the buyer and held that a contract was only concluded at
the point of breaking the seal, adopting the following classification:

> "In my opinion the only acceptable view is that the supply of proprietary software for
> a price is a contract sui generis . . . it is . . . unacceptable to analyse the transaction in
> this case as if it were two separate transactions relating to the same subject matter.
> There is but one contract".[51]

On this view, shrink-wrap contracts are characterised as a tender of software
by the supplier with an offer to complete the bargain in terms of the copyright
owner's conditions—giving the purchaser a right of election between accepting

---

[48] The sale and purchase of computer software stored in a computer disk has been held to con-
stitute a sale and supply of goods, to which the Sale of Goods Act 1979 and the Supply of Goods and
Services Act 1982 apply. See the decision of *St Albans City and District Council v International
Computers Limited* [1996] 4 All ER 481, where the Court of Appeal confirmed the first instance
analysis of limitation clauses and the application of implied terms in relation to the supply of goods.
Glidewell LJ addressed the initial question of whether software is "goods" under the Sale of Goods
Act 1979 and Supply of Goods and Services Act 1982. Section 61 Sale of Goods Act 1979 and s 18
Supply of Goods and Services Act 1982 define "goods" so as to include "all personal chattels other
than things in action and money". His Lordship stressed that it is necessary to distinguish between
the program and the disk carrying the program, and took the view that a disk would clearly fall
within this definition but a program, of itself, would not be regarded as "goods". It has to be asked
whether this distinction was material, for Glidewell LJ went on to hold that any defect in the program would amount to a defect in the disk. The implied condition of fitness for purpose, as implied
by statute, accordingly applied to the sale and supply in question. The case shows how uncomfort-
ably computer programs fit into the existing sale of goods framework, and in particular, notions of
sale and property. See Scott, "Software as "goods": nullum simile est idem" (1987) 3 CL&P 133. On
the *St Albans* case, see further Elizabeth Macdonald "The Council, the Computer and the Unfair
Contract Terms Act 1977" (1995) 58 MLR 585.

[49] Graham Smith writes: "What, then, is software? It is suggested that the answer is that at least
where it is supplied on a physical medium it should be regarded as physical property, like a book or
record, even though the nature of the contract under which it is supplied will vary, depending on the
circumstances". See Reed, *Computer Law*, 3rd edn at p 56.

[50] [1996] FSR 367. For further commentary, see Gringras "The Validity of Shrink-wrap Licences"
[1996] 4 Int J of Law and Information Technology (No 2) 77; Smith "Shrink-wrap Licensing in the
Scottish Courts" [1996] Int J of Law and Information Technology (No 2) 131; Euan Cameron
"Major Cases—the Scrutiny of Computer Contracts: At Last" (1996) 10(2) *International Review of
Law, Computers and Technology* 331.

[51] Ibid at 377. Lord Penrose took the view that the contract is not a sale of goods contract, otherwise the dominant purpose of the contract (to acquire the right to use the software) is subordinated
to the medium on which it is stored. For Graham Smith's reaction to Lord Penrose's views see Smith
[1996] 4 Int J of Law and Information Technology (No 2) 131 at 135.

the conditions that are imposed by the copyright owner, or rejecting the goods. What is encouraging is that Scottish Courts appear to endorse the view that shrink-wrap licences have legal effect[52]—at least in Scotland, and this has been heralded by one writer as reflecting commercial reality.[53] However, Lord Penrose's judgment may be validly criticised for the dogmatic view that the user of software has always to make his purchase subject to a licence to use the same,[54] and that an unconditional contract would not have given the purchaser any right to use the software.[55] This could explain the reluctance of Lord Penrose to find an agreement at the point when the telephone order was made by Adobe, since the licence terms were not known to the user at this juncture.[56]

(iii) Validating shrink-wraps under English law

10.26   The lack of privity, preventing a copyright owner from suing on a contract, should not be viewed as an obstacle to shrink-wrap validity, since copyright infringement is founded upon the lack of authorisation, regardless of contract. The more pertinent issue is one of incorporation, whether licence terms have been brought sufficiently to the notice of the user, alongside his contract of sale or otherwise.

10.27   A number of practical solutions have been offered.[57] For example, incorporating in a registration card which normally contains "user group" benefits (such as free upgrades, magazines, promotional offers , etc) a statement that the purchaser has seen, read and agrees to be bound by the terms of the licence; or alternatively, the adoption of shrink-wrap terms "as a practice of the trade" for the purposes of implying terms.[58]

---

[52] Lord Penrose relied on the Scottish exception to privity—*ius quaesitum tertio*, which gives a right to the copyright owner (non-contracting party) to adopt the contract between end-user and supplier, and sue on it. The closest English law comes to this doctrine is the principle in *St Martin's Property v MacAlpine* [1993] 3 WLR 408. Here the House of Lords accepted that a party to an English contract, who had purported but failed to assign the benefit of the contract to a third party, could recover damages suffered by that third party as a result of defective performance on the contract. It has been offered as a solution to validate shrink-wraps under English law (Bainbridge [1996] 12 CLSR 310), but arguably is limited, since the copyright owner does not acquire direct rights under the contract, and has to rely on the seller to sue on his behalf. The seller's's concern does not normally venture beyond the purchase price.

[53] See Bainbridge *Software Copyright Law*, 3rd edn (1997) at p 216.

[54] In particular, see Smith, *supra*, n 51 at 143 *et seq*.

[55] Lord Penrose took the view that there was a need to incorporate licence conditions in the interests of the software industry and the legislative policy of the CDPA (*supra*, n 50 at 377–380). It should be said his Lordship obviously adopted the concerted view of both parties, accepting in their pleadings that it is standard practice for manufacturers to include in packaged software end-user licence conditions (*supra*, n 50 at 378). One wonders whether this view truly reflects commercial reality, since much computer software, such as computer games, is already supplied without any attempt to lay down licence conditions.

[56] The situation would be different if a course of dealing could be established prior to a telephone order, in which case the licence conditions may be implied.

[57] See eg Goodger, "Beta Plus for Effort: Beta Minus for Clarity?" [1996] 11 EIPR 636.

[58] Ibid at 637. Courts will invariably accept shrink-wrap practice; see eg the licence in *Microsoft v Electrowide* [1997] FSR 580, which was completed on shrink-wrap terms and upheld.

Michael Silverleaf QC has suggested the following approach towards vali- **10.28** dating shrink-wrap licences under English law: such a contract may be regarded as concluded when the sale is made, but subject to an implied term permitting the customer to reject the software within a reasonable time if he does not wish to agree to the terms of the licence conditions.[59] Two questions arise with this approach. First it is not clear whether such an implied term would be upheld in an English court and the question turns on whether it is essential to lend business efficacy to a commercial transaction, bearing in mind that a term cannot be implied merely because to do so would appear reasonable in all the circumstances.[60] Secondly, the question still remains as to how the rightholder enforces his licence terms; and this would be determined by whether the rightholder was regarded as a party to the contract of sale (subject to proper incorporation), or whether the licence forms a separate contract.

Whilst the *Beta* judgment should be commended for bringing to the fore many **10.29** of the legal issues concerning shrink-wrap licences, and for the ultimate validation of the same through the imaginative invocation of the doctrine of *ius quaesitum tertio* under Scots law, it provides, at best, limited assistance to an English Court deciding the validity of such a licence.

Quite apart from the contract of sale, if the terms and conditions of the **10.30** licence governing software use are sufficiently brought to the notice of the buyer, he will be taken to have accepted them on the breaking of the seal or undertaking whatever steps necessary to show the manifestation of assent.[61] In this situation the Court may create a contractual licence on these terms.

If on the other hand, the terms are not brought to the user's notice, or he **10.31** breaks open a software package not having read the terms of the licence, then these terms would not have been incorporated, and it is argued that his "use" rights over the software are governed by section 50C CDPA, with the contractual provisions fettering such rights being implied in the circumstances, subject to the CDPA provisions against exclusory contract.

(d) Buyer's Remedies against the Software Supplier

In the situation where the buyer acquires a computer program, and upon break- **10.32** ing the seal, discovers that he is bound by overly restrictive terms, he may arguably sue his supplier for breach of conditions of sale implied by the Sale of Goods Act 1979. Quite apart from the condition as to merchantable quality and

---

[59] See Silverleaf, "Beta v Adobe" *Commercial Lawyer* (February 1996) at 7.

[60] See *Hamlyn v Wood* [1891] 2 QB 499 at 491.

[61] Compare the position in Netherlands, where under Dutch law, shrink-wrap licences may be enforceable provided that users are aware of their existence and terms before an agreement is formed. See *Coss Holland BV v TM Data BV Computerecht* 1997/2, pp 63–65. See further Grosheide, "Shrink wrap License" WPNR 1997/6260, pp 153–54. See *infra*, para 10.36, for a discussion on enhancing the enforceability of licence conditions.

fitness for purpose,[62] section 12 implies a condition that in a sale, the seller has a right to sell the goods. Typically the power to confer title is concurrent with the right to sell, but an exceptional situation arises where the seller has the power to confer good title on a buyer, but no "right to sell" the goods.[63] In *Niblett v Confectioners' Materials*,[64] the defendant, a US company, sold 3,000 tins of preserved milk to the plaintiffs. When the goods arrived in England they were detained by customs authorities on the ground that their labels infringed the trade mark of a well-known English company. It was held that since the English company could have obtained an injunction to restrain the sale, the defendant had no right to sell them. Similarly, a software user may be able to argue that the supply of software, which, without further agreement with the copyright owner, could not be used without infringing copyright, would be in similar breach of the term implied by section 12.[65]

10.33 The buyer may also wish to bring a restitutionary claim against the supplier, on the ground of a total failure of consideration.[66] He would face difficulties, since technically he had received good title to the physical disk containing the software.

(e) Shrink-Wrap Licences in the USA: possible application?

(i) Case law in the USA

10.34 Several US courts[67] have considered the validity of shrink-wrap licences. In the earliest case to analyse the enforceabilityof shrink-wrap licences, the Fifth Circuit in *Vault v Quaid*[68] held that such licences are unenforceable as "contracts of adhesion".[69] In *Step-Saver DataSystems v Wyse Technology*[70] the Third Circuit reached a view that a shrink-wrap licence was unenforceable because the bargain between the publisher and end-user had already been made before the end-user saw the licence.[71] More recently, in *ProCD v*

---

[62] See s 14 Sale of Goods Act 1979.
[63] Atiyah, *Sale of Goods*, 8th edn (1990) at p 85.
[64] [1921] 3 KB 387.
[65] However, such an argument is an extension of *Niblett*, since it is a situation where goods (software) are in fact obtained (unlike in *Niblett*), but where the end-user is restricted as to activities which may be performed in relation to the goods—arguably a lesser impediment.
[66] eg *Rowland v Duvall* [1923] 2 KB 500.
[67] *Step Saver Data Systems v Wyse Technology and the Software Link* 939 F.2d 91 (3rd Cir 1991); *Arizona Retail Systems Inc v The Software Link Inc* 831 F.Supp 759 (D.Ariz 1993); *Vault Corporation v Quaid Software Ltd* 857 F.2d 255 (5th Cir 1988); and most recently, *ProCD v Mathew Zeidenberg* 908 F.Supp 640 rev'd 86 F.3d1447 (7th Cir 1996). For a more detailed discussion, see Gringras [1996] 4 Int J of Law and Information Technology 77 at 99 *et seq.*
[68] *Supra*, n 67.
[69] *Supra*, n 67 at 269–270. "Contracts of adhesion" are described as contracts which are offered on a non-negotiable"take it or leave it" basis, by a party in a superior bargaining postion.
[70] *Supra*, n 67.
[71] *Supra*, n 67 at 103. The Third Circuit applied Art 2–207 of the Uniform Commercial Code ("Battle of the Forms" provision) to reach the view that the shrink-wrap licence was not part of the

Zeidenberg[72] (4 January 1996) a Federal Court in Wisconsin ruled that a shrink-wrap agreement contained in CD-ROM telephone directory packages was not binding under the US Uniform Commercial Code.[73] This was subsequently overturned on appeal.[74] In upholding the validity of shrink-wrap licences under the Code, Judge Easterbrook noted that "[t]ransactions in which the exchange of money precedes the communication of detailed terms are common in transactions such as insurance contracts, movie tickets, and airline tickets . . . a buyer may accept by performing the acts the vendor proposes to treat as acceptance. And that is what happened".[75] The facts supporting this ruling merit attention.

In *ProCD* the defendant made data from the plaintiff's proprietary **10.35** "SelectPhoneTM"database (including a comprehenseive national telephone listing of more than 95 million telephone listings from more than 3,000 telephone directories) available over the Internet. This was contrary to the terms of a shrink-wrap licence that was included *inside* the packaging, and the plaintiff placed a notice on the outside of the box stating that the use of the database was subject to the terms and conditions of the enclosed licence, which provided, inter alia, for a "home use" restriction.[76] The CD-ROM disks were also encoded such that the licence would appear on the screen and the user was not permitted to proceed until he indicated his acceptance of the licence terms. The user was provided with a right of refusal if the terms of the enclosed licence was thought to be objectionable. The licence, as prescribed, was held enforceable, the Court reasoning that the defendant had ample notice that the purchase was subject to licence terms, and was given an opportunity to review and reject it.[77] The Court observed that as in other transactions where the exchange of money occurs before the communication of the detailed terms, the defendant accepted the contract by using the software after having had the opportunity to read and reject the shrink-wrap licence.[78]

---

contract established between the parties. The publisher "did not clearly express its unwillingness to proceed with the transaction undless its additional terms were incorporated into the parties' agreement".

[72] *Supra*, n 67. It is significant that *ProCD* is the first decision to directly consider the enforceability of shrink-wrap licences.

[73] *ProCD v Zeidenberg* 908 F.Supp 640 at 655–656. The District Court discussed the then-proposed Art 2–2203 of the Uniform Commercial Code (discussion draft of 10 September 1994) which provided for the validation of shrink-wrap licences subject to proper review and manifest assent by the consumer. The Court considered the proposal as evidence that shrink-wraps licences were invalid under current law, otherwise the proposed change would have been unnecessary.

[74] 86 F.3d 1447 (7th Cir 1996). See further, Joseph Wang "ProCD Inc v Zeidenberg and Article 2B: Finally, the Validation of Shrink-Wrap Licences" (1997) 15 J of Computer & Information Law 439 at 448–453.

[75] *ProCD, supra*, n 73 at 1451–1452.

[76] cf para 10.15.

[77] *ProcD, supra*, n 73 at 1450–1453.

[78] Ibid, at 1452. Interestingly, the Judge said in obiter that if the defendant had opened the package and found the terms of the licence to be objectionable, he could have prevented the formation of the contract by simply returning the product and having his money refunded. This would not be the position under English law.

10.36   *ProCD* does emphasise one feature of enforceability of mass market licences which this work has tried to emphasise—the proper incorporation of licence terms.[79] Particularly for software that is distributed over the Internet, the best approach appears to be the "click-on" licence, which requires that the consumer register his or her acceptance to the terms of the licence on the screen before being permitted to use the software. As in *ProCD*, the click-on method can also be used for software distributed through the post, from a retail store, or pre-installed in a personal computer. It may be the most effective method of incorporation—instead of the ambiguous conduct of simply refraining from returning software or other uncertain action the user clicks on a box on the screen stating that he or she accepts the terms of the shrink-wrap licence.[80]

10.37   Ultimately English courts should exercise due caution if and when they choose to import the reasoning in US cases. There are substantial differences between the USA and the United Kingdom concerning the governance of mass-market licences, most notably the copyright preemption doctrine,[81] copyright misuse doctrine,[82] state legislative efforts aimed at dealing with shrink-wrap validity,[83] the originally mooted implementation of a new Article 2B to the Uniform Commercial Code, and most recently, the Draft Uniform Computer Information Transactions Act 1999 ("Draft UCITA").[84]

---

[79] *Supra*, paras 10.30–10.31.

[80] See Moore, Hadden, "On-Line Software Distribution: New Life for 'Shrinkwrap' Licences?" *The Computer Lawyer* (April 1996); Ramos, Verdon "Shrinking and Click-on Licences after ProCD v Zeidenberg" *The Computer Lawyer* (September 1996) 1 at 5.

[81] See s 301 US Copyright Act 1976. Preemption is a doctrine which limits state law analogues to Federal property rights in the interests of conformity. See US Supreme Court decisions *Sears and Roebuck* 376 US 225 (1904); *Compco Corp v Day Bite* 376 US 234 (1964); *Bonito Boats v Thundercraft Boats* 489 US 141 (1989). The doctrine has been argued to extend to ubiquitous contractual restrictions on reverse engineering and fair use. See David Rice "Public Goods, Private Contract and Public Policy: Federal Preemption of Software Licence Prohibitions against Reverse Engineering" (1992) 53 U.Pitt L. Rev 543; Merges (1995) 93 Mich. L Rev (essentially arguing that a dominant contract form can operate as a form of private legislation which restricts federal rights as much as state law); Friederick Kessler "Contracts of adhesion—some thoughts about the Freedom of Contract" (1943) 43 Colum L Rev 629 (defining the notion of "private legislation" in the context of adhesion contracts); Maureen O'Rouke "Drawing the Boundary between Copyright and Contract: Copyright Preemption of Software Licence Terms" (1995) 45 Duke LJ 479 at 557. For the application of the preemption doctrine to shrink-wrap licences, see *Vault v Quaid* (*supra*, n 67 at 270) and *ProCD v Mathew Zeidenberg* (ibid at 1455).

[82] *Lasercomb American Inc v Reynolds* 911 F.2d 970 at 978 (4th Cir 1990). In England there is a statutory provision for intervention by the Minister to impose compulsory licences in cases of abuse: see s 144(1) CDPA. But it is not clear how this limited power might be used and its very existence militates against the idea that there is some more extensive power inherent in the common law.

[83] In the 1980s the states of Illinois and Louisiana passed Software License Enforcement Acts which made licences take effect, subject to their provisions, as contracts. Both Acts were ultimately undone; Louisiana's by virtue of preemption under Federal law (following *Vault v Quaid*, *supra*, n 67) and Illinois' by appeal. For a historical account charting the failure of state shrink-wrap legislation, see Kaufman, "The enforceability of State 'shrink wrap' licence statutes in *Vault Corp v Quaid Software*" (1988) 74 Cornell Law Rev 222.

[84] Drafted by the National Conference of Commissioners on Uniform State Laws, Denver, Colorado, 23–30 July 1999.

(ii) Draft UCITA: the enforceability of mass market licences

The Draft UCITA is the latest attempt of US legislators to implement a uniform **10.38**
state law applicable to transactions in computer software and other forms of
digital information. The last few years of debate over the proposed Article 2B to
the Uniform Commercial Code[85] has finally given rise to a separate Federal draft
law, sanctioning, inter alia, mass market informational licensing[86] in the electronic age.[87] Section 211 of the latest Draft UCITA provides:

"(a)   A party adopts the terms of a mass-market license . . . only if the party agrees
       to the license, by manifesting assent or otherwise, before or during the party's
       initial performance or use of or access to the information . . .

(b)   If a licensee does not have an opportunity to review a mass-market license or a
       copy of it before becoming obligated to pay and does not agree, by manifesting
       assent or otherwise, to the license after having that opportunity, the licensee is
       entitled to a return. . .and, in addition, to:

       (1)   reimbursement of any reasonable expenses incurred in complying with
             the licensor's instructions for return or destruction of the computer infor-
             mation or, in the absence of instructions, incurred for return postage or
             similar reasonable expense in returning it; and

       (2)   compensation for any reasonable and foreseeable costs of restoring the
             licensee's information processing system to reverse changes in the system
             caused by the installation".

Section 211 provides for the enforceability of shrink-wrap licences, and protects the licensee, by providing for "manifesting assent"[88] and remedies (reim-
bursement of expenses and restoration costs) if he is deprived of an opportunity
to review the licence.

The validity of the shrink-wrap licences in the USA will be put beyond all **10.39**
doubt in the future implementation of Draft UCITA. From a conflict of laws
perspective, if US law is the stated choice of law and English Courts chose to
apply it, under the Uniform Computer Information Transactions Act (if

---

[85] For an instructive guide on the various view points to date, see "Symposium: Intellectual
Property and Contract Law in the Information Age: The Impact of Article 2B of the Uniform
Commercial Code on the Future of Transactions in Information and Electronic Commerce" (1998)
13(3) Berkeley Technology L J 809. One of the most important concerns was how Article 2B's provisions allowed software developers unilaterally to impose restictive terms (which were enforced if
assented to) which circumvented public policy limitations imposed by copyright law. It has been
argued that this state of affairs has been perpetuated by the *ProCD* decision, since copyright policy
was not held in that case to override the restricitve condition within the licence: Samuelson, "Does
Information Really Have to be Licensed?" 41(9) *Communications of the ACM* (September 1998) 15
at 16–17.

[86] The paradigm transaction contemplated by the Draft UCITA is a licence of computer information, rather than a sale of goods.

[87] See George Graff "The Evolution of the Uniform Computer Information Transactions Act"
Vol 14(2) *Computer Law Association Bulletin* 47.

[88] A manifestation of assent requires conduct, including a failure to act, or statements, indicating
assent and that the person has reason to know that, in the circumstances, this will be the case: s 112
Draft UCITA.

enacted), a shrink-wrap licence could potentially bind an English software user.[89]

III. IMPLIED LICENCES AND USERS' RIGHTS IN SOFTWARE TRANSACTIONS

10.40 This section analyses the relevance of implied licences to software copyright law under Anglo-Commonwealth law.[90] This analysis is derived from a general template of how implied licences arise generally (notably in relation to parallel importation), and their relevance to patent and copyright laws. There is also a recent case in Singapore which addressed the question of the implied licence and the extent to which it could be argued as a defence to *primary infringement*,[91] an argument which may be of relevance to UK copyright jurisprudence in the future. This section proposes to analyse how and to what extent the implied licence may be used as a vehicle for eroding the primary rights of the copyright owner.

(a) Implied Licences: General Principles

10.41 In cases where a work is made by an independent contractor to be used by another for certain purposes, in circumstances where the copyright is retained by the author, some licence to use the work must be implied in favour of the latter if the contract governing the transaction is silent on this point. In such a situation, the general principle to be applied is:

> "the engagement for reward of a person to produce material of a nature which is capable of being the subject of copyright implies a permission, or consent, or licence in the person giving the engagement to use the material in the manner and for the purpose in which and for which it was contemplated between the parties that it would be used at the time of the engagement".[92]

---

[89] See further Gringras [1996] 4 Int J of Law and Information Technology 77 at 104–109.

[90] The author takes the view that a comparison with US law in the area of implied licences presents little if any utility, largely due to the differences in the latter's first sale doctrine and anti-trust legislation. This is perhaps reflected in similar comparisons drawn in the arena of parallel imports, where it has been observed that "[t]here is no consistency in approach across the different categories of intellectual property, nor is there much coherence in the treatment of parallel imports involving the same subject matter. Different countries purporting to apply the same legal principles also often arrive at completely contradictory results". See Rothnie, *Parallel Imports* (1993), ch 5 . In addition, US courts also impose a "constructive implied licence" as a matter of law, as seen in *Sega v Accolade* (District Court). See further Stern "An ill-conceived analysis of reverse engineering of software as copyright infringement: Sega Enterprises v Accolade" [1992] 11 EIPR 407 at 410.

[91] *Creative Technology v Aztech*, *infra*, at para 10.63 *et seq.*

[92] See *Beck v Montana Constructions Pty Ltd* (1963) 80 WN (NSW) 1578 at 1581–1582, approved by the UK Court of Appeal in *Blair v Osborne & Tomkins* [1971] 2 QB 78. See also *Redwood v Chappell & Co.* [1982] RPC 109 at 128 (per Goff J: "The test to be applied . . . [is] an objective one . . . whether viewing the facts objectively, the words and conduct of the alleged licensor, as made known to the alleged licensee, in fact indicated that the licensor consented to what the licensee was doing").

In *Acohs v Bashord* (Fed Court, Australia), Meckel J, applying the above proposition, stated that if copyright material is prepared for a particular purpose, then there is an implied permission, consent or licence to use that material to carry out that purpose. This purpose is to be determined objectively, by reference to the contract entered into by the parties, and the factual matrix in which the transaction took place.[93]

Copinger and Skone James have stated that the implied licence extends no **10.42** further than to that which is necessary to give business efficacy to a contract, and to allow use of the work for the purposes which were in contemplation of both parties at the time the contract was made, but no further.[94]

For the purposes of copyright, the question to settle is: *what is the extent of* **10.43** *permitted use?* It is debatable whether a user's implied right can go beyond mere access to cover otherwise infringing acts, for example, printing or downloading material.[95] This question is addressed below, by reference to the development of the "implied licence" in patent and copyright laws.

(b) Implied Licences and Patent Law: *Betts v Willmott*

Section 60(1) Patents Act 1977 defines what constitutes infringement under **10.44** patent law:

> "(1)   Subject to the provisions of this section, a person infringes a patent for an invention if, and only if, while the patent is in force, he does any of the following things in the United Kingdom in relation to the invention *without the consent of the proprietor of the patent*, that is to say:
> (a)   where the invention is a product, he makes, disposes of, offers to dispose of, uses or imports the product or keeps it whether for disposal or otherwise; . . ."
> (emphasis added)

---

[93] *Acohs v Brashford* (1997) 144 ALR 528 at 548 (Fed Court, Australia). In this case the defendants counter-claimed against the plaintiffs, alleging copyright infringement in respect of the reproduction of 43 material safety data sheets (MSDSs). The Court took the view that these MSDSs were prepared by the defendants with the intention that they be used for a particular purpose—the provision of ready access of the information contained in the MSDSs for safety-related purposes. In this situation the law implies a licence to the MSDSs to carry out these purposes. In the regulatory and factual matrix, the Court found that it was within the parties' contemplation that MSDSs commissioned by manufacturers and importers were to be made available and accessible at workplaces through various means.

[94] See *Copinger and Skone James on Copyright*, 13th edn (1991) at para 8–147, and references cited therein. See also *Codelfa Construction v State Railway Authority of New South Wales* (1982) 149 CLR 337 at 345–346 (per Mason J); discussed in *Castlemaine Tooheys Ltd v Carlton & United Breweries Ltd* (1987) 10 NSWLR 468 at 486–487; *Devefi v Mateffy Perl Nagy* (1993) 113 ALR 225 at 240. See also the two-part test discussed in *Trumpet Software v OzEmail* (1996) 34 IPR 481 at 500, in relation to shareware: (i) whether the supposed condition is necessary to give business efficacy, in the light of the fundamental purpose of shareware, which is that of evaluation, and (ii) whether it is so obvious that it "goes without saying" (*following BP Refinery (Westernport) v Shire of Hastings* (1977) 180 CLR 266 at 283).

[95] See Hector MacQueen "Copyright and the Internet" in Edwards, Waelde (eds) *Laws and the Internet—Regulating Cyberspace* (1997) at pp 89–91.

A question which has derived from this broad provision is the extent to which a patentee can continue to control dealings in a patented article after it has been sold. In relation to a domestic sale, it has been held by the Privy Council in *National Phonograph Co. of Australia v Menck*[96] that a purchaser of a patented article will not be bound by any restrictions on its use unless the restrictions be brought home to the purchaser before the purchase is completed.[97] Lord Shaw justified this proposition by reference to the all-important 1871 decision of *Betts v Willmott*. As this case has come to adopt a wider significance, its facts merit discussion.

10.45   In *Betts*[98] the owner of an English patent (for metallic capsules of tin and lead compressed together so as to seal corks into bottles) manufactured the article in England, and in France through an agent. The agent had been instructed not to sell any articles for export to England since the owner intended exclusive domestic production for the English market. The owner discovered the defendant, Willmott using the articles in England. Willmott had acquired them from a wholesaler who did not buy the articles from the owner in England. The owner, Betts, failed in his suit because, inter alia, he was unable to prove that the use or sale in England was unauthorised—Willmott successfully raised the possibility that the articles were manufactured and acquired in France. It was held by Lord Hatherley LC:

> "When a man has purchased an article he expects to have control of it, and there must be some clear and explicit agreement to the contrary to justify the vendor in saying that he has not given the purchaser his licence to sell the article, or to use it wherever he pleases as against himself. He cannot use it against a previous assignee of the patent, but he can use it against the person who himself is proprietor of the patent, and has the power of conferring a complete right on him by the sale of the article".[99]

In *Betts* the patentee could not argue the territoriality of his English patent in order to enjoin the defendant's use of a lawfully acquired article in France.[100] The case was decided as a matter of general commercial convenience,[101] given the breadth of a patent owner's exclusive rights (including use and disposal).[102] Commercial convenience and the normal expectations of purchasing goods led to *the implication of consent in the absence of any explicit agreement to the contrary*. In this situation the territorial nature of the patent is rendered in abeyance.[103]

[96] See *National Phonograph Co. Australia v Menck* [1911] AC 336 (PC).
[97] Ibid at 353–354. See also the judgment of Wills J in *Incandescent Gas Light Co. v Cantelo* 12 Rep. Pat. Cas 262.
[98] Ibid. See *Betts v Willmott* (1871) LR 6 Ch 239.
[99] (1871) LR 6 Ch at 245.
[100] In the words of the patentee's counsel: "if it was made by the Plaintiff's agent abroad, that fact would not legalize its sale in this country, in violation of the English patent" (1871) LR 6 Ch at 242; see also the report of Bett's evidence under cross-examination, ibid at 241.
[101] See Rothnie, *Parallel Imports*, *supra*, n 90 at p 128.
[102] In the twentieth century this is reflected in s 60 Patents Act, *supra*, para 10.43.
[103] This is to be contrasted with the situation when the importer is a licensee of a foreign patent, in which case territoriality prevails; see *Glaces v Tilghman's* (1833) 53 ChD 1 at 8; cf the

As the following sections illustrate, this principle has wandered into the field   **10.46**
of copyright.

(c) Implied Licences and Copyright Law

(i) Generally

Implied licences undoubtedly have a place in copyright law;[104] as evident from   **10.47**
the example when a letter is written to a newspaper with a view to publication—
since copyright remains with the writer, a licence to publish is clearly implied.[105]
The implied licence has gained prominence in the domain of parallel importation, notably, as a defence of consent to secondary infringement. This is discussed in the next section.

(ii) Copyright and parallel importation: the importation of Betts v Willmott

A detailed analysis of how the CDPA can be used to deal with parallel importa-   **10.48**
tion lies outside this work. Generally there are two options[106] available to the
copyright owner. The first is by way of sections 22–23 CDPA; the other option
is holding the parallel importer liable for the primary infringement of the distribution right.[107] The latter is useful in a situation when the mens rea of the defendant cannot be sufficiently ascertained for the purposes of sections 22–23
CDPA.

For the purposes of the present discussion, the *Betts v Willmott* principle has   **10.49**
been raised in relation to sections 22–23 CDPA. As identified by Laddie, *et al*,
two lines of defence[108] are available to the parallel importer who is sued under
these provisions: (i) did the conduct of the UK copyright owner, his licensee or
agent create an implied licence, in respect of the transaction now complained;
and (ii) was the article an "infringing copy" as defined by section 27 CDPA. The
latter, which involves a study of the merits of the "hypothetical manufacturing
requirement",[109] is not relevant for present purposes. However, (i) raises the
issue of the copyright owner's implied consent.

---

interpretation of this case given by Laddie, *et al*, *Modern Law of Copyright and Designs*, Vol 1 at
para 18.19, n 3. For general exposition on the impact of the sale of products marketed abroad, see
Vitoria, *et al*, *Encyclopaedia of United Kingdom and European Patent Law*, Vol 1 at para 4–304; see
also Cornish, *Intellectual Property*, 3rd edn (1995) at para 6–15.

[104] *Supra*, n 4.
[105] For other examples of implied licences in copyright law, see *Copinger and Skone James on
Copyright*, 13th edn (1991) at para 8–158.
[106] See Laddie *et al*, *supra*, n 103 at para 18.15.
[107] See s 18 CDPA.
[108] See Laddie, *et al*, *supra*, n 103 at para 18.18.
[109] For further exposition see Laddie, *et al*, *supra*, n 103 at para 18.27 *et seq*; Rothnie, *Parallel
Imports*, *supra*, n 90 at p 199 *et seq*.

10.50   It is at this juncture that writers have sought to import the principle in *Betts v Willmott* into copyright law.[110] Laddie, *et al* have strenuously argued *Betts* to be applicable as a principle of general law—in the nature of an estoppel[111] and as a "rule of reason",[112] and not one that is peculiar to the law of patents as such.[113] In their view, the correct test in relation to implied licences in copyright law depends on the answer to the following question:

> "having regard to the conduct of the plaintiff or his privies, would a reasonable man believe he was getting a right to re-sell in the home market?"[114]

10.51   The process of extending the application of *Betts v Willmott* to copyright begins with the distinction between copyright and patent laws.

(iii)   Time Life v Interstate Parcel Express

10.52   These differences came to light in the High Court of Australia's decision of *Time-Life International v Interstate Parcel Express Co.*[115] The plaintiff was a wholly owned subsidiary of Time Inc, and was appointed the exclusive licensee throughout the world (apart from the USA and Canada) for its copyrights in various literary works. Experiencing difficulties with obtaining supplies from Time-Life, the defendant procured shipments of the books in the USA (from a wholesaler who did not impose any restrictions at the point of sale) and sold the books in Australia at a competitive price.

10.53   The plaintiff sued for infringement of its Australian copyright in the books by import and sale. The defendant made two primary arguments: (i) it had the right to import the books as an implied term of the contract of sale; and (ii) by analogy with the law of patents and *Betts*, that an unrestricted sale carried with it the right to import the books into Australia. Both grounds were rejected by the High Court. Argument (i) failed because it was unnecessary to lend business efficacy to the contract in question.

10.54   Stephen J rejected the analogy with patent law by raising its differences with copyright, in that the sale of a copy of the work involves no retention by the copyright owner of any rights over the use and subsequent dealings in it.[116] Gibbs J also adopted a similar course in rejecting the defendant's arguments.[117] Both judges agreed that the need for the implied licence in patent law did not exist in copyright because the exclusive rights conferred on the patentee included the power to control and prohibit dealing in the patented article even after sale.

---

[110] Most notably, Laddie, *et al, supra*, n 103.

[111] Ibid at para 18.19.

[112] Ibid at para 18.21.

[113] Ibid at para 18.22.

[114] Ibid at para 18.21.

[115] (1977) 138 CLR 534.

[116] Ibid at 549–553. Without an implied licence, a purchaser might not lawfully put patented goods to use, in the absence of express restriction at the point of sale.

[117] Ibid at 542–543.

The reasoning of *Time-Life* has since been adopted in numerous other cases[118] (and in one case to an inconvenient result),[119] including the English Court of Appeal in the case of *Polydor Ltd v Harlequin Record Shop*.[120] In this case it was held that Harlequin had infringed Polydor's rights as an exclusive licensee in the United Kingdom of copyright in certain sound recordings. Consent from the licensee was absent, and Templeman LJ relied on the *Time-Life* decision to advance the proposition that the necessary consent could not be implied from the unrestricted sale of sound recordings in Portugal by Portuguese licensees (associated with Polydor).[121] **10.55**

The rejection of a *Betts v Willmott* defence in the *Time-Life* case has been criticised by Laddie, *et al* as a case of "making an invalid induction", in that either the copyright owner was somehow retaining a "power" over the copy in respect of future dealings (thus justifying the application of *Betts*) or he could not succeed. However, sections 22–23, 27 CDPA clearly apply to parallel importation, and regulate subsequent sales. **10.56**

With respect this ignores the fundamental and valid distinction drawn in the *Time-Life* case, between the exclusive rights which are provided under the two regimes; and in particular, that copyright, by its statutory definition, does not embrace subsequent sale (except for pirated copies, subject to the finding of mens rea) and use.[122] Even if the *Betts* principle was applied to copyright, such an application is only about implied intent, which a copyright owner can displace simply by giving adequate notice of restrictions against transfers between **10.57**

---

[118] See decision by the Full Federal Court in *Computermate Products (Aust) Pty Ltd v Ozi-Soft Ltd* (1988) 12 IPR 87; also *Star Micronics v Five-Star Computers* (1990) 18 IPR 225 at 230 (decision of Davies J, Federal Court). More recently, see the decision of the Singapore Court of Appeal decision in *Creative Technology v Aztech Systems* [1997] FSR 491 at 505–508. cf the Canadian case of *North American Systemshops v King* [1992] 27 CPR (3d) 367, which adopts a disturbingly broad proposition: "the sale by the plaintiff of its product over the counter constitutes the implied granting by the plaintiff of an implied permission to the purchaser to do whatever the purchaser wished with the product" (at 376).

[119] See *Bailey v Boccaccio Pty Ltd* (1986) 6 IPR 279 (NSW), where trade mark and copyright infringement was asserted against the sale of parallel imports of *Bailey's Irish Cream*. The plaintiffs succeeded on the ground of copyright infringement in respect of the bottle's label design, even though under trade mark law they failed in respect of the same. Laddie, Prescott and Vitoria make much of this as an adverse consequence of the "*Time-Life* doctrine"; see Laddie, *et al, supra*, n 103 at para 18.21. It is however submitted that legislative intervention is the best means of avoiding a similar situation, where copyright law is seen as undermining trade mark law. See further the recommendations in the Report of the Copyright Law Review Committee, *The Importation of the Copyright Act 1968* (AGPS, Canberra, 1 September 1988), at pp 3–7. The Australian Government announced on 18 March 1992 that it would amend the Copyright Act to prevent the use of packaging copyright to protect exclusive distribution and importation. See further Lahore, *Intellectual Property Law in Australia: Copyright* (Law Book Company, Looseleaf) at para 4.11.457 *et seq.*

[120] [1980] FSR 362.

[121] Ibid at 365–366. Laddie, *et al*, try to distinguish this case by arguing that a *Betts* defence was not advanced, since the whole issue turned on the presence or absence of consent; thus *Polydor* is no authority on the point; see Laddie *et al, supra*, n 103 at para 18.22, n 2. This is arguably a distinction without a difference, since consent is the reflection of a licence (express or implied), and Templeman LJ did consider *Betts v Willmott* themes within the *Time-Life* case.

[122] On the other hand the argument could be made that since copyright does not embrace their subsequent sale and use, the implied permission should arguably be stronger, cf *Time-Life*.

national markets.[123] If the objective is to increase the tolerance for parallel importation, surely the means were ill-conceived. Thus the effect of adopting a *Betts* principle for copyright would be, at best, to require a copyright owner to place an express restriction, in order to prevent parallel importation. This is conceded by Laddie, *et al*,[124] who also accept that the *Betts* principle cannot be "blindly carried over to copyright law without reflecting on the different nature of subject matter".[125] The case for importing *Betts v Willmott* into copyright law is evidently not without restrictions and uncertainty.

10.58   Notwithstanding the above-expressed reservations about importing *Betts v Willmott* into the field of copyright law, there may be a hint that increasing use is being made of the *Betts* argument, *outside* the parallel importation context.[126] The following subsection considers further extensions, particularly where, in the context of primary infringement of software copyright, the implied licence may, if taken too far, override the exclusive rights of the copyright owner.

(d) Further Extensions of the *Betts v Willmott* Principle

10.59   In at least two specific examples, the *Betts*-originated implied licence has come to encroach upon the primary rights of a copyright owner.

(i) Software licensing

10.60   In respect of the enforceability of software licences under English law, Smith has suggested, in response to the *Beta v Adobe* decision,[127] that Lord Penrose appeared to take the view that when a copyrighted article is sold the contract is not complete until the terms of a licence are agreed. It was suggested that the software contract could have been concluded at the time the telephone order was made, and that in reality such a contract is complete when it is made and there are no express licence terms unless these are introduced at the time the contract is made. An analogy has been drawn with the sale of patented articles in cases like *Betts v Willmott*.[128] In this situation two distinctions fail to be made.

---

[123] See the view taken by Professor Cornish, *Intellectual Property*, 3rd edn (1995) at para 12–15, especially n 46 where it is remarked: "With a bit of effort any producer in the know could thus prevent parallel imports". See however, *Roussel Velat v Hockley* [1996] RPC 441.

[124] See Laddie, *et al*, *supra*, n 103 at para 18.23.

[125] Ibid at para 18.22

[126] There has been a recent British extension of the "Betts" license in the area of trade mark exhaustion in the context of parallel importation. In *Zino Davidoff SA v A & G Imports Limited* [1999] 3 All ER 711, a trade mark infringement action involved the parallel importation of above name into the UK even outside the EEA. Laddie J took the view that under English law, although a trade mark owner does not automatically exhaust its European trade mark rights by putting goods on the market outside the EEA, the trade mark owner can be held to have impliedly consented to the goods calling into the EEA if it sold goods to the purchaser without restricting the rights on where they may be sold (whether by markings or any notice) (ibid at p 722–3).

[127] Discussed *supra*, at para 10.25.

[128] See Graham Smith, "Shrink-wrap licensing in the Scottish Courts" [1996] 4 Int J of Law and Information Technology (No 2) 131 at 145.

The first is separating the contract of sale from the software licence itself. **10.61**
This distinction was one that Lord Penrose unfortunately did not choose to
draw in *Beta v Adobe*, in preference of a *sui generis* classification. However if
this argument were to be accepted, it is inconceivable that a shrink-wrap or
other licence can ever be enforceable, save in the situation where the licence
terms are incorporated at the time when an order for particular software is
made to a supplier or retailer, through whatever medium. This is hardly a reflection of commercial reality. The consequence of adopting such a view would be
that software developers will be anxious to impose express conditions to bind
users at the earliest opportunity.

Secondly, this analysis does not recognise the all-important difference **10.62**
between patent and copyright, alluded to above.[129] However it is arguable that
computer programs by their nature provide greater impetus to draw analogies
with patent law, since mere use (loading in RAM or ROM) does amount to an
infringement of the reproduction right. Notwithstanding this similarity, it is
submitted that this difference (owing to the nature of the subject-matter) is not
sufficient to override the larger differences in the statutory rights which are provided under the patent and copyright regimes. In any event the Software
Directive has also acknowledged this feature of computer software by providing for the necessary users' rights in Artcle 5.

(ii) Rights of disassembly/testing in Singapore

The "*Betts v Willmott* implied licence" featured in a recent software copyright **10.63**
decision from Singapore: *Creative Technology v Aztech Systems*.[130] In this case
Creative Technology alleged first, that Aztech Systems had disassembled the
firmware of Creative's Sound Blaster Card; and secondly, that the admitted
copying by Aztech of the software which accompanied the Soundblaster, TEST-
SBC,[131] for testing and analysis amounted to copyright infringement.[132] On the
first issue the Court of Appeal reversed the factual findings of the trial judge,[133]

---

[129] See discussion of the *Time-Life* case, *supra*, paras 10.52–10.57.

[130] [1997] 1 SLR 621 (Singapore Court of Appeal; judgment of the Court delivered by Lai Kew
Chai J). Also reported in [1997] FSR 491.

[131] TEST-SBC is a computer program that is supplied with every purchase of the Sound Blaster
card. Its primary function is to run tests on a Sound Blaster card that is installed in a personal computer. Aztech admitted to using this program to determine how Creative's card responded to undoc-
umented commands. To facilitate this analysis, Aztech made use of DEBUG, a commonly supplied
software tool to load TEST-SBC in a computer's RAM, so as to disassemble the target program in
whole or in Part. DEBUG was used by Aztech to ascertain how Creative's card responded to hex
commands, and returned values.

[132] Creative argued successively that their copyright in TEST-SBC was infringed when Aztech
loaded a copy of it into the RAM of the computer for testing and disassembly carried out by the
DEBUG program. A copy, no matter how transitory, is a reproduction and within the exclusive
rights of the copyright holder. For a detailed examination of the facts of the decision, and other comments, see Stanley Lai, "Recent Developments in Copyright Protection and Software Reverse
Engineering in Singapore—a Triumph for the Ultra-protectionists?" [1997] 9 EIPR 525.

[133] *Aztech Systems v Creative Technology* [1996] 1 SLR 683 (decision of Lim Teong Qwee JC).
The action originated as a "threats" action brought by Aztech against Creative Technology.

and concluded that Aztech had the "means, motive and opportunity" to disassemble Creative's firmware.[134]

10.64   On appeal the substantive issues of law arose from the admitted copying by Aztech of Creative's entire TEST-SBC program, and running it with the DEBUG program for the purposes of "understanding functionality in order to make a non-infringing, compatible product".[135] Aztech argued, inter alia, that its copying of TEST-SBC fell within the rights inherent in the lawful ownership of a copy of the software, where such use was not for an "unreasonable purpose",[136] relying on *Betts v Willmott*.[137] At first instance this was accepted by the trial judge.[138]

10.65   The Court of Appeal, in reversing the trial judge, took the firm view that the proposition advanced by Aztech was untenable. Citing the *Time-Life* decision, the court took the view that *Betts v Willmott* had no application in Singapore copyright law; to hold otherwise would be "tantamount to making a mockery of the provisions of the Singapore Copyright Act".[139] The Court further recognised the differences between the exclusive rights of both copyright and patent regimes, and noted that Aztech had to amend the original *Betts* proposition, which contemplated unfettered use in the absence of clear restrictions to "use for any reasonable purpose".[140]

10.66   It is argued that there are dangers to the type of argument made by Aztech in the *Creative* case. First, "use for any reasonable purpose" is ill-defined, and for a country that does not implement a legislative equivalent to the EC Software Directive, it is highly suspect whether Aztech's use of TEST-SBC could be considered as "reasonable". Secondly, the original *Betts* proposition, as delivered by Lord Hatherley LC did not contemplate a *motive* of use.[141] Thirdly, such a proposition would also be tantamount to compromising the standard which governs the imposition of implied terms in general contract law. Arguably, Aztech sought to transform this from a test of necessity to lend business efficacy to a given transaction, to a test of "reasonableness"—a suggestion which has been unequivocally rejected by the House of Lords.[142]

10.67   Ultimately the question is raised as to whether an implied licence may be used to subrogate the rights of the copyright owner, in the interests of user, eg the conferment of disassembly rights, as in *Creative v Aztech*. The foregoing sections have alluded to the dangers of a reckless, albeit imaginative deployment of

---

[134] *Supra*, n 130 at 633.
[135] *Supra*, n 130 at 635.
[136] This argument originated in para 35A(4) of Aztech's Defence to Counterclaim (on file with author).
[137] It was not a matter of surprise that this argument was made, given that Peter Prescott QC was counsel for Aztech.
[138] *Supra*, n 133 at 710.
[139] *Supra*, n 130 at 640.
[140] *Supra*, n 130 at 639.
[141] See para 10.45 ("use it wherever [*not however*] he pleases as against himself").
[142] *Liverpool City Council v Irwin* [1977] AC 239 at 265H.

the *Betts* principle, and it is submitted that Lord Hatherley's original proposition should firmly remain within, and not depart from, the patent context.

(iii) Relevance to UK copyright law

A *Betts*-type proposition has thus far not ventured into any software copyright **10.68** decision or litigation in the United Kingdom. It is anticipated that arguments similar to those mounted in Singapore's *Creative v Aztech* litigation could find their way here, and, in all likelihood, be pleaded in the alternative[143] to the general copyright derogations under Articles 5(2), (3) and 6 Software Directive, and the express contractual prohibitions contained in Article 9(1) Software Directive and section 296A(1) CDPA.

This speculation is made in response to the wording of Article 5(3) Software **10.69** Directive. It is recalled this provision partly states that a lawful user shall be entitled, without the authorisation of the rightholder, to observe and test the functionality of a program, so as to discover its underlying ideas. However, it concludes with the following phrase:

> "if he does so while performing any of the acts of loading, displaying, running, transmitting or storing the program which *he is entitled to do*" (emphasis added).

In other words, a lawful user is still very much constrained by the scope of any applicable software licence, or authorisation by the copyright owner. Such a reading is supported by Recital 19 of the Software Directive, which states that a person having a right to use a computer program should not be prevented from performing acts necessary to observe, study or test the functionality of a program, *provided* that such acts do not infringe the copyright in the program. For this reason, Laddie, *et al* regard Article 5(3) to be a "tame" provision, since a copyright owner is free to restrict his licence to a limited purpose.[144] A similar view could be reached of section 50C CDPA.

The argument could be made that in order to overcome this inadequacy, the **10.70** sale of software had to be accompanied by an implied licence to use the purchased software for any reasonable purpose. It is suggested that a UK court should set its face against such an argument,[145] for to hold otherwise would be "tantamount to making a mockery of the provisions"[146] of the CDPA and Software Directive.

---

[143] Alongside other defences such as fair dealing for research and private study, *supra*, at para 7.4 *et seq*.

[144] See Laddie, *et al*, *supra*, n 103 at para 20.46. The authors regard Art 5(3) as a provision that at the very least lacks transparency; ibid at para 20.50.

[145] A restricted view should be taken. See *Fylde Microsystems v Key Radio* [1998] FSR 449, where Laddie J refused to grant an implied licence for a general right of exploitation of the plaintiff's software in favour of the defendants, in circumstances where the defendant was the plaintiff's sole client. His Lordship reasoned that the plaintiff had undertaken four years of developmental work for which it would have been left without recompense if such a licence was found (ibid 461–462).

[146] *Creative v Azech*, *supra*, n 130, perhaps as close as a Commonwealth Court has ever come to the equivalent of a US copyright preemption or misuse doctrine.

(e) Shareware and Implied Licences

10.71   The recent case of *Trumpet Software v OzEmail*[146] illustrates how the Australian Federal Court defined an implied licence in relation to shareware.[148] The defendants had distributed the plaintiff's shareware through two computer magazines; and in the process altered the plaintiff's shareware program so that it would direct users to connect to another Internet access service. The Court found that the defendants had infringed the plaintiff's reproduction and distribution rights.

10.72   Applying the relevant tests,[149] the Court determined that the shareware licence carried the following implied term in respect of the software in question:

> "it be distributed in its entirety and without modification, addition or deletion. The whole purpose of evaluation is to enable the end user to evaluate the product as produced by the author".[150]

IV. CONCLUSION

10.73   This chapter has explored areas of software copyright law where copyright and contract law have an actual or potential interrelationship; and the ramifications for authors' and users' respective rights. The following conclusions are reached.

10.74   For the purposes of ascertaining validity, shrink-wrap licences do not lend themselves to a traditional contractual analysis under English law. It is likely that an English Court would adopt an incremental, case-by-case approach without setting out a clear principle of prima facie validity. The Scottish case of *Beta v Adobe*, whilst being the first UK case to pronounce on the validity of a shrink-wrap licence, provides, at best, limited assistance to an English Court.

10.75   A study of shrink-wrap licences in the USA indicates little scope for cross-fertilisation and application in the United Kingdom (beyond emphasising the enforceability of "click-on" licences), especially on issues pertaining to formation. As discussed above, the earlier cases in the USA did not support the enforceability of such licences.[151] *ProCD v Zeidenberg* could be considered a milestone in terms of the tolerance shown by the judiciary towards the enforceability of shrink-wrap licences. Together with the ensuing Article 2B debate, the status quo in the USA has arguably been altered, with the ubiquity of shrink-wraps, the proliferation of software distribution across the Internet, and new

---

[147] (1996) IPR 481 (Fed Court, of Australia, Heerey J). See further note by Fitzgerald [1996] 6 CTLR 245.

[148] The nature of shareware is discussed by Heerey J in (1996) IPR 481 at 484–485; and Kelleher "Shareware Licences for Software" [1998] EIPR 140.

[149] *Supra*, paras 10.41–10.43.

[150] *Supra*, n 147 at 500.

[151] See cases discussed *supra*, in para 10.34 *et seq*.

legislation.[152] The latest US legislative initiatives (Draft UCITA) reflect the increasing importance of contractual and informational licensing, possibly eclipsing the importance of copyright in the future.[153] For the future the extent to which contractual overrides are permissible remains key.

Turning to implied licensing, there are inherent dangers to importing the principle in *Betts v Willmott*, which originated in patent law, into the copyright context. The fundamental reason lies in the kind of rights conferred by both regimes. This is true not only in relation to parallel importation (*Time-Life*); but equally where it is argued that a lawful user of software enjoys unlimited right of use, as long as it does not extend to an "unreasonable purpose" (*Creative v Aztech*). Such an extension to the original proposition in *Betts v Willmott* should not be accepted, lest it results in the serious erosion of a monopoly right, further unsettling the fragile balance of rights which has been argued for elsewhere in this work.

10.76

In sum, this chapter has sought to demonstrate the significant role played by implied or express contractual licensing in defining the scope of rights within copyright in software transactions. It can truly be said that contract and intellectual property laws "have always co-existed not only peacefully, but in an aggressive interaction between ordinarily consistent and mutually supportive fields".[154]

10.77

---

[152] Samuelson, "Does Information really have to be licensed?" 41(9) *Communications of the ACT* (September 1998) 15 at 16.

[153] Raymond Nimmer (Reporter for the Art 2B Project) perceives a growing importance for contract law in the new information environment because in the new world of digital information intellectual property constructs do not match up very well with new forms of commercial exploitation of digital information, such those involving "transmission, extraction and access". See Nimmer "Breaking Barriers: The Relationship between Contract and Intellectual Property Law" (1998) 13 Berkeley Tech LJ 827 at 829.

[154] See Nimmer, *supra*, n 153 at 829.

11

General Conclusion

This work has identified specific topics within the general subject of software **11.1**
copyright for discussion, in the hope of addressing concerns for the development
of the subject within the United Kingdom.

The principal thesis is that a new methodology for non-literal infringement **11.2**
analysis should be adopted in the United Kingdom, founded on the growing
body of US jurisprudence. This conclusion is arrived at from a study of US decisions, commentary and writings from leading academics, which reinforce the
conviction that, given the idiosyncrasies of computer software, and the need to
operate within the copyright frame, this is the best approach for the future.
Ferris J paved the way for the application of the *Altai*-type of infringement
analysis. This book takes the approach further, through a study of the subsequent judicial treatment of *Altai*, suggesting a uniform structure for the identification of "abstraction" levels within software.[1] The work has explored
particular limiting doctrines within the *Altai* formulation, in the hope of establishing a case for their application in the United Kingdom. The proposed limiting analysis is also argued to apply to user interface elements, including video
games. In this area of copyright law, it has been recognised that the resolution
of doctrinal tensions, as well as the continued elaboration of analytical techniques, is essential to the law's maturation on this subject.[2]

The study of software reverse engineering is largely comparative. Although **11.3**
there is some evidence that the EU Software Directive is setting the agenda for
interoperability in the future, the work has also investigated the operation of the
fair use doctrine in the USA, exploring the "transformative use" concept for the
future treatment of software reverse engineering, notwithstanding the obvious
impact of *Sega v Accolade*, and *Atari v Nintendo*.[3] Moreover the discussion of
Fair Use is not irrelevant to UK copyright,[4] particularly when one considers the
continued relevance and applicability of the fair dealing defence to practices
such as "black-box" testing[5] and pre-Directive decompilation.[6]

---

[1] The systematic method used to develop computer programs makes the abstractions test more
evidently applicable to computer software than other types of works. See 4 *Nimmer on Copyright*
§10.03[F][1] at 13–121.

[2] Remembering the words of Benjamin Cardozo: "The implications of a decision may in the beginning be equivocal. New cases, by commentary and exposition extract the essence. At last there emerges
a rule or principle which becomes . . . a point of departure, from which new lines will be run, from
which new courses will be measured": Cardozo *The Nature of the Judicial Process* (1921) at p 48.

[3] *Supra*, paras 6.44 *et seq.*

[4] *Supra*, paras 7.19–7.20.

[5] *Supra*, paras 7.21–7.22

[6] *Supra*, paras 7.4–7.77

11.4   This work has also considered other defences and permitted acts, such as error correction and maintenance, including the latter's coverage of "normative" corrections.[7] It is also been tentatively argued that the right of error correction extends to disassembly for the purposes of effecting such correction. The scope of the *British Leyland* defence has also been discussed, observing its diminishing relevance to software copyright,[8] largely through its subsequent restrictions to situations of repair.[9]

11.5   Concerning the future challenges for this subject in the United Kingdom, the work identifies four distinct areas.

I. APPLICATION OF UK COPYRIGHT TO THE WWW

11.6   The author is of the view that in the *Shetland Times* decision, Lord Hamilton's classification of a website as a "cable programme service" is "arguable" under section 7(1) CDPA, but disagrees with his Lordship's holding that the operative "interactivity" exception (section 7(2) CDPA) is inapplicable to web-browsing. In addition several provisions of the CDPA[10] are shown to be potentially applicable to web-based infringements.

II. THE DIGITAL AGENDA

11.7   The aftermath of the WIPO Treaties (1996) has seen various initiatives put forward to advance their implementation. As part of its topical coverage of software copyright law in the United Kingdom, this work has focused on two pertinent areas, the treatment of temporary copies in the course of Internet operations and provisions against the circumvention of technical protection systems. With the former, the book questions the efficacy of the obligatory exception in Article 5 of the Proposed Directive. On the latter issue, the work outlines the initial threat to reverse engineering from early proposals,[11] culminating in the latest EU[12] and US[13] proposals, and suggests necessary amendments to be made to section 296 CDPA.[14]

---

[7] *Supra*, paras 7.30.
[8] *Supra*, paras 7.38–7.40.
[9] *Canon v Green Cartridge*, *supra*, paras 7.38–7.40; followed in *Mars v Tecknowledge*, discussed *supra*, paras 7.47–7.48.
[10] eg ss.6(1), 24(2), 72 CDPA.
[11] *Supra*, para 8.24.
[12] See Art 6 Proposed Directive, discussed *supra*, in para 8.26.
[13] Digital Millennium Copyright Act, discussed *supra*, in para 8.25.
[14] *Supra*, para 8.27.

III. UK DATABASE LEGISLATION

The work acknowledges the strength of protecting sub-programs as compila- **11.8**
tions, and scrutinises the effect of database amendments on software copyright.
Apart from the anomalies created by the latest amendments with reference to
database copyright generally, and the unsatisfactory non-treatment of computer-generated works, some discussion is devoted to the overlap between software copyright and database protection, concluding with a caution against the
use of the new (*sui generis*) database right to protect uncopyrightable "database
components" within computer programs.

IV. THE INTERFACE BETWEEN CONTRACT AND COPYRIGHT

Considering the validity and enforceability of shrink-wrap licences under **11.9**
English law, the work ultimately concludes that privity of contract is strictly a
"red herring" and an unnecessary distraction to a validity analysis. A licence can
exist quite independently, although not frequently, apart from a contract, and it
is suggested that the validity of such a licence comes down to the sole issue of
incorporation of licence terms, subject to provisions of the Software Directive
and CDPA which operate against exclusory contract.

The work concludes with a study of implied licences, cautioning against their **11.10**
use to subvert the exclusive rights of the copyright owner in future software litigation, with the seeds of this approach sowed in an inappropriate extension of
a patent law-based proposition. It is also anticipated that implied licences will
play a greater role with the online dissemination of shareware[15] and usage.

This work has attempted to bring to the fore various issues confronting soft- **11.11**
ware copyright practice in the years to come. It is hoped that the English Courts
and legislators will heed the warnings of ultra-protectionism, manifested in its
various forms, as shown by this work. By way of final comment, it is observed
that UK software copyright practice is approaching a global dimension.
International and regional standards will continue to affect this subject in a way
that legal practitioners, judges and academics can ill-afford to ignore. This work
has just been a small (bordering on insubstantial) attempt to raise this aware-
ness for the next millennium, in which the continued, laborious struggle of
adapting old to new will take on an even more enhanced, sustained and aggressive vigour.

---

[15] See *Trumpet Software v OzEmail*, discussed *supra*, in para 10.71 *et seq.*

Appendix

Technical Background

Appendix

Technical Background: Software Design, Functionality, Reverse Engineering and Internet Issues

This appendix to the main work seeks to provide a technical account of soft- **A.1** ware development and functionality, serving as background to the substantive legal discussion. There are five major sections; (1) the software designing process—an overview; (2) how a computer functions; (3) the reverse engineering process; (4) an evaluation of the "clean room" procedure; and (5) technical issues and the Internet. The Appendix aims to acquaint the reader with the some of the technical detail forming the background[1] to the legal discussion of this work.

I. THE SOFTWARE DESIGNING PROCESS: AN OVERVIEW

This section presents an overview of the mechanics of the software design **A.2** process. This process is a matter of defining the functions of the program at increasing levels of specificity, to varying degrees of abstraction,[2] at all times relying on the fundamental principle that all computer systems are organised on a hierarchial principle.[3]

---

[1] See Kidwell, "Software and semiconductors: why are we confused?" (1985) 70 Minn L Rev 533, 535–540, where it is suggested that some of the confusion about applying existing law to software is attributable to the nature of software.

[2] At one level a computer has been described as a device for storing, moving, adding, subtracting or comparing numbers by electronic means, one step at a time. This arrangement is known as "Von Neumann Architecture", and stipulates that no matter how difficult the task, it can be organised such that the processor is never called upon to perform more than one simple step at a time. Thus the art of computer programming may be thought of as "progressively transforming a task through successive levels of hierarchy such that it emerges as a series of simple one step instructions". See Laddie, *et al Modern Law of Copyright*, 2nd edn, Vol 1 at para 20.11. This should be contrasted with "fifth generation computer systems" (which make use of parallel processors) and neural networks.

[3] Explained in Laddie, *et al*, *supra*, n 2, Vol 1at paras 20.8–20.17; Christie "Designing Appropriate Protection for Computer Programs" [1994] 11 EIPR 486 at 491–493. Hence the phenomena of "top-down" programming; where a programmer starts with a general idea of what the program is to accomplish, and moves in steps towards the ultimate goal of producing specific code that can operate the computer correctly. See Dahl *et al* (eds), *Structured Programming* (1972); Booch *Software Engineering with ADA* (1983); Wirth "Program Development by Stepwrite Refinement" (1971) 14(4) Comm ACM; Schneider and Bruell *Advanced Programming and Problem Solving with Pascal* (1981) at pp 164–188; *Whelan v Jaslow* 797 F.2d 1222 at 1229 (3rd Cir 1986); 4 Nimmer §13.03[F][1] 13–119–13–128.

A.3   The highest level is an analysis of the problem which defines the general functions to be carried out and the order in which they are performed. Each of these functions can then be analysed in more detail until the program is sufficiently well specified to allow the various parts to be given to programmers to write the coding (set of instructions). These sets of instructions may be called "algorithms", the complete analysis of a problem which if followed exactly produces a unique solution for each set of inputs.[4] Since they constitute sets of instructions for accomplishing a logical process, these algorithms are often expressed in the form of a flowchart.

A.4   The programmer's task is to write his program in a computer language such as "C". In doing this he may well use standard pieces of code from a library (which might be developed in-house or brought in) to perform frequently used functions such as the production of screen windows or menus. In some cases the prototype version or parts of the final code will be produced using a program generator or fourth-generation language ("4GL") which takes a standardised, high level description of the program and generates detailed code to perform the various functions. Some routines may be written in assembly code, which is essentially a set of mnemonics for object code which another program translates directly into that code.[5] Once all the sections are complete, they are combined together to produce a complete version in source code (which is in human readable form). In order to run the program and so that it can be distributed in a form that gives the user as little information as possible about the details of the program (thus reducing the danger of copying) the source code is used as input for another program, the compiler.[6] The compiler transforms the program into object code, a machine readable form which will have linked to it the standard pieces of code for the program to run as a stand-alone or executable file.[7] The compiled code will be run to test it, and any errors which are detected will be corrected in the source code and recompiled.[8] Very few computer programs of any size are error-free and as these errors (or "bugs") surface and become identified, software houses will choose to issue updated and improved versions.

---

[4] An algorithm exists at a level of abstraction whose place in the hierarchy lies somewhere between a program specification (written in a high level language) and the computer program itself. For doubts as to whether "algorithms" per se constitute copyrightable subject-matter, see Laddie, *et al, supra*, n 2 at para 20.15.

[5] This is normally done when the programmer needs to drive the hardware directly, or where speed is required, as it gives very precise control over the program's operation.

[6] Otherwise known as a "translator"; *infra*, at paras A.16–A.18.

[7] For a technically accurate discussion of source and object code in the legal literature, see Samuelson, "CONTU revisited: The case against copyright protection for computer programs in machine readable form" (1984) Duke LJ 663 at 672–689.

[8] A computer program has thus to be created in a series of successive stages: (i) identification of the goals to be achieved; (ii) analysis of the tasks to be implemented; (iii) writing of the system specifications (in progressively greater levels of detail); (iv) implementation of the system in the form of a high level language computer program; (v) translation into low level computer language; and (vi) testing, identification and the correction of errors (known in the trade as "debugging"). It has said that perhaps 90 per cent of work goes into stage (vi) and subsequent maintenance. See Laddie *et al, supra*, n 2 at para 20.13.

The final process is to produce documentation which the user will need to **A.5** operate the program. The completed product is the package of any object code version and documentation.

II. HOW A COMPUTER FUNCTIONS

By way of technical background to the main work, what follows is a discussion **A.6** of the fundamental workings of a computer, its hardware, software, user interface and other instruction sets. This section is divided into the following subsections; (a) information storage in a computer; (b) computer software and its operating instructions; (c) translators and compilers; (d) operating systems; (e) the user interface; (f) macros, parameters and microcode.

(a) Information Storage in a Computer

Every computer has component called "storage" or "memory", which retains **A.7** information. Storage is almost always a kind of magnetic medium, in which the circuitry of the computer can distinguish a series of ones and zeros:

"00011111000101010101111000000011101010101...001"

How a computer finds anything in such a long and cryptic sequence of digits is a wonderment. There is in fact an implicit structure superimposed on the storage. There is a pattern to how information is represented there and that pattern is the key to interpreting that information.

The typical computer is designed to accommodate 256 different items, or **A.8** characters.[9] By writing all the possible combinations of a pair of 0s and 1s one obtains:

0	0
0	1
1	0
1	1

If all the possible combinations are written for three digits, each of which can be 0 or 1, the following list is generated:

0	0	0
0	0	1
0	1	0
0	1	1
1	0	0
1	1	0
1	1	1

---

[9] This includes 26 upper-case letters, 26 lower-case letters, 10 decimal digits, and a variety of special characters such as "+, –, *, @, ?" etc.

It may be seen from the above that adding another digit merely reproduces the entries in the previous group, once preceded by a "0" and once preceded by "1". The addition of another digit doubles the number of possibilities. Similarly, using four digits allows 16 entries, using seven digits yields 128 entries, and using eight digits provides for 256 entries in such a listing. Machine language is all about assigning one entry to each character, and through this a sequence of characters can be represented by their corresponding sequences of 0s and 1s.

A.9   It is seen that information storage in a computer takes the form of the assignment of characters to 0 and 1 patterns. One common system for such assignment is called the American Standard Code for Information Interchange (or "ASCII"). The ASCII standard actually used seven-digit patterns, allowing 128 possible characters, but most computers have been designed around eight digits, allowing for future expansion to 256 different characters. By way of illustration, the following is a portion of ASCII 7-bit code:

0100000	(space)
0100001	!
01000010	"
0100011	#
. . .	. . .
0101010	*
0101011	+
0101100	"
. . .	. . .
0110000	0
0110001	1
0110010	2
0110011	3
0110100	4
. . .	. . .
1000001	A
1000010	B
1000011	C
. . .	. . .
1001010	J
1001011	K
1001100	L
. . .	. . .
1100001	a
1100010	b
1100011	c
. . .	. . .
1101010	j
1101011	k
1101100	l
. . .	. . .
1110101	u

1110110	v
1110111	w
1111000	x
1111001	y
. . .	. . .

The eight-digit patterns used in most computer are called bytes, and the 0s **A.10** and 1s themselves, which can be viewed as binary choices, or binary digits, are usually referred to as bits. Thus each byte contains eight bits.

Storage is normally organised into bytes, each consisting of eight bits; each **A.11** byte represents a character in storage. In order to access this information, each byte position or location in storage is associated with its position number, or "address", starting with zero. For example, an instruction in programming might be to cause a particular number, say 3, to be placed in byte location 74.

A distinction should also be made between the different types of storage. **A.12** Random Access Memory (RAM) storage is that in which any location can be accessed, and if so desired, changed. The other kind of storage is called read-only memory (ROM) storage, in which one can read values in various locations in any sequence, but these values cannot be changed or written. They can only be read.

(b) Computer Software and Operating Instructions

This section examines what a program actually accomplishes with operating **A.13** instructions. The typical instruction might have the following structure; (i) what operation to perform; (ii) what to do it to; (iii) where to put the result and (iv) where to find the next instruction.[10] Given that an instruction must include these four components, and that the central processing unit must be able to analyse every instruction to find those components, it is clear that each instruction must conform to a standard format, or structure. For example, in a particular computer an instruction might consist of 36 bits, allocated in the following sequence:

operation	register	result location	next instruction location
11110010	0011	000011101010	111000101010

In the above example, the first group or field represents the operation code (with the 8 bits allowing the 256 possible codes for this purpose). The second field shows the number of a register in the ALU (*infra*) containing the data on which this particular operation will be carried out. The third field provides the address of the location in storage where the result is to be placed after the computation, and the fourth field indicates the location of the next instruction.

---

[10] See Bernard Galler *Software and Intellectual Property Protection* (Quorum Books, 1995) at pp 147–151.

A.14   Instructions in 0s and 1s are tedious for any programmer to produce, and thus this led to written instructions in the form of alphabetic codes and symbols (otherwise known as "assembler instructions"), such as:

read	a, b, c
load	3, a
add	3, b
sub	3, c
store	3, x
print	a, b, c, x

The intent of this sequence is to read three values into storage locations to be referred to as "a", "b" and "c", then load the value in location "a" into Register 3 of the Arithmetic/Logic Unit (ALU) of the Central Processing Unit (CPU),[11] then add the value in location "b" to the value in Register 3, subtract the value in location "c" from the value in Register 3, store the result in a storage location called "x" and finally print the values in locations "a", "b", "c" and "x". Previously a programmer would then laboriously translate each instruction manually into the corresponding 0s and 1s before entering them into the computer for execution. This process of "manual translation" consisted of looking up the binary code for "add", or "store", etc, selecting specific storage addresses for "a", "b", "c" and "x", and then writing it all out in binary form, in 0s and 1s, and was a very tedious and error-pone exercise.[12] This was before the introduction of the "assembler" program.

A.15   What the last example really wanted to accomplish was to bring in as input the values for a, b and c:

$$x = a + b - c$$

What a programmer sought to accomplish was to write more abstract and user friendly versions (to him), for example:

read a, b, c
ompute x = a + b − c
print a, b, c, x

or

read (a, b, c) and print (a, b, c, and x = a + b − c)

These more abstract versions are written in a high-level language.

[11] The CPU comprises two main components. The most visible part is the Arithmetic/Logic Unit (ALU), which consists of a number of registers, each capable of temporarily holding one or more bytes. The contents of these registers are involved in arithmetic computation, such as adding numbers, and also in logical decisions, such as testing for positive or negative numbers in order to decide which of several possible courses of action to undertake next. The other component of the CPU is the Control Unit. The activities of the Control Unit are generally hidden from anyone using the computer. Its primary role is to co-ordinate the actions of all of the other parts of the system so they occur at just the right moment and have precisely the desired effect.

[12] In practice most programmers use octal or hexadecimal representation for binary values, because these forms are more compressed and easier to write. The octal representation is based on the number 8, and the hexadecimal on the number 16, just as the decimal representation is based on the number 10.

(c) Translators and Compilers

Programs are now written in very high level languages whenever possible.[13] **A.16**
Previously it was difficult to take complex statements, such as "read (a, b, c) and
print (a, b, c, and x = a + b − c)", and determine what object code was needed
to carry out the corresponding computation. On average, about ten assembler-
level instructions are needed for each high-level language. For example, simple
statements like:

set x = y

would generate only two instructions:

load   1, y
store   1, x

while some high-level statements generate many more instructions than ten.

Assemblers appeared as early as 1950,[14] but it took until 1956 for FORTRAN **A.17**
(Formula Translator) to be considered the first high-level language translator.
Currently there are many such languages,[15] and an important segment of the
software designing process is creating and marketing translators, called "compilers", which enable various high-level languages to run on a wide variety of
computers.

Each of these high-level languages in which programs are written requires a **A.18**
translator to convert statements from the respective language into object code
(0s and 1s).[16] There is debate as to whether such translators should be considered part of the operating system (explained below) or regarded as application
programs in their own right.[17]

---

[13] This is because high-level languages are easy to use and understand; see further the note
"Copyright Protection of Computer Program Object Code" (1983) 96 Harvard L.Rev 1723 at
1724–1725.

[14] Assemblers appeared very early in the life of the computer industry; see Campbell-Kelly,
"Programing the EDSAC", *Annals of the History of Computing* (1980) Vol 2 at p 26.

[15] From time to time attempts have been made to standardise a language for all to use, but with
little success. A few languages are more commonly used than the rest, eg FORTRAN, COBOL,
PL/1, BASIC, Pascal, C, C++, Ada, LISP, etc. Over the years special languages appeared for speci-
fying the actions of numerically controlled milling machines, for solving particular kinds of mathematical equations and for solving problems using artificial intelligence techniques. See Sammet,
Programing Languages: History and Fundamentals (Englewood Cliffs, NJ, Prentice-Hall, 1969)
which contains descriptions of about 200 languages.

[16] For good illustrations of how the translation process takes place, see Galler, *supra*, n 10 at pp
155–160.

[17] A controversy that has yet to reach the British shores. The view that is taken by some US writers is that compiler programs are separate programs capable of independent copyright protection.
Compiler programs are used to transform one set of materials into another form. In many cases the
use of the compiler creates no additional copies other than are implicit in the licence to use the program. However in some cases the compiler places portions of its own code on the medium that eventually holds the compiled program. They are described as "run-time" modules, which transform
code each time the program is placed into operation. If the original use of the compiler was authorised, the question of whether creating copies of run-time modules in a new program should be a
non-infringing partial copy depends on the nature of the modules. The question may be identified

(d) Operating Systems

A.19 A library of packaged programs, often called subroutines or utility programs, is one of the many components forming the typical operating system on a computer. The operating system[18] is software (eg Microsoft's Windows 95/98 or Windows 3.11) which is usually provided or sold by the vendor of the hardware, whose role is to co-ordinate the uses of the various software components that are available to serve the user and make it easier to use the computer system. The operating system determines the order in which user application programs will be executed, which resources such as storage space, disk facilities and execution time will be allocated to each program, and how much different users of a system will be charged.

A.20 Operating systems also provide translators for programs written in high-level languages. When a program is written, eg in PASCAL, the "Pascal translator" must be called upon to translate the program into the object code version so it can be executed.

A.21 To the user, operating systems provide many services. They include a complete library of utility programs, and they provide input and output services. They also keep track of files or documents that the user creates. In most systems, eg Microsoft Windows, the files are organised with directories and subdirectories maintained by the operating system. Other services include file and document management, the addition/removal of hardware, modem detection, virus scans and other housekeeping tasks. It is material to remember that an operating system is software that consists of many programs.[19]

A.22 For copyright purposes, the distinction between operating systems and application programs has been an issue in several US cases, as discussed elsewhere in this work.[20]

as one of distinguishing code from the process it creates. The copyright issue is determined by whether these "run-time modules" constitute copyrightable expression. The view has been taken, notably by Raymond Nimmer, that if the run-time modules are not expression, the compiler copyright stops at the copy of the program itself that was licensed. If the modules constitute expression, the compiler copyright is extended into subsequent works; see Nimmer, *The Law of Computer Technology*, 2nd edn at 1–48.

[18] To be immediately contrasted with application software. See Kutten, *Computer Software: Protection/Liability/Law/Forms* (1991) §102 at 1–3; also Menell, "An analysis of the scope of copyright protection for applications programs" (1989) 41 Stanford L Rev 1045 at 1051.

[19] What has complicated the situation is that for efficiency reasons, some aspects of some operating systems have been embedded into hardware, significantly obsfucating the distinction between hardware and software.

[20] See *Apple Computer v Formula International* 725 F.2d 521 (9th Cir 1994), in which the defendant admittedly copied Apple operating system programs, but argued that machine-resident programs (operating system) that do not directly produce visual images or other expression that the computer discerns should be excluded from copyright. The Court rejected this argument and held that the programs contained expression that did not merge with their idea. Evidence was adduced in the District Court that there were numerous ways to write operating systems capable of running 98 per cent of all existing application programs used with the Apple computers. The 9th Circuit assumed that an operating system which accommodated this percentage of the application programs performs the same function as the Apple system and thus represents an alternative way of

(e) The User Interface

In many ways the user interface of a computer program is the most important **A.23**
component of a software system,[21] and its design takes up a substantial part of
the programming effort.[22] It is the means by which a user directly interacts[23]
with a particular application, and as such it is the most important factor influ-
encing the customer's decision to buy. Consequently the protection of so-called
"look and feel" aspects of a computer program are among the most litigious
areas in software copyright.[24]

The user interface, being the "face and voice" of a particular program, is also **A.24**
influential on judges, many of whom mistakenly regard similar screen displays
as probitive evidence of copyright infringement, regardless of coding. Thus two
programs with different texts eg VP-PLANNER and LOTUS 1–2–3, can have
completely equivalent behaviour.[25]

By way of illustrating the interaction between user and computer, suppose **A.25**
that a program has been developed for a bank, allowing it to keep track of its
customer loans. The programmer may prompt the user, eg a bank officer, to
input data, by programming following input request (or "input format"):

Example: in PASCAL language

```
writeln    ('Enter Balance, Rate, Starting Month and Year,',
           'Ending Month and Year, and Monthly Payment')
readln     (Bal, Rate, Imonth, Iyear, Lmonth, Lyear, Payment)
```

---

implementing the same process. Similar facts arose in *Apple Computer v Franklin* 714 F.2d 1240 (3rd
Cir 1983), where Franklin's primary argument was that operating system programs in machine form
should be per se excluded from copyright because an operating system program is an unpredictable
process or method of operation. This was rejected by the 3rd Circuit. Although the *Franklin* decision is generally regarded as establishing the copyrightability of operating system programs in
machine form, the Court actually decided that operating system programs are not per se excluded
and that the critical consideration is whether more than a limited number of ways exist to express
the idea underlying the operating system—a narrower issue. Both these cases should be re-assessed
in the light of *Lotus v Borland International*, discussed *supra*, at paras 4.24–4.32.

[21] It is said that a well-composed user interface is frequently the precise feature that renders a
computer program successful: Ben Schneiderman, *Designing the User Interface: Strategies for
Effective Human-Computer Interaction* 2nd edn (1992), p 11.

[22] See Frederick P Brooks, *The Mythical Man-Myth: Essays on Software Engineering* (1982) at p
20 (stating that one-half the program design effort should be devoted to user interface design).

[23] The type of interaction varies. In some programs, screen menus provide an interface permitting users to select an item by typing a numeric digit or alphabetic character; in other programs,
users interface with the program by selecting icons with mouse: see Corington & Downing, *Barron's
Dictionary of Computer Terms*, 3rd edn (1992) at p 343.

[24] See Chapter 4.

[25] These were two famous examples: the VP-PLANNER program developed by Paperback
Software and the TWIN program developed by Mosaic Software. The behaviour of each was virtu-
ally identical to that of Lotus 1–2–3, a feature that was boasted in the VP-Planner manual. See *Lotus
Development Corp Paperback Software* 740 F.Supp 37, 69–70. Neither imitator had any access to
Lotus source code.

Example: in FORTRAN language

```
  1    WRITE (0, 600)
600    FORMAT ('1ENTER BALACE, RATE, STARTING MONTH,',
       X 'YEAR, ENDING MONTH, YEAR, MONTHLY PAYMENT')
       READ (5,700) BAL, RATE, IM, IYEAR, LM, LYEAR, X PAY
700    FORMAT (F9.2, F5.3, 2(13,15), F7.2
```

The corresponding input format appears on screen:

ENTER BALANCE, RATE, STARTING MONTH, YEAR, ENDING MONTH,
YEAR, MONTHLY PAYMENT

The input format in the above example lacks visual appeal and imagination; in
this instance the programmer is in all likelihood assuming that the user would
not necessarily be using the program constantly, and would only appreciate a
simple reminder of the order in which the data values should be entered. This
type of user interface can best be described as "textual".

A.26   On the other hand, if that program was marketed to compete with others, the
programmer would most likely spend a considerable amount of time designing
the user interface so it would be pleasing to the eye, and it might even make use
of colour. Another set of choices available to the programmer, depending on the
capabilities of the user's workstation, is in the presentation of prompts on the
screen. The program fragments shown in the above example are really oriented
towards input devices that display one line at a time from a keyboard. Given the
availability of a two dimensional presentation on a screen, the programmer
could choose the location of the prompts on the screen and allow the user to
enter the values in appropriate positions on the screen in any order. The programmer might then want to ask that a signal be given when all of the values
have been entered. This might take the form of a click of the mouse button when
the cursor is in a certain location on the screen, or the depression of a particular
key on the keyboard.

A.27   Modern workstations and pentium computers are not restricted to lines containing characters. The screens used today can put different colour or shade of
colour at every point on the screen (called a "pixel"). As a result, elaborate
graphical user-interface-generating programs have become available, so every
application programmer can create extremely friendly screen presentations.
Many users are now accustomed to the "desktop metaphor", in which the illu-
sion is created of working with pieces of paper on a desktop.[26] We have all, to
some extent, adapted to the so-called "WIMP" environment—the environment
of windows, icons, mice and pull-down menus.[27]

---

[26] The very similarity of some of these graphical user interfaces has led to significant litigation,
as in *Lotus v Paperback*, *Apple v Microsoft*, and most recently, *Lotus v Borland International*; discussed *supra*, at para 4.24 *et seq*.
[27] See Bainbridge, *Software Copyright Law*, 3rd edn (1997) at pp 87, 305.

(f) Other Interfaces

The term "interface" may carry the "mystique of the technical inner sanctum",[28]   **A.28** but really has no specific technical meaning in programming.[29] Put simply, interfaces may be described as features or elements[30] of a program that are necessary for machine-machine or program-program relationships, and their corresponding interaction with the operating system. What is common to interfaces is that copying or using them may be necessary for the creation of interoperable programs.[31] It has been suggested[32] that the more important interfaces divide into three categories: (i) the interface between hardware and software; (ii) the interfaces between programs; and (iii) communication protocols.[33]

(g) Macros, Parameters, Microcode, Look-up and Compression Tables

This final sub-section considers three technical issues which have appeared in   **A.29** recent litigation: macros, parameter lists, microcode, look-up and compression tables. Their technical aspects are reviewed below:

(i) Macros

The term "macro" is a shortened form of "macro-instruction". The idea is to   **A.30** create a new kind of short-hand notation for commonly used sequences of ordinary instructions, so a person writing a program will not have to write out long sequences of very similar instructions over and over again. Often a group

---

[28] See Miller, 106 Harv L Rev 977 at 1034.

[29] Clapes, *Software, Copyright and Competition: The "Look and Feel" of the Law* (1989) at pp 181–182. See also Alfred Z Spector, "Software, Interface and Implementation" Jurimetrics J (Fall 1989) 79 at 86 n 1 (listing a broad variety of examples of "interface").

[30] See for example, "operating system calls", "parameter structures" and "input and output formats of application programs" discussed in Zimerman "Baystate: Technical Interfaces not Copyrightable—on to the First Circuit" 14(4) *Computer Lawyer* (April 1997) 9 at 9–10.

[31] As discussed elsewhere in this work, many Courts have ruled elements to be unprotectable and non-infringing when they underwrite compatibility: see eg *Gates Rubber v Bando* 9 F.3d 823 at 838 (10th Cir 1993); *Bateman v Menomics* 79 F.3d 1532 at 1546–1547 (11th Cir 1996); *Sega Enterprises v Accolade* 977 F.2d 1510 at 1520 (9th Cir 1992) (9th Circuit held that the intermediate copying of "system interface procedures" is a fair use when it is "the only means of gaining access to [the] unprotected aspects of the program", namely ideas and functional concepts required for compatibility).

[32] See Karl H Pilny "Legal Aspects of Interfaces and Reverse Engineering—Protection in Germany, the United States and Japan" (1992) 23 IIC 196 at 202–204.

[33] Holding particular relevance for intranet and Internet links, communication protocols are a convention according to which the communicating partners agree on setting up, realising and closing down a communication link. A communication protocol consists of three parts (1) the control data sent via the link before the transfer of user data; (2) the data format which localises both the control and communication data; and (3) the data sequence which determines the sequence of communication (ibid at 203–204).

of programmers will agree on a common set of macros and put them into a library for their joint use.[34]

A.31   In the programming context, the usual treatment of macros is for the programmer to write the name of the macro as a statement in the source code program. The source code language translator then substitutes for the macro name the actual sequence of instructions specified in an earlier definition of the macro. Not only does the person who specifies the macro choose which macros to create, but also the sequence of instructions to use in the definition of each macro.[35]

A.32   Apart from programmers' macros, modern application programs (eg WordPerfect, Microsoft Word and Lotus 1–2–3) also contain an extensive facility for users to create their own "macros", which shorten oft-used commands, and increase the efficiency of the work. Such commands have more recently been the focus of attention in the Courts.[36]

(ii) Parameters

A.33   Parameters are part of sub-routines, or procedures contained in a program. The name of the sub-routine, such as "readln",[37] is used to invoke its action, and the instructions which comprise the sub-routine are then executed. When the sub-routine finishes its computation, control returns to the original program at the point from which the sub-routine was invoked.[38] A sub-routine may be called any number of times by another program, at different points in the latter. Moreover each time a sub-routine is called, it may be given different data on which to work; ie different parameters may be specified.

A.34   For example, a frequently used sub-routine in mathematical computation is the calculation of a square root. Every standard library of pre-packaged sub-routines includes a sub-routine for the square root, usually called "SQRT", and invoked as:

$$SQRT \ (x)$$

---

[34] An example of such a concept outside the computer field (although probably implemented by a computer) can be found in the video cassette recorder (VCR). A typical VCR system provides a menu of commands on the screen of the TV set; the commands can be selected on the remote control device to direct the VCR to do sequences of commands packaged together. The sequences could be executed by pushing various buttons one after the other, but mistakes can be made. The choice of packaged commands presented on the screen represents the manufacturer's prediction as to which command sequences a typical consumer would find useful, eg "Play-Rew-Power Off"; "Go to Zero-Stop"; "Go to Zero-Play"; "Go to Rec Start-Play"; "Rew-Power Off"; "Rew-Eject-Power Off"; "Rew-Play"; "Rew-Timer Rec".

[35] More powerful macro facilities even provide for the specification of parameter values at each invocation of the macro, causing specific changes to occur during the substitution of the instruction sequence, thus tailoring the sequence to the actual context in which it is invoked.

[36] See *Lotus v Borland*; and more recently in Australia, *Powerflex v Data Access* 37 IPR 436 (1997). For a technical discussion of *Powerflex v Data Access*, see further Hunter [1998] EIPR 98.

[37] See the example *supra*, in A.25.

[38] For a more thorough illustration of how sub-routines work, see *infra*, n 65 and accompanying text.

which means: call the square root sub-routine, and specify that this time the square root of the value of the variable "x" is required. The important observation to make is that in relation to parameters, there are many choices to be made, in selecting which computations to package into sub-routines, which variables to specify as parameters, which order to list them in the description, etc. Thus if two programmers using identical parameter lists on identically specified sub-routine collections, it is unlikely that they worked independently of each other, otherwise they would have made some choices differently. In less mathematical applications, the variety of choice is even greater, further impacting both copyright and infringement analyses.

(iii) Microcode

Microcode is a basic level of software in a computer system. In essence it is narrow band programing to interpret the instruction sets and basic operations of microprocessors, such as Intel 8086 and 80386 chips. Instead of wiring in the behaviour of the control unit[39] so it cannot be changed, one treats the control unit as if it were a small computer within the overall computer, and then programs the control computer to interpret operation codes. This kind of programming for the inner computer is called micro-programming, and the instructions for that inner computer are called micro-instructions, or microcode. With microcode, changes or additions to the behaviour of the control unit, such as the proper interpretation of old or new operation codes, can be made by altering the microprogram instead of redesigning a major part of the hardware.[40]   **A.35**

In micro-programming the central processing unit's primary responsibility is to obtain an instruction from storage, break that instruction into its components (the operation code, the address of the data on which it is to operate, the address of the location where the result is to be put, and the address of the next instruction), and then co-ordinate and direct the actions of the various parts of the computer system so as to carry out the intended effect of the original instruction. Suppose the required instruction to be executed is an "Add" function: **A.36**

Add   10045   14   23167   55012

where the number 10045 represents the address of the data to be used as one value in the addition, the number 14 indicates that Register 14 in the ALU[41] is the place to find the other value to be added, the number 23167 indicates the

---

[39] *Supra*, n 11.

[40] Hence the flexibility of microcode. The designer of a new computer would usually leave a number of possible operation codes unused in order to be able to adjust to unforeseen circumstances. Later when the computer is in use, and the pattern of customers' programs become more apparent, certain very desirable operation codes could be "built in" by assigning them as yet unused operation codes.

[41] *Supra*, n 11.

storage address where the result is to be placed, and the number 55012 points to the address of the next instruction. The programmer will want to ensure that values arrive at various registers at the right time; that the registers are conditioned to received new values; that these values are routed through the addition device at just the right time; that the result is routed to the proper storage location; and that the storage unit is ready to receive a new value after having just sent a value to the ALU.

A.37   To carry out the "Add" instruction illustrated above, the control unit may require the following sequence of microinstructions:

```
Add:
    load      a,x          load      b,r              (1)
    setup     c                                       (2)
    add       a,b          get       next             (3)
    store     c            end                        (4)
```

which would be interpreted by the control unit as follows:

- In parallel, load two hidden registers "a" and "b" with the contents of the location referred to in the first data field of the instruction, called "x" here, and having the address 10045 in the above example, and in the second field, called "r", and in the above example, Register 14.
- Send the address where the result is to be put, called the "c" field of the instruction, and 23167 in the example, to the storage unit so it can prepare to receive a value.
- Send the values from the internal registers "a" and "b" to the addition unit, and at the same time start the necessary process to obtain the next instruction, by sending the address of the next instruction, in the example 55012, to the storage unit. Since the addition does not involve the storage unit, these two independent activities can be carried out in parallel.
- Store the result of the addition directly into the storage unit, which already has been prepared to receive a value and put it into the correct place. The second half of the microinstruction indicates that this is the end of the microsequence. The control unit concludes the interpretation of this sequence of microinstructions and begins to interpret the next instruction.

A.38 Another possible microsequence for the above instruction can take the following form:

```
Add:
    load      a,r1         load      b,r2
    add       a,b          get       next
    store     r2           end
```

Yet another possible microsequence for the same operation might be:

```
Add:
    load      b,x          load      a,r
              add          a,b       setup     c
              get          next      store     c
              end
```

These two versions are comparatively faster than the original, since they take only three cycles, thus improving the performance of the computer when adding two values. At the same time it is observed that these two alternate microsequences for the interpretation and execution of the "Add" operation show the possibility of different choices which can be made by different microprogrammers.

It follows that a collection of carefully designed, high-performance microc- **A.39** ode sequences constitutes valuable intellectual property. Consequently, the copyrightability of microcode has been confronted, and been resolved by US courts.[42]

(iv) Look-Up Tables

In *Autodesk v Dyason*[43] it will be recalled that "Widget C" contained instruc- **A.40** tions (from a 127-bit look-up table) to the computer on which it was run, requiring the latter to send a "challenge" to the AutoCAD lock.[44] On receipt of the challenge, Widget C compares it with the correct response which it ascertains from the look-up table. If the two correspond, Widget C allows the AutoCAD program to continue running. The 127-bit look-up table was randomly generated (in a "pseduo random sequence", or "stochastic" way); but was essential for the AutoCAD lock to function; and any device which was to perform the function of the AutoCAD lock was required to have the look-up table reproduced in the same form.

(v) Huffmann Compression Tables

In *Powerflex v Data Access*,[45] the Huffman Compression Table, which was **A.41** accorded copyright protection by the Full Federal Court, is used in the compression and decompression of files. Huffman encoding is a form of statistical encoding,[46] which identifies certain sequences within data, which are then coded so that they are represented by few bits. Initially the encoder scans through the file and generates a table of occurrences of a given character. The

---

[42] In *NEC Corp v Intel Corp* 643 F.Supp 590 (ND Cal 1986) it was held that microprograms are essentially the same as any other computer programs and that neither the legislative history nor the language of the US Copyright Act distinguishes between types of programs. See also *Allen-Myland v IBM* 746 F.Supp 520 (ED Pa. 1990) where it was held that microprograms related to an IBM mainframe system (the 3090 system) were copyrightable.

[43] *Autodesk v Dyason* (1992) 22 IPR IPR 163; *Autodest v Dyason (No 2)* (1993) 25 IPR 33; discussed *supra*, at paras 6.67–6.72.

[44] For details on the working of the AutoCAD lock, see the exposition by Dawson J in (1992) 22 IPR 163 at 168–169.

[45] *Data Access Corporation v Powerflex Services* (1996) 33 IPR 194; *Powerflex Services v Data Access Corporation* (1997) 37 IPR 436; discussed further, *supra*, para 6.73–6.75.

[46] For a comparison between Standard binary coding and Huffman binary coding, see Huner [1998] EIPR 98 at 102.

codes are then assigned to minimise the number of encoded bits.[47] As with the look-up table in *Autodesk v Dyason*, in order to read a file compressed with a particular Huffmann table, the exact same table must be used in the decompression.

III.   REVERSE ENGINEERING PROCESSES: A TECHNICAL BACKGROUND

A.42   This section forms a technical precursor to Chapter 6, which discussed the legal regimes that govern the process of software reverse engineering. Through the following account one attempts to set the scene for the technical truths of software reverse engineering to emerge; ultimately emphasising that disassembly or the supposed process of "decompilation" are procedures which are often treated with over-simplification.

A.43   The primary purpose of software reverse engineering is to investigate the functionality and underlying ideas of a computer program, either through a static or dynamic examination of the program's object code. There are generally four different ways by which the process may be effected:

- by reading program documentation;
- by observing the program in operation by use in a personal computer;
- by performing a static examination of the individual computer instructions contained within a program; or
- by performing a dynamic examination of the individual computer instructions as the program is being run on a computer.

The process of reverse engineering has often been dismissed by its opponents as an easy means by which a competitor can erase the lead time advantage obtained by the original developer:

> "any successful software product can be copied and decompiled with a flick of a console key, without significant investment or risk. Thus a decompiler can erase the lead time advantage of the program developer and significantly reduce the originator's market for the authored work".[48]

Computer programmers have routinely used reverse engineering to make up for inadequate program documentation for the past 30 years, documentation which either fails to provide sufficient details of the ideas embodied within the program, or is completely absent.[49]

---

[47] See William Buchanan, *Mastering Global Information Systems* (Macmillan, 1997) at pp 79–80.
[48] See Irving Rapport, "EC Threatens Software Protection" *San Francisco Recorder*, 22 February 1990 at 6 (writing as IBM's general counsel).
[49] This is well illustrated by the numerous books and publications which have emerged augmenting well respected and popular software products. Such books are the product of software reverse engineering.

(a) An Illustrative Example of the Need for Software Reverse Engineering

The example has been given[50] of a company, X Co, which seeks to produce a **A.44** competitive version of the Lotus 1–2–3 spreadsheet program. X Co first has to consider what information is available for analysis. Lotus Development Corporation would have a blueprint of the overall design of its 1–2–3 program. However, it would keep, as all software companies do, the human readable source code[51] as a closely guarded trade secret. X Co will also look at the actual product that is commercially distributed, including any user documentation which explains how the program can be used, and the object code[52] that controls the computer when the 1–2–3 program is loaded. X Co will not have access to Lotus 1–2–3's design documentation nor will it have access to its source code. The only information that is available to it is first, user documentation and second, the actual code that makes up the 1–2–3 program itself.

In order to produce a competing product, X Co must understand certain **A.45** attributes of Lotus 1–2–3; namely (i) functionality; (ii) the user interface (the external appearance and the way in which the user controls what 1–2–3 does); and (iii) datafile formats (computer representations by which previously stored information can be input into Lotus 1–2–3, and the representations output by the same).

Much of the information that X Co requires in order to create a design for a **A.46** competing product can be obtained from the documentation provided with purchase. For example, its user manual provides a useful description of how to make Lotus 1–2–3 perform various calculations. The program itself also provides an experimental test-bed that can be used to verify that the program works as described by the documentation. X Co's programmer can obtain significant information about user interfaces by merely using Lotus 1–2–3, often deriving clues of the minor workings just by observing the program's external behaviour. Together, external observation and documentation will provide X C. with much of the information it would require about the functionality of Lotus 1–2–3, with the exception of "bugs" (areas where the program malfunctions) or where the documentation is erroneous and incomplete.

The more cynical of programmers[53] adopt the general rule that program doc- **A.47** umentation is incomplete and inaccurate in providing the material information. A thorough examination of the object code is necessary, hence the role of software reverse engineering. Let us take the Net Present Value mathematical function in Lotus 1–2–3. Suppose X Co's programmer makes the observation that under certain specific circumstances, it computes a result that is a few cents different from the same calculation done using Borland's Quattro Pro. If X Co is

---

[50] See Laird "Software Reverse Engineering in the Real World" 19(3) *U Dayton L.Rev* 843 (1994).
[51] *Supra*, at para A.4.
[52] Ibid.
[53] See eg Laird, *supra* n 50 at 843. The author wishes to acknowledge the utility of this and other papers of Dr Laird as invaluable resources to the preparation of this section.

creating a competing product, it has to make a judgement call: whether it should be "compatible" with this possibly erroneous calculation. Should X Co's product produce the same results as Lotus 1–2–3 even though those results are slightly in error? From the programmer's point of view, the answer is clear: if one wishes to compete with an existing product, there should be no measurable difference, at least with such things as standard calculations, between one's own product and the existing product. In the absence of any documentation or explanation as to why the 1–2–3 Net Present Value function does what it does, X Co's only recourse is to examine the object code for the 1–2–3 program itself.

A.48   Another example has been given where X Co wishes to create a video game to run on the Nintendo SNES base unit. Unless the game cartridges that plug into the base unit are produced under licence and manufactured by Nintendo, the games they contain will not run in the SNES base unit.[54] There is an immediate obstacle confronting X Co—the lock-out mechanism.[55] Nintendo uses two special purpose computer chips, one in the game cartridge and one in the SNES base unit. These purpose built central-processing chips are dedicated to the specific task of interrogating each other, passing pseudo-random segments of 0s and 1s back and forth to each other. If one chip fails to send a correct digit, fails to send it at the right time, or fails to pause for the correct length of time, the other chip, detecting the imposter, can stop the SNES base unit from running the game program in the cartridge. One of the key questions addressed by this book is: given that X Co wishes to produce games for SES, should it be forced to sign a licence agreement with Nintendo, or is it lawful that X Co could elect to derive the inner workings of the special computers and produce a computer chip which is capable of generating the correct responsive signals with the lock-out mechanism?[56]

A.49   Suppose X Co elects not to become a Nintendo licensee, either because it cannot afford to, or because it objects to being held to ransom. In this scenario, there is no information available for X Co's programmer to be able to write a game for the Nintendo base unit, eg how to control the various chips in the base unit which control the display, or control the sound generator. In this scenario the only recourse for X Co, in the absence of a licence from Nintendo, is to analyse the following components of the Nintendo SNES system:

- the base unit's hardware and software;
- the game cartridge's software;

[54] *Supra*, n 50.

[55] The rise of reverse engineering by third party software developers in turn has led some computer manufacturers to seek technological protection against unwanted competitors. For a discussion of this technological one-upmanship, see Marshall Leafer, "Engineering Competitive Policy and Copyright Misuse" (1994) 19 U. Dayton L. Rev 1087, 1096–1097. Within the video game industry, several system manufacturers have developed specialised "lock-out" programs that limit access to their hardware to program disks or cartridges that contain the "key"; see further *Sega v Nintendo* 977 F.2d 1510 at 1515 (9th Cir 1992); *Atari v Nintendo of America Inc.* 975 F.2d 832 at 836 (Fed Cir 1992).

[56] This is a different question from asking whether X Co should be able to copy the coding within the special lock-out chip. All X Co needs to do is to understand the programming regime governing the pseudo-random stream of 0s and 1s, and the pauses which occur in this data stream.

- the actual lock-out chip.

Through this process X Co hopes to write games that will run on the SNES base unit and will also emulate the behaviour of the lock-out chip on the game cartridge so that the base unit will permit the game program to run. In practice this translates into two questions: (i) how to write games for the base unit, and (ii) how to make a lock-out chip that will be accepted by the lock-out chip in the base unit. It has been observed that observing the data stream between the two chips would be "time consuming" and "error prone".[57] In the US it is also not open to the reverse engineer to obtain a deposit copy of the source code from the Copyright Office through fraudulent means.[58]

A.50   X Co will be forced to take the more laborious route of physically reverse engineering the lock-out chips—removing the protective plastic that encapsulates the chip, and creating photomicrographs of the read-only memory containing the relevant data-generating code. In many special-purpose microcomputers, the 0s and 1s that make up the program are not laid out in systematic fashion, either for reasons of engineering simplicity, or in some cases, to discourage reverse engineering. X Co would most likely not be able to make any sense of the 0s and 1s that make up the interfacing programs until they had also reverse engineered the chip itself.[59] In its observation of the base unit, the observation of the silk-screened notations visible on some of the integrated circuits might give engineers some clues as to their functions. Careful observation of the printed circuit board's wiring will add to these ideas, but many of the more complex special purpose chips will either leave no markings, or bear only proprietary markings that mean nothing to the outside world.

A.51   X Co's engineers will undoubtedly realise that the only certain method of determining how to write a game is to examine the object code contained within existing Nintendo games, so as to ascertain how these games initialise the various components of the SNES base unit, and produce and generate graphic images and music.

(b) Techniques of Software Reverse Engineering

A.52   It is possible to list the various strategies that are available to companies that wish to investigate the functionality of competing programs. They are discussed in ascending order of utility and effectiveness.[60]

---

[57] See Laird, (1994) 19 U. of Dayton L Rev 843 at 854.
[58] See *Atari v Nintendo* 975 F.2d 832 (Fed Cir 1992).
[59] eg is an ADD instruction 0011 or 1010? It all depends on how the central processing unit that forms the heart of the computer chip has been designed.
[60] See Laird, op cit.

(i) Reading user documentation

A.53 This is perhaps the least adequate technique, as user documentation is by definition insufficient for the purposes of offering the programmer a real idea as to how and why a program's coding is structured in a particular way.[61]

(ii) "Black-box" operations

A.54 The entire plaintiff's computer program/chip is viewed as a black-box, and the engineer in this instance merely observes what it does and how it performs, with a view to inferring what must be going on inside the program. Through the empirical observation of program inputs and outputs, the programmer is only making a reasonable guess as to how the program's coding is structured.[62] This inspection fails to ascertain information as fact, and moreover is unable to reveal the precise cause for apparent errors.

(iii) Examination of the circuit board

A.55 In some instances this static examination is conducted in order to identify the actual program to be reverse engineered amidst a circuit board with a dozen integrated circuit chips mounted on it. Typically some of the chips are marked with manufacturers' code numbers; others are unmarked.[63] Programmers start from a position of ignorance; they must first examine the physical details of the circuit board, look up data sheets for those chips that are marked, an attempt to infer additional information about the unmarked chips. Ostensibly engineers can determine the electrical connections laid out in a circuit board. From this they can speculate what chips contain read-only memory (so-called "ROM chips"), and are therefore candidates for further examination. There are two primary techniques to examine the contents of ROM chips:

---

[61] For a different view see Edmund Weiss, "The Next Wave of User Documentation" *Computer World*, 9 September 1985 at ID/15: "Gradually the developers of systems and products have become aware of a trade-off. They saw that good documentation saves money: Having good manuals costs less than not having them. Every incompleteness, every error, every unclear or obsolete instruction has its price. And that price almost always involves personal services: training, consulting, telephone hotlines, field visits or late-night trips to the operations centre".

[62] Duncan Davidson, "Common Law, Uncommon Software" (1986) 47 U Pitt L Rev 1037 at 1080-1084, discussing the black-box metaphor and a model for how it might be used in resolving copyright disputes. Under the Davidson Model, "black-box testing" is lawful. See Hart, "Legal Protection of Computer Programs: Decompilation, Reverse Engineering and the EC Directive" [1993] 1 *The International Computer Lawyer* 10, in which "black-box" reverse engineering is described as a process in which the desired information about how a program functions is obtained by inputting data into the computer system, running the program and then looking at the resulting outputs. Through an "iterative" process of changing the input and observing the changing outputs, it may be possible to determine how the program functions.

[63] Often this is a deliberate strategy to make the identification of the chip's purpose so much more difficult.

- **electronic technique**: which can be implemented in two ways depending on whether the ROM chip can be removed from the circuit board. If the chip can be removed, it can be placed into a test rig and its contents read out directly as a set of 0s and 1s. If the ROM chip cannot be removed form the board without damaging it and preventing its contents from being read out, programmers will need to devise a mechanism for "looking inside" the unit in question while it is switched on and running. An "in-circuit emulator" is commonly used to read the coding.

- **physical technique**: involves "deprocessing" the ROM chip by removing the outer layer of protective plastic and exposing the small silicon chip itself. Acid is used to etch away some of the outermost layers of the chemicals deposited on the silicon chip and photomicrographs can be taken of the circuitry that makes up the ROM chip itself. At suitable magnification, a trained engineer can discern the actual 0s and 1s stored in the ROM chip.

The above techniques yield an image of the ROM's contents, the actual 0s and 1s presented to the CPU. The task for the programmer is to decode these 0s and 1s and define what instructions and what data will be presented to the CPU.

(iv) Examination of a program in the computer's memory

A computer uses a numeric representation that is even simpler than decimal— **A.56** the binary system (base 2 rather than base 10).[64] Memory locations in a computer system store the characters of the alphabet using a simple encoding system. Incoming keystrokes are converted to their appropriate number, and then the numbers are converted into their respective letters appearing on the screen (video display unit). For example, "A" does not equal "1" but "65". In binary this appears as 1000001. Other characters are assigned to the first 65 numbers, 0–64; including "non-graphic" characters that are not visible on the computer screen. (eg carriage return, tab, etc). The entire upper/lower case alphabet, special characters such as parenthesis, and a percentage sign take up the remaining numbers up to 255. It was stated earlier that this encoding is recognised by the acronym, ASCII,[65] invented by the American National Standards Institute.

As mentioned earlier,[66] in the computer's memory, binary digits are stored in **A.57** groups of eight or "bits" and these groups of eight are known as "bytes". To identify each byte in memory, each is assigned an "address". The address is just a number, starting from "0" and increasing by "1".

---

[64] eg the decimal number 123 (which represents hundred, 2 tens and 3 ones) will appear as 1111011 in binary. This represents 1 "64", 1 "32", 1 "16", 1 "8", 1 "2" and 1 "1" which totals up to 123 in decimal. Seeing binary with column headers helps:

6432168421
1 1 1 1011

[65] American Standard Code for Information Interchange, *supra*, para A.9.

[66] Ibid.

(c) Binary Notation and Hexadecimal Representation

A.58 Opponents to reverse engineering claim that programmers need only look at the binary data as it is stored in a computer's memory, without having to make an intermediate copy of the program under examination.[67] It is submitted that this is an impractical and inefficient way of looking at binary notation, especially when eight source code lines can be represented by as many as 50 pages of unrelenting raw binary data. In practice the print-outs of data made would constitute infringing copies in their own right, and any handwritten annotations that programmers may write into the print-out could given rise to works of adaptation under the Copyright Designs and Patents Act 1988.

A.59   To understand adequately the binary image, programmers must convert binary notation into a human comprehensible form (noting that this is only a conversion, no new information is being added to the underlying binary image). The first of several conversions will be to group the binary digits into 8-bit bytes as follows:

```
00000000  00000010  00000001  00001011  00000000  00000000  01000000  00000000
00000000  00000000  00100000  00000000  00000000  00000000  00001110  11111100
00000000  00000000  00000110  10000100  00000000  00000000  00100000  00100000
00000000  00000000  00000000  00000000  00000000  00000000  00000000  00000000
00100100  00010111  01000111  11101111  00000000  00000100  00100010  00000010
```

This conversion improves the engineer's ability to study the contents of the computer's memory. Yet it is still almost impossible to know where on the screen a particular byte is located. To be practical, the engineer must be able to display memory in such a way that he can see both the instructions to the computer and the memory locations contained in those instructions, including any embedded ASCII characters. Instead of displaying the contents of memory in binary, an engineer could use a compressed but readable form of binary—hexadecimal. Hexadecimal is base 16 arithmetic. To convert to hexadecimal, binary digits are grouped together in groups of four and placed under normal binary headings as follows:

Binary	Hexadecimal
0000	0
0001	1
0010	2
0011	3
0100	4
0101	5
0110	6
0111	7

[67] The case is made that loading binary data into RAM does not constitute a permanent fixation of data. This argument was advanced by Sega in *Sega v Accolade* 977 F.2d 1510 (9th Cir 1992) and was accepted by the lower Court.

Binary	Hexadecimal
1000	8
1001	9
1010	A
1011	B
1100	C
1011	D
1110	E
1111	F

Hexadecimal notation, or "hex" notation demands "numbers" to represent the values which correspond to the decimal values 10,11,12,13,14 and 15 and so the first few letters of the alphabet are used. Numbers may be written eg as "1FH"—which denotes that "1F" is to be taken in hex form. Hex representation carries the advantage of compressing the amount of memory space, since each hex digit represents 4 binary digits.

(d) The "Hex Dump"

A hex dump is a conversion of ordinary binary notation into hexadecimal nota- **A.60** tion and ASCII representation, and offers a new representation of binary data. It should be said a hex dump does not add any new information. An example of a hex dump is listed as follows:

```
0000:   00 02 01 0b 00 00 40 00    00 00 20 00 00 00 0e fc    ......@     ......l
0010:   00 00 06 84 00 00 20 20    00 00 00 00 00 00 00 00    ........    ........
0020:   24 17 47 ef 00 04 22 02    e5 81 49 f3 18 04 23 cc    $ . Go .. "  e . Is .. #L
```

In the above example, the memory address of the first byte on the line is shown first. This address is also shown in hexadecimal. Two groups of eight bytes follow, with each byte's value being shown in hexadecimal (the grouping makes it easier to count off across the line). On the far right, again grouped in two groups of eight, comes the same data, but this time displayed as ASCII characters. Those bytes that have values that do not correspond to "visible" characters like letters and numbers (such as carriage return and tab) are shown as a period.

A hex dump is the first representation of the computer program's object code **A.61** which improves the understanding of the software engineer. Opponents to reverse engineering have argued that a reverse engineer has no need to proceed further, since object code can be read directly at this point.[68] The view has been

---

[68] See Clapes, "Confessions of an Amicus Curiae: Technophobia, law and creativity in the digital arts" (1993) 19 U Dayton L Rev 903 at 943; "when software is processed by a computer, the ideas, concepts and principles, along with the expression sought to be imparted can be perceived by the user. If the computer user happens also to be a programmer, by observing what happens on the computer's monitor screen, disk drives, loudspeakers or printer when the computer is under the control of a program, the programmer can learn a great deal about those ideas in the program that are not readily perceived by the casual user". The author goes on to cite Vinje, "The Development of

taken by proponents that it is completely impractical for a programmer to work with hex dumps. While it would be possible for them to read this slightly simpler representation and decode it, it is still impossible for the engineer to read and understand the program in sufficient detail.[69] Moreover the computer instructions together with the bytes which contain them, have to be ascertained.

(e) Disassembly and Disassemblers

A.62   A hex dump is inadequate for two reasons: it still remains difficult first, for the engineer to locate the first instruction in the program; and secondly, to use that first instruction as the starting point for a journey through the maze of instructions in the program. For example, the engineer needs to be ever-vigilant of "branch" and "jump" instructions which prevent a computer from executing adjacent instructions one after another.

A.63   In order to overcome these problems, the engineer takes a few lines of hex code and manually "disassembles" them. Disassembly is the conversion of hex notation into assembly language, which explains what each instruction is telling the CPU to do. In this process the programmer can not only decode what each instruction is, but how many bytes it occupies. From this he refers to the user manual, to obtain a quick reference chart showing each of the instructions in numerical order. For example, when examining a string of bytes, say "4e 56 00 00 df" the engineer can narrow his search by looking in the manual only for instructions which have "4e" as their first byte. From this they are also able to discern what the next byte is, and when the next instruction is most likely to start. This process, which is known as "manual disassembly" is repeated for subsequent instructions.

A.64   Manual disassembly, as described above, is extremely time-consuming. It can take up to one minute to decode each instruction and to double-check the results. Modern programs may have at least 300,000 instructions, and programmers can take many months to arrive at a disassembled listing. It should also be noted that disassembled listing is a set of raw, low-level instructions that will be executed by the CPU. There are no comments nor symbolic variable names to guide a programmer.

A.65   Since the early 1950s, every computer manufacturer has provided basic software which could disassemble program code back into assembly language in just moments. Such software is called a "disassembler". But disassemblers have limitations. The engineer must still know where the instructions begin. In many systems, code and data are intermixed; small blocks of code will be followed by data, and then more code and more data, etc. The use of a disassembler is also

Interoperable Products Under the EC Software Directive" *Computer Lawyer* (November 1991) 1 at 4; describing screen displays of hexadecimal object code as a means of obtaining information about a program.

   [69] See Laird, 19 U Dayton L Rev 843 at 870–871.

a time-consuming process. The engineer has to disassemble some part of the program, inspect the results and, using instinct as much as logic, make adjustments as to where the disassembler starts disassembling instructions (coding) and where it skips over data.

Through much coaxing, trial and error, a disassembled listing is then pro-   **A.66** duced. No new information is added, only the representation of the binary patterns in memory has been changed. There is an absolute one-on-one relationship between the instructions that a disassembler outputs and their bit patterns in memory.

The biggest obstacle to reverse engineering is the absence of information pre-   **A.67** sent in the output of a disassembler. Moreover the instructions and their operands appear in detail, but engineers have no information as to (i) what these instructions are actually doing; (ii) why they are doing what they are doing; and (iii) when, in the overall program's execution, these instructions might be carried out. The purpose of a particular set of instructions is further shrouded by fact that most instructions are not executed sequentially. There could be a jump to a part of a program or a particular sub-routine which the engineer has not yet disassembled. See the following example:

00a0:	linkw	a6, #0
00a4:	addl	#−0x10, a7
00aa:	moveml	#0, sp@
00ae:	movl	#0, a6@ (−4)
00b6:	movl	a6@ (−4), d0
00ba:	jsr	0x0afc: 1 —This is a jump out of sequence to a different sub-routine
00c0:	movl	0x0200, a6@ (−0x10)

Note the "jsr" function at location 00ba. This instruction tells the computer not to execute the following instruction at 00c0, but to "jump" out of sequence to another part of the program.[70] It is this information that eludes the reverse engineer.

(f) "Decompilation"

The frequency of use of the term "decompilation" in the course of debate   **A.68** leading to the adoption of the EU Software Directive, and elsewhere,[71] could

---

[70] "Jsr" means "jump sub-routine" and is used to direct the processor to break sequence, follow the instructions contained in the specified sub-routine and then return to execute the instruction following the "jsr". A sub-routine is a small self-contained group of instructions used to perform a specific function. The computer stops executing the main program, and starts executing the sub-routine code. When the sub-routine is complete, the computer returns to the main code.

[71] See David Hamilton, "US criticizes Japan on Panel Software" *Wall Street Journal*, 10 November 1993 at B5: "United States companies, like IBM say they are particularly concerned about a form of reverse engineering known as 'decompilation'. In that procedure, software engineers 'translate' a computer program's ones and zeroes of binary code into a more readable

reasonably lead one to assume that "decompilation" was a term of art. Yet in truth "decompilation"[72] is not a technical term, being merely the contrived antonym of "compilation", which is a term of art.[73] As part of common parlance, "decompilation" describes the process of disassembling object code, in an attempt to recreate the original, or as near as possible to the original source code. Programmers have to try and understand the particular instructions in the final disassembled listing. "Decompilation" takes place in the following stages.

(i) Insertion of comments

A.69   In the first stage, the engineer adds his own comments to the disassembly listing. Every sub-routine has to be examined, and disassembled. If the sub-routine itself contains a "jsr" instruction which transfers control to other sub-routines,[74] then these sub-routines must be disassembled and understood.

A.70   After considerable study the engineers can make intelligent guesses as to what some of these sub-routines are doing by examining the object code. They may insert symbolic names in their disassembly listing as a reminder of what the code was doing. Through these means, the engineer can gradually add to his understanding of what the code appears to be doing, per instruction, per sub-routine and per symbolic label. Experienced programmers are quick to stress that at this stage they are adding their own ideas and labels to coding which otherwise would not contain the higher level information which they crave.[75]

(ii) Creation of a flow chart

A.71   After long weeks of research, disassembly, commentary, analysis and actual observation of the program running under the control of a diagnostic program, the engineer can make a leap to a higher level of abstraction and create his own flow chart. At this juncture, the engineer begins to see the overall "shape" of the program under analysis

---

language. That translated version can be easily modified and 'recompiled' into a new program that is only slightly different from the original, a prospect that unnerves many US software companies".

See also Andrew Pollack, "US Protesting Japan's Plan to Revise Software Protection" *New York Times*, 22 November 1993 at D2: "American officials say decompilation involves copying software, which is illegal. There are legal ways, they say, to find out how a program works. In addition, they say, once a program has been decompiled it can be changed somewhat and recompiled into a new program in a way that makes it hard to tell whether the original had been copied".

[72] See also Johnson-Laird "Technical Description of Decompilation" (1992) 16 Computer L Rep 469.

[73] This is certainly the view of Dr Andrew Johnson-Laird.

[74] This is known as "nesting" (sub-routines calling sub-routines calling sub-routines). Nesting may occur to 20/30 levels in modern object code, especially object code generated by an "optimising" compiler that translates the original source code, optimises the object for execution, and then links it with prefabricated libraries of fine-tuned object code sub-routines prepared by specially skilled systems programmers.

[75] See Laird, (1994) 19 U Dayton L Rev 843 at 879.

(iii) Creation of the source code

After the "flow chart" stage, most programmers ask their colleagues to write **A.72**
source code corresponding to the specifications as revealed through the flow
chart. This "clean room" technique[76] may lend considerable assistance to dis-
proving any charge of "slavish copying" since the second programmer does not
have direct access to the disassembled listing, and will in all probability produce
a different source code.

Whilst it may be shown that both codes may be identical at parts, this is not **A.73**
necessarily "slavish copying". Many lines are absolutely standard for any program written, for example, in the "C" language.[77] The similarities which emerge
may be a direct product of the constraints under which the programmers have
developed the program.[78] On the other hand, programmers have on occasion
faithfully reverse engineered, and consequently reproduced a mistake in the
original program. Such an occurrence in a defendant's product would constitute
a "fingerprint" which has in other circumstances been used as "proof" of copyright infringement.

(g) What Does Reverse Engineering Reveal?

Reverse engineering can only reveal information contained within the binary **A.74**
code that is being studied. The skilled engineer is able to obtain precise but partial information about what a program does, as opposed to why it does it. The
following information may be revealed through the various reverse engineering
techniques discussed above

- information concerning the user interface—that is the visual and audio
  interface perceived by someone using the program;[79]
- information concerning internal interfaces[80]—certain interface specifications are crucial for interoperability. Computer manufacturers have
  argued that "decompilation is not standard industry practice in developing original computer programs".[81] This is disputed since it is most

---

[76] See further discussion, *infra*, paras A.77–A.79.
[77] See the detailed hypothetical "SENSATEMP" example by Laird in (1994) 19 U Dayton L Rev
843 at 881–887.
[78] A factor which Courts undoubtedly should take into account when considering non-literal
similarity between programs.
[79] It could be argued that disassembling the user interface is impractical since information can be
obtained more easily by black-box observation of the program in operation.
[80] An interface is a software "connection" between one body of software and another. Andrew
Johnson-Laird has defined an "interface" as "a point in an information processing system through
which information passes without any intentional change to its format or its meaning". See Laird,
(1994) 19 U Dayton L Rev 843 at 897.
[81] See Amicus Brief by the Computer and Business Equipment Manufacturers' Association in
Sega v Accolade 977 F.2d 1510 (9th Cir 1992) at p29.

unlikely that "original computer programs" are developed in isolation from all other programs;[82]

- information concerning internal and external data structures—the existence and purpose of internal data structures can only be analysed by observing the program placing data into, or retrieving data from the various data fields within the structure. Data files can also be analysed by creating special test data with predetermined data values in each data field;

- information concerning the overall static structure of the object code—revealing how the object code is laid out when the program is loaded into memory to be run on the computer;[83]

- information on some aspects of the algorithms used by the program under scrutiny. However, in the absence of detailed information, the reverse engineer can at best only observe how the program performs.[84] Further analysis is inhibited by not seeing all of the program's code in action;

- information concerning the dynamic structure and execution sequence in which parts of a program are executed by computer.

A.75 On the other hand, reverse engineering can never recreate any of the original higher levels of abstraction information contained in design documentation, specifications, business plans and other preparatory material of the original software developer. It also is unable to reveal the original source code, complete with programmer's comments. Original data structures, complete with data fields that might be set aside for future use, are also not revealed. Above all while disassembly may assist in perception, it does little to determine the rationale behind the original design.

A.76   The point to be emphasised from the above section is that in the absence of direct copying, reverse engineering techniques, particularly those of disassembly and "decompilation" are strictly *not* substitutes for hard work.[85]

---

[82] eg for Microsoft Word for Windows to remain a viable commercial product, it must interoperate flawlessly with eight other major software products: (i) Microsoft Windows, (ii) Microsoft Disk Operating Systems, (iii) Adobe Type Manager, (iv) Word for Windows, (v) Alki's Master Word extensions to Word for Windows, (vi) Norton's Desktop for Windows, (vii) Stac Electronics' Stacker Software, (viii) QEMM (Computer Memory Manager).

[83] The static structure of object code is vastly different from the static structure of the source code. The source code has been translated by a Compiler program and glued together with other object code by a Linker program. The final object code is more a product of the Compiler and the Linker than the programmer who wrote the source code.

[84] It is not at all unusual that only 10 to 30 per cent of the object code is executed during the normal operation of a modern program. The remaining 70 to 90 per cent is reserved for error-handling and special conditions that the reverse engineer might not be able to recreate.

[85] This is stressed by numerous writers on the subject. See for example, Laird, *supra*, n 72 at 895–901; Jacobs "Copyright and Compatibility" (1989) 30 Jurimetrics J 91 at 102; Daughtey, "Reverse Enginering of Software for Interoperability and Analysis" (1994) 47 Vand L Rev 145 at 151–152.

IV. THE "CLEAN ROOM" PROCEDURE

A technique of software examination and creation which, in the view of some **A.77** writers,[86] serves to ensure immunisation against infringement claims is the "clean room" procedure. The procedure involves two groups of programmers. The first group examines the original program, extracts its specifications (functions, ideas and interfaces) and transmits the specifications, and not the original program, to the second group, which attempts to produce independently a computer program with similar characteristics.[87] By making literal copying difficult or impossible for the second team that writes the new program, this procedure arguably helps to rebut any assertion or inference that the final product was produced as a result of copying.[88]

Yet many are sceptical of the legality of this procedure,[89] especially if the **A.78** resulting program contains such a high degree of resemblance.[90] Much is determined by what the first team does. If it uses decompilation (prima facie an infringing act, subject to the fair use defence[91] or Software Directive provisions) to ascertain the underlying functions and specifications of the target program, then the legality of the decompilation is the determinant. If the decompilation is not legal, the use of a clean room technique will not render the end result lawful.[92] Nor can it be said that the clean room protocol offers an *alternative* to decompilation in extracting specifications.[93]

An inaccurate view has been somewhat formed of *Computer Associates v* **A.79** *Altai* as suggesting a presumptive legality of clean room procedures,[94] but *Altai* involved the admitted copying by defendants, who then rewrote the program

[86] See eg Stephen Davidson "Reverse Engineering and the Development of Compatible and Competitive Products under US Law", 10th Annual Computer Law Institute (PLI Patents, Copyrights, Trademarks & Literary Cause Handbook Series No 259, 1988), at 407, 432–433.

[87] See Clapes, *Software, Copyright an Competition: The "Look and Feel" of the Law* (1989) at pp 153–154.

[88] See further, Bernard Galler, *Software and Intellectual Property Protection* (Quorum Books, 1995) at pp 125–131.

[89] See eg Lake, Harwood and Olson "Tampering with Fundamentals: a Critique of Proposed Changes in EC Software Protection" *Computer Law* (December 1989) at 1, 7.

[90] See Clapes, *supra*, n 84 at 153, where it is said that if the level of resulting similarity between both programs is very high, inference that the "clean room" procedure was somehow circumvented would be very difficult to overcome.

[91] Professor Julie Cohen has argued that it is no greater a risk to allow a competitor continued access to the copied work than to make the "clean room" procedure a precondition for a finding of fair use (in *Sega*, Accolade had used such a procedure, a fact that weighed heavily in its favour). Courts, in assessing decompilation would easily require that clean room procedures be followed and documented. The burden would then shift to the copyright owner to show that the protected material was taken. Cohen (1995) 68 Southern Cal L Rev 1091 at 1124.

[92] See Miller "Copyright Protection for Computer Programs, Databases, and Computer-Generated Works: Is Anything New Since CONTU?" (1993) 106 Harv L Rev 977 at 1025.

[93] In *Sega v Accolade* 977 F.2d at 1526 (1992), Judge Reinhardt overturned the District Court's finding that "clean room" procedures provide an alternative to decompilation.

[94] See Office of Technology Assessment, *Finding a Balance: Computer Software, Intellectual Property and Technological Change* (1992) at p 140.

using the clean room protocol to correct the infringement. As such the defendants primarily worked from a non-infringing program,[95] and this has to be distinguished from other fact situations.

V.   TECHNICAL ISSUES AND THE WWW

(a) Hypertext Markup Language Runs the WWW

A.80 The World Wide Web[96] (WWW) operates on a text-based language called HTML[97] (HyperText Markup Language). The text contained in triangular brackets ("<" and ">") are the HTML directives that determine (in a manner that is similar to the embedded codes used by word processing programs) how the text is to be formatted, and the points of insertion of graphics into text.[98] The potency of HTML is illustrated by the following statement:

<img src="http://lcweb.loc.gov/copyright/mb100.gif>

This statement contains a link to another computer system and directs the web-browser program on the user's computer in the following (or equivalent) terms:

> "This is a citation to an image source (img src). Use the HyperText Transfer Protocol (http) to go to the computer site named 'lcweb' in the domain loc.gov (the Library of Congress website) and in the subdirectory 'copyright', retrieve the graphic image file (gif), called 'mb100'."

As this webpage is being displayed on the computer screen, its constituent components are being retrieved from different computers. There is no limit imposed on the number of remote sites which can be used, nor on the physical locations of those sites.

(b) Identification of Computers on the WWW

A.81 The WWW is a massive network of computers and servers.[99] Each computer is identified by means of a numeric "Internet Protocol Address". An IP address contains four groups of three digits; each digit can have a value from 0 to 255. The full statement "http://www . . . ." is the URL ("Universal Resource

---

[95] See *Computer Associates v Altai*, District Court Decision 775 F.Supp 544 at 554 (EDNY, 1991).

[96] A popular misunderstanding is that the WWW is the Internet. In fact the WWW is only one of the many information services available on the Internet. One of its primary advantages is that it encompasses most of the other Internet protocols, such as FTP (File Transfer Protocol), GOPHER, Newsgroups and Email. See further Cricket Liu, *et al Managing Internet Information Services* (1994) 1 at 20–22 ; Harley Hagn and Rick Stout *The Internet Complete Reference* (1994) at pp 68–69.

[97] See Ian S Graham, *The HTML Sourcebook* (1995), ix.

[98] Graham, ibid at p 21.

[99] April Major, "Copyright Law Tackles Yet Another Challenge: The Electronic Frontier of the World Wide Web" (1998) 24 Rutgers Computer & Technology L J 75 at 78–83.

Locator")[100]—the string of characters which identifies the communication protocol used (http) and the IP address of the server site. The protocol which administers this addressing system is the "TCP/IP" (Transmission Control Protocol/Internet Protocol).

(c) Data Transfer on the WWW

Data files are reduced into smaller "data packets" for the purposes of transfer. **A.82** Each data packet comprises (1) sender's IP address and port number; (2) recipient's IP address/port number; and (3) data contents. Each data packet has to pass through a hierarchical series of "routers". Routers receive multiple, incoming data feeds from individual computers in a home, company or Local Area Network (LAN). Thereafter they attach forward copies of these data packets to local or wide area routers which are electronically closer to the destination IP address.

(d) JAVASCRIPT and APPLETS[101]

JAVA is an Internet programming language,[102] which by definition is plat- **A.83** form-neutral, and, inter alia, may be used to write executable programs within HTML. A designer may create an executable program in the form of a "Java Appelet", which is stored in the designer's computer in Java Byte code and interpreted in a user's computer by a program called a Java Virtual Machine.[103]

(e) Hyper-Linking

(i) Linking

Hyper-linking is the means by which one document could refer a web-browser **A.84** to another webpage. A webpage does not have to link to the default home page of a particular site. It can link to any particular page. This secondary entry

---

[100] The underlying URL of a link "hotspot" on a webpage comprises four elements; the HTML elements of the URL ("<AHREF=. . .>") that are common to all URLs; the domain name of the website; the directory structure of the web-server (eg "/stores/council"); and the HTML filename of a particular webpage.

[101] See Hollander "A Primer; Java for Lawyers: What is all the hype about?" Vol 15 (6) *Legal Tech* (September 1997) p 5; Hollander "Java for Lawyers: a Primer" Vol 2 (5) *The Internet Newsletter Legal & Business Aspects* (August 1997) at p 5.

[102] A most useful work on the JAVA language and technology is Joe Webber, *et al*, *Using Java 1.1*, 3rd edn.

[103] Some writers regard a Java Applet to be protected as a literary work in its own right: see eg Gringras *Laws of the Internet* (1997) at pp 182–183.

by-passes any advertising text and images which may be present in a home page. This was the background to the complaint in *Shetland Times v Wills*.[104]

(ii) Framing

A.85 A variation to linking is "framing". The remote user's web-browser display is subdivided into a set of rectangular windows or frames—each of which can be manipulated independently; or the text can be scrolled up or down. Framing is accomplished by using the provisions of the HTML language—the first step is to define a "frame set", which divides the screen into different sections (eg see the CNN interactive homepage <http://www.cnn.com>). Typically a "site index" appears on the left of the page and remains there, regardless of which page is being displayed.[105]

(iii) Prevention of linking

A.86 Any site can prevent a link to one of its pages by including in its webpages a small program—written in JAVASCRIPT (a net interpreted programming language developed by Sun Microsystems) that can detect (a) that its page is being framed and (b) that the site performing the framing is a particular host site. The web-browser detects the Javascript program and interprets each statement in the program when it is first encountered. For example:

> Example of a Javascript program that prevents a given webpage from being framed
>   <Head>
>   <Title>Frame killers/Title>
>   <Script Language=Javascript>
>   <!Hide from non-javascript browsers if (self!=stop) top.location.replace ("noframe.htm")//done hiding—>
>   </script>
>   </Head>
>   <Body>
>   <Font Size=+2>
>   This page cannot be framed.
>   </Font>
>   </Body>
> (The above program must be saved in a file called "noframe.htm" as it relies on the knowledge of its own filename)

It is also possible to include a Common Gateway Interface (CGI) script on a webpage, which would automatically direct a user to the advertising page, or incorporate advertisements into a particular page as originally presented.

---

[104] *Supra*, para 8.12 *et seq*. For similar litigation in the USA, see *Ticketmaster Corp. v Microsoft Corp* No.97–3055 DDP (CD Cal 1997), discussed in Effross "Withdrawal of the Reference: Rights, Rules and Remedies for Unwelcomed Web-Linking" (1998) 49(4) South Carolina Law Rev 651 at 656–658.

[105] See further *Washington Post Co v Total News* No 97 Civ 1190 (PKL) (SDNY 1997), discussed in Effross, ibid at 659–660.

(f) Caching

(i) Copying on the WWW: Caching

Another activity that is ubiquitous on the Internet is the process of caching.[106] **A.87**
Caching refers to the storing of copies of material from an original source site
(eg a webpage) for later use when the same material is requested again, thereby
obviating the need to go back to the original source for the material. To establish the necessary implications for the reproduction right and exceptions
thereto, "caching" has to be studied to (i) determine its purpose; (ii) ascertain its
various forms; (iii) ascertain its attributes, particularly in relation to transience;
and (iv) ascertain its "integral" nature or otherwise.

(ii) Purpose of caching

The purpose of caching is to facilitate user access to a particular website, obvi- **A.88**
ating the need to route data packets from the host server, where the original
material is stored. The primary purpose of caching is to speed up repeated access
to data and to reduce network congestion resulting from repeated downloads of
data.[107]

(iii) Types of caching

It is impossible to predict how many such caches exist in a particular connec- **A.89**
tion. There are generally four types of caching.

- **Mirror Caching**. Also known as "caching servers". These occur when a
  frequently accessed website is downloaded to another server in anticipation that the information will be required sometime in the future. It
  relieves net traffic, since a user will avoid the need to read the page from
  the original source.
- **Web Caching**. Many Internet Service Providers operate "web caches", of
  which there are two kinds; "pull-caches" and "push-caches". The content
  of pull-caches is determined by which pages are requested by the users—
  they respond to actual demand for webpages from remote sites, and store
  the most frequently accessed webpages. Push-caches work by receiving
  pages from remote sites in anticipation of demand. In this way time-consuming reloads are avoided.

---

[106] See generally Perrit Jr *Law and the Information Superhighway* (1996) at pp 434–436 (1996).
Caching is particularly important with images since these are a greater time drain. Two variations
of caching have been identified, "soft stores" (which stay alive for the session) and "hard stores"
which put the cache on disk. See Dimitris N Chorafas, *Network Computers versus High
Performance Computers* (Redwood Books, 1997) at pp 38–39.
[107] See Lloyd "Liabilities for the contents of on-line sources" (1995) 3(3) *International Source of
Law and Information Technology* 273 at 292.

- **Proxy Caching**. This occurs when a Local Area Network (LAN) or corporate in-house network stores frequently used material. Alternatively, ISPs also may store on their servers for a certain period of time webpages that have been previously requested by their users. On request, such pages would be downloaded from server rather than original source.
- **User Caching**. A user's web-browser, eg Netscape or Internet Explorer, caches the webpages accessed during a particular browsing session ("Back" and "Forward" functions). Netscape eg has a cache file which stores all the webpages browsed by the user over time. If the user does not clean out his cache, the material (copyright infringing or otherwise, and perceptible) remains as a file in a subdirectory in the user's hard disk.

(iv) The attributes of caching

A.90 To answer the question of whether a temporary copy is made each time a webpage is cached, much depends on what is meant by "temporary". Applying a duration test, if "temporary" means "not-permanent", then to a large extent, mirror, web and proxy caches are temporary copies. They may be cleaned out on a daily or weekly basis. If a user does not clean out his cache, then the material is stored permanently. Caching solves the problem of net congestion but creates several others:

- "Net lag" and stale webpages, by the storage of perishable information. The consequence of too many caches is that the website may be updated, but caching servers may still hold copies of outdated material.[108] However there are techniques for embedding cache control instructions into a webpage's HTML, determining how long any web caches should "live" before removal.
- Companies whose sites are cached are unable to establish exactly how many people are "hitting" their sites.
- Caching can also adversely affect companies whose income derives from selling advertising space on their webpages. In order to increase advertising income companies often show a different advertisement each time the site is viewed. A number of adverts are "rolled", hence multiplying each page's earnings. The caching server stores only one copy of the popular pages, thus benefitting only one advertiser. For this reason, such companies object to caching.
- Caching may jeopardise security, since cached "access" information (eg passwords) may allow unauthorised users to obtain unlimited access.[109]

---

[108] Hence the loss of version control; see Schlachter "Caching on the Internet" *Cyberspace Lawyer* (October 1996) at 43.

[109] See David Hayes, "Application of Copyright Rights to Specific Acts on the Internet" Vol 15(8) *Computer Lawyer* (August 1998) 1 at 4.

(v) Is caching necessary or "integral"?

Caching speeds up access to web material, but is not technologically indispens-   **A.91**
able to browsing. It is a tool of convenience, not necessity. As a function,
caching can be disabled. This carries ramifications for the exception to the
reproduction right as proposed in the Proposed EU Directive[110] and the potential application of the implied licence.[111] Caching has stemmed primarily from
current transmission bandwidth limitations, resulting from at least two causes:
first, usage of the Internet has grown in the last two years at a rate that is dis-
proportionate to the ability to build the infrastructure necessary to support the
increased usage;[112] secondly, much of the infrastructure now in place was not
designed for the online-centric model of usage.

---

[110] Discussed *supra*, at paras 8.35–8.38.
[111] See Gringras, *Laws of the Internet* (London, Butterworth, 1996) at pp 204–207.
[112] There is already emerging an "Internet 2" or "I2"—a separate network being pioneered by the
University Corporation for Advanced Internet Development (UCAID) to achieve greater transmission speeds than currently available. See further Lange, "Technology 1998 Analysis & Forecast: The
Internet" *IEEE Spectrum* (January 1998) at 37–39.

Index